CROSSING THE STRAIT

China's Military Prepares for War with Taiwan

Edited by
Joel Wuthnow
Derek Grossman
Phillip C. Saunders
Andrew Scobell
Andrew N.D. Yang

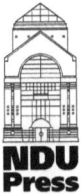

National Defense University
Press
Washington, D.C.
2022

*This book is dedicated to Rear Admiral Eric McVadon,
U.S. Navy (Ret.), and Alan D. Romberg in appreciation
for decades of friendship and their many contributions
to PLA studies and cross-strait relations.*

CONTENTS

Even as Russia's invasion of Ukraine has turned attention to Europe, China is continuing meticulous preparations for a conflict with another democracy—Taiwan. For more than 30 years, China's People's Liberation Army (PLA) has identified Taiwan and the United States as its major opponents and a conflict in the Taiwan Strait as its main contingency. China's Communist Party would prefer to win without fighting, but it has tasked the PLA to develop the military means to coerce Taiwan's leadership and to be prepared to seize and occupy the island. Under Chinese leader Xi Jinping's tenure, PLA reforms and fast-paced modernization have increased the military threat to Taiwan.

The 2022 National Defense Strategy makes clear that the United States will continue to prioritize peace and stability in the Indo-Pacific region. China is the pacing challenge for the Department of Defense and Taiwan is the pacing scenario. Any use of force by the PLA against Taiwan would have serious consequences for U.S. national interests and for the future of Taiwan's democracy. To meet this challenge, policymakers and strategists need high-quality insights into Chinese strategic decisionmaking, Chinese military capabilities, and PLA plans, policies, and systems. We also need to continue refining our own joint warfighting concepts and capabilities.

National Defense University's Center for the Study of Chinese Military Affairs is a leading source of high-quality, objective analysis on China and the Chinese military. For more than 15 years, the center has partnered with the RAND Corporation and Taiwan's Council on Advanced Policy Studies to organize an annual conference on the Chinese military. This volume is the fruit of a November 2020 conference focused on providing an up-to-date public assessment of the Chinese military threat to Taiwan.

The book provides a detailed analysis of the political and military context of cross-strait relations, with a focus on understanding the Chinese decision calculus and options for using force, the capabilities the PLA would bring to the fight, and what Taiwan can do to strengthen its defenses. It concludes that the PLA has made major advances to prepare itself for a conflict across the Taiwan Strait, but also faces continued challenges and vulnerabilities in some areas. The book offers suggestions on how Taiwan and the United States can work together to improve Taiwan's defenses and increase stability across the Taiwan Strait. It is highly recommended reading for students and policy practitioners focused on China, Taiwan, and the Indo-Pacific region.

MICHAEL T. PLEHN, Lt Gen, USAF
President, National Defense University

ACKNOWLEDGMENTS

This volume is the latest publication from a longstanding series of annual conferences on the People's Republic of China's People's Liberation Army, sponsored by Taiwan's Council on Advanced Policy Studies (CAPS), the RAND Corporation, and the U.S. National Defense University (NDU). For their continued support, we are grateful to the leaders of our respective institutions, including CAPS Secretary-General Andrew N.D. Yang; RAND's National Defense Research Institute Director Jack Riley, Arroyo Center Director Sally Sleeper, Project Air Force directors Jim Chow and Ted Harshberger, and Acting Director Anthony Rosello; NDU Presidents Vice Admiral Frederick J. Roegge, USN, and Lieutenant General Michael T. Plehn, USAF; and Institute for National Strategic Studies (INSS) Director Laura Junor-Pulzone.

The chapters were originally presented at the 2020 conference, which was held virtually from November 18 to 20. For keeping things on track, we thank the moderators: Cortez Cooper, Mark Cozad, T.X. Hammes, Andrew Scobell, Cynthia Watson, and Andrew N.D. Yang. Also contributing to a successful conference behind the scenes were RAND colleagues Mark Cozad and Derek Grossman; RAND IT specialists Sonia Wellington, David Cherry, and Carmen Richard; INSS Dean of Administration Catherine Reese; and INSS colleagues Brett Swaney, Kira McFadden, and Kevin McGuiness. On the Taiwan side, CAPS thanks Yi-Su Yang and Zivon Wang. The final roundtable also enriched the conference by providing wider perspectives on Chinese military threats and policy responses. The panelists included Admiral Richard Chen, Taiwan Navy (Ret.), Michael Coullahan,

David Finkelstein, Rear Admiral Michael McDevitt, USN (Ret.), the Honorable Randall Schriver, and Andrew N.D. Yang.

The discussants took time out of their busy schedules to offer constructive verbal and written feedback that helped transform conference papers into book chapters. The discussants included Fiona Cunningham, Bonnie Glaser, Derek Grossman, Kristen Gunness, Scott Harold, Yuan-Chou Jing, Ma Chengkun, Che-Chuan Lee, Joanna Yu Taylor, and Kharis Templeman. Several chapter authors also received helpful feedback from other colleagues.

We were fortunate to collaborate with the excellent team once again at NDU Press, which shepherded our earlier volumes *The PLA Beyond Borders: Chinese Military Operations in Regional and Global Context* (2021) and *Chairman Xi Remakes the PLA: Assessing Chinese Military Reforms* (2019), and others. The team includes NDU Press Director William T. Eliason, Executive Editor Jeffrey D. Smotherman, Senior Editor John J. Church, and Internet Publications Editor Joanna E. Seich. We also thank many others who helped turn this into a polished volume, including the editing team at VTR Technical Resources and Lisa Yambrick and proofreader and indexer Susan Carroll. We also would like to thank Jill A. Schwartz and Cameron R. Morse at the Defense Office of Prepublication and Security Review for their help in stewarding this publication through the review process.

Finally, the editors would like to acknowledge Tiffany Batiste, Margaret Baughman, CDR Jason Brandt, Maj H.C. Carnice, CAPT Bernard Cole (Ret.), Jessica Drun, Xiaobing Feng, Sarah Gamberini, LTC Joshua Goodrich, Christine Gramlich, MAJ Michelle Haines, Kyle Harness, Danielle Homestead, Col Kyle Marcrum, Capt Joshua L. Nicholson, Corrie Robb, MSgt Daniel Salisbury, Meghan Shoop, CPT Dereck Wisniewski, LtCol John Kintz, Lt Col Jeffrey Wright, MAJ Justin Woodward, Beth Wootten, and CPT Xiaotao Xu for their help in proofreading the manuscript.

Map 1. Taiwan

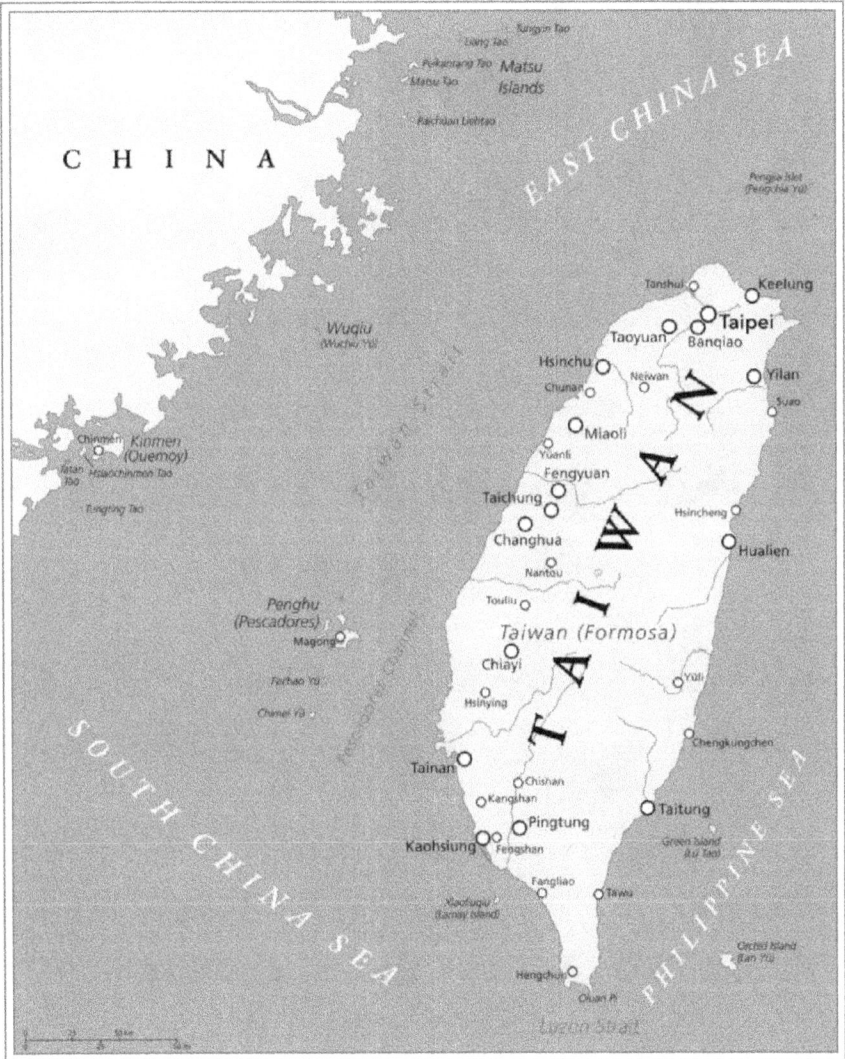

Crossing the Strait:
PLA Modernization and Taiwan

Phillip C. Saunders and Joel Wuthnow

In an atmosphere of increasing U.S.-China strategic competition, Taiwan stands out as the issue with the greatest potential to trigger a major war between the United States and the People's Republic of China (PRC), two nuclear-armed powers. The stakes are high for both countries and for the 23 million people of Taiwan. Moreover, the issue is becoming increasingly militarized as China's military, the People's Liberation Army (PLA), seeks to develop the capabilities needed to achieve unification through coercion, including in the face of potential U.S. military intervention on Taiwan's behalf.

This introductory chapter begins with a concise review of how the current situation developed, including a review of the policy positions and the stakes for China, Taiwan, and the United States. It then reviews the impact of PLA modernization on the cross-strait military balance and on the PLA's ability to execute the major military options available to Chinese leaders. The third section reviews the current debate on when the PLA might be able to conduct the most demanding option—an amphibious invasion of Taiwan—and what factors might influence the Chinese calculus about whether to pursue forced unification. The fourth section presents five key findings from the book, followed by brief summaries of the individual chapters. The conclusion considers the relative role of military and political factors in determining deterrence and stability in the Taiwan Strait.

Background and Stakes of the Taiwan Issue

For Chinese Communist Party (CCP) leaders, Taiwan is an integral part of China that was forcibly seized by Japan in 1895 following the Sino-Japanese War and which became a haven for the Republic of China (ROC) government and military after their 1949 defeat in the Chinese Civil War. Taiwan is thus connected both to the Chinese nationalist goal of restoring China's sovereignty and territorial integrity after the so-called century of humiliation and to the CCP's final political victory over the Chinese Nationalist Party (the Kuomintang, or KMT). CCP leaders have pledged their commitment to the goal of unification and have repeatedly expressed willingness to fight to prevent Taiwan independence, including in the 2005 Anti-Secession Law that authorizes the use of "non-peaceful means" if necessary. Taiwan's status is a sensitive domestic political issue, with CCP leaders vulnerable to criticism by nationalists inside and outside the party if they are viewed as too weak in defending China's "core interest" in sovereignty and territorial integrity. Since 2017, CCP leaders have linked Taiwan unification to "the great rejuvenation of the Chinese people," which is to be achieved by 2049, creating an implicit deadline.[1]

For the United States, support for Taiwan coalesced in the context of early Cold War anti-Communist sentiment: Washington supported the ROC as the sole legitimate government of all China for more than two decades. Taiwan's status was a major issue in the U.S. opening to China in the 1970s, with U.S. political leaders seeking to avoid the domestic and international costs of abandoning Taiwan to the Communist regime in China. The eventual solution, worked out in three U.S.-China joint communiques, was for the United States to terminate its defense treaty with the ROC and withdraw U.S. military forces from Taiwan, shift diplomatic recognition to the PRC, and maintain only unofficial relations with the people on Taiwan. Beijing asserted that Taiwan was an integral part of China, while the United States acknowledged this position without formally accepting it.[2] The United States enacted the 1979 Taiwan Relations Act (TRA) to provide the legal basis for its unofficial relations with Taiwan. Among other things, the TRA requires the United States to make defensive arms available to Taiwan and states that it will "consider any effort to determine the future of Taiwan by other than peaceful means, including by boycotts or embargoes, a threat to the peace and security of the Western Pacific area and of grave concern to the United States." The TRA also states that U.S. policy is to retain the capability to resist the use of force or coercion to undermine Taiwan's security.[3]

Although the United States does not have a formal commitment to defend Taiwan, the TRA's language and decades of policy have linked the credibility

Map 2. Pratas and Taiping islands, marked in black

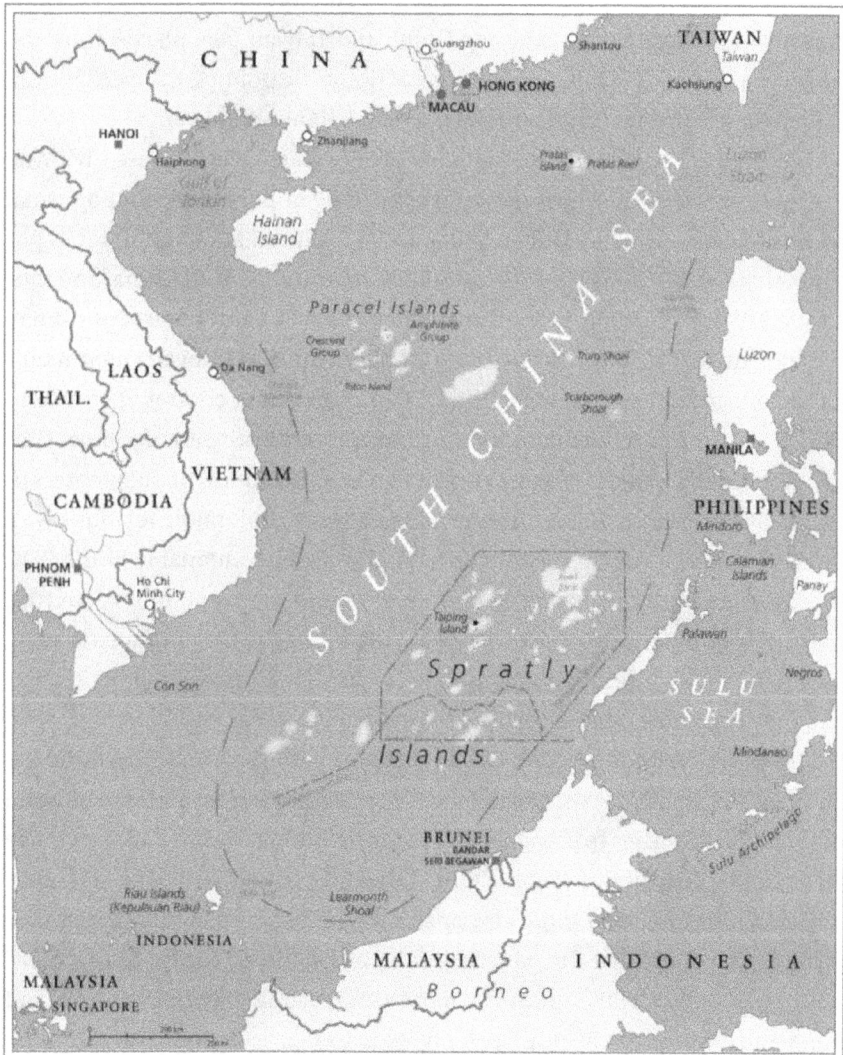

of U.S. regional alliance commitments to its actions regarding Taiwan. U.S. stakes deepened further with Taiwan's democratization in the late 1980s and early 1990s, which increased Taiwan's appeal relative to the authoritarian PRC regime and strengthened U.S. political sympathy and support for Taiwan, especially in Congress.[4] Moreover, some U.S. strategists have come to view a Taiwan not under PRC control as having significant geopolitical value in limiting PLA power projection capability.[5] Recent testimony by a Biden administration official implied that U.S. policy might accept this view and seek to prevent unification rather than simply shape the procedural conditions under which negotiations between China and Taiwan take place.[6] Thus, the stakes are high for Washington in terms of domestic politics, the credibility of U.S. alliance commitments, and the regional balance of power.

For more than two decades after its 1949 defeat in the Chinese Civil War, the authoritarian KMT government ruling Taiwan benefited from a formal security alliance with the United States and U.S. diplomatic support for its position that the ROC was the sole legitimate government of all China, and thus entitled to membership in the United Nations (UN) and control of China's permanent seat in the UN Security Council.[7] The KMT government maintained the goal of overthrowing the CCP and regaining control of Mainland China, agreeing that the mainland and Taiwan were both part of a larger China. Like the PRC, the ROC government rejected the notion of dual representation and insisted that countries choose between diplomatic relations with the PRC or the ROC. This position eventually became untenable as the ROC was expelled from the United Nations in 1971 and more and more countries switched diplomatic relations to the PRC, including the United States in 1979. This left Taiwan internationally isolated, with few formal diplomatic allies and only unofficial relations with most major countries.

Taiwan's attitude toward China changed with democratization in the late 1980s and early 1990s, which ended KMT authoritarian rule and allowed other political parties to compete for power, including the pro-independence Democratic Progressive Party (DPP). Taiwan's government (and its policy toward China) became more responsive to the concerns of the native Taiwanese who constitute the majority of the population.[8] The traditional ROC position is that the ROC government has sovereignty over both Taiwan and Mainland China, but in practice only exercises jurisdiction over the main island of Taiwan; various offshore islands such as the Penghus, Pratas/Dongsha, Matsu, Jinmen, and Wuchiu; and Taiping/Itu Aba Island in the South China Sea.[9] (See map 2 showing Pratas/Dongsha Island and Taiping/Itu Aba Island, respectively.)

The issue of Taiwan's relationship with China is highly contested, but public opinion on Taiwan strongly supports the continuation of the current status quo and the population increasingly identifies as Taiwanese rather than Chinese.[10] Credible PRC threats to use force deter a declaration or referendum that would formally assert Taiwan's independence. At the same time, the current DPP government has refused to acknowledge that Taiwan is part of China, arguing that Taiwan is already an independent sovereign state and that a formal declaration of independence is unnecessary. This position is in great tension with the PRC's "one China principle" and ultimate goal of unification as well as the KMT's acceptance of the 1992 Consensus, which involved a vague commitment to one China.[11] This disagreement about Taiwan's exact status relative to China is the fundamental basis of the political dispute between Beijing and Taipei.

Despite these differing interpretations, this ambiguous "one China" framework has served the minimal needs of political leaders and people in China, Taiwan, and the United States for more than 40 years, supporting economic growth, development of robust cross-strait economic and cultural ties, and political development of Taiwan's democracy. Although political tensions have waxed and waned over time, the CCP's "reform and opening up" policy and the interest of the Taiwan government and business community in exploiting economic opportunities in China have allowed cross-strait trade and investment to grow to the point where China is Taiwan's largest market, and the two economies are deeply intertwined despite Taiwan government efforts to reduce economic dependence on the mainland.

Nevertheless, long-term political, military, and economic trends are eroding the stability of the status quo and increasing the potential for military conflict.[12] China's policy toward Taiwan shifted from its initial emphasis on "liberating Taiwan" by force to a focus on achieving "peaceful unification," but CCP leaders have refused to rule out the use of force, either to prevent Taiwan independence or to compel unification under certain conditions.[13] Taiwan's status is fundamentally a political question, but the military balance between China and Taiwan and between China and the United States is an increasingly important factor shaping cross-strait relations.

The importance and sensitivity of these issues is illustrated by China's response to Taiwan President Lee Teng-hui's June 1995 unofficial visit to the United States. Lee's visit triggered a military crisis that included the PLA firing ballistic missiles near Taiwan's two main harbors prior to the March 1996 presidential election and President Bill Clinton ordering the deployment of two U.S. aircraft carriers to waters near Taiwan as a military show of force.[14] Since then, a Taiwan contingency has become the principal focus of Chinese military modernization, and the PLA has assumed that the U.S. military would intervene on Taiwan's behalf in a conflict. This has fueled PLA efforts to develop the capabilities necessary to invade Taiwan, including advanced antiaccess/area-denial (A2/AD) systems to counter a potential U.S. military intervention. The PLA's successes in military modernization and reform increasingly challenge Taiwan's ability to defend itself in the face of numerically and qualitatively superior Chinese forces and raise the costs and risks of U.S. intervention on Taiwan's behalf.

A Changing Military Balance

The military balance between Taiwan and China has shifted decisively in Beijing's favor over the last three decades. Taiwan has historically benefited from the inherent defensive advantages provided by its island geography and a technological edge based on access to advanced U.S. weapons and training. PLA modernization has eroded Taiwan's technological advantage, and the PLA now maintains qualitative advantages across the spectrum of conflict. Taiwan's conventional force capabilities are outmatched by the PLA's size and advantages in personnel, weapon systems, and defense budgets. The table compares Taiwan military forces with the PLA's Eastern and Southern theater commands (TCs) that would be most involved in a Taiwan scenario to establish a baseline of the conventional military challenge Taiwan faces.[15]

In addition to the forces depicted in the table, the PLA Rocket Force operates 100 ground-launched cruise missile launchers, 250 short-range ballistic missile launchers, and 250 medium-range ballistic missile launchers with the collective capability of firing at least 1,900 missiles.[16]

Table. Comparison of PLA and Taiwan Military Forces

Capability	PLA Eastern and Southern TCs	Taiwan
Ground Force Personnel	416,000	88,000 (active duty)
Tanks	6,300 across PLAA	800
Artillery Pieces	7,000 across PLAA	1,100
Aircraft Carriers	1 (2 total)	0
Major Surface Combatants	96 (132 total)	26
Landing Ships	49 (57 total)	14
Attack Submarines	35 (65 total)	2 (diesel attack)
Coastal Patrol Boats (Missile)	68 (86 total)	44
Fighter Aircraft	700 (1,600 total)	400
Bomber Aircraft	250 (450 total)	0
Transport Aircraft	20 (400 total)	30
Special Mission Aircraft	100 (150 total)	30

Source: *Annual Report to Congress:* Military and Security Developments Involving the People's Republic of China 2021 (Washington, DC: Office of the Secretary of Defense, 2021), 161–162.

The PLA has several options to apply its military capabilities against Taiwan, including low-level military coercion, coordinated missile and air-strikes, a blockade, and a full-fledged invasion of the island. (These options are detailed and assessed more fully in the chapters by Mathieu Duchâtel and Michael Casey in this volume.) However, even with China's considerable military advantages, there would still be significant costs and risks in trying to resolve Taiwan's status by force.

The PLA has periodically employed military coercion against Taiwan in the form of targeted military exercises, demonstrations of force, and deployments. These actions have sought to signal China's capability and resolve while staying in the gray zone—that is, below the level of lethal force. However, low-level coercion could potentially grow to include limited use of lethal force, such as seizing offshore islands controlled by Taiwan or kinetic attacks against Taiwan's infrastructure. Some actions have come in response to specific Chinese concerns about possible movement toward Taiwan independence, such as the 1995–1996 Taiwan Strait Crisis and PLA deployments in 2008 during the final months of Chen Shui-bian's presidency. Although China used only limited military coercion for most of Ma Ying-jeou's presidency (2009–2016), it has ramped up military pressure against Taiwan since then, citing Tsai Ing-wen's refusal to accept the 1992 Consensus as justification. These actions have included island landing exercises, circumnavigation of Taiwan by PLA Navy aircraft carriers and aircraft, and repeated intrusions into Taiwan's Air Defense Identification Zone.[17] The PLA appears to have escalated the number and intensity of these actions in 2020 and 2021 to increase military pressure on Taiwan.

A joint firepower strike campaign would employ PLA missile and air strikes to inflict sufficient damage to compel Taiwan to accept Chinese terms. The first phase would employ precision strikes to degrade Taiwan's air and missile defenses and achieve air superiority. A second phase of attacks would strike military and infrastructure targets to inflict punishment on Taiwan's leaders and population. China has the military capabilities to inflict heavy punishment on Taiwan, but these attacks would generate significant international reaction and provide time for the United States to mobilize and deploy forces. Moreover, the historical record indicates that strategic bombing campaigns tend to produce rallying effects rather than cause leaders and the public to surrender.[18] Taiwan also has its own offensive missile capabilities that it could use to mount limited strikes against the mainland in response. Taiwan's 2021 Quadrennial Defense Review and 2019 National Defense Report address these realities in depth and highlight the training, defense spending increases, and foreign military sales acquisitions to significantly add risk and cost to this option for the PLA.[19]

A joint blockade campaign would employ kinetic blockades of maritime and air traffic to Taiwan to cut off vital imports. The blockade would likely include mines, missile strikes, and possible seizures of Taiwan's offshore islands and could be tailored in scope and intensity.[20] A full blockade could employ the entire suite of PLA capabilities, including electronic warfare, cyber warfare, and information operations. Chinese submarine warfare capabilities and the PLA's ability to launch antiship cruise missiles and ballistic missiles from a variety of platforms would greatly complicate Taiwan's defenses. A blockade would disrupt commercial shipping in the region and generate significant international reactions. The extended duration of the blockade necessary to compel Taiwan into accepting Chinese terms would have substantive military, economic, and political costs and provide time for the international community to impose sanctions and for the U.S. military to deploy forces to intervene militarily. This option carries substantial costs and risks with uncertain prospects of compelling Taiwan to capitulate.

A joint island landing campaign would involve a full amphibious invasion that might build on prior blockade and strike campaigns. This option has the highest military costs and risks but offers the prospect of a decisive military victory. The PLA routinely exercises the military skills that would be employed in an amphibious invasion.[21] An invasion would require a massive mobilization of PLA forces, equipment, and logistics capabilities. The first phase would involve efforts to degrade Taiwan's air and naval defenses in preparation for an amphibious assault. The PLA would utilize precision ballistic and cruise missile strikes against Taiwan's air and missile defenses, precision long-range artillery, airstrikes with medium-range bombers and fighters, and antiship cruise missile and submarine attacks against Taiwan's naval assets. Taiwan would employ its air and missile defense and air force and naval assets to defend targets and contest PLA efforts to gain maritime and air superiority.[22] The PLA would then need to execute an amphibious assault to establish a beachhead on Taiwan and an airborne/air assault attack to try to seize an airfield and a port facility that could allow the PLA to use civilian transportation assets to provide air and sea lift. The PLA would then have to land sufficient ground combat forces to defeat Taiwan's ground forces and provide sufficient ammunition, fuel, and other supplies to support these forces during combat operations.

Since the 1995–1996 Taiwan Strait Crisis, the PLA has assumed that the United States would intervene in a Taiwan conflict and has sought to deter or delay U.S. intervention via an array of A2/AD capabilities that would raise the costs and risks for U.S. forces operating near China.[23] These include advanced diesel submarines, which could attack U.S. naval forces deploying into the Western Pacific; surface-to-air missiles such as the Russian S-300, which could target U.S. fighters and bombers; and antiship cruise and ballistic missiles optimized to attack U.S. aircraft carrier battle groups.[24] China has invested in a range of accurate conventional missiles that could target the bases and ports the U.S. military would use in a conflict, including most recently the DF-17 intermediate-range ballistic missile with a hypersonic glide vehicle. China has also sought to exploit U.S. military dependence on space systems by developing a range of antisatellite capabilities that could degrade, interfere with, or directly attack U.S. satellites and their associated ground stations. It has invested in cyber capabilities to collect intelligence and to degrade the U.S. military's ability to employ computer networks in a crisis or conflict. In a conflict, the PLA would attempt to use multidomain attacks to paralyze U.S. intelligence, communications, and command and control systems and force individual units to fight in isolation, at a huge disadvantage.[25] China is also likely to deal with the risks of U.S. intervention by seeking to win a quick victory before the United States could fully deploy its forces to the theater, thereby presenting the United States with a hard-to-reverse fait accompli.

The implications for the U.S. ability to defend Taiwan are significant. While the PLA has not caught up to the U.S. military in aggregate military capabilities, it does not need parity to frustrate U.S. intervention in a short conflict on its immediate periphery.[26] The RAND Corporation's 2015 evaluation of U.S.-China military force capability trends found that the United States had "major advantages" in 7 of 10 critical capability areas in a Taiwan scenario in 1996 but that by 2017 the United States would have clear "advantages" in only three categories, and the PLA would enjoy advantages in two: its ability to attack U.S. airbases and carriers.[27] China's advances in ballistic missiles, cruise missiles, and modern diesel attack submarines now give it capabilities it did not have during the 1995–1996 standoff, which might affect how the U.S. military chooses to forward deploy forces.[28]

Of course, Taiwan and the United States are not standing still. Taiwan's Overall Defense Concept, described in the chapters by Alexander Chieh-cheng Huang and Drew Thompson, seeks to use asymmetric capabilities to increase the challenges for invading PLA forces. These include investments in rapid mine deployments and mobile missile platforms that would target invading forces and complement Taiwan's geographic advantages. The concept also includes investments to make Taiwan's forces more survivable and effective in preventing a post-landing breakout. Taiwan's 2021 Quadrennial Defense Review and 2019 National Defense Report spend considerable time highlighting the training, defense spending increases, and foreign military sales acquisitions to add risk and cost to PLA military options.[29]

The Department of Defense (DOD) is working to adapt U.S. weapons and operational concepts to fight the PLA in an A2/AD environment, including increased forward deployment of forces and supplies to overcome the "tyranny of distance." This thinking is evident in the 2018 National Defense Strategy and in the joint concept of "globally integrated operations" that seeks to leverage information and U.S. global capabilities to achieve decisive strategic effects in regional contingencies. At the request of Congress, then U.S. Indo-Pacific Command commander Admiral Philip Davidson developed a 6-year, $20 billion investment program for the U.S. military to "regain the advantage" over China in the Indo-Pacific region. Congress appears likely to continue to fund this request.[30]

The U.S. Services all have active efforts under way to adapt systems and doctrine to meet A2/AD threats, with a clear focus on China. For the Navy, this involves efforts to disrupt the "kill chain" necessary for Chinese missiles to locate and target U.S. carriers and to develop the ability to operate and reload ship armaments from a diverse set of nontraditional port facilities. For the Air Force, this involves efforts to develop both standoff and penetrating platforms[31] and improve the Service's ability to conduct expeditionary, distributed operations from austere airfields with reduced logistics and maintenance requirements, which the Air Force calls Agile Combat Employment.[32] The Army has created new "multidomain task forces" that combine artillery and precision strike capabilities with a range of cyber, electronic warfare, space, and intelligence capabilities to operate within and degrade an adversary's A2/AD capabilities. The initial pilot program was conducted under U.S. Army Pacific, and the first operational task force has been established at Joint Base Lewis-McChord, which is aligned to the Indo-Pacific theater.[33] The Marine Corps has made a major shift in its force modernization over the next decade to improve its ability to conduct expeditionary advanced base operations in contested environments.[34]

Secretary of Defense Lloyd Austin III has repeatedly described China as the "pacing challenge" for DOD. In a December 2021 speech, he highlighted how DOD has been stepping up its efforts on China:

Our China Task Force sharpened the Department's priorities and charted a path to greater focus and coordination. We made the Department's largest-ever budget request for research, development, testing, and evaluation. And we're investing in new capabilities that will make us more lethal from greater distances, and more capable of operating stealthy and unmanned platforms, and more resilient under the seas and in space and in cyberspace.

We're also pursuing a more distributed force posture in the Indo-Pacific— one that will help us bolster deterrence, and counter coercion, and operate forward with our trusted allies and partners.

And we're developing new concepts of operations that will bring the American way of war into the 21ˢᵗ century, working closely with our unparalleled global network of partners and allies.

Austin highlighted "integrated deterrence" as the cornerstone concept of a new National Defense Strategy that was released in early 2022. He described it as "integrating our efforts across domains and across the spectrum of conflict to ensure that the U.S. military—in close cooperation with the rest of the U.S. Government and our allies and partners—makes the folly and costs of aggression very clear."[35]

Assessing the Risks

Most military analysts would agree that the PLA has made considerable military advances. Secretary Austin stated in December 2021 that "two decades of breakneck modernization" have put the PLA on pace "to become a peer competitor to the United States in Asia—and eventually around the world."[36] In its 2021 annual report, the U.S.-China Economic and Security Review Commission found that "improvements in China's military capabilities have fundamentally transformed the strategic environment and weakened the military dimension of cross-strait deterrence."[37]

The PLA clearly has the capability to apply low-level coercive pressure and to conduct air and missile strikes against Taiwan and probably has the capability to execute a blockade absent U.S. intervention. Disagreements come in assessing the PLA's capability to execute the most demanding military option—an amphibious invasion of Taiwan—especially in the face of U.S. intervention. The Office of the Secretary of Defense 2021 report on the PLA highlights the challenges and risks:

Large-scale amphibious invasion is one of the most complicated and difficult military operations, requiring air and maritime superiority, the rapid buildup and sustainment of supplies onshore, and uninterrupted support. An attempt to invade Taiwan would likely strain PRC's armed forces and invite international intervention. These stresses, combined with the PRC's combat force attrition and the complexity of urban warfare and counter-insurgency, even assuming a successful landing and breakout, make an amphibious invasion of Taiwan a significant political and military risk for Xi Jinping and the Chinese Communist Party.[38]

Some have expressed concern that the PLA might acquire the ability to mount an invasion soon. In March 2021, Admiral Philip Davidson, then commander of U.S. Indo-Pacific Command, told Congress that China's threat to Taiwan could manifest "in the next six years."[39] Davidson's judgment was not a coordinated U.S. Government position, and other DOD officials have not repeated this assessment.[40] Davidson's successor, Admiral John Aquilino, declined to offer a specific time estimate but testified that China considers establishing control over Taiwan to be its "number one priority" and that "this problem is much closer to us than most think."[41] The U.S.-China Economic and Security Review Commission judged in its 2021 report that "PLA leaders now likely assess they have, or will soon have, the initial capability to conduct a high-risk invasion of Taiwan if ordered to do so."[42] Similarly, Taiwan Minister of Defense Chiu Kuo-cheng told the Taiwan legislature that Mainland China will have the ability to mount a full-scale invasion of Taiwan by 2025, though he also noted that Chinese leaders would still "need to think about the cost and consequence of starting a war."[43]

Oriana Skylar Mastro argued in *Foreign Affairs* in July 2021 that advances in military modernization mean that Chinese leaders now consider a military campaign to take back Taiwan "a real possibility" and that "once China has the military capabilities to finally solve the Taiwan problem, Xi could find it politically untenable not to do so" due to strong nationalist pressures.[44] She sketches PLA military options and argues that the PLA could already execute the less demanding scenarios, while noting that an amphibious assault on the island "is far from guaranteed to succeed." Nevertheless, Mastro argues that "Chinese leaders' perceptions of their chances of victory will matter more than their actual chances of victory." She argues that China would hope for a short, decisive campaign that would limit costs, but might believe that it has social and economic advantages that would help it prevail over the United

States in a protracted war. She acknowledges that economic and diplomatic costs of war would be part of Beijing's decision calculus but argues that Chinese leaders may believe that these costs are significantly less than U.S. decisionmakers and analysts assume. Mastro concludes that Xi "may believe he can regain control of Taiwan without jeopardizing his Chinese dream."

Other scholars question various aspects of this assessment. In a rejoinder published in the next issue of *Foreign Affairs*, Rachel Esplin Odell and Eric Heginbotham argue that the PLA's chances of succeeding in a cross-strait invasion are poor today and will remain so for at least a decade.[45] They cite limitations in PLA lift and logistics capability and argue that "the PLA still lacks the naval and air assets necessary to pull off a successful cross-strait attack. Just as important, it suffers from weaknesses in training, in the willingness or ability of junior officers to take initiative, and in the ability to coordinate ground, sea, and air forces in large, complex operations." Odell and Heginbotham also question whether CCP leaders are eager to resolve the situation with force, noting that "although some of these options are more realistic than others, all would carry immense risk. . . . Beijing is unlikely to attempt any of them unless it feels backed into a corner." Similarly, Bonny Lin and David Sacks agree that "it is far from clear that China could defeat Taiwan's military, subdue its population, and occupy and control its territory. Nor is it clear that the PLA could hold off any U.S. forces that came to Taiwan's aid or that Beijing would be willing to undertake a campaign that could spark a larger and far more costly war with the United States."[46] They cite the likely costs of using force, arguing that "a Chinese invasion would invite significant international political, economic, and diplomatic backlash that could undermine China's political, social, and economic development goals. It would also spur the formation of powerful anti-China coalitions, bringing to fruition Beijing's long-standing fear of "strategic encirclement" by powers aligned against it." Thus, despite the PLA's considerable modernization gains over the last 20 years, experts continue to debate whether and when it will be able to invade at a cost and risk acceptable to CCP leaders.

Key Conclusions

This edited volume contributes to the debate by addressing the problem at three levels: China's decisionmaking calculus, its military capabilities and operations, and potential policy responses by Taiwan and the United States.

It contains up-to-date analysis from multiple perspectives, including scholars from the United States, Taiwan, and France and analysis by academics, think-tank experts, and government analysts. The analysis draws on a wide range of sources, including PLA internal writings about military campaigns and the logistics and transportation requirements for an invasion of Taiwan.

The analysis also looks beyond hardware to consider how recent organizational reforms and revised command and control arrangements would affect the PLA's ability to conduct complicated, high-risk integrated joint operations in the face of opposition by Taiwan and U.S. military forces. It builds on previous books produced from the Taiwan's Council of Advanced Policy Studies–RAND Corporation–National Defense University conference series.[47] The analysis also digs deeper into some underappreciated areas, such as PLA urban warfare, logistics, and airborne capabilities.

While looking at China's military threat to Taiwan through different lenses, the contributors to this volume reached several common conclusions.

First, any Chinese decision to use force is much more likely to result from a deliberate cost-benefit calculus incorporating both domestic and external considerations than from unintended escalation. Andrew Scobell emphasizes domestic economic and political resilience as keys to the use of force—a Chinese Communist Party that sees itself as "ascendant" and buffered from sanctions and other predictable consequences might accept the risks of a war to resolve a remaining obstacle to "national rejuvenation," while a party struggling to govern a "stagnant" mainland might conclude that the risks outweigh the benefits. Other authors assess that upgraded hardware and a more cohesive command structure following the reforms could increase the leadership's confidence in the PLA's ability to act decisively while keeping escalation at an acceptable level.

Political trends in Taiwan are also likely to inform China's calculus. Phillip Saunders argues that low support for unification in Taiwan, which has diminished further with China's dismantling of individual freedoms in Hong Kong and repression against ethnic Uighurs in Xinjiang, has reduced China's confidence in the prospects for a settlement based on a "one country, two systems" model. For Beijing, the closing of other options increases the relative attractiveness of military intimidation (and the potential use of force should coercion fail) to prevent a slide toward Taiwan independence in the near term and to convince Taiwan's leadership to accept reconciliation on China's terms in the future. Nevertheless, as Mathieu Duchâtel notes, Beijing might be cautious about more provocative tactics short of war, such as the seizure of one of Taiwan's outlying islands, that leave Taiwan's leadership intact and might galvanize *greater* support for independence, rather than cowing Taiwan's public.

For some authors, the U.S. factor is also prominent in Chinese decision-making. Drew Thompson and Alexander Chieh-cheng Huang both argue that increasing military coordination between the two sides and continued U.S. arms sales are essential for improving Taiwan's defenses, thus enhancing deterrence by denial and raising the stakes for Beijing, which would prefer not to have to fight a war with the United States. From a military perspective, however, Michael Casey emphasizes that Chinese anticipation of U.S. intervention—which is already assumed in PLA doctrinal writings—encourages Beijing to prefer an invasion over less extreme options, such as a blockade, that would give the United States time to mobilize forces across the Western Pacific and assemble a broader coalition.

Second, while the prospects for peaceful unification are narrowing, China's menu of military intimidation and warfighting options is expanding. Peacetime saber-rattling, which is most useful in dissuading Taiwan's pursuit of de jure independence, has become more routine and varied. Joshua Arostegui assesses that Beijing has used amphibious exercises to intimidate Taiwan's public: while part of the annual training cycle, the PLA has publicized some exercises to underscore China's resolve and capabilities to Taiwan and the United States. Mathieu Duchâtel tracks the dramatic expansion of Chinese fighter incursions across the midline of the Taiwan Strait and the increasing tempo and complexity of PLA Air Force (PLAAF) and naval aviation flights within Taiwan's southwestern Air Defense Identification Zone. Such operations serve multiple goals, such as normalizing more intense military activities, testing U.S. resolve, deterring Taiwan independence, and catering to a nationalistic domestic audience.

Authors also discuss a variety of military measures that Beijing has not yet employed. Duchâtel assesses that the PLA could seize an outlying island such as Dongsha/Pratas to gradually extend its control over territory currently held by Taiwan—a higher risk version of the "salami-slicing" tactics that China has used in the South China Sea. He also describes an escalating series of cyber attacks against Taiwan, including targeting civilian infrastructure, as a possible next step in China's pressure campaign.[48] Higher forms of coercion discussed in Chinese writings, and likely within current PLA capabilities, include missile bombardments or a maritime, air, and information blockade. As Michael Casey discusses, these campaigns could be used in isolation to attempt to force Taiwan's leaders to the negotiating table or to set conditions for an invasion. Joshua Arostegui notes that China's amphibious forces, though essential to an island landing, would also help safeguard critical sea lanes during a blockade.

The most significant Chinese military threat to Taiwan, as discussed in many scholarly and media publications, remains a full invasion.[49] As Casey demonstrates, the concepts for a landing are well established within PLA doctrinal writings. Numerous chapters in this volume, as discussed below, flesh out how various PLA forces and systems are being improved to tackle the challenges of crossing the strait with sufficient force, after attrition, to establish a foothold. A question that has received much less attention is what comes next. Chinese writings sometimes assume that any resistance would quickly collapse, though as Sale Lilly points out, the PLA has increased urban warfare training, developing skills that could become relevant if Taiwan does not easily concede.

Third, the PLA is making wholesale changes to ready itself for higher end Taiwan contingencies. Several chapters address the implications of reforms carried out during the Xi Jinping era. Conor Kennedy, Roderick Lee, and Joshua Arostegui all highlight the conversion of pre-reform divisions into brigades as a key part of the "below the neck" reforms that took place in 2017. Kennedy notes that the PLA Army's watercraft units, which complement the navy's sealift assets, have been "brigadized," with newer ships coming online to replace those of Cold War vintage. Lee sketches the PLAAF Airborne Corps' transition from divisions to brigades, which increases those units' maneuverability, and catalogues their structure and hardware. Arostegui argues that the army's shift to a flatter brigade structure encourages greater "initiative and independence" for its six amphibious brigades. He also notes that the relocation of forces has allowed for "improved mobilization timelines."

Other chapters assess how the reforms generated a more cohesive "system of systems," bringing together the PLA's diverse capabilities. Joel Wuthnow argues that a joint command structure, modeled in part on the U.S. system, allows theater commanders greater control over conventional forces while strengthening the ability of the Central Military Commission to allocate "national assets," such as the Strategic Support Force or long-range Rocket Force conventional missiles that might be used for counterintervention purposes or to deter other rivals during a Taiwan crisis. Chieh Chung describes a similar centralization of PLA logistics forces, which are now better postured to allocate and redeploy munitions and other supplies along an extended front. He also provides a rare look inside China's mobilization system, which has been reconfigured so that multiple provinces—some of them far from the Taiwan Strait—are mobilized to facilitate the flow of materiel during a conflict.

Contributors also describe new hardware and equipment that would allow the PLA to better execute its primary cross-strait operations. Kennedy argues that the launch of multiple Type-075 large-deck amphibious ships, which carry 30 helicopters, would increase the PLA's ability to deliver forces across the strait. His chapter also describes the potential enlistment of civilian merchant ships, including high-capacity roll-on/roll-off vessels and semi-submersible ships, to reduce the PLA's sealift deficit.[50] Arostegui highlights new ZLT-05 amphibious fighting vehicles, whose 105-millimeter assault guns will "improve commanders' ability to direct fires in optimal conditions," while Roderick Lee suggests that the new 4x4 tactical vehicles in the PLAAF Airborne Corps will "improve the mobility and lethality of those units equipped with [them]." No less important, Chieh Chung anticipates that logistics bases will soon be upgraded with specialized equipment to accelerate the loading and unloading of supplies.

Fourth, despite recent reforms and new capabilities, the PLA continues to wrestle with challenges in hardware, organization, training, and doctrine. A common observation concerns insufficient military air- and sealift to transport multiple echelons of troops and equipment across the strait. Kennedy describes the attention to civilian shipping as a response to insufficient "gray hull" sealift, though this approach raises questions about how well civilian assets would perform in a combat environment. Kennedy also suggests that difficult tidal conditions would reduce the utility of some of those assets. Lee identifies a similar shortfall of military airlift, which the PLA could resolve by accelerating production of transport aircraft by 2030; the more challenging problem is the limited capacity of mainland airfields to handle frequent sorties in a compressed timeframe. He also argues that the PLAAF Airborne Corps will face difficult choices in how to employ those forces (such as between offensive and defense ground operations). In the logistics arena, Chung describes continuing constraints in warehouse capacity and medical supplies, which could impede operations.

PLA reforms strengthened parts of the organizational structure but might have created new weaknesses. Joshua Arostegui observes that the army's drive to emphasize combined arms battalions as the basic maneuver unit could lead to overburdened command and staff at lower levels who would be "faced with vulnerabilities resulting from networked command and information systems; competing requirements from subordinate, lateral, and higher units; and operations in a complex electromagnetic environment." He also notes that marine corps units remain nonstandardized and thus less able to be plugged into an army-centric amphibious campaign. Joel Wuthnow describes tensions in the joint command structure between a recognition that commanders at the operational and tactical levels need to be empowered to make difficult decisions and a simultaneous effort during the Xi era to increase centralized decisionmaking and strengthen the role of party committees throughout the PLA.

Authors also describe a variety of training and doctrinal impediments. Sale Lilly notes that while the PLA has increased its urban warfare training, it might have drawn the wrong lessons from U.S. experiences, highlighting the allure of "decapitation strikes" and avoiding serious analysis of the drawn-out insurgencies that U.S. forces faced in Afghanistan and Iraq. He concludes that the PLA may be unprepared for a protracted resistance. The lack of combined arms and joint training could also reduce the PLA's battlefield effectiveness: Arostegui notes that amphibious units rarely participate in opposition force training, and older army watercraft units barely train at all, while Lee finds that the PLAAF Airborne Corps has not conducted joint training (which would be essential to support amphibious troops). Casey observes that PLA doctrine has not been updated for over a decade, though a joint operations outline approved by the Central Military Commission in November 2020 could set the stage for updated joint doctrine.[51]

Finally, opportunities remain to strengthen Taiwan's defense. Wuthnow argues that the PLA's Leninist organizational culture—which emphasizes careful decisionmaking, along with a shift to a "system of systems" architecture where the failure of a given system could have broader implications for the cohesiveness of China's military operations—supports operational concepts that confront PLA decisionmakers with unforeseen and difficult-to-resolve dilemmas. This requires precision-guided munitions combined with cyber and information operations.[52] Chung similarly contends that Taiwan should target China's centralized logistics systems and networks to slow the PLA's ability to mobilize and sustain forces.

Several authors also encourage Taiwan to strengthen its asymmetric warfighting capabilities to deter or delay a PLA invasion. Casey suggests that limited sealift could require the PLA to focus its landing on just one part of the island, which would allow Taiwan to concentrate its limited munitions. He also argues that large amphibious ships, which could become high-value targets in a cross-strait campaign, are better suited for global power projection operations. Kennedy suggests that Taiwan's Overall Defense Concept, which prioritizes investments in antiship missiles, could exacerbate PLA concerns about the likely attrition of its amphibious forces and therefore enhance deterrence. Drew Thompson notes that Taiwan has either built or procured several key systems associated with the concept, including modern sea mines, fast attack vessels, Harpoon coastal defense missiles, howitzers, and Stinger missiles.

Nevertheless, Taiwan's defenses remain troubled by factors beyond China's military threat. According to Huang, domestic problems include recruitment shortfalls as Taiwan shifts to an all-volunteer force, the need to maintain expensive legacy systems that have less utility in a war, such as fighters and large surface ships, and a population that has trouble "imagining an actual war." He also worries that the Overall Defense Concept's singular focus on preparing for invasion could leave Taiwan less well-prepared for gray zone coercion and other problems, such as a blockade. Thompson argues that while Taiwan has made progress in hardware, it needs to focus more on personnel issues, including strengthening the reserve force and on stockpiling critical supplies to weather a blockade. Huang and Thompson both argue that U.S. and Taiwan defense establishments could work to improve Taiwan's posture, though progress requires a higher level of political and fiscal commitment from Taiwan.

Outline of the Book

This edited volume is divided into four parts. The first considers the political and strategic calculus informing Chinese decisions toward Taiwan. In chapter 1, Phillip Saunders evaluates three logics underlying Beijing's choices over the past three decades—what he terms *leverage, united front,* and *persuasion.* He argues that authoritarian political trends in China; sharply declining support for unification in Taiwan, driven in part by the cautionary example of Hong Kong; and shifts in Taiwan's domestic politics have reduced the viability of a conciliatory path to unification and increased Beijing's focus on more coercive tools. In chapter 2, Andrew Scobell suggests that China's calculus on the costs, risks, and benefits of using force will be shaped by the country's trajectory. He describes four scenarios, arguing that Beijing would likely be most war-prone in an "ascendant" future, where Taiwan remains a singular obstacle to national greatness, or in an "imploding" future, where the Chinese Communist Party bets its future on a risky conflict.

The second part of this volume explores Chinese military options along the spectrum of conflict. Mathieu Duchâtel considers gray zone tactics below the level of armed conflict in chapter 3. He explains why military and political factors could lead Beijing to move beyond its recent expansion of coercive operations in Taiwan's Air Defense Identification Zone and consider even more provocative moves, including incursions into Taiwan's territorial seas and airspace, an intensified cyber campaign, or the seizure of one of Taiwan's key offshore islands. Such actions, despite their risks, could be seen as useful in manufacturing a "series of crises" that demonstrate resolve while creating a pretext for escalation above the gray zone.

The following chapters explore how PLA combat operations across the Taiwan Strait might unfold. In chapter 4, Michael Casey details the three primary cross-strait campaigns discussed in PLA doctrinal writings: joint firepower strike, joint blockade, and joint island landing. For each campaign, Casey describes PLA assessments of critical decision points, operational phasing, and military requirements, while also relaying how Chinese writings discuss the task of countering U.S. or other foreign intervention. In chapter 5, Sale Lilly addresses how the PLA is preparing for resistance on the island in the post-landing phase of an invasion. He documents more frequent PLA urban warfare training over the last decade, though he suggests that PLA authors, influenced by the fall of Saddam Hussein in 2003, may be overly optimistic about the chance of a quick victory.

The third part of this volume dives deeper into specific Chinese forces and systems that would be critical to a cross-strait campaign, beginning with the landing forces. In chapter 6, Joshua Arostegui describes the structure of the PLA's amphibious units. He argues that a recent shift from divisions to brigades improved the PLA's ability to conduct a blockade or a landing, though inadequate sealift means that these forces are likely most useful in the near term in deterring Taiwan independence through exercises held on the mainland. Arostegui also explains the division of labor between the army, whose six amphibious brigades are focused on cross-strait operations, and the PLA Navy Marine Corps, which prepares for more diverse missions. In chapter 7, Roderick Lee sketches the composition of the PLA's airborne forces. He explains how the reformed PLAAF Airborne Corps would be instrumental in an island seizure, though he identifies limited airlift, airport capacity, and training as possible constraints.

Another pair of chapters looks more closely at PLA logistics requirements. Conor Kennedy, in chapter 8, argues that the PLA might address a shortfall in military sealift by using civilian merchant ships to ferry some troops and equipment across the Taiwan Strait. Reviewing Chinese technical publications, he finds that the PLA is exploring how forces could be moved ashore both with and without an operational port. In the latter case, there are signs that the PLA is investigating how to use artificial harbors, like the Mulberry harbors used in the Normandy invasion. In chapter 9, Chieh Chung describes the PLA's new logistics structure and catalogues its prodigious logistics needs for a cross-strait campaign in three areas: materiel, medical support, and transportation. He also explains how recent improvements in China's mobilization system could lead to a more efficient transition of society from a peacetime to a wartime footing.

Chapter 10 by Joel Wuthnow discusses how reforms have created a command structure better suited to joint operations. In the Taiwan context, the Eastern Theater Command conducts contingency planning and joint training in peacetime and would oversee ground, naval, and air forces during a campaign. Nevertheless, the command structure remains prone to problems of centralized or consensus-oriented decisionmaking and other issues that could reduce the effectiveness of PLA operations. He suggests that Taiwan and the United States could exploit these problems during a crisis through rapid and hard-to-predict operations that force overwhelmed leaders to make difficult decisions under strenuous circumstances.

The final part of this volume focuses on improving Taiwan's defenses. In chapter 11, Alexander Chieh-cheng Huang argues that the Overall Defense Concept has shown promise in positioning Taiwan to withstand a PLA landing but is less useful in countering Chinese gray zone coercion or other PLA combat operations, such as a blockade. He recommends a refinement of the concept, underwritten by a consensus that needs to be strengthened across Taiwan's political landscape. In the final chapter, Drew Thompson considers the capabilities needed to prevail in the fight "Taiwan cannot afford to lose," suggesting that Taiwan should continue to develop its asymmetric approaches, giving more attention to personnel and logistics issues. He also suggests ways to strengthen U.S.-Taiwan defense cooperation, including more intensive bilateral planning and integration of Taiwan's sensors with U.S. standoff strike weapons.

Conclusion

The analysis in this volume suggests that the PLA already has the capability to apply low-level coercive pressure and conduct air and missile strikes against Taiwan. The PLA likely also has the capability to execute a blockade absent U.S. intervention. However, these military options would leave the sitting Taiwan government intact, would provide time for U.S. forces to intervene, and would likely entail considerable diplomatic, economic, and military costs in addition to the risk of escalation into a major war with the United States.

A cross-strait invasion could potentially be decisive but probably lies beyond current PLA capabilities given known gaps in airlift, sealift, and logistics, as well as other limitations identified by the contributors to this volume. The PLA is working hard to improve its capabilities and rectify its shortfalls. However, the U.S. and Taiwan militaries are also improving their capabilities, including by acquiring new weapons, developing new operational concepts, and improving fighting effectiveness in confronting the PLA. The PLA has made considerable progress over the last 20 years in building the capabilities necessary for an invasion and in closing the qualitative gap with the U.S. military, but future progress is not guaranteed.

A full assessment of CCP decisionmaking about Taiwan must include both costs and risks.[53] Costs are the known diplomatic, military, and economic losses that CCP leaders would expect if they decided to use force to try to resolve the issue of Taiwan's status. Risks include estimates of additional costs that China *might* have to pay depending on how the conflict unfolds. These could be calculated by multiplying the potential additional costs by the probability that China would ultimately have to pay them. These costs and risks could potentially be assessed by outside analysts, but, ultimately, it is the subjective assessments of CCP and PLA leaders that matter most.[54] The operational challenges the Russian military encountered in its invasion of Ukraine and the political and economic sanctions imposed on Moscow following the invasion will likely cause Chinese leaders to increase their estimates of the possible costs and risks of taking military action against Taiwan.

Within the military sphere, there are considerable uncertainties in assessing how a military conflict might play out. If the United States does not intervene and Taiwan's will to resist collapses quickly, China might achieve its political goals at a lower-than-expected cost without having to execute an invasion. However, Chinese leaders cannot assume this outcome and would have to be prepared for less favorable results, including stiff Taiwan resistance and rapid U.S. intervention. As this volume discusses, the PLA currently has specific capability gaps that hinder its ability to successfully execute an invasion. The PLA also has broader weaknesses, including in senior leadership command ability, limited experience with conducting integrated joint operations, and lack of combat experience. Moreover, there are no real-world examples of advanced militaries using the full suite of advanced information-warfare capabilities against equally capable adversaries; neither are there examples of two nuclear-armed countries fighting a major war against each other. The difficulty of assessing the likely outcome of a military conflict—and the high costs of protracted war or nuclear escalation—will give leaders in China and the United States strong incentives to try to avoid a conflict.

Moreover, there are considerable nonmilitary costs and risks that extend beyond the correlation of forces. In the case of a U.S.-China conflict over Taiwan, PRC risks include a military failure that might jeopardize the political survival of top CCP leaders, the potential for a protracted war that threatens China's economy and political stability, and a postwar situation with a powerful and hostile United States and other countries more willing to participate in an anti-China coalition. These costs might occur even if the PLA successfully achieves its operational objectives. If the PLA continues to make up ground in its military modernization, deterrence might rest more heavily on these nonmilitary factors.

CCP statements that China would prefer to pursue peaceful unification with Taiwan are logical considering the high costs and risks of resolving the issue with force.[55] This highlights the need for greater attention to the political foundations of cross-strait relations and of U.S.-China relations. As noted above, neither China, nor Taiwan, nor the United States is fully satisfied with the current framework of cross-strait relations. Nevertheless, this framework has met the minimal requirements of all three sides for more than 40 years.

For this situation to continue, restraint and political creativity will be necessary on all sides. Beijing will need to continue to reemphasize its objective of peaceful unification and find creative ways to move beyond the "one country, two systems" framework that has little appeal on Taiwan. This will require recognizing the high costs and risks of seeking a military solution and that efforts to achieve a decisive military force advantage will have extremely negative effects on U.S.-China relations and on regional stability, which in turn will affect China's economy and domestic stability. Even in the absence of a conflict, the costs of seeking PRC military superiority are likely to continue to rise.

Taiwan leaders will need to acknowledge the high risks of not only formally declaring independence but also of foreclosing the possibility of unification at some future date under more favorable circumstances. Such restraint would likely be necessary to maintain U.S. support, which is critical if Taiwan is to maintain its current de facto sovereignty in the face of China's power advantage. Although heightened U.S.-China strategic competition has created new opportunities for Taiwan to improve relations with Washington, more adversarial U.S.-China relations that include significant economic decoupling would have negative consequences for cross-strait relations. Taiwan leaders might ultimately have to consider whether a negotiated political arrangement that preserves much of Taiwan's current de facto sovereignty is preferrable to a hostile relationship with China that damages Taiwan's economy and security environment.[56]

Washington will need to not only weigh its stakes and obligations to Taiwan but also consider its obligations under the communiqués that it signed with China as part of normalizing relations. Recent years have seen a steady blossoming of the relationship between the U.S. and Taiwan governments and of that between the U.S. and Taiwan militaries. Beijing opposes any increase in U.S.-Taiwan cooperation, but developments that further erode U.S. "one China" commitments could prompt China to take limited military action to reestablish limits on unofficial U.S. relations with Taiwan. The United States has historically focused on encouraging a peaceful, noncoercive environment for cross-strait relations rather than pursuing a specific resolution of Taiwan's status. The United States should continue that policy and not adopt a policy of preventing unification.

If Chinese leaders conclude that the prospects of peaceful unification have disappeared, then the potential for war over Taiwan—despite its known high costs and unfathomable risks—would increase dramatically. The United States must be careful that actions intended to deter a conflict do not end up precipitating one.

Notes

[1] "Full Text of Xi Jinping's Report at 19th CPC National Congress," Xinhua, October 18, 2017, available at <http://www.xinhuanet.com/english/special/2017-11/03/c_136725942.htm>.

[2] At the time, the Republic of China (ROC) government also asserted that Taiwan was an integral part of China.

[3] For a concise overview of the Taiwan Relations Act and U.S. policy, see Richard C. Bush, *A One-China Policy Primer*, East Asia Policy Paper 10 (Washington, DC: Brookings Institution, March 2017), available at <https://www.brookings.edu/research/a-one-china-policy-primer/>.

[4] For a mainstream case on why Taiwan matters to the United States, see *Toward a Stronger U.S.-Taiwan Relationship: A Report of the CSIS Task Force on U.S. Policy Toward Taiwan* (Washington, DC: Center for Strategic and International Studies, 2020), available at <https://csis-website-prod.s3.amazonaws.com/s3fs-public/publication/201021_Glaser_TaskForce_Toward_A_Stronger_USTaiwan_Relationship_0.pdf>.

[5] Elbridge Colby, "The United States Should Defend Taiwan," *National Review*, December 2, 2021, available at <https://www.nationalreview.com/magazine/2021/12/20/the-united-states-should-defend-taiwan/>.

⁶ Assistant Secretary of Defense for Indo-Pacific Security Affairs Ely Ratner described Taiwan as a "critical node within the first island chain, anchoring a network of U.S. allies and partners—stretching from the Japanese archipelago down to the Philippines and into the South China Sea—that is critical to the region's security and critical to the defense of vital U.S. interests in the Indo-Pacific." See Ely Ratner, Statement to the Senate Foreign Relations Committee, *Hearing on The Future of U.S. Policy on Taiwan*, 117ᵗʰ Cong., 1ˢᵗ sess., December 8, 2021, available at <https://www.foreign.senate.gov/imo/media/doc/120821_Ratner_Testimony1.pdf>. For a critical assessment of Ratner's testimony, see Paul Heer, "Has Washington's Policy Toward Taiwan Crossed the Rubicon?" *The National Interest*, December 10, 2021, available at <https://nationalinterest.org/feature/has-washington%E2%80%99s-policy-toward-taiwan-crossed-rubicon-197877>.

⁷ The United States initially adopted a policy of "letting the dust settle" after the Chinese Communist Party (CCP)'s 1949 victory in the Chinese Civil War, but the People's Republic of China (PRC)'s decision to "lean to one side" by joining the socialist bloc, and especially its intervention in the Korean War in October 1950, solidified U.S. support for the ROC. The *Mutual Defense Treaty Between the United States of America and the Republic of China* was signed in December 1954 and took effect in March 1955.

⁸ Mainlanders who arrived in 1949 and their descendants make up about 14 percent of the population in Taiwan.

⁹ This position is expressed in the 1992 *Act Governing Relations between the People of the Taiwan Area and the Mainland Area*, which distinguishes between territory under ROC and PRC jurisdiction in the period "before national unification." Laws and Regulations Database of the Republic of China, *Act Governing Relations between the People of the Taiwan Area and the Mainland Area*, Mainland Affairs Council, amended July 24, 2019, available at <https://law.moj.gov.tw/Eng/LawClass/LawAll.aspx?PCode=Q0010001>.

¹⁰ Kat Devlin and Christine Huang, "In Taiwan, Views of Mainland China Mostly Negative," Pew Research Center, May 12, 2020, available at <https://www.pewresearch.org/global/2020/05/12/in-taiwan-views-of-mainland-china-mostly-negative/>.

¹¹ The Chinese Nationalist Party (the Kuomintang) regards the 1992 Consensus as involving "one China, separate interpretations" and interprets the "one China" that Taiwan belongs to as the Republic of China. The CCP regards the 1992 Consensus as acknowledging that China and Taiwan are both part of the same sovereign political entity.

¹² See Phillip C. Saunders, "Long-Term Trends in China-Taiwan Relations: Implications for U.S. Taiwan Policy," *Asian Survey* 45, no. 6 (November/December 2005), 970–991; Susan A. Thornton, "Whither the Status Quo? A Cross-Taiwan Strait Trilateral Dialogue," National Committee on American Foreign Policy, December 17, 2021, available at <https://www.ncafp.org/read-new-cross-strait-trilateral-report/>.

¹³ At various times CCP leaders have mentioned several factors that might justify the use of force, including formal declaration of Taiwan independence; movement toward Taiwan independence; internal unrest in Taiwan; Taiwan's acquisition of nuclear weapons; indefinite (*sine die*) delays in the resumption of cross-strait dialogue on unification; and foreign military intervention in Taiwan's internal affairs. See *Annual Report to Congress: Military and Security Developments Involving the People's Republic of China 2021* (Washington, DC: Office of the Secretary of Defense, 2021), 115–116, available at <https://media.defense.gov/2021/nov/03/2002885874/-1/-1/0/2021-cmpr-final.pdf>.

[14] John W. Garver, *Face Off: China, the United States, and Taiwan's Democratization* (Seattle: University of Washington Press, 1997); Robert S. Ross, "The 1995–1996 Taiwan Strait Confrontation: Coercion, Credibility, and the Use of Force," *International Security* 25, no. 2 (Fall 2000), 87–123. See also James R. Lilley and Chuck Downs, eds., *Crisis in the Taiwan Strait* (Washington, DC: NDU Press, 1997).

[15] *Military and Security Developments Involving the People's Republic of China 2021*, 161–163.

[16] Ibid., 163.

[17] Ibid., 98–99.

[18] See Robert Pape, *Bombing to Win: Air Power and Coercion in War* (Ithaca, NY: Cornell University Press, 1996); Heather Venable and Sebastian Lukasik, "'Bombing to Win' at 25," *War on the Rocks*, June 25, 2021, available at <https://warontherocks.com/2021/06/bombing-to-win-at-25/>.

[19] *2021 Quadrennial Defense Review* (Taipei: Ministry of National Defense, 2021), available at <https://www.ustaiwandefense.com/tdnswp/wp-content/uploads/2021/03/2021-Taiwan-Quadrennial-Defense-Review-QDR.pdf>; and *2019 National Defense Report* (Taipei: Ministry of National Defense, 2019), available at <https://www.ustaiwandefense.com/tdnswp/wp-content/uploads/2020/02/Taiwan-National-Defense-Report-2019.pdf>.

[20] *Military and Security Developments Involving the People's Republic of China 2021*, 116.

[21] Ibid., 117.

[22] Ibid., 120.

[23] Roger Cliff et al., *Entering the Dragon's Lair: Chinese Antiaccess Strategies and Their Implications for the United States* (Santa Monica, CA: RAND, 2007).

[24] For a discussion of naval aspects of People's Liberation Army (PLA) antiaccess/area-denial capabilities, see Michael McDevitt, *China as a Twenty-First-Century Naval Power: Theory, Practice, and Implications* (Annapolis, MD: Naval Institute Press, 2020).

[25] The PLA calls this "systems attack" or "systems confrontation." See Jeff Engstrom, *Systems Confrontation and System Destruction Warfare: How the Chinese People's Liberation Army Seeks to Wage Modern Warfare* (Santa Monica, CA: RAND, 2018). For an earlier analysis, see Thomas J. Christensen, "Posing Problems Without Catching Up: China's Rise and Challenges for U.S. Security Policy," *International Security* 25, no. 4 (2001), 5–40.

[26] For an influential assessment of how much ground the Chinese military has made up relative to the United States, see Eric Heginbotham et al., *The U.S.-China Military Scorecard: Forces, Geography, and the Evolving Balance of Power, 1996–2017* (Santa Monica, CA: RAND, 2015), available at <https://www.rand.org/pubs/research_reports/RR392.html>.

[27] "An Interactive Look at the U.S.-China Military Scorecard," RAND Project Air Force, available at <https://www.rand.org/paf/projects/us-china-scorecard.html>. RAND defined *advantage* to mean that one side could achieve its primary objectives in an operationally relevant period while the other side would have trouble doing so.

[28] For example, the U.S. Air Force ended its 16-year continuous bomber presence on Guam in late April 2020, although it has continued rotational deployments. See Stephen Bryen, "Why the U.S. Withdrew Its Bombers from Guam," *Asia Times*, April 28, 2020, available at <https://asiatimes.com/2020/04/why-the-us-withdrew-its-bombers-from-guam/>; Mikaley Kline, "B-1s Train with JASDF, Return to Andersen Air Force Base for BTF Deployment," Andersen Air Force Base Web site, September 11, 2020, available at <https://www.andersen.af.mil/News/Features/Article/2345627/b-1s-train-with-jasdf-return-to-andersen-air-force-base-for-btf-deployment/>; Lee Jeong-ho, "China Releases Footage of 'Guam Killer' DF-26 Ballistic Missile in 'Clear Message to the U.S.,'" *South China Morning Post*, January 28, 2019, available at <https://www.scmp.com/news/china/military/article/2183972/china-releases-footage-guam-killer-df-26-ballistic-missile-clear>.

[29] *2021 Quadrennial Defense Review; 2019 National Defense Report.*

[30] Mallory Shelbourne, "INDOPACOM Wants $20B Over the Next Six Years to Execute National Defense Strategy," *Inside Defense*, April 2, 2020, available at <https://insidedefense.com/daily-news/indopacom-wants-20b-over-next-six-years-execute-national-defense-strategy>; Tony Bertuca, "White House Report on China Sets Stage for New Indo-Pacific Investments," *Inside Defense*, May 21, 2020, available at <https://insidedefense.com/daily-news/white-house-report-china-sets-stage-new-indo-pacific-investments>; Jim Inhofe and Jack Reed, "The Pacific Deterrence Initiative: Peace Through Strength in the Indo-Pacific," *War on the Rocks*, May 28, 2020, available at <https://warontherocks.com/2020/05/the-pacific-deterrence-initiative-peace-through-strength-in-the-indo-pacific/>.

[31] Alex Grynkewich, "The Future of Air Superiority, Part III: Defeating A2/AD," *War on the Rocks*, January 13, 2017, available at <https://warontherocks.com/2017/01/the-future-of-air-superiority-part-iii-defeating-a2ad/>.

[32] Brian M. Killough, "The Complicated Combat Future of the U.S. Air Force," *The National Interest*, February 9, 2020, available at <https://nationalinterest.org/feature/complicated-combat-future-us-air-force-121226>.

[33] Sean Kimmons, "Army to Build Three Multi-Domain Task Forces Using Lessons from Pilot," Army News Service, October 15, 2019, available at <https://www.army.mil/article/228393/army_to_build_three_multi_domain_task_forces_using_lessons_from_pilot>.

[34] David H. Berger, "Notes on Designing the Marine Corps of the Future," *War on the Rocks*, December 5, 2019, available at <https://warontherocks.com/2019/12/notes-on-designing-the-marine-corps-of-the-future/>; "Expeditionary Advanced Base Operations (EABO)," Headquarters Marine Corps, August 2, 2021, available at <https://www.marines.mil/News/News-Display/Article/2708120/expeditionary-advanced-base-operations-eabo/>; Michael R. Gordon, "Marines Plan to Retool to Meet China Threat," *Wall Street Journal*, March 22, 2020, available at <https://www.wsj.com/articles/marines-plan-to-retool-to-meet-china-threat-11584897014>.

[35] Lloyd J. Austin III, speech, Reagan National Defense Forum, Department of Defense, December 4, 2021, available at <https://www.defense.gov/News/Speeches/Speech/Article/2861931/remarks-by-secretary-of-defense-lloyd-j-austin-iii-at-the-reagan-national-defen/>.

[36] Ibid.

[37] U.S.-China Economic and Security Review Commission, *Report to Congress 2021* (Washington, DC: Government Publishing Office, November 2021), 387, available at <https://www.uscc.gov/sites/default/files/2021-11/2021_Annual_Report_to_Congress.pdf>.

[38] *Military and Security Developments Involving the People's Republic of China 2021*, 117.

[39] Philip Davidson, Testimony Before the Senate Armed Services Committee, *U.S. Indo-Pacific Command Review of the Defense Authorization Request for Fiscal Year 2022, and the Future Years Defense Program*, 117th Cong., 1st sess., March 9, 2021, available at <https://www.armed-services.senate.gov/imo/media/doc/21-10_03-09-2021.pdf>.

[40] Fred Kaplan claims that Davidson did not clear his testimony with the Pentagon in advance; the 6-year estimate is not in the written testimony but came in response to a question. See the discussion in Fred Kaplan, "Will China Really Invade Taiwan?" *Slate*, November 9, 2021, available   at   <https://slate.com/news-and-politics/2021/11/china-taiwan-invasion-philip-davidson-military-threat.html>.

[41] Admiral John Aquilino, Testimony Before the Senate Armed Services Committee, *To Consider the Nomination of Admiral John C. Aquilino, USN, for Reappointment to the Grade of Admiral and to Be Commander, U.S. Indo-Pacific Command*, 117th Cong., 1st sess., March 23, 2021, available at <https://www.armed-services.senate.gov/imo/media/doc/21-14_03-23-2021.pdf>; Brad Lendon, "Chinese Threat to Taiwan 'Closer to Us Than Most Think,' Top U.S. Admiral Says," CNN, March 24, 2021, available at <https://www.cnn.com/2021/03/24/asia/indo-pacific-commander-aquilino-hearing-taiwan-intl-hnk-ml/index.html>.

[42] U.S.-China Economic and Security Review Commission, *Report to Congress 2021*, 387.

[43] Lawrence Chung, "Beijing 'Fully Able' to Invade Taiwan by 2025, Island's Defence Minister Says," *South China Morning Post*, October 6, 2021, available at <https://www.scmp.com/news/china/military/article/3151340/beijing-capable-taiwan-invasion-2025-islands-defence-minister>.

[44] Oriana Skylar Mastro, "The Taiwan Temptation: Why Beijing Might Resort to Force," *Foreign Affairs* 100, no. 4 (July/August 2021), 58–67.

[45] Rachel Esplin Odell and Eric Heginbotham, "Don't Fall for the Invasion Panic," *Foreign Affairs* 100, no. 5 (September/October 2021), 216–220.

[46] Bonny Lin and David Sacks, "Force Is Still a Last Resort," *Foreign Affairs* 100, no. 5 (September/October 2021), 222–226.

[47] Phillip C. Saunders and Andrew Scobell, eds., *PLA Influence on China's National Security Policymaking* (Stanford: Stanford University Press, 2015); Andrew Scobell et al., eds., *The People's Liberation Army and Contingency Planning in China* (Washington, DC: NDU Press, 2015); Phillip C. Saunders et al., eds., *Chairman Xi Remakes the PLA: Assessing Chinese Military Reforms* (Washington, DC: NDU Press, 2019); Joel Wuthnow et al., eds., *The PLA Beyond Borders: Chinese Military Operations in Regional and Global Context* (Washington, DC: NDU Press, 2021).

[48] For additional discussion, see Ying-Yu Lin, "A New Type of Cross-Border Attack: The PLA's Cyber Force," in Wuthnow et al., *The PLA Beyond Borders*, 295–310.

[49] See, for example, Ian Easton, *The Chinese Invasion Threat: Taiwan's Defense and American Strategy in Asia* (Washington, DC: Project 2049 Institute, 2017); Lonnie Henley, *PLA Operational Concepts and Centers of Gravity in a Taiwan Conflict*, Testimony Before the U.S.-China Economic and Security Review Commission, 117th Cong., 1st sess., February 18, 2021; "T-Day: The Battle for Taiwan," Reuters, November 5, 2021, available at <https://www.reuters.com/investigates/special-report/taiwan-china-wargames/>.

[50] For additional analysis, see J. Michael Dahm, *Ferry Tales: The PLA's Use of Civilian Shipping in Support of Over-the-Shore Logistics* (Newport, RI: China Maritime Studies Institute, 2021); Thomas Shugart, "Mind the Gap: How China's Civilian Shipping Could Enable a Taiwan Invasion," *War on the Rocks*, August 16, 2021, available at <https://warontherocks.com/2021/08/mind-the-gap-how-chinas-civilian-shipping-could-enable-a-taiwan-invasion/>.

[51] For a more thorough discussion, see David M. Finkelstein, *The PLA's New Joint Doctrine: The Capstone of the New Era Operations Regulation System* (Arlington, VA: CNA, 2021).

[52] For a fuller analysis, see Joel Wuthnow, *System Overload: Can China's Military Be Distracted in a War over Taiwan?* China Strategic Perspectives No. 15 (Washington, DC: NDU Press, 2020).

[53] We assume, based on past experience, that CCP leaders make decisions on a rational cost-benefit basis.

[54] The role of perception and misperception in Beijing's decisionmaking calculus vis-à-vis Taiwan should not be underestimated. See Andrew Scobell, "Perception and Misperception in U.S.-China Relations," *Political Science Quarterly* 135, no. 4 (Winter 2020), 637–664.

[55] Although some argue that China has given up hope of peaceful unification, CCP leaders continue to emphasize a preference for peaceful unification in speeches. See Xi Jinping, "Speech at Meeting Marking the 110th Anniversary of the Revolution of 1911," *China Daily*, October 9, 2021, available at <http://www.news.cn/english/2021-10/13/c_1310242627.htm>. Also see Michael D. Swaine, "Recent Chinese Views on the Taiwan Issue," *China Leadership Monitor* 70, December 1, 2021, available at <https://www.prcleader.org/swaine-3>.

[56] See Richard C. Bush, *Difficult Choices: Taiwan's Quest for Security and the Good Life* (Washington, DC: Brookings Institution Press, 2021).

China's Decisionmaking Calculus

CHAPTER 1

Three Logics of Chinese Policy Toward Taiwan: An Analytic Framework

Phillip C. Saunders

For Chinese Communist Party (CCP) leaders, Taiwan is an integral part of Chinese territory that was forcibly seized by Japan in 1895 following the Sino-Japanese War and became a haven for the Republic of China (ROC) government and military after their 1949 defeat in the Chinese Civil War. Taiwan is thus connected both to the Chinese nationalist goal of restoring China's sovereignty and territorial integrity after the so-called century of humiliation and to the CCP's final political victory over the Chinese Nationalist Party (the Kuomintang, or KMT). Since the founding of the People's Republic of China (PRC) in October 1949, core elements of CCP policy toward Taiwan have remained constant. CCP leaders have insisted that the PRC is the sole legitimate government of China and that Taiwan is an integral part of Chinese territory that cannot be allowed independence and must eventually be unified with the PRC.[1] Although the ROC government continues to exercise jurisdiction over Taiwan and various other islands, the PRC has sought to make acceptance of its "one China principle" a condition for diplomatic relations and has prevailed on most countries and the United Nations to accept this position.[2]

The core principles of PRC policy toward Taiwan have remained constant, but there has been variation in the policies, strategies, and tactics CCP

35

leaders have employed to deter Taiwan independence and make progress toward unification. The PRC initially declared its intent to "liberate Taiwan" by force, but this ambition was frustrated by the operational challenges of an amphibious invasion and by U.S. military intervention after the outbreak of the Korean War in 1950. In 1979, the PRC announced a new policy of "peaceful unification" while reserving the right to use force under some circumstances. Beijing subsequently elaborated its vision for what peaceful unification might look like, advancing a "one country, two systems" model that would allow Taiwan to keep its capitalist system and its military and to enjoy a high degree of autonomy. This model was eventually applied to Hong Kong and Macao, which became special administrative regions within the PRC in 1997 and 1999, respectively.

The CCP's insistence that the PRC is the sole legitimate government of China led PRC leaders to refuse to recognize the ROC government or have direct contacts with its leaders, but the two sides eventually found ways to negotiate through party-to-party and semi-official channels, especially the PRC's Association for Relations Across the Taiwan Strait (ARATS) and Taiwan's Straits Exchange Foundation (SEF).[3] The peaceful unification policy and "one country, two systems" formula elaborated under Deng Xiaoping from 1979 to 1982 continues to define the basic parameters of PRC policy toward Taiwan, but there have still been significant variations over time.[4] This chapter presents an analytic framework to help analyze and explain those variations.

China's policy toward Taiwan is the product of a complex policymaking process that involves senior leadership competition, domestic political considerations in a nationalistic policy environment, and PRC assessments of political conditions in Taiwan, the United States, and the broader geopolitical forces at play in the Indo-Pacific region. Mapping the relevant policy actors within China and understanding the content and context of PRC policy debates are challenging analytic tasks: the political sensitivity of policy toward Taiwan creates strong incentives for exaggerated nationalist views in public writings and speeches and encourages Chinese scholars to conform to the preferences of senior leaders in internal writings provided as policy inputs.[5] Moreover, because Taiwan policy has significant implications for the political standing of senior CCP leaders, the circle of key decisionmakers is relatively small and policy initiatives are closely held. As a result, the debates taking place in public and at lower levels of the Chinese system may not actually re-flect the views and concerns of senior CCP leaders making policy decisions.[6] The poor quality of available information on high-level internal debates makes analyzing Chinese policy toward Taiwan a challenge.

An alternative way of understanding China's approach toward Taiwan fo-cuses on three distinct causal logics: leverage, united front, and persuasion. This analytic framework offers considerable explanatory, analytical, and per-haps even predictive power in assessing Beijing's positions. In particular, it provides a means of understanding the mix of coercion and inducements in PRC policy toward Taiwan at any given moment of time while highlighting PRC strategies and tactics that persist despite the ups and downs of cross-strait relations. It also provides a concise way to think about the interests and relevance of different PRC policy actors in the policymaking and policy im-plementation process. One key finding is that changes in Taiwan politics and identity, the authoritarian turn in China, and the PRC's implementation of "one country, two systems" in Hong Kong have made the united front and persuasion logics less effective and could lead CCP leaders to rely more heav-ily on leverage and coercion in the future. This raises questions about the continued viability of the PRC's policy of seeking peaceful unification.

This chapter outlines the three logics and their respective approaches to Taiwan, illustrates some implications of the coexistence of multiple logics for PRC policy, and applies this analytic framework to explain shifts in the PRC policy approach toward Taiwan under different Taiwan leaders from Lee Teng-hui to Tsai Ing-wen. It then considers the relevance of each logic go-ing forward considering recent political developments in China, Taiwan, and Hong Kong and how shifts in relevance might affect China's policy choices as Beijing considers a shift from deterring Taiwan independence toward the more ambitious and difficult goal of achieving unification.

Three Logics of Chinese Policy Toward Taiwan

A causal logic is not a policy, strategy, or tactic. Rather, it is the underlying reasoning about how specific policies, strategies, or tactics are supposed to help achieve or advance a policy objective. A causal logic explains the "ways" in an ends-ways-means chain that connects actions to policy goals. Causal logics can be useful in grouping policies, strategies, and tactics that work in similar ways into conceptual baskets, highlighting hidden commonalities. The rest of this section discusses the PRC's objectives and explores three distinct causal logics evident in its policy toward Taiwan.

China's Taiwan policy has two primary objectives: preventing Taiwan from attaining independence and achieving unification of China and Taiwan. China's most urgent objective is preventing Taiwan independence. Even though the Taiwan government currently exercises jurisdiction over Taiwan and various islands, most of the international community does not recognize Taiwan as a sovereign state separate from China. A formal statement or referendum declaring Taiwan independence would present PRC leaders with a major crisis involving China's core interest in sovereignty and territorial integrity. Chinese leaders have repeatedly and credibly declared a willingness to fight to prevent Taiwan independence.[7]

The CCP's ultimate objective is to achieve unification by bringing Taiwan under the political control of the PRC.[8] The question is how best to accomplish that goal at an acceptable cost and risk and in a reasonable period. CCP leaders have been careful not to establish a precise deadline for unification, which would limit flexibility and present unpalatable choices as the deadline approached and turned into a de facto ultimatum. At that point Beijing would either have to publicly back down or use force regardless of the costs, risks, and political circumstances. China has not set an explicit deadline for unification, but Xi Jinping stated in 2013 and 2019 that the Taiwan issue "should not be passed down generation after generation."[9] Since 2017, CCP leaders have linked Taiwan unification to "the great rejuvenation of the Chinese people" that is to be achieved by 2049, creating an implicit deadline that still leaves some room for maneuver.[10]

Leverage

Leverage interprets China's relations with Taiwan in terms of a zero-sum view of relations across the strait. It is a measure of one party's potential ability to use military, economic, and diplomatic coercion to impose costs on the other.[11] Leverage is an implicit and passive form of coercion that exists and could influence behavior even absent specific threats by one side to employ coercion for deterrent or compellent ends.[12] However, leverage manifests as coercion once one side makes active threats to use force, pressure, or punishment if the other does not take specific actions (compellence) or refrain from tak-ing specific actions (deterrence). As Thomas Schelling noted, effective coer-cion requires that threats be accompanied by credible assurances that the threatened costs will not be imposed if the other side complies with the de-mands.[13] Deterrence is generally easier to achieve than compellence, but this finding depends on what is being demanded in the deterrent and compellent cases.[14] For Taiwan, the costs of accepting unwanted unification are consider-ably higher than the lost benefits of foregoing desired independence, making it easier for the PRC to deter Taiwan independence than to coerce Taiwan into accepting unification. This conclusion is also consistent with prospect theory (see Andrew Scobell's chapter in this volume).

China's ability to deter Taiwan from moving toward independence rests on its capacity to use its economic and diplomatic power to impose costs and to deny Taiwan international recognition and its military ability to threaten the island with unacceptable punishment. This leverage is translated into de-terrence by the PRC's conditional threat to employ coercive means if Taiwan takes actions to proclaim its status as an independent entity separate from China. The more leverage China has, the greater Beijing's confidence that it can deter Taiwan independence. This logic suggests a focus on efforts to in-crease Chinese strength and to weaken Taiwan via diplomatic isolation, eco-nomic dependence, and an end to U.S. arms sales to Taiwan.

This logic also implies that China could eventually achieve unification by increasing its leverage to the point where Taiwan's diplomatic, econom-ic, and military position becomes untenable in the face of potential Chinese coercive threats. This logic assumes that at some point China could confront Taiwan and force capitulation or that Taiwan's leaders would ultimately have to make the best deal they could from a position of weakness. The more lever-age China has, the sooner that day will come and the more the deal will reflect PRC interests. At the limit, leverage could be converted into coercive efforts to employ economic and military power to compel Taiwan to accept unification or the use of military means to achieve unification by force.

Sophisticated versions of this logic embrace the idea of making fur-ther economic and even diplomatic concessions to Taiwan that increase its dependence on Beijing's continued good will, thus generating addi-tional leverage.[15] China could then remove or threaten to remove these

concessions in the future as a coercive tactic, creating an economic or domestic political crisis for Taiwan leaders.

Leverage is best understood as potential coercive power that CCP leaders can choose to employ as circumstances dictate. This includes ramping up
political, economic, or military pressure to punish perceived Taiwan moves
toward independence or to try to coerce Taiwan into accepting the PRC "one
China" position or the PRC agenda for cross-strait relations. CCP leaders might
also choose to decrease pressure on Taiwan to support cross-strait political initiatives or to reward Taiwan actions that signal interest in a closer relationship
with the mainland (or that promise restraint in pushing toward independence).
While leverage can always be banked for future use, employing leverage by
coercing Taiwan is a tactical calculation based on PRC objectives at a given
moment in time, expectations about how effective coercion could be, and the
positive or negative externalities in terms of other PRC policy goals.

PRC leaders rely on coercion to deter Taiwan leaders from pursuing independence. The PRC has consistently refused to rule out the use of force if
Taiwan takes overt actions toward independence and has built military capabilities to make this threat credible. At the same time, China has limited the
circumstances under which it says it would employ force to assure Taiwan
that restraint in pursuing independence will be reciprocated with Chinese
restraint in not employing force.[16] PRC leaders have preserved a degree of
ambiguity about exactly which actions would prompt it to use force, both to
preserve flexibility in deciding how to respond and to prevent Taiwan from
taking incremental actions that stop just short of Beijing's red lines. China has
sometimes taken specific actions to reinforce its deterrent threats, including
two rounds of ballistic missile tests in the 1995–1996 Taiwan Strait Crisis and
passing the Anti-Secession Law in 2005 that laid a legal basis for "non-peaceful actions" in the event of Taiwan independence.

China has also periodically employed limited coercion to compel Taiwan to accept its definition of the relationship between China and Taiwan or
to enter political talks about unification. Despite good cross-strait relations
during Taiwan President Ma Ying-jeou's two terms in office (May 2009–May
2016), China began using various coercive measures in 2015 to pressure Ma
to begin formal talks about Taiwan's political status. When Ma's successor,
Tsai Ing-wen, refused to accept the 1992 Consensus as the political basis for

cross-strait dialogue, the PRC responded by encouraging Taiwan's diplomatic allies to switch recognition to the PRC, applying economic pressure by limiting Chinese tourist visits to Taiwan, and conducting military exercises and deployments aimed at Taiwan.[17]

Leverage has some inherent drawbacks and limitations. The most extreme forms of coercion, such as the use of brute force to achieve unification, have very high economic, military, and diplomatic costs and risks, including the possibility of a nuclear conflict with the United States. Beijing's desire to avoid these costs is why Chinese leaders consistently express a preference for peaceful unification. Even limited forms of economic and military coercion aimed against Taiwan damage China's peaceful image and lead other countries to be concerned about Chinese intentions and cautious about cooperation that would leave them vulnerable to Chinese coercion. Taiwan could also take some actions to reduce China's leverage, such as improving its defense capabilities and diversifying its economic relationships to make itself less vulnerable to Chinese coercion. The high costs and risks of the PRC employing force to achieve unification might also make coercive threats that would be sufficient to compel Taiwan to accept unification seem less credible. Finally, PRC willingness to employ extreme coercive threats to compel Taiwan to accept a unification agreement undercuts the credibility of any assurances that Beijing would abide by the agreement's terms.

United Front

United front tactics have a rich history in the CCP's approach to domestic and international politics. A *united front* is a means for communist parties to cooperate with non-communist parties and groups by finding common ground and downplaying differences. The CCP has an elaborate organizational infrastructure to engage various domestic and international groups, some of which falls under the heading of the CCP United Front Work Department.[18] Because the CCP seeks to maintain its monopoly on power and maximize its ability to dictate outcomes—goals not shared by non-communist political actors—such cooperation is inherently limited and restricted to areas where short-term interests overlap. Although the CCP seeks to enlist non-communist parties and groups to work on behalf of CCP goals, in practice united front tactics are most useful in building coalitions to oppose shared threats.[19]

(CCP efforts to enlist support for its positive goals are better captured by the logic of persuasion, considered below.)

In the Taiwan context, the CCP defines the principal threat as individuals or groups who advocate Taiwan independence. For example, China's 2019 defense white paper refers to the "very small number of 'Taiwan independence' separatists and their activities."[20] In December 2020, the CCP issued an updated version of its united front work regulations, which described the mission of united front worked aimed at Taiwan as

> *Implementing the CCP Central Committee's work on Taiwan, adhering to the "One-China Principle," broadly uniting Taiwan compatriots at home and abroad, developing and strengthening Taiwan's patriotic reunification force, opposing Taiwan's secessionist activities, and continuing to promote peace in the motherland for the process of reunification and jointly realize the great rejuvenation of the Chinese nation with one heart.*[21]

Although the regulations include some positive objectives such as strengthening "reunification forces" in Taiwan, a united front logic emphasizes opposition to a common threat or enemy by cooperation with groups and individuals that might not support the CCP's ultimate objectives.

The primary focus of CCP united front tactics has been on strengthening opposition to pro-independence leaders and political parties (such as the Democratic Progressive Party [DPP], the Taiwan Solidarity Union, and the New Power Party) and their policy initiatives (such as constitutional referenda and de-Sinification of the educational system). China's efforts have included building formal party-to-party ties with the KMT and People First parties, mobilizing international actors to oppose Taiwan independence as a threat to regional stability, and reaching out to members of the DPP to wean them away from support for Taiwan independence. China has also employed united front tactics by organizing retired officer dialogues, encouraging Taiwan business leaders operating in the mainland to oppose separatist activities and support unification, and engaging Taiwan mayors and local government officials.[22]

Although the Taiwan independence movement has been the primary target of CCP united front tactics, Beijing has also tried to build a united front against Japan by harnessing anti-Japanese sentiment in Taiwan over the issue of the Senkaku/Diaoyu Islands. The islands are claimed by Japan, Taiwan, and the PRC (which asserts that the islands belong to Taiwan, which is part of the PRC). Especially after Japan's nationalization of some of the islands in 2012, when the Japanese government purchased three of the islands from a private Japanese owner, the CCP has tried to use the issue to drive a wedge between Taiwan and Japan and to make common cause with Taiwan groups that support Taiwan's claims to the islands. China has followed similar tactics with respect to Taiwan's territorial claims in the South China Sea, trying to appeal to nationalists in Taiwan by asserting that it is more willing to stand up for Chinese territorial claims than the government in Taipei.

United front tactics have some inherent limitations in the Taiwan context. There are political actors in Taiwan who identify as Chinese and oppose independence because they believe that Taiwan is part of a larger China, but few of them are eager to subject Taiwan to CCP control as part of the PRC. Moreover, the political power of this group has declined over time due to Taiwan's democratization and generational change that has reduced personal ties to mainland China.[23] Others in Taiwan oppose movement toward independence on the practical grounds that it might precipitate a devastating war, but this pragmatic view yields support for maintaining the political status quo rather than for political talks aimed at unification. Public opinion polls consistently indicate that this "conditional preference" for the status quo rather than independence is the dominant view in Taiwan.[24] From a PRC viewpoint, this suggests that tactics based on a united front logic are much more effective in preventing Taiwan's movement toward independence (largely due to concerns about precipitating a war) than in convincing actors in Taiwan and elsewhere to embrace unification.

Persuasion

Persuasion focuses on convincing key actors (especially in Taiwan, but also in the international community) that unification is an acceptable or even desirable outcome. This is a judgment made partly in the context of alternatives, including China's threat to use force. However, this logic emphasizes CCP efforts to increase the benefits and reduce the potential costs of unification for key actors in Taiwan and to promulgate a positive vision of what life would be like as part of the PRC.

One line of effort involves reassuring Taiwan that unification would not cause fundamental changes in Taiwan's political system (via Deng Xiaoping's "one country, two systems" proposal and subsequent offers to allow Taiwan to keep its own military, not have PRC troops on its soil, have substantial autonomy over its affairs, and so forth). Another involves demonstrating the value of a closer relationship between China and Taiwan by providing economic opportunities and facilitating a larger international presence (with the potential for even greater benefits if Taiwan accepts unification). A third involves efforts to influence conceptions of identity in Taiwan in ways that emphasize cultural and historical ties with China and make unification more acceptable.

Persuasion has limitations in the Taiwan context. Because this logic involves projecting a positive vision of Taiwan's role in a future unified China, people in Taiwan will judge the vision's appeal based on expectations of the political future of the PRC and the CCP, the specific terms offered, and the credibility of the CCP's pledge to respect those terms in the future when Taiwan would have limited ability to enforce a bargain with Beijing. China's rapid economic growth and rising power could have potential appeal for people in Taiwan, offering significant economic opportunities and the chance to be associated with a country that has growing international influence. However, Taiwan already enjoys significant economic access because CCP leaders believe this is beneficial for the Chinese economy, allowing Taiwan to enjoy most of these potential benefits without a more formal political relationship. Moreover, the growing authoritarian trend in China and crackdown on political expression over the last decade make a closer political association with the PRC much less attractive.

China's various formulations of what "one country, two systems" might look like in Taiwan include several specific assurances if Taiwan accepts peaceful unification. These include pledges that Taiwan would enjoy a high degree of autonomy, could manage local affairs without interference, would be able to retain its armed forces, and could keep its current socioeconomic system.[25] However, some of these assurances have been weakened in recent PRC speeches about Taiwan, and they must be judged against PRC pledges in other contexts, such as the high degree of autonomy promised to Hong Kong in the reversion agreement. The PRC's efforts to roll back democratic institutions and impose a political crackdown in Hong Kong in the name of security have severely damaged the CCP's credibility with the Taiwan public. In this context, persuading Taiwan people of the benefits of unification is an increasingly difficult task. Finally, the PRC's conditional threat to use force if Taiwan declares independence and its increasing military pressure undercut efforts to persuade Taiwan leaders and people that they can achieve security, prosperity, and a sufficient degree of freedom and autonomy as part of a unified China.

Implications of Multiple Causal Logics

What are the implications of the three logics underlying Chinese policy? Using multiple logics can explain several important points about Chinese policy. These include patterns of continuity and change in PRC policies toward Taiwan, coalition-building on policy decisions, and how the fungibility of policy tools across the three logics shapes the positions of PRC policy actors.

A starting point is to view Chinese policy from the perspective of a unitary actor responding rationally to changing assessments of the threat of Taiwan independence and opportunities to move toward unification. Since policies derived from the three logics have varying utility for the separate goals of deterring independence and achieving unification, China's policy mix should shift over time based on changes in its assessment of threats and opportunities. This approach could be used to tease out the evolving mix of Chinese policies. Such a perspective also suggests that if Beijing feels that the threat of Taiwan independence has declined and opportunities for unification have increased, then China's policy mix might shift in the direction of policy measures that make sense under the logic of persuasion. Conversely, if the threat of independence has increased, Beijing is likely to lean more heavily on tools that rest on leverage and united front logics to deter movement toward Taiwan independence.

This approach could be helpful in revealing patterns of continuity and change in PRC policy. In terms of continuity, the PRC has consistently refused to rule out the use of force to deter Taiwan independence, continued united front efforts aimed at groups in Taiwan that might be mobilized to oppose independence and support unification, and sought to articulate and demonstrate the benefits that unification might have for Taiwan. PRC policy toward Taiwan has largely stayed within the principles and parameters established from 1979 to 1982 under Deng Xiaoping, but there have been significant variations over time in the use of coercive measures to deter independence and encourage political talks on unification; to mobilize groups in Taiwan to oppose specific leaders, parties, and policies that Beijing regards as promoting separation from China; and to provide or deny economic benefits to specific groups in Taiwan. Viewing these changes in terms of shifts in the relative importance of the three logics is a parsimonious way to describe and analyze changes in Chinese policy.

A second point is that the existence of multiple logics could affect prospects for building domestic coalitions on Taiwan policy within the PRC. A number of PRC actors have important interests in Taiwan policy: economic and local officials want to use Taiwan trade and investment to increase economic growth. Businesses seek technology from Taiwan to move up the knowledge ladder. Political leaders want to win points with nationalists for moving toward unification (and avoid losses if Taiwan moves toward independence). Foreign Ministry officials regard isolating Taiwan internationally as a core part of their mission. The military feels a special responsibility for defending China's sovereignty and territorial integrity, especially by achieving unification.[26]

If a policy makes sense under all three logics, then Chinese leaders would find it easier to build a consensus on that policy even if the rationales that individual actors use to support the policy are different or mutually inconsistent. For example, China's liberalization of fruit imports from southern Taiwan increases Taiwan's dependence on the mainland market (potentially creating economic leverage), creates new economic interests for a traditional DPP constituency (potentially drawing them into a united front), and shows that closer political ties with the mainland could produce important economic benefits for Taiwan (demonstrating potential benefits of unification). The corollary is that China finds it harder to adopt policies that make strong sense from one logic, but which are counterproductive from other perspectives.[27] For instance, facilitating Taiwan's participation in the World Health Assembly makes sense in terms of united front logic and persuasion logic but undercuts efforts to increase Chinese leverage by isolating Taiwan.[28]

A third point involves the extent to which influential policy actors are associated with tools that are fungible across the different logics or tools that only make sense under one logic. Chinese businesses and local PRC leaders focused on expanding cross-strait economic contacts benefit from the fact that their preferred policies potentially make sense under all three logics.[29] Such policies make Taiwan more dependent economically on the PRC, generating leverage that might be used in the future to reward favored groups with opportunities, to punish those viewed as enemies, and to provide benefits to the Taiwan people that demonstrate the gains from improved cross-strait relations.

Conversely, the People's Liberation Army (PLA) is heavily associated with military tools, such as developing ballistic missiles and deploying them opposite Taiwan, which make sense only under the logic of leverage and might have negative effects on other policy goals. If Chinese policy actors are only relevant under one logic (leverage), then they would tend to support policies that make sense under that logic and oppose those that are costly or counterproductive from their institutional point of view. Thus, many in the PLA support accelerated military modernization to generate more leverage and oppose substantive military confidence-building measures that might reduce or constrain China's ability to generate and employ military power. A focus on competing policy logics and the utility of tools under each logic could potentially help identify the likely positions of key Chinese actors, help predict their positions in terms of supporting or opposing specific policy measures, and help assess the relative influence of different actors in the PRC policy process.

The CCP has a deliberative process for policymaking about Taiwan, with decisions generally made at the top of the system based on input from lower levels.[30] This does not mean, however, that the unitary rational actor model explains all policy decisions. In practice, CCP policy toward Taiwan appears to be the product of a relatively cautious, bureaucratic process with multiple competing players operating within a policy environment with well-established principles and constraints. In such a system, powerful actors such as the military could invoke the logic of leverage to resist proposals that might hurt their institutional interests (even if these might advance PRC goals by winning support from people in Taiwan). Conversely, less-influential actors might need to frame their policy proposals in terms of multiple logics to build consensus in adopting them. Viewing policy debates from the perspective of multiple causal logics can add richness to analysis of the bureaucratic and political interests of the different groups involved in making and implementing China's policy toward Taiwan. Finally, it is important to remember that some PRC statements and actions may be the product of bargaining between policy actors or reflect domestic political calculations rather than any expectation that they would advance PRC policy goals.

The Three Logics Framework and Historical Analysis of Cross-Strait Relations

This section sketches the mix of the three logics in China's policy during different political administrations in Taiwan. Because this chapter focuses on PRC policy toward Taiwan, it might appear logical to follow the conventional path of organizing the analysis in terms of successive CCP top leaders. It is certainly true that there are important and distinctive policy developments associated with each leader.

Deng Xiaoping launched China's "opening up and reform" policy that emphasized stability and placed a higher priority on the contributions Taiwan could make to PRC economic development. He also shifted policy from "liberating Taiwan" to "peaceful unification" and proposed the "one country, two systems" model for unification. Jiang Zemin (1989-2002) proposed a path toward unification in his "eight points" speech. He also approved ballistic missile tests near Taiwan ports following Lee Teng-hui's 1995 visit to the United States and increased PLA budgets after the 1995–1996 Taiwan Strait Crisis. Hu Jintao (2002–2012) supported the 2005 Anti-Secession Law to strengthen deterrence of Taiwan independence. Xi Jinping (2012–present) has emphasized improvements in PRC military capabilities, exhibited greater willingness to employ coercion and pressure against Taiwan, and placed greater stress on achieving unification.

In practice, however, changes in PRC policy toward Taiwan have been driven primarily by PRC assessments of the intentions of different Taiwan leaders and the balance between the urgency of the perceived threat of Taiwan independence and the perceived opportunity to improve relations and move toward unification. China's policy has remained within the framework of principles and parameters established by the early 1980s under Deng. Even Xi Jinping, widely viewed as the most powerful PRC leader since Deng, continues to operate within this basic framework.

Lee Teng-hui (1988-1994). Lee's time as president can be divided into two phases. As the first Taiwan president to be born on the island, Lee navigated through the KMT's mainlander-dominated factional politics to attain power after Chiang Ching-kuo's death in 1988 and to pursue democratization and the end of the authoritarian governance structures that marked KMT rule. Taiwan elites accepted the reality that Taiwan was never going to conquer the PRC, focused on implementing democratic governance of the territory that Taiwan did control, and began efforts to develop a working relationship with the PRC. The governments Lee led during this period included mainlanders committed to eventual unification with China and policies that reflected the KMT's mainlander-dominated factional politics. Notable actions included Taiwan's 1991 *Guidelines for National Unification*, which were based on a "one China" foundation and articulated a three-stage process that would culminate in planning for the unification of a "democratic, free, and equitably prosperous China."[31] Taiwan and China also expanded economic ties and established the semi-official SEF-ARATS mechanism in 1991 as a channel for cross-strait dialogue and coordination.

Lee Teng-hui (1995–2000). Lee eventually consolidated his power base within the KMT, replacing many older party and government officials with native-born appointees. In January 1995, Jiang Zemin sought to lay out a positive PRC roadmap for improving cross-strait relations that might appeal to people in Taiwan with his eight points speech. Lee spurned Jiang's initiative and launched a successful lobbying effort to win permission to visit the United States and give a speech at Cornell University, which ultimately triggered the 1995–1996 Taiwan Strait Crisis. PRC policies subsequently emphasized building economic leverage and accelerating military modernization, coupled with united front tactics targeting conservative elements within the KMT that might support unification and oppose movement toward Taiwan independence. Lee's 1999 announcement that cross-strait relations were best characterized as "special state-to-state relations" reinforced PRC suspicions that Lee had a pro-independence agenda and led to a suspension of the ARATS-SEF channel until June 2008.

Chen Shui-bian (2000–2008). PRC suspicions of Chen and the pro-independence DPP were partly offset by his moderate inauguration speech and KMT control of the Legislative Yuan throughout his tenure in office, which constrained Chen's ability to pursue independence through legislative means. However, Chen's pursuit of de-Sinification and referendums asserting Taiwan's independent status raised concerns and prompted the PRC to pass the Anti-Secession Law in 2005 as a warning of its willingness to pursue "non-peaceful means" to prevent Taiwan independence. Economic ties continued to grow despite the absence of cross-strait political dialogue. The PRC continued to pursue economic and military leverage and intensified united front efforts to harness the KMT to oppose Chen and prevent moves toward Taiwan independence.

Ma Ying-jeou (2008–2016). Ma's involvement in previous cross-strait dialogue and willingness to expand and deepen cross-strait ties reduced CCP concerns about Taiwan independence and provided new opportunities to deepen and institutionalize cross-strait ties, including by establishing the "three links" (direct mail, transport, and trade) and negotiating the Economic Cooperation Framework Agreement. PLA modernization continued, but China was careful to avoid provocative military exercises in the strait. United front tactics were less useful with the KMT in power, but the CCP tried to create an anti-Japanese united front focused on the Senkaku/Diaoyu Islands, which Ma defused by negotiating an agreement that gave Taiwan fishers access to fishing grounds near the islands.[32] The CCP also allowed limited Taiwan participation in some international organizations such as the World Health Assembly. Both sides explored the notion of a peace accord that might pave the way for eventual unification.[33] In 2014, Ma's attempt to push the Cross-Strait Service Trade Agreement through the legislature sparked the student Sunflower movement opposing further expansion of cross-strait economic ties.[34] CCP leaders eventually grew frustrated at Ma's ability to control the cross-strait agenda and began applying economic and military pressure on Taiwan to begin talks on political issues.

Tsai Ing-wen (2016–present). PRC leaders were deeply suspicious of Tsai due to her role in Lee's cabinet, including her involvement in developing the "two states theory" and her DPP party affiliation. Tsai made some accommodating gestures in her inauguration speech but refused to accept the 1992 Consensus. Chinese leaders chose to use this as a rationale to break off ARATS-SEF contacts rather than seek a mutually acceptable formulation that could serve as a political basis for cross-strait contacts.[35] China has applied various forms of economic, diplomatic, and military pressure, including restrictions on tourists coming to Taiwan, ending previous restraint on peeling away Taiwan's diplomatic allies, successfully opposing Taiwan's participation in international organizations, resuming military exercises opposite Taiwan, and using air force and navy maneuvers near Taiwan to exert pressure on Tsai and the Taiwan military (for a discussion on these operations, see the chapter by Mathieu Duchâtel in this volume). China tried to increase united front approaches to the KMT and to DPP local officials, including allegations of illegal funding and influence operations to support some KMT candidates. These efforts had some success in the 2018 Taiwan local elections but faltered in the face of anti-China sentiment in the aftermath of the Hong Kong protests. The PRC made few efforts under the persuasion logic: the conditions offered for peaceful unification in Xi Jinping's 2019 Taiwan policy speech were less generous than those that had previously been offered.[36] The table describes the perceived mix of threat and opportunity under different Taiwan leaders and PRC policy efforts under each of the three logics.

Table. Three Logics in Historical Perspective

Taiwan Leader	Perceived Threat of Independence	Perceived Opportunity to Improve Cross-Strait Relations	Leverage	United Front	Persuasion
Lee Teng-hui (1988–1994)	Limited due to influence of KMT mainlanders	National Unification Guidelines reaffirmed goal of unification; establishment of semiofficial dialogue; 1992 Consensus	Increasing cross-strait economic ties; incremental progress in PLA modernization	Efforts to engage KMT; efforts to engage Taiwan business and retired military	Jiang Zemin's "8 points" speech; benefits of cross-strait trade
Lee Teng-hui (1995–2000)	Increasing, especially after 1995 U.S. visit and 1999 "two states theory"	Lee rejected Jiang's 8 points proposal; cross-strait dialogue suspended by PRC in 1999	Increasing economic ties; 1995–1996 missile tests; increasing PLA budgets after 1996	Efforts to engage conservative "deep blue" elements in KMT; efforts to engage Taiwan business and retired military	Benefits of cross-strait trade

Taiwan Leader	Perceived Threat of Independence	Perceived Opportunity to Improve Cross-Strait Relations	Leverage	United Front	Persuasion
Chen Shui-bian (2000–2008)	DPP independence platform, Taiwanization, and pro-independence actions create deep suspicion	Economic ties separated from political tensions; cross-strait dialogue remained suspended	Increasing economic ties; PLA modernization accelerates; PLA emphasis on deterrence; Anti-Secession Law (2005)	Increased efforts to engage opposition KMT via party-to-party channels	Benefits of cross-strait trade
Ma Ying-jeou (2008–2016)	Receding due to KMT control of executive and legislative branches and acceptance of 1992 Consensus	Opportunity to deepen and institutionalize cross-strait ties; expansion of cross-strait semi-official contacts; PRC hope for start of political dialogue	Increasing economic ties; PLA modernization continues; military balance shifts in PRC's favor	Efforts to build anti-Japan united front	Cross-strait agreements that benefit Taiwan; expanded international space; diplomatic truce; limits on PLA exercises aimed at Taiwan; PRC growth and status have some appeal
Tsai Ing-wen (2016–present)	Tsai's refusal to accept 1992 Consensus heightens PRC suspicion; restraint on sovereignty issues not acknowledged; DPP control of executive and legislative branches heightens PRC concerns	PRC refuses to deal directly with Tsai and the DPP; breaks cross-strait semi-official contacts	PLA exercises aimed at Taiwan resume; PLA military pressure on Taiwan increases; diplomatic truce ends; economic pressure exerted through limits on PRC tourism; squeezing of Taiwan's international space; linkage between unification and great rejuvenation of the Chinese people	Increased efforts to engage opposition KMT and DPP local leaders; PRC efforts to influence 2018 local and 2020 national elections	Benefits of cross-strait trade; Xi Jinping's 2019 speech laying out benefits of unification less generous than Jiang's 8 points

Key: DPP: Democratic Progressive Party; KMT: Kuomintang; PLA: People's Liberation Army; PRC: People's Republic of China

This concise historical review illustrates how the three logics may help explain PRC policies toward Taiwan in different periods, including patterns of continuity and change. Policies that made sense under all three logics, such as expanding economic relations with Taiwan, continued throughout despite leadership changes in Taiwan and the PRC and significant ups and downs in cross-strait relations. Efforts to develop military leverage over Taiwan, strongly supported by powerful PLA leaders, accelerated after the 1995–1996 Taiwan Strait Crisis, but CCP leaders exercised tight control over the timing and amount of military coercion applied against Taiwan. This may be explained partly in terms of the continuing high costs and risks of using lethal military force, but concerns about undermining political initiatives aimed at building support in Taiwan for unification were also a factor in determining whether and how the PRC applied military coercion.

The review also suggests findings about the employment of policies associated with the three logics in different political conditions. The logic of building leverage applies throughout all periods and the PRC has consistently employed coercive threats to deter potential movement toward Taiwan independence. Variation has come in terms of PRC efforts to use military shows of force when it perceived the need to reinforce deterrence and in PRC decisions about whether to apply accumulated leverage in an attempt to coerce Taiwan leaders to move toward unification.

The potential utility of united front tactics largely depends on whether the KMT is in power or in opposition. It is relatively easy for the CCP and the KMT to cooperate in opposing the DPP and its policies aimed at promoting a separate Taiwan identity or promoting independence. When the KMT is in power, however, PRC pressure to move toward unification highlights the differences in ultimate goals and places the KMT in the untenable position of acting against the preference of most of the Taiwan people to maintain the status quo. Under these conditions, united front tactics lose much of their effectiveness. PRC efforts to substitute an anti-Japan united front over the Senkaku/Diaoyu Islands issue or to rally Taiwan support against Southeast Asian claimants for the Spratly Islands have been ineffective.

China's willingness to emphasize tools under the persuasion logic ebbs and flows with conditions. In the early period of Lee's presidency and during Ma's term in office, the PRC made a number of positive gestures as part of its efforts to improve cross-strait relations and build support in Taiwan for unification. However, when the PRC feels the need to oppose moves by a pro-independence Taiwan leader, as in the later period of Lee's presidency and during Chen's term in office, coercion is used even though it undercuts PRC efforts to build support for unification.

One interesting implication of this historical analysis is that it suggests Chinese policy has been driven more by PRC assessments of the threats and opportunities caused by political developments in Taiwan (and to a lesser degree in the United States) than by leadership changes or domestic political developments in the PRC. Chinese policy toward Taiwan over the past 40 years has tended to follow a consistent, fairly conservative set of principles initially articulated by Deng. Policy changes have generally come in reaction to developments in Taiwan rather than proactive PRC efforts to influence conditions on the island. This may be due to the political sensitivity of the Taiwan issue and the nationalist policy environment in the PRC, both of which discourage creative proposals that might have more appeal to people in Taiwan.

Looking to the Future

Can this analytic framework help predict future PRC policy toward Taiwan? This section reviews Taiwan survey data on identity, party affiliation, and preferences on independence and unification and the implications for Taiwan politics and policy toward the mainland. It considers the relevance of the leverage, united front, and persuasion logics going forward and how shifts in their relevance might affect China's future policy choices. It then considers PRC perceptions about the risks of Taiwan independence and whether PRC politics are likely to shift from an emphasis on deterring Taiwan independence toward the more ambitious and difficult goal of achieving unification.

Survey data in Taiwan over the last 30 years shows an increasing sense of Taiwan identity, a consistent preference for maintaining the cross-strait status quo coupled with decreasing interest in unification and increasing party affiliation with the DPP and declining affiliation with the KMT. Data from the December 2021 survey by National Chengchi University's Election Study Center show that 62.3 percent of respondents identify as Taiwanese, 31.7 identify as both Taiwanese and Chinese, and only 2.8 percent identify as

Chinese. The long-term trendlines show Taiwanese identity increasing dramatically over time (from just 17.6 percent in 1992 to 62.3 percent in 2021) and a gradually decreasing, but still significant, number of respondents who self-identify as both Taiwanese and Chinese.[37]

Preferences about unification versus independence are more complicated to analyze, but the survey data show a consistent preference for maintaining the status quo for now (the choice of 85.6 percent of respondents in the most recent survey) rather than moving quickly toward unification (1.4 percent) or independence (6 percent). There is declining interest in the option of unification, with a peak of 22 percent favoring rapid or eventual unification in 1996 but only 7.4 percent in the 2021 survey. Although declining from its 2006 peak of 38.7 percent, 28.4 percent of respondents want to maintain the status quo and decide at a later date, keeping eventual unification open as a potential option.[38] A more detailed analysis that probes conditional preferences by examining "easy" or "hard" scenarios for unification and independence concludes that "clear pluralities [of status quo respondents] are willing to have easy independence, but strong majorities are not willing to accept unification even in the easiest scenario."[39]

The survey data also show that a plurality of Taiwan citizens (45.5 percent) identify as independents or did not report a party affiliation in 2021. DPP affiliation is volatile but has averaged about 27–28 percent from 2015 to 2021, while KMT affiliation has declined significantly from a peak of 39.5 percent in 2011 to 17.1 percent in the 2021 survey.[40]

The survey data suggest a Taiwan electorate that increasingly identifies as Taiwanese, is cautious about moving away from the status quo, and has declining interest in unification. For the PRC, these results should be good news in terms of deterring Taiwan independence and bad news in terms of achieving unification. The DPP's road to winning the presidency, assembling a majority in the Legislative Yuan, and ambition to become a permanent ruling party has required it to move away from the pledge to declare independence in its original platform to a more moderate position that can win support from the Taiwan public.[41] This democratic filtering effect has produced more pragmatic and cautious DPP candidates, although this may be tested if the current vice president, William Lai Ching-te—who declared himself "a political worker who advocates Taiwan independence" in 2017 while serving as premier—wins the DPP nomination in 2024. While the Taiwan electorate and outside observers regard DPP leaders such as Tsai Ing-wen as pragmatic and moderate, PRC officials and analysts view them with deep suspicion, citing past statements and actions as evidence of their independence inclinations.

The identity and unification/independence preference data cited suggest the Taiwan public is relatively content with the status quo, averse to taking risks, and has limited interest in unification. This presents the PRC with a difficult challenge in persuading Taiwan leaders and the Taiwan public to accept unification. China's recent trend toward more authoritarian politics and decreased freedom of expression makes unification with the PRC less attractive to a Taiwan public used to living in a democratic society. Beijing's crackdown on democracy and civil rights in Hong Kong has led many people in Taiwan to conclude that CCP leaders cannot be trusted to live up to the terms of a negotiated agreement. This suggests that PRC policies, strategies, and tactics that rely on persuasion may be less effective in the future because it will be increasingly difficult to convince a reluctant Taiwan public that China's vision of future unification is better than the current status quo. The PRC might ultimately have to threaten the current status quo to push Taiwan to accept unification—an approach that would challenge U.S. policy that opposes unilateral changes to the status quo by either China or Taiwan.

United front tactics may also have less utility for the PRC in the future. Demographic changes and declining interest in unification among the Taiwan electorate will make it harder for parties supporting unification to win power, as the KMT's dwindling party identification figures suggest. In 2021, KMT party chair Johnny Chiang proposed adjustments in KMT policies toward China that might have more appeal to the Taiwan public, but party elders such as Lien Chan and Ma Ying-jeou weighed in against him and Chiang was defeated in his bid for reelection. New KMT chair Eric Chu promptly sent a letter to Xi Jinping reaffirming the 1992 Consensus and calling for cooperation in opposing Taiwan independence.[42] This outcome is consistent with the CCP's united front logic, but this approach is unlikely to have much appeal in Taiwan politics, especially given continuing PRC military coercion against Taiwan. The result may be a KMT that becomes increasingly marginalized and perhaps incapable of functioning as an effective opposition party. At the same time, the DPP's relatively cautious and incremental approach on policy toward China makes it difficult to use opposition to Taiwan independence as a political rallying cry.

The declining utility of policies associated with united front and persuasion logics leaves CCP leaders increasingly reliant on policy instruments based on leverage and coercion. These tools are likely to be effective in deterring overt moves toward Taiwan independence, given pragmatic Taiwan leadership, a risk-averse Taiwan public, and the high costs of war for Taiwan, the United States, and China.

At present, the most likely source of conflict would be a Chinese leadership that redefines its red lines about which actions promoting Taiwan independence are unacceptable and decides that it must use a show of force to deter "creeping independence." PRC complaints about deepening U.S.-Taiwan military cooperation and U.S.-Taiwan relations taking on an increasingly official dimension highlight this risk. Beijing opposes any increase in U.S.-Taiwan cooperation, but developments that further erode the U.S. "one China" commitments made in the three communiques could prompt China to take limited military action to reestablish limits on U.S. unofficial relations with Taiwan, as it did in 1995–1996.

The longer term issue is whether the PRC can remain patient about its ultimate goal of achieving unification or whether CCP leaders will conclude that a distinctive Taiwan identity is becoming consolidated, which would permanently separate Taiwan from China. The United States is a factor in this calculus, given heightened U.S.-China strategic competition and the suggestion by some U.S. strategists that U.S. geostrategic interests require preventing Taiwan's unification with China.[43] Some U.S. analysts worry that China is likely to attack Taiwan as soon as it has the military capability to do so or that nationalistic pressures might force PRC leaders to make a risky decision to use force.[44] As other chapters in this volume document, the CCP has invested significant resources to develop military options for unification, even though the PLA has not yet put all the necessary pieces in place for an invasion.

Xi Jinping and CCP leaders in Beijing are clearly not satisfied with the political status quo in Taiwan. Yet they also appear to have implicitly accepted that conditions will not be ripe for unification for some time and have recently reiterated their faith in the Taiwan people and their commitment to the policy of peaceful unification.[45] Although nationalist pressures exist and might be growing, CCP control over the media and propaganda apparatus and the ability to tolerate or suppress public protests make it unlikely that such pressures will force CCP leaders to take unwanted actions, such as starting a conflict that China might not win.[46] Moreover, CCP leaders could create political room to maneuver by toggling between emphasizing the easy-to-achieve goal of deterring Taiwan independence or the more ambitious but harder-to-accomplish goal of unification as circumstances warrant.

The most likely PRC approach for the near term is continued pressure on Taiwan's DPP government to accept the 1992 Consensus coupled with efforts to accumulate additional political, economic, and military leverage to strength Beijing's coercive options for dealing with Taiwan and the United States. The PRC is also likely to continue to employ united front tactics and to seek to persuade the Taiwan public that unification would have positive benefits, despite the declining effectiveness of these lines of effort. Press reports suggest that the CCP's National Party Congress in fall 2022 is likely to adopt a new guiding policy on Taiwan that may provide a clearer sense of the PRC's policy direction.[47]

Conclusion

CCP leaders may ultimately decide that time and political trends in Taiwan are moving against the PRC and that force will be necessary to achieve unification despite the high political, economic, and military costs and risks. Such a decision would be based on the leadership's assessment of the perceived costs and risks of various courses of action and of the perceived costs of inaction in terms of accepting Taiwan independence or losing the chance for unification. Andrew Scobell's chapter in this volume discusses the potential CCP leadership calculus in more detail, and the chapters by Mathieu Duchâtel and Michael Casey discuss the pros and cons of available PRC military options. It is worth emphasizing that all of China's top leaders have repeatedly stated that they are willing to fight, if necessary, to protect China's core interest in sovereignty and territorial integrity.

Taiwan and the United States can take some actions to reduce the likelihood of CCP leaders reaching the point where a costly and risky decision to use force appears to be the PRC's best course of action. One line of effort involves concerted efforts to improve Taiwan's defenses and focus them on increasing the costs and risks of PRC military options, as discussed in the chapters by Drew Thompson and Alexander Huang. These efforts should focus on concrete actions to improve military capability rather than symbolic measures of U.S. support for Taiwan. Ukraine's resistance to Russia's February 2022 invasion demonstrates that targeted investments in defense can be effective against a more powerful military. The U.S. military is also increasing its emphasis on developing new capabilities and operational concepts to prevail in a conflict with the PRC over Taiwan. However, it is equally important to influence the other side of the CCP leadership calculus by keeping the possibility of peaceful unification alive. This suggests that Taiwan should not definitively rule out the possibility of unification if conditions change in China. For the same reason, U.S. policy should continue to focus on process (for example, any unification must be achieved peacefully with the consent of the Taiwan people) rather than explicitly oppose unification regardless of the circumstances. Placing the PRC in a position where war is the only option for achieving unification would increase the risks of a military conflict with potentially devastating consequences for China, Taiwan, and the United States.

The author thanks Michael Glosny, Joel Wuthnow, Bonnie Glaser, Thomas Christensen, Stapleton Roy, and Isaac Kardon for helpful comments on earlier drafts and Jessica Drun for research assistance.

Notes

[1] See *The Taiwan Question and Reunification of China* (Beijing: State Council Information Office and Taiwan Affairs Office, August 1993), available at <https://www.fmprc.gov.cn/ce/ceno/eng/ztxw/twwt/t110654.htm>; Richard C. Bush, *Untying the Knot: Making Peace in the Taiwan Strait* (Washington, DC: Brookings Institution Press, 2005); Alan D. Romberg, *Rein in at the Brink of the Precipice: American Policy Toward Taiwan and U.S.-PRC Relations* (Washington, DC: The Henry L. Stimson Center, 2003), 225–227.

[2] As of this writing, Taiwan maintains diplomatic relations with 13 United Nations member states and the Vatican. Note that the U.S. "one China" *policy* does not accept all elements of the PRC "one China" *principle*. For a full explication of U.S. policy, see Romberg, *Rein in at the Brink of the Precipice*. For a concise explanation, see Richard C. Bush, *A One-China Policy Primer*, East Asia Policy Paper 10 (Washington, DC: Brookings Institution, March 2017), available at <https://www.brookings.edu/research/a-one-china-policy-primer/>.

[3] See Bush, *Untying the Knot*, 35–45.

⁴ For a recent statement showing the endurance of these principles, see Xi Jinping, "Speech at a Meeting Marking the 110ᵗʰ Anniversary of the Revolution Of 1911," Xinhua, October 9, 2021, available at <https://www.mfa.gov.cn/ce/ceus//eng/zgyw/t1913454.htm>.

⁵ Some People's Republic of China (PRC) academics and think tank analysts have privately indicated that some experts hesitate to challenge the preconceptions of PRC policymakers in their internal writings. Author's discussions with PRC scholars and analysts, 2016–2018.

⁶ A senior PRC academic noted privately that even fairly senior officials within the Taiwan Affairs Office (Taiban) might not be privy to Xi Jinping's real thinking or aware of the content of forthcoming policy statements on Taiwan. Discussion with the author, 2018.

⁷ One of the things that distinguishes Chinese core interests from lesser interests is a willingness to fight to defend core interests.

⁸ Some solutions proposed by scholars involve a confederation that would include both the PRC and the Republic of China (ROC) as equals, but official PRC proposals envision a unified Taiwan that is a subordinate part of the PRC.

⁹ Xi first stated this in a 2013 meeting with Vincent Siew, Taiwan's representative at the 2013 Asia Pacific Economic Cooperation Summit, and reiterated it in his 2019 New Year's speech. See "China's Xi Says Political Solution for Taiwan Can't Wait Forever," Reuters, October 6, 2013, available at <https://www.reuters.com/article/us-asia-apec-china-taiwan/chinas-xi-says-political-solution-for-taiwan-cant-wait-forever-idUSBRE99503Q20131006>; Richard C. Bush, "8 Key Things to Notice from Xi Jinping's New Year Speech on Taiwan," *Brookings Institution*, January 7, 2019, available at <https://www.brookings.edu/blog/order-from-chaos/2019/01/07/8-key-things-to-notice-from-xi-jinpings-new-year-speech-on-taiwan/>.

¹⁰ "Full Text of Xi Jinping's Report at 19ᵗʰ CPC National Congress," Xinhua, October 18, 2017, available at <http://www.xinhuanet.com/english/special/2017-11/03/c_136725942.htm>.

¹¹ An analogy could be drawn with potential energy (leverage) and kinetic energy (coercion).

¹² For example, a weaker state might choose to forgo actions that it knows or expects would antagonize a stronger state that has significant leverage over it, even if that stronger state has not made specific deterrent threats.

¹³ Thomas C. Schelling, *The Strategy of Conflict* (Cambridge, MA: Harvard University Press, 1960); Thomas C. Schelling, *Arms and Influence* (New Haven: Yale University Press, 1966).

¹⁴ This argument originates with Schelling, who emphasizes higher costs due to the greater visibility of concessions and the likelihood of concessions leading to additional demands in the compellence case. Schelling, *Arms and Influence*, 69–91. More recent formulations ground this conclusion in prospect theory, which draws on social psychology to argue that the perceived costs of giving up something one already has are valued more highly than prospective gains of attaining something one wants. See Gary Schaub, Jr., "Deterrence, Compellence, and Prospect Theory," *Political Psychology* 25, no. 3 (June 2004), 389–411.

¹⁵ See Albert Hirschman, *National Power and the Structure of Foreign Trade* (Berkeley: University of California Press, 1945).

[16] Chinese Community Party (CCP) leaders have mentioned several actions that might justify the use of force, including formal declaration of Taiwan independence, movement toward Taiwan independence, internal unrest in Taiwan, Taiwan's acquisition of nuclear weapons, indefinite (*sine die*) delays in the resumption of cross-strait dialogue on unification, and foreign military intervention in Taiwan's internal affairs. See *Annual Report to Congress: Military and Security Developments Involving the People's Republic of China 2021* (Washington, DC: Office of the Secretary of Defense, 2021), 115–116, available at <https://media.defense.gov/2021/nov/03/2002885874/-1/-1/0/2021-cmpr-final.pdf>.

[17] The Kuomintang regards the 1992 Consensus as involving "one China, separate interpretations" and interprets the "one China" as the ROC. The CCP regards the 1992 Consensus as acknowledging that China and Taiwan are both part of the same sovereign political entity. The term *1992 Consensus* was coined by Su Chi in 2000 as shorthand for the 1992 agreement that allowed the Association for Relations Across the Taiwan Strait–Straits Exchange Foundation talks to move forward. See Yu-Jie Chen and Jerome A. Cohen, "China-Taiwan Relations Re-Examined: The '1992 Consensus' and Cross-Strait Agreements," *University of Pennsylvania Asian Law Review* 14, nos. 1/2 (2019), 1–40, available at <https://scholarship.law.upenn.edu/cgi/viewcontent.cgi?article=1039&context=alr>.

[18] See Larry Diamond and Orville Schell, eds., *China's Influence & American Interests: Promoting Constructive Vigilance* (Stanford: Hoover Institution, 2018), appendix I, available at <https://www.hoover.org/research/chinas-influence-american-interests-promoting-constructive-vigilance>.

[19] This is partly because united fronts to oppose common enemies divert attention from the incompatibility of the CCP's ultimate goals with those of other members of the united front.

[20] *China's National Defense in the New Era* (Beijing: State Council Information Office, July 2019), available at <https://english.www.gov.cn/archive/whitepaper/201907/24/content_WS5d3941ddc6d08408f502283d.html>.

[21] Translation adapted from Russell Hsiao, "Political Warfare Alert: CCP Updates United Front Regulations Expanding Foreign Influence Mission," *Global Taiwan Brief* 6, no. 3 (February 10, 2021), available at <https://globaltaiwan.org/2021/02/vol-6-issue-3/>.

[22] See June Teufel Dreyer, "China's United Front Strategy and Taiwan," *Taiwan Insight*, February 19, 2018, available at <https://taiwaninsight.org/2018/02/19/chinas-united-front-strategy-and-taiwan/>.

[23] Moreover, the author's personal conversations suggest that for many Taiwan people increased contacts with the PRC through employment, study, or tourism tend to reinforce an awareness of differences rather than build a sense of shared identity.

[24] Emerson M.S. Niou, "Understanding Taiwan Independence and Its Policy Implications," *Asian Survey* 44, no. 4 (August 2004), 555–567, available at <https://doi.org/10.1525/as.2004.44.4.555>.

[25] See "Ye Jianying on Taiwan's Return to Motherland and Peaceful Reunification," September 30, 1981, available at <http://www.china.org.cn/english/7945.htm>; "Jan 30, 1995: President Jiang Zemin Puts Forward Eight Propositions on Development of Relations Between Two Sides of Taiwan Straits," *China Daily*, January 30, 2011, available at <https://www.chinadaily.com.cn/china/19thcpcnationalcongress/2011-01/30/content_29715090.htm>. Also see Bush, *Untying the Knot*, 36–39.

[26] Ibid.

²⁷ This may be conceptualized as the extent to which a policy proposal has positive externalities (which facilitates coalition-building) or negative externalities (which highlights tradeoffs and generates opposition from groups whose interests would be harmed).

²⁸ This circle is somewhat squared by China's approach of making Taiwan's participation contingent on Beijing's approval each year, which generates continuing leverage for China.

²⁹ In some cases, China might consciously decide to limit cross-strait economic activities that would increase competition and hurt politically important constituencies in Taiwan.

³⁰ See Michael D. Swaine, "Chinese Decision-Making Regarding Taiwan, 1979–2000," in *The Making of Chinese Foreign and Security Policy in the Era of Reform, 1978–2000*, ed. David M. Lampton (Stanford: Stanford University Press, 2001), 289–336; Bonnie S. Glaser, "The PLA Role in China's Taiwan Policymaking," in *PLA Influence on China's National Security Policymaking*, ed. Phillip C. Saunders and Andrew Scobell (Stanford: Stanford University Press, 2015), 166–197.

³¹ See National Unification Council, *Guidelines for National Unification*, March 4, 1991, available at <https://www.mac.gov.tw/en/news_content.aspx?n=bec36a4a0bb0663c&sms=bf821f021b282251&s=d0017062a39af1c0>.

³² Tetsuo Kotani, "The Japan-Taiwan Fishery Agreement: Strategic Success, Tactical Failure?" *Center for Strategic and International Studies*, October 20, 2015, available at <https://amti.csis.org/the-japan-taiwan-fishery-agreement-strategic-success-tactical-failure/>.

³³ See Phillip C. Saunders and Scott L. Kastner, "Bridge Over Troubled Water? Envisioning a China-Taiwan Peace Agreement," *International Security* 33, no. 4 (Spring 2009), 87–114.

³⁴ David G. Brown and Kevin Scott, "A Breakthrough and a Deadlock," *Comparative Connections* 16, no. 1 (May 2014), available at <https://cc.pacforum.org/2014/05/a-breakthrough-and-a-deadlock/>.

³⁵ Alan D. Romberg, "Tsai Ing-wen Takes Office: A New Era in Cross-Strait Relations," *China Leadership Monitor*, no. 50 (Summer 2016), available at <https://www.hoover.org/research/tsai-ing-wen-takes-office-new-era-cross-strait-relations>; and Alan D. Romberg, "The First 100 Days: Crossing the River While Feeling the Stones," *China Leadership Monitor*, no. 51 (Fall 2016), available at <https://www.hoover.org/research/first-100-days-crossing-river-while-feeling-stones>.

³⁶ See Bush, "8 Key Things to Notice from Xi Jinping's New Year Speech on Taiwan."

³⁷ "Taiwanese/Chinese Identity (1992/06–2021/12)," Election Study Center, National Chengchi University, January 10, 2022, available at <https://esc.nccu.edu.tw/PageDoc/Detail?fid=7800&id=6961>.

³⁸ "Taiwan Independence vs. Unification with the Mainland (1994/12–2021/12)," Election Study Center, National Chengchi University, January 10, 2022, available at <https://esc.nccu.edu.tw/PageDoc/Detail?fid=7801&id=6963>.

³⁹ Nathan Batto, "Unification, Independence, SQ, and Polling," *Frozen Garlic*, January 10, 2022, available at <https://frozengarlic.wordpress.com/2022/01/10/unification-independence-sq-and-polling/>. Also see the article Batto cites by Hsiao Yi-ching [蕭怡靖] and Yu Ching-hsin [游清鑫], "Re-Examining the 6-Itemed Measurement of Citizen's Preference on the Issue of Independence vs. Unification in Taiwan: A Proposed Advancement" [檢測台灣民眾六分類統獨立場：一個測量改進的提出], *Taiwanese Political Science Review* [台灣政治學刊] 16, no. 2 (November 2012), 67–118, available at <https://www.tpsr.tw/zh-hant/zh-hant/paper/jian-ce-tai-wan-min-zhong-liu-fen-lei-tong-du-li-chang-yi-ge-ce-liang-gai-jin-de-ti>.

⁴⁰ "Party Preferences (1992/06–2021/12)," Election Study Center, National Chengchi University, January 10, 2022, available at <https://esc.nccu.edu.tw/PageDoc/Detail?fid=7802&id=6964>.

41 This shift included a 1995 pledge by Democratic Progressive Party (DDP) Chair Shih Ming-teh [施明德] that the DDP would not declare independence if it won the presidency, downplaying the Taiwan independence plank in the party platform, and eventually claiming that Taiwan is already an independent sovereign state so that a declaration of independence is unnecessary. See Batto, "Unification, Independence, SQ, and Polling."

42 Nathan Batto, "Change Under Chu? Never Mind," *Frozen Garlic*, September 27, 2021, available at <https://frozengarlic.wordpress.com/2021/09/27/change-under-chu-never-mind/>.

43 Elbridge Colby, "The United States Should Defend Taiwan," *National Review*, December 2, 2021, available at <https://www.nationalreview.com/magazine/2021/12/20/the-united-states-should-defend-taiwan/>. Also see Assistant Secretary of Defense for Indo-Pacific Security Affairs Ely Ratner's testimony before the Senate Foreign Relations Committee where he describes Taiwan as a "critical node within the first island chain." Ely Ratner, Statement to the Senate Foreign Relations Committee, 117th Cong., 1st sess., December 8, 2021, available at <https://www.foreign.senate.gov/imo/media/doc/120821_Ratner_Testimony1.pdf>.

44 Oriana Skylar Mastro, "The Taiwan Temptation: Why Beijing Might Resort to Force," *Foreign Affairs* 100, no. 4 (July/August 2021), 58–67.

45 Xi, "Speech at a Meeting Marking the 110th Anniversary of the Revolution Of 1911"; Liu Jieyi, "Video Speech at the Meeting to Commemorate the 110th Anniversary of the Revolution of 1911 in Hong Kong," September 24, 2021.

46 See Jessica Chen Weiss, *Powerful Patriots: Nationalist Protest in China's Foreign Relations* (New York: Oxford University Press, 2014).

47 Amber Wang, "'Only a Matter of Time' Before Taiwan Has No Allies, Chinese Vice Foreign Minister Says," *South China Morning Post*, January 18, 2022, available at <https://www.scmp.com/news/china/diplomacy/article/3163815/only-matter-time-taiwan-has-no-allies-chinese-vice-foreign?utm_source=rss_feed>.

CHAPTER 2

China's Calculus on the Use of Force: Futures, Costs, Benefits, Risks, and Goals

By Andrew Scobell

The People's Republic of China (PRC) considers Taiwan a rogue province—the last holdout from the long-suspended Chinese Civil War.
Since 1979, the PRC has formally adopted a policy of "peaceful reunification" and officially embraced a strategy of political reconciliation with the
island. Despite this significant change from the Mao Zedong–era mantra of
"liberation," it is noteworthy that the PRC's Communist rulers have refused to
renounce the use of armed force to unify Taiwan with the mainland. Indeed,
for decades the central warfighting scenario for the People's Liberation Army
(PLA) has been the Taiwan Strait.

Most observers assume that, when it comes to Taiwan, the ruling Chinese
Communist Party (CCP) is gravely serious about optioning the use of armed force.
Unification with Taiwan is a CCP central objective and the PLA's most important
military objective.[1] Yet any use of armed force across the Taiwan Strait would entail a major military operation the likes of which the PLA has not conducted in
more than 40 years.[2] Moreover, four decades of mostly conciliatory and peaceful
cross-strait ties have provided a foundation for an unprecedentedly vibrant and
dense web of relations between the island and the mainland. These interactions
have produced considerable prosperity and economic dynamism for the PRC.

Is Beijing prepared to use armed force against Taiwan in the 21st century? Under what circumstances might Beijing be prepared to use force across the strait? In the previous chapter, Phillip C. Saunders explored an array of measures short of the use of force that Beijing could pursue to advance its goal of national unification. This chapter unpacks the assumption that Beijing is prepared to use armed force, considering the circumstances under which the PRC might use force, the ends force might serve, and how force might be employed. China's calculus regarding the use of force against Taiwan will be explored by considering five variables: alternative futures, costs, risks, benefits, and goals.

This chapter adopts a medium- to long-term perspective (looking out 10 to 30 years) to assess Beijing's calculus of coercion against Taiwan. There are two main reasons for this perspective. First, the Taiwan issue is not likely to be resolved peacefully in the near term, and a cross-strait standoff will likely persist for decades. Both sides are adamant in their respective stances: Beijing is highly unlikely to renounce its claim on the island in the near future, and Taipei will almost certainly refuse to concede to the PRC's demands to unify under the auspices of the CCP. Second, neither Beijing nor Taipei is likely to engage in extreme behavior in the coming months or years because leaders on both sides of the Taiwan Strait are currently operating in the domain of gains. In other words, at present, Beijing and Taipei both assess that their own respective situations are acceptable, and neither is disposed to take costly actions that risk losing what they already possess.

The chapter is organized into four sections. The first section sketches out the framework and approach employed, including assumptions, concepts, and definitions. The second section describes Beijing's grand strategy and outlines alternative futures for China. The third section builds on these alternative futures by exploring five alternative Taiwan Strait scenarios sketched out according to a range of possible cost-benefit calculations that Beijing might make. The final section offers some tentative conclusions.

Framework and Approach

This section first identifies fundamental assumptions and defines key terms and concepts. It then outlines a framework adapted from prospect theory to analyze China's calculus of coercion against Taiwan.

Assumptions

This chapter makes four fundamental assumptions. First, it assumes that Taiwan will continue to be a high priority for the ruling CCP. Beijing classifies Taiwan as a "core interest" [*hexin liyi*, 核心利益]—the PRC's version of what the United States would label a "vital national security interest."[3] This designation underscores the island's continuing central importance to the CCP and strongly suggests that Beijing believes Taiwan is worth fighting for. Indeed, authoritative Chinese documents articulate this very position. The 2019 PRC Defense White Paper states, "China must be and will be reunited. . . . We [China] make no promise to renounce the use of force and reserve the option of taking all necessary measures. . . . The PLA will resolutely defeat anyone attempting to separate Taiwan from China and safeguard national unity at all costs."[4]

Second, this chapter assumes that the PRC's political and military rulers are fundamentally rational within the bounds of their particular situational context.[5] However, all individuals possess cognitive biases; psychological factors, including perceptions and misperceptions, also play significant roles in decisionmaking.[6] While Taiwan clearly constitutes an emotional and even personal issue for CCP and PLA leaders, the regime's approach to the issue is largely logical and pragmatic. Hence, decisions by the PRC's senior political leadership about a course of action vis-à-vis Taiwan almost certainly will be made after weighing the perceived costs, benefits, and risks against the desired goal. Since regime perpetuation remains the highest priority, deliberations about the use of force against the island include consideration of the essentiality of such action to the continued rule by the CCP and the risks to the Party's survival in the case of a serious military setback.

Third, this chapter assumes that any decision to use military force against Taiwan will be made by the top echelon of CCP leaders. The PRC's senior political leadership has decided every significant employment of armed force since 1949, always pursuant to the wishes of the most prominent individual at the apex of the power structure. This includes Mao Zedong (1949–1976), Deng Xiaoping (1978–1989), Jiang Zemin (1989–2002), Hu Jintao (2002–2012), and Xi Jinping (2012–present). For the purposes of analytic elegance, this chapter treats PRC senior leadership as a unitary rational actor. However, this is not to say that multiple individuals and entities will not influence the outcome. Indeed, while the ultimate decision will be made at the top, this decision will almost certainly be made only after input from, or in consultation with, military leaders.[7] In this chapter, *Beijing* is used as shorthand for the PRC's top political and military leaders and *Taipei* refers to Taiwan's top political and military leaders.

Fourth, this chapter assumes that, under most circumstances, the PRC's military leaders will obey the orders of their political superiors and execute a campaign plan against Taiwan. Indeed, where Taiwan is concerned, "there is no evidence that the PLA has ever acted in contradiction to [CCP] orders."[8] This dictum has certainly been the case for the largest military operations, including the dispatch of armed forces into Korea in 1950 and the invasion of Vietnam in 1979.[9] The cases of the military being directed to restore order in the late 1960s during the most tumultuous phase of the Cultural Revolution and the PLA being ordered to clear the streets of Beijing in 1989 after weeks of popular protests are each complicated and convoluted. And yet, in both instances, once the paramount leader issued clear-cut orders, the armed forces obeyed.[10]

Definitions and Concepts

This chapter defines the use of armed force in expansive terms.[11] It does not require actual combat between the armed forces of two states, any loss of life, or a formal declaration of war.[12] An instance of the use of force involves the employment of overt military or paramilitary power, including the explicit credible threat of military or paramilitary action backed by troop movements, exercises, missile or artillery tests, or the construction or expansion of military installations at or beyond a state's boundaries.[13] This definition, as applied to China, is broader than actual warfighting and encompasses combat and noncombat actions by other elements of the PRC's armed forces, including the People's Armed Police, the China Coast Guard, and the People's Militia.

According to this definition, it is clear that the PRC has been willing to use armed force against Taiwan on multiple occasions since 1949. The Taiwan Strait has been the location of battles and skirmishes, as well as artillery barrages and serial crises, across the decades. These crises have involved troop movements, military exercises, missile tests, and periodic credible threats of the use of violence.[14] This chapter, however, focuses on Beijing's decision-making calculus for launching major large-scale military operations against

Taiwan—invasion, blockade, and fire strikes (see Michael Casey's chapter in this volume for details on each of these campaigns). Lesser actions will receive only limited attention.

Beijing will weigh the anticipated costs of the use of armed force against Taiwan with the anticipated benefits. Political and military leaders will assume that achieving their objective concerning Taiwan will almost certainly incur significant costs, although expected costs may not be equivalent to actual costs. The costs could be material or nonmaterial. The former includes military costs (budgetary allocations for the effort, the human toll in personnel killed and wounded, and equipment and armaments destroyed), economic costs (direct and indirect via sanctions and changed partner behavior), and diplomatic costs (sanctions and damage to bilateral relations with a range of countries). Nonmaterial costs include the impact on the reputation of the Party or PLA in the eyes of the Chinese people. There might also be costs to China's image as a peaceable power outside of the country. The nonmaterial costs could be net positive or negative depending on the outcome of the operation. As for benefits, Beijing must consider what it currently possesses compared with possible future benefits. Beijing's decision to employ force against Taiwan would involve some form of cost-benefit analysis, although these assessments would be subjective, based on incomplete information, and prone to cognitive biases.

Risk Management

While a cost-benefit analysis would be a key component of any decision-making calculus about whether to launch a large-scale military campaign against Taiwan, it almost certainly would also involve some evaluation of the associated risks. A key factor would be the degree of military and political risk acceptable to PRC leaders. Such an assessment of risk would be situationally dependent and colored by the outlook of decisionmakers in Beijing at a particular point in time. Chinese leaders may be quite conservative and risk averse under some circumstances, while under other circumstances they may be more adventurous and risk acceptant. These risks are explored in five scenarios later in the chapter.

A review of the PRC's use of armed force across the decades reveals that Beijing has long demonstrated a willingness to take calculated risks.[15] However, that level of risk tolerance has fluctuated over time. This chapter uses prospect theory to explore China's calculus of coercion vis-à-vis Taiwan and of when, why, and how Beijing might use armed force against the island.

Prospect theory suggests that an actor is more likely to be risk averse when operating in the domain of gains and risk acceptant when operating in the domain of losses.[16] In essence, individuals tend to fear losing something they already possess more than they value gaining something they do not have. Take, for example, the behavior of a gambler at a casino. An individual who is on a winning streak is often more cautious in subsequent wagers to protect his winnings. An individual who is on a losing streak, by contrast, is likely more daring in subsequent wagers to compensate for earlier losses. Of course, an individual on a winning streak could become overconfident and emboldened, while an individual after a string of losses could decide it is time to leave the casino.

Whether it be the case of a casino gambler or of Beijing weighing a decision to use large-scale force in the Taiwan Strait, the psychological impact of an actor assessing whether he or she is operating in the domain of gains or in the domain of losses will be significant. Under most circumstances, Chinese leaders emphasize protecting what they already possess. In the domain of gains, Beijing may be risk averse and focused more on successfully deterring Taiwan from pursuing independence and sustaining regime perpetuation than on achieving unification.

In a time of crisis or conflict, however, if Chinese leaders perceive that they have lost or are in imminent danger of losing what they already have, their coercive calculus regarding Taiwan would likely change. In the domain of losses—if Taiwan is assessed to be independent or almost independent, and/or if PRC regime survival is at stake—Beijing may be more disposed to risk using armed force to achieve unification or ratcheting up coercion to accelerate unification. Indeed, Chinese leaders do perceive that domestic political security and the status of Taiwan are intimately intertwined.[17] Hence, when in the domain of gains, Chinese leaders would focus on risk-averse strategies to perpetuate CCP rule, whereas in the domain of losses Chinese leaders would pursue risk-acceptant strategies aimed at ensuring CCP survival (see the next section).

The logic of prospect theory is readily applicable to extreme situations, such as when an actor has recently experienced either a series of spectacular wins or devasting losses. In the China-Taiwan context, these extreme situations would occur during political-military crises and deliberations over whether to use large-scale armed force (see below).[18] However, top-level Chinese leaders have more on the line concerning Taiwan than does a high-stakes casino gambler—not only large sums of money but also sizable armed formations and expensive military assets, as well as sustaining CCP rule.

This chapter adopts a modified version of Kai He's political survival prospect model in formulating two propositions.[19] First, when PRC leaders' political survival status is framed in the domain of gains, they are more likely to behave in an accommodating way and select risk-averse coercive courses of action (COAs) vis-à-vis Taiwan. Second, when PRC leaders' political survival status is framed in the domain of losses, they are more likely to behave in a coercive way and select risk-acceptant coercive COAs concerning Taiwan.

Although no eventuality can be ruled out, Taiwan's leaders recognize that an extreme action or declaration would automatically trigger a harsh response from Beijing, which almost certainly would include the use of armed force. There is also always the possibility that a small step or series of incremental steps by Taipei may provoke the PRC.[20] Yet Beijing would be reluctant to engage in any extreme action in the near term because Chinese leaders remain uncertain that using armed force against Taiwan would be successful. In other words, the risks are too great and the costs too high. The CCP is currently operating in the domain of gains, and hence, PRC leaders are risk averse and reluctant to incur costs associated with the use of armed force against Taiwan. At present, China's economy remains robust because the country seems to have weathered COVID-19 better than any other Great Power in the world, and the CCP enjoys strong popular support. Therefore, discussion about the increased likelihood of Beijing using force against the island in 2020 constituted stimulating but unsubstantiated speculation.[21]

The mainland defense establishment is currently involved in a comprehensive reorganization and upgrading of weaponry and training; however, these transformations will take a decade or two to complete.[22] It is far too early for China's armed forces to be reaping the fruits of Xi's massive defense overhaul that was initiated in 2015. Commander in chief Xi's admonitions to the military to "fight and win informatized wars" remain aspirational. The PLA candidly acknowledges that it remains in the process of mechanization, with informatization as the next challenge.[23] Ongoing organizational restructuring is necessary but insufficient to realize this goal: more inputs must be incorporated, and more time needs to elapse. China's military has embraced a "system of systems approach"[24] as it plans for a future of conducting "integrated joint operations," whereby the PLA will master "very complex combinations of systems and subsystems to [be able to] kinetically or non-kinetically defeat or paralyze key point nodes in enemy operational systems all within the enemy's decision cycle."[25] Hence, the PLA would prefer to postpone military action against Taiwan at least until the 2030s. Of course, circumstances could change; if Beijing assesses that its situation has become bleak, then CCP and PLA leaders could become more risk acceptant.

Beijing's Grand Strategy and Alternative China Futures

PRC political and military leaders are best characterized as ambitious alarmists, focused on the medium and long term.[26] While conventional scholarly wisdom defines Beijing's paramount goal as *regime survival*, this term is rather misleading in ordinary circumstances.[27] The word *survival* implies that the mindset of China's Communist rulers is one of desperation—that they are fearful of near-term collapse or being overthrown. This could be so in a crisis or conflict situation as noted above. But in ordinary circumstances, CCP leaders are less worried about the end coming next week, next month, or next year than they are about being able to meet the challenges of the medium and long term. While day-to-day vigilance is essential, CCP leaders are consumed with regime perpetuation, which means paying considerable attention to planning. If CCP leaders were consumed with immediate threats, why would they put so much effort into formulating and implementing multiyear over-the-horizon planning in areas ranging from economics and technology to national defense?

The PRC possesses a *grand strategy*, defined as "the process by which a state relates long-term ends to means under the rubric of an overarching and enduring vision to advance the national interest."[28] Nevertheless, adoption of this long-term view does not imply that there is no near-term possibility of military action against Taiwan. Indeed, the dynamics and factors discussed in this chapter will also be in play in the coming few years. Yet, as long as its calculus of coercion regarding Taiwan remains in the domain of gains, Beijing is unlikely to decide to use armed force against the island—and the near-term outlook seems relatively positive.

In thinking about China's long-term future out to 2050, it is useful to consider a range of scenarios depending on the degree of success Beijing might have in executing its grand strategy. China's grand strategy since 2004 can be labeled *national rejuvenation*.[29] Beijing has four strategic priorities that have been consistent across the decades: maintaining political control and social stability, sustaining economic growth, advancing science and technology, and modernizing the national defense establishment.[30] Broad targets have been identified in each of these areas to be attained in the coming decades.[31] In national defense, the target is the PLA becoming a "world-class military" by midcentury. As M. Taylor Fravel notes, this does not mean "being the single best" but rather "to be among the best."[32] In Beijing's eyes, the gold standard for a world-class military is the U.S. Armed Forces. Being a true peer or near-peer competitor of the U.S. national defense establishment is therefore the overarching goal.

Recent RAND research has sketched out four alternative futures depending on how successful CCP leaders would be in achieving their grand strategic goals in the coming decades.[33] In a *triumphant China* future, Beijing is remarkably successful in realizing its grand strategy. In an *ascendant China* future, Beijing is successful in achieving many, but not all, of the goals of its grand strategy. In a *stagnant China* future, Beijing fails to achieve its long-term goals. In an *imploding China* future, Beijing is besieged by a multitude of problems that threaten the existence of the Communist regime. Currently, Beijing appears to be on an ascending China trajectory, although the specter of a stagnant China may be looming. Whatever the future holds for China, central to Beijing's calculus of coercion toward Taiwan will be the level of risk it is prepared to tolerate and the costs it is willing to accept versus the perceived benefit. Risk tolerance and cost acceptance will likely fluctuate according to the degree of success that China achieves in realizing its grand strategic goals.

Targeting Taiwan? Alternative Cross-Strait Scenarios

Unification with Taiwan is implicitly part and parcel of the PRC fully attaining its grand strategy of national rejuvenation, although no explicit deadline or timeline has been identified for realizing this outcome.[34] In the meantime, maintaining the status quo in the Taiwan Strait, which entails deterring any perceived steps by Taiwan toward de jure independence, is a high priority. Beijing thus has little motivation to resort to a major use of armed force. Status quo, however, is defined differently by each of the major actors in this drama—China, Taiwan, and the United States. But, objectively speaking, each actor has been responsible for some related change. In the 1990s and the 2000s, change was driven by developments on the island: democratization and efforts by political leaders to expand Taiwan's international space. In the 2010s, particularly the latter part of that decade, the change came from the United States, as Washington gradually sought to enhance its relationship with Taipei in official and quasi-official ways. Will it be the PRC's turn to drive change in the 2020s and beyond?

Unsurprisingly, the PRC has never been a completely passive actor across the decades. Yet, from Beijing's perspective, it has been quite consistent and unwavering in its approach to the island. Beijing believes that change has been instigated by Taiwan and the United States, while "change" on its part has been only in reaction to actions by Taipei or Washington. Nevertheless, the PRC itself has changed, if only by growing economically stronger and more militarily powerful. As a result, the China-Taiwan balance of power has become ever more skewed in favor of the PRC. If significant change in the cross-strait status quo occurs during the 2020s or in subsequent decades, it would likely be triggered by Beijing.

To explore Beijing's calculus on the launch of a large-scale military campaign against Taiwan in a more concrete manner, it is useful to examine five specific scenarios, considering for each the levels of benefit and cost, Beijing's risk propensity in conjunction with alternative Chinese future, and possible outcomes (see table 1). The five notional scenarios—each framed in terms of relative cost and benefit accruing to Beijing—are:

- low cost/high benefit
- high cost/high benefit
- low cost/no benefit
- very high cost/low benefit
- ultimate cost/no benefit.

Beijing's priorities and goals vis-à-vis Taiwan are likely to vary according to the alternative future China follows. Thus, the level of risk PRC rulers are prepared to entertain (see table 2) and the cost-benefit assessment they make (see table 1) will likely depend on the future scenario in which they find themselves.

Scenario 1: Low Cost/High Benefit

This scenario would most likely play out in a future in which the CCP achieves stunning success in attaining its grand strategic objectives. A triumphant China would view unrealized unification with Taiwan as especially frustrating.[35] However, in this scenario, cross-strait unification could occur peacefully if Taipei concludes that further stalling or resistance is futile in the face of an overwhelming and growing imbalance of hard power in favor of Beijing. PRC assurances, if credible, could make this undesirable outcome more acceptable to the people of Taiwan.[36] In a triumphant future, achieving complete national unification would be a top CCP priority, although Beijing would tend to

Table 1. Unification by Force: Cost/Benefit, Futures, Scenarios, and Military Campaigns

COST / BENEFIT (unification)	LOW	HIGH
ACHIEVED	TRIUMPHANT FUTURE Taiwan succumbs to coercion without a major use of force	ASCENDANT FUTURE Scenario 1 INVASION
FAILURE	STAGNANT FUTURE Scenario 2 BLOCKADE	IMPLODING FUTURE Scenario 3 and Scenario 4 FIRESTRIKE/FIRESTRIKE

Table 2. Beijing's Calculus of Coercion Against Taiwan: Priorities, Goals, and Risks

FUTURE	PRIORITY	GOAL	RISK PROPENSITY
Triumphant	Top	Solve	Risk averse
Ascendant	High	Compel/Solve	Risk tolerant
Stagnant	Medium	Deter/Manage	Risk tolerant
Imploding	Low	Distract	Risk acceptant

be risk averse. Hence, if Taipei did not readily accept outright peaceful reunification, then PRC leaders would intensify an array of measures, including using the military, paramilitary, and nonmilitary means to coerce (or persuade) Taiwan into accepting unification. These measures would not involve large-scale use of armed force. Rather, this effort would constitute a whole-of-government and whole-of-society COA conducted entirely below the threshold of actual military conflict. From Beijing's perspective, this would be a low cost/maximum benefit COA (see table 1). Beijing might also consider this COA low risk because it would conclude that the United States, Japan, and other countries would be hesitant to confront an extremely powerful and triumphant China. Moreover, Taipei might harbor grave doubts over whether third countries would continue to back the island and thus would be more likely to succumb to Beijing's coercion.

Scenario 2: High Cost/High Benefit

This scenario would most likely unfold if Beijing were able to achieve many, but not all, of its grand strategic goals. For an ascendant China future, unrealized unification with Taiwan would almost certainly be near the top of the agenda (see table 2). Taiwan would be "a significant source of frustration" across the decades as the PRC approached midcentury.[37] CCP leaders would feel considerable self-imposed pressure to complete national unification, especially as high-profile commemorations approached, notably the centenary of the PLA and the PRC in 2027 and 2049, respectively. This latter date would carry special psychological weight because of Xi's designation of midcentury as the deadline for realizing national rejuvenation. While popular expectations could likely be managed, top CCP leaders could feel psychologically burdened by their own failure to deliver on a prominent and publicly announced commitment. Hence, there could be a sense of urgency to compel Taipei to accept unification, and Beijing might be risk tolerant (see table 2) and prepared to bear considerable costs (see table 1) to achieve the goal.

Chinese leaders might conclude that the prospects for unification were promising enough to seek final resolution via invasion. Under such circumstances, Beijing could be ready to pay a high cost, and PRC civilian and military leaders might be more prepared to solve the Taiwan issue once and for all. In other words, Beijing would aim to seize control of the island via armed force. As a top priority, PRC and PLA leaders would be willing to accept a high price for attaining the goal—including significant military losses, considerable damage to the Chinese economy, and diplomatic ostracism.

However, while significant costs in blood and treasure would be acceptable in the event of success, Beijing would be wary of risking a high-profile military catastrophe because top leaders would worry that this could call into question their judgment within a key constituency—the PLA. This uncertainty could mean that all campaign options would be on the table and that Chinese leaders would be prepared to engage in a protracted military effort to achieve unification. Yet Beijing could begin with less risky military operations and gradually increase the costs of resistance to Taipei.[38] This method could include a military operation to seize one of Taiwan's offshore islands (as described in Mathieu Duchâtel's chapter in this volume). Beijing could then ratchet up military operations to a blockade and then a fire strike campaign.

Scenario 3: Low Cost/No Benefit

This scenario would likely take place in a stagnant China future. In such circumstances, unification with Taiwan would be less of a priority (see table 2) since Beijing would confront a considerable number of other serious challenges. Nevertheless, the island's continued de facto independent status would remain a matter of "frustration."[39] Beijing would likely be inclined to manage cross-strait relations while staying alert to a Taipei tempted to opportunistically exploit the CCP's difficulties to move closer to independence. This situation could prompt Beijing to be risk tolerant (see table 2) while undertaking low-cost coercive actions (see table 1). The goal would be to deter Taipei from moving toward independence and work to manage cross-strait relations (see table 2). Under such circumstances, the CCP would be most likely to launch coercive activities below the threshold of war, including stepping up military exercises and missile tests in the vicinity of Taiwan, increasing incursions into the island's waters and airspace, and conducting multiple barrages of cyber attacks against the island.

These PRC provocations would likely generate alarm and anger in Taiwan and heighten concern in Washington that Beijing might gear up for large-scale military action against the island. In response, the United States would issue stern public and private warnings to Beijing and ramp up its air and naval presence in the vicinity while urging restraint to Taipei. In the face of this U.S. response, if Taipei refrained from high-profile pro-independence actions and inflammatory pro-independence rhetoric, the PRC would be unlikely to escalate. Indeed, Beijing would likely wind down its provocations and declare victory. The PRC would claim that it had successfully deterred separatists in Taipei from achieving independence, similar to how Beijing declared victory following the 1995–1996 Taiwan Strait Crisis.[40] Yet in reality, the benefits achieved and costs incurred would be low (see table 1): no tangible progress on unification but no major costs in military hardware or casualties, along with a likely modest but discernible hit to China's already stagnant economy after weeks of elevated tensions in the Taiwan Strait.

Scenario 4: Very High Cost/Low Benefit

This scenario would likely play out in a future beset by daunting multiple crises at home and abroad. In an imploding China future, Taiwan would be a low priority for Beijing.[41]

Emboldened by a mainland roiled by chronic chaos, Taipei could take steps that amount to a unilateral declaration of independence. Under these circumstances, Beijing's only alternative might be to respond with a large-scale use of armed force. PRC leaders would realize that doing so would be a high-risk (see table 2) and high-cost operation (see table 1). Beijing would perceive that the very survival of the regime was at stake and hence prepare to roll the dice. Launching a large-scale military operation against Taiwan would invite U.S. intervention. Given the level of chaos and turmoil within the borders of the PRC, the PLA would experience considerable challenges as it prepared to mount fire strikes and/or an amphibious invasion of Taiwan. These difficulties would delay preparations, and indicators of mobilization would probably be readily discernible to Taipei and Washington. As such, the armed forces of Taiwan and the United States would likely have a week or more of warning, giving them time to prepare for a Chinese attack.

Thus, the potential for the PRC to be decisively defeated by the combined military responses of Taiwan and the United States would be high. The upshot could easily be regime collapse or the ouster of one or more top CCP leaders, who would become the scapegoats of a colossal and humiliating military failure in the Taiwan Strait. The costs would be high in terms of military losses and domestic political fallout without any discernible benefit—save the regime just barely staving off collapse. Indeed, the scope and array of crises in an imploding future might overwhelm the regime and call into question the assumption of Beijing as a unitary actor. The pressures could fracture the Party and the armed forces. This future would generate considerable volatility in the outcomes and implications, which would be difficult to predict. In an imploding China with fractured political elites but a relatively unified PLA, the specter of a military coup could loom. A cohesive military could proclaim it was acting on behalf of the CCP and scapegoat the ousted political leadership for the cross-strait fiasco and political-economic morass.

A more likely variant of this scenario would be deep fissures in both the CCP and the PLA, which would increase the potential for risk-prone behavior by one or more Chinese actors. Such a situation raises the real prospect of multiple armed factions deciding to launch missile strikes against Taiwan. This possibility is frighteningly plausible if Taipei decided to take advantage of a mainland in complete chaos to formally declare itself a separate and independent state, with heightened expectations that some third countries might be brave enough, in the face of a PRC in total disarray, to officially recognize Taiwan as a sovereign state. In this variant, regime survival would be far more tenuous, and interventions by third countries would be highly plausible. These interventions could be prompted by the desire to secure loose nuclear warheads and ballistic missiles, stabilize conditions and contain refugee outflows, seize territory, and/or carve out spheres of influence. Third-country interventions might be executed unilaterally, with little or no coordination between states, or they might be conducted multilaterally with close cooperation or coordination. Nevertheless, third-country interventions would not necessarily preclude the survival of a rump PRC.[42]

Scenario 5: Ultimate Cost/No Benefit

This scenario would also likely happen in an imploding China future beset by daunting multiple crises at home and abroad. These circumstances would make unification with Taiwan a low priority for Beijing.[43] Nevertheless, faced with specific developments in the Taiwan Strait, Beijing could feel pressure to use armed force. A plausible scenario would be a Beijing desperate to distract the Chinese people from upheaval at home. Rather than top leaders purposely launching a diversionary war, Beijing could initiate heightened provocations in the Taiwan Strait with the intention of keeping these acts below the threshold of war and avoiding the use of large-scale military operations.[44] PRC leaders would be risk acceptant in terms of the potential for unintended escalation (see table 2) because they would perceive themselves as operating in the domain of losses, with the survival of CCP rule on the line. The goal behind instigating provocations against Taiwan would be a desperate attempt to rally support for a regime in crisis and build a semblance of unity among disparate factions. Under these circumstances, however, PRC leaders would be reluctant to accept a high cost, especially in terms of military losses since the armed forces would be needed to deal with internal unrest.

In the end, Beijing could pay the ultimate cost without accruing any benefit (see table 1). Beijing would be playing an intricate two-level game: a provocation in the Taiwan Strait would not only aim to rally domestic constituencies around the flag but also seek to signal to external audiences in Taipei, Washington, and elsewhere not to trifle with a PRC in distress.[45] At the same time, with multiple major crises, Beijing would seek a low-cost action to preserve its forces and capabilities for other contingencies, and thus aim to avoid large-scale use of armed force.

Despite Beijing's desire to keep actions in the Taiwan Strait at the level of a "diversionary spectacle,"[46] a series of miscalculations and misperceptions could trigger a set of action-reaction spirals that would escalate to a massive conventional conflict and perhaps even a nuclear exchange with the United States.[47] The result would almost certainly be the complete collapse of CCP rule.

Conclusion

At the start of the third decade of the 21st century, three centenaries loomed for Beijing: those of the CCP in mid-2021, of the PLA in 2027, and of the PRC in 2049. Each of these commemorations serves not only as a celebration of regime accomplishments but also as a reminder of unfinished business. The issue of Taiwan was certainly the most significant piece of unfinished business in July 2021, and this sentiment will likely remain in August 2027, and perhaps in October 2049.

A—if not *the*—key determinant in Taiwan's future will be the status of the PRC because Beijing's readiness to employ armed force against the island is likely to correlate with the CCP's perceived degree of success in achieving its grand strategic goals in the coming decades. The higher the level of overall success, the more willing Beijing will be to accept higher costs, but at the same time less willing to accept risk, to realize unification. Meanwhile, the greater the degree of failure in achieving its grand strategic goals, the less willing Beijing will be to accept higher costs but the more willing it will be to tolerate risk. Fortunately, the most ominous alternative Chinese futures for Taiwan are also the least likely: a triumphant China or an imploding China. In the former, Beijing could be prepared to use force no matter the cost, although PRC leadership is likely to be risk averse. In the latter, Beijing could be prepared to use force against the island and willing to take considerable risks to do so. Nevertheless, the most likely futures—an ascending China or a stagnant China—while less ominous for Taiwan, also hold significant peril for the island. In the former, Beijing could experience considerable pressure to "do something" about Taiwan and be risk tolerant. In the latter, Beijing would be risk tolerant and cost averse.

Taiwan will certainly persist as a long-term regime priority, but Beijing's specific short-term goals vis-à-vis Taiwan will inevitably fluctuate according to changing conditions. The PRC's calculus of coercion against the island will be determined by how Beijing weighs costs, benefits, and risks against specific short-term goals. These assessments will change in the coming decades depending on the future trajectory of the PRC.

Notes

[1] See, for example, Bonnie S. Glaser, "The PLA Role in China's Taiwan Policymaking," in *PLA Influence on China's National Security Policymaking*, ed. Phillip C. Saunders and Andrew Scobell (Stanford: Stanford University Press, 2015), 166.

[2] Arguably, an operation to unify Taiwan would be unprecedented in the People's Republic of China's (PRC's) military history. Yet the People's Liberation Army (PLA) has engaged in operations to seize islands before. Far and away the most significant and challenging of these was the 2-month-long campaign to capture Hainan Island in the spring of 1950.

³ Xi Jinping told PLA delegates to the National People's Congress in March 2014 that "national sovereignty, security, and development interests" constitute the PRC's core interests. See Feng Yahui and Duan Xinyi, "Xi Jinping Attends PLA Delegation Plenary Meeting" [习近平出席解放军代表团 全体会议], *People's Daily* [人民网], March 12, 2014, available at <http://lianghui.people.com.cn/2014npc/n/2014/0312/c376707-24609511.html>.

⁴ State Council Information Office of the People's Republic of China, "Section II: China's Defensive National Defense Policy in the New Era," in *China's National Defense in the New Era* (Beijing: Foreign Languages Press, 2019), available at <http://www.xinhuanet.com/english/2019-07/24/c_138253389.htm>.

⁵ Herbert A. Simon, *Models of Man: Social and Rational* (New York: John Wiley & Sons, 1957).

⁶ Martie G. Haselton, Daniel Nettle, and Paul W. Andrews, "The Evolution of Cognitive Bias," in *Handbook of Evolutionary Psychology*, ed. David M. Buss (New York: John Wiley & Sons, 2005), 724–746.

⁷ For the ways in which military leaders provide input or consultation, see Saunders and Scobell, *PLA Influence on China's National Security Policymaking*.

⁸ Glaser, "The PLA Role in China's Taiwan Policymaking," 167.

⁹ Andrew Scobell, *China's Use of Military Force: Beyond the Great Wall and the Long March* (New York: Cambridge University Press, 2003), chapters 4, 6.

¹⁰ Ibid., chapters 5, 7.

¹¹ This draws on Andrew Scobell, "Reassessing China's Use of Military Force," in *The PLA Beyond Borders: Chinese Military Operations in Regional and Global Context*, ed. Joel Wuthnow et al. (Washington, DC: NDU Press, 2021), 183–197.

¹² Scobell, *China's Use of Military Force*, 10.

¹³ This definition is a revised version of the one that appears in Scobell, *China's Use of Military Force*, 9–10. The original version omitted reference to paramilitary forces and included the phrase "in a border area."

¹⁴ See, for example, Thomas E. Stolper, *China, Taiwan, and the Offshore Islands* (Armonk, NY: M.E. Sharpe, 1985); and James R. Lilley and Chuck Downs, eds., *Crisis in the Taiwan Strait* (Washington, DC: NDU Press, 1997).

¹⁵ See, for example, Scobell, "Reassessing China's Use of Military Force"; and Allen S. Whiting, "China's Use of Force, 1950–96, and Taiwan," *International Security* 26, no. 2 (Fall 2001), 103–131.

¹⁶ Daniel Kahneman and Amos Tversky, "Prospect Theory: An Analysis of Decision Under Risk," *Econometrica* 47, no. 2 (March 1979), 263–292.

¹⁷ Timothy R. Heath, "The 'Holistic Security Concept': The Securitization of Policy and Increasing Risk of Militarized Crisis," *RAND Blog*, June 27, 2015, available at <https://www.rand.org/blog/2015/06/the-holistic-security-concept-the-securitization.html>.

¹⁸ See, for example, Kai He, *China's Crisis Behavior: Political Survival and Foreign Policy After the Cold War* (New York: Cambridge University Press, 2016).

¹⁹ Ibid., 43. These two propositions, which are focused on the use of force, are modified versions of four hypotheses formulated by Kai He to analyze Chinese crisis behavior.

²⁰ There is, for example, a small but nontrivial possibility that a Democratic Progressive Party president after Tsai Ing-wen could press more vigorously toward the goal of de jure independence for Taiwan.

[21]   See, for example, Tim Willasey-Wilsey, "The Question: Why Would China Not Invade Taiwan Now?" *Military Review* 100, no. 5 (September–October 2020), 6–9. The essay originally appeared June 4, 2020, in the *Cipher Brief*, available at <https://www.thecipherbrief.com/the-question-why-would-china-not-invade-taiwan-now>. For a more plausible analysis, see Dan Blumenthal, "Is China Getting Ready to Start a War over Taiwan?" *The National Interest*, October 29, 2020, available at <https://nationalinterest.org/blog/reboot/china-getting-ready-start-war-over-taiwan-171611>.

[22]   Andrew Scobell et al., *China's Grand Strategy: Trends, Trajectories, and Long-Term Competition* (Santa Monica, CA: RAND, 2020), 96.

[23]   See, for example, Michael S. Chase et al., *China's Incomplete Military Transformation: Assessing the Weaknesses of the People's Liberation Army (PLA)* (Santa Monica, CA: RAND, 2015). See also Andrew Scobell, "China's Post-Pandemic Future: Wuhan Wobbly?" *War on the Rocks*, February 3, 2021, available at <https://warontherocks.com/2021/02/chinas-post-covid-future-wuhan-wobbly/>.

[24]   See, for example, Jeffrey Engstrom, *Systems Confrontation and System Destruction Warfare: How the Chinese People's Liberation Army Seeks to Wage Modern Warfare* (Santa Monica, CA: RAND, 2018).

[25]   Scobell et al., *China's Grand Strategy*, 85.

[26]   Ibid., 25–26.

[27]   See, for example, John W. Garver, *China's Quest: The History of the Foreign Relations of the People's Republic of China* (New York: Oxford University Press, 2016).

[28]   Scobell et al., *China's Grand Strategy*, 5.

[29]   Ibid., 17–18.

[30]   Ibid., 18–19.

[31]   For details, see ibid., chapters 3, 4, 5.

[32]   M. Taylor Fravel, "China's 'World-Class Military' Ambitions: Origins and Implications," *The Washington Quarterly* 43, no. 1 (2020), 85–99, quotes on 85.

[33]   Scobell et al., *China's Grand Strategy*, 102–111.

[34]   Xi has implied that national rejuvenation will be achieved by 2050. See Xi Jinping, "Chinese Communist Party 19th National Congress Report" [中国共产党第十九次全国代表大会报告], October 28, 2017, available at <http://www.mofcom.gov.cn/article/zt_topic19/zywj/201710/20171002661169.shtml>.

[35]   The notional *triumphant China* scenario is described in Scobell et al., *China's Grand Strategy*, 105. In this scenario, by 2050, the Taiwan issue has been resolved, although the resolution process is unspecified.

[36]   See, for example, Phillip C. Saunders and Scott L. Kastner, "Bridge over Troubled Water? Envisioning a China-Taiwan Peace Agreement," *International Security* 33, no. 4 (Spring 2009), 87–114.

[37]   Ibid., 107.

[38]   Statement of Lonnie Henley, *PLA Operational Concepts and Centers of Gravity in a Taiwan Conflict*, Testimony Before the U.S.-China Economic and Security Review Commission Hearing on Cross-Strait Deterrence, February 18, 2021, available at <https://www.uscc.gov/sites/default/files/2021-02/Lonnie_Henley_Testimony.pdf>.

[39]   Scobell et al., *China's Grand Strategy*, 108.

[40]   Andrew Scobell, "Show of Force: Chinese Soldiers, Statesmen, and the 1995–1996 Taiwan Strait Crisis," *Political Science Quarterly* 115, no. 2 (June 2000), 227–246.

[41] Taiwan's status and Beijing's disposition vis-à-vis Taipei is not addressed in this future. See Scobell et al., *China's Grand Strategy*, 109–111.

[42] Indeed, the continued existence of some form of a weakened Chinese government—although not necessarily a communist one—could be extremely useful to these third countries, which would be unlikely to want to occupy China indefinitely. A weak and pliant Chinese government could permit third countries to shape a postintervention domestic political solution deemed conducive to establishing a more stable future China. Such a Chinese government could be one with redrawn borders and/or reconfigured political institutions.

[43] Scobell et al., *China's Grand Strategy*, 109–111.

[44] Diversionary wars are far less frequent than is widely believed. See Amy Oakes, *Diversionary War: Domestic Unrest and International Conflict* (Stanford: Stanford University Press, 2012).

[45] Robert D. Putnam, "Diplomacy and Domestic Politics: The Logic of Two-Level Games," *International Organization* 42, no. 3 (Summer 1988), 427–460.

[46] Oakes, *Diversionary War*.

[47] Inadvertent escalation between the United States and China is more likely than is widely assumed for two reasons. First, Beijing believes it is skilled at escalation control and crisis management. Second, dyadic interactive cognitive dynamics increase the impact of misperceptions in U.S.-China relations in times of crisis or confrontation. On the former, see Lonnie D. Henley, "War Control: Chinese Concepts of Escalation Management," in *Shaping China's Security Environment: The Role of the People's Liberation Army*, ed. Andrew Scobell and Larry M. Wortzel (Carlisle Barracks, PA: Strategic Studies Institute, 2006), 81–104. On the latter, see Andrew Scobell, "Perception and Misperception in U.S.-China Relations," *Political Science Quarterly* 135, no. 4 (September 2020), 637–664.

II

PLA Operations and Concepts for Taiwan

CHAPTER 3

An Assessment of China's Options for Military Coercion of Taiwan

Mathieu Duchâtel

President Tsai Ing-wen has described People's Liberation Army (PLA) Air Force (PLAAF) operations inside Taiwan's Air Defense Identification Zone (ADIZ) and approaching the Taiwan Strait's median line that was established in 2019 as "Chinese Communist aircraft harassing Taiwan."[1] The use of coercive military power is not new in China's Taiwan policy: the 1995–1996 crisis is a textbook case.[2] *Military coercion* is the use or threat of using military power to "seek changes in the behavior" of a state "by making the choice preferred by the coercer appear more attractive than the alternative, which the coercer wishes to avoid."[3] Military coercion differs from *gray zone operations*, which are defined as "an operational space between peace and war, involving coercive actions to change the status quo below a threshold that, in most cases, would prompt a conventional military response, often by blurring the line between military and nonmilitary actions and the attribution for events."[4] Coercion does not exploit ambiguity around attribution between military and nonmilitary means, even though in some Taiwan Strait scenarios nonmilitary assets or cyber attacks that raise an attribution challenge could be used to enhance coercion. This chapter defines military coercion in the context of the Taiwan Strait as hostile operations that involve the limited use of military assets and aim to lay the foundations for Taiwan's future capitulation. This definition excludes high-end combat scenarios such as a missile strike campaign, a blockade, or a large-scale invasion of Taiwan.

What factors might convince Beijing that military coercion is an attractive option? This chapter examines five possible motives for China to carry out further military coercion against Taiwan:

- employing deterrence
- gradually establishing a position of military superiority
- expanding China's administrative control inside Taiwan's ADIZ and possibly over some of Taiwan's outlying islands
- securing domestic political gains
- testing U.S. resolve.

China has real options, a record of calculated risk under Xi Jinping, and concerns regarding the future course of the U.S.-China-Taiwan security triangle. China also lacks realistic soft alternatives to "seduce" the Taiwan population given the rejection of China's preferred framework for "one country, two systems" in Taiwan and the lack of attractiveness of China's governance model under Xi. This unique combination of factors makes the use of military coercion likely, but not certain. China's future decisions will reflect a cost-benefit analysis regarding the outcomes and consequences of coercive actions for Taiwan's international position and domestic morale. Actions that erode the position of Taiwan and the resolve of the Taiwan public to resist might be undertaken, but not without a larger assessment of their possible costs.

The chapter is divided into four main sections. The first section proposes an analytical framework based on available sources and the record of the use of military power in territorial disputes under Xi to assess Chinese thinking on military coercion and understand how Beijing evaluates gains and costs. The second section analyzes the benefits China seeks from its current campaign of military coercion against Taiwan, which consists of air force operations in Taiwan's ADIZ and approaching the median line of the strait. The third section explores how this framework may apply to three future scenarios of military coercion against Taiwan: PLA operations in Taiwan's territorial waters and airspace, PLA seizure of an offshore island held by Taiwan, and a PLA cyber campaign. The conclusion details implications for maintaining the status quo in the Taiwan Strait, which is understood as the survival in Taiwan of a democratic system of separation of powers that protects a free and open society.

Possible Gains of Military Coercion

An analytical framework to evaluate how Beijing assesses the benefits and costs of coercion in the Taiwan Strait should combine two elements: patterns in China's use of coercive power under Xi and patterns in China's Taiwan policy. During Xi's tenure, nonpeaceful means have been increasingly used as a tool to advance Chinese interests in territorial disputes. In addition to Taiwan, this assertiveness has been on display in the East and South China seas and in the 2020 Himalayan border clashes with India during the COVID-19 pandemic. Since 2012, China has effectively seized control of Scarborough Shoal and between 300 and 1,000 square kilometers of Indian territory across the Line of Actual Control (LAC), established a dominant military presence in the Spratly Islands vis-à-vis other claimants, and established a permanent coast guard presence in the territorial sea of the Diaoyu/Senkaku Islands, allowing China to argue that the effective administration of the islands is de facto shared. These actions exhibit a common pattern of offensive behavior to transform the territorial status quo. They constitute a change of scale compared with what some analysts described as Chinese assertiveness in maritime disputes under the leadership of Hu Jintao, which mainly materialized in an intensification of China's law enforcement and naval presence in the East and South China seas in 2007–2008.[5]

China's Taiwan Strait dispute differs in many ways from its territorial disputes with Japan, Vietnam, the Philippines, Malaysia, Brunei, and India. Key differences include the Chinese Communist Party (CCP)'s definition of cross-strait relations as the continuation of the Chinese Civil War, the operational challenge of defeating an island of 24 million people supported by the United States, the degree of cross-strait economic integration, and the importance for many Chinese interest groups to access Taiwan capital and technology. Integrating Taiwan into the People's Republic of China is without question the highest strategic priority, enshrined in the Chinese constitution and central to the strategic rivalry between China and the United States. A cost-benefit analytical framework should not only consider the specifics of the cross-strait security equation but also incorporate the more general views on the use of military power in China's current strategic environment and Xi's appetite for risk in managing territorial disputes. This section combines these two elements to describe five possible motivations for coercion against Taiwan: competitive military advantage gains, expanding administrative control, punishment/deterrence, testing U.S. resolve, and catering to domestic political gains. It then examines the factors Beijing may consider in assessing the risks of a coercive campaign.

Competitive Military Advantage Gains

An essential component of Chinese policy under Xi is building a position of superiority in terms of intelligence, readiness, and force deployment. The PLA and law enforcement agencies have enhanced their presence to affect the balance of power in territorial disputes. This strategy is a pattern in the East and South China seas and in border disputes with India. The regular presence of the China coast guard in the territorial sea and contiguous zone in the Diaoyu/Senkaku Islands, for instance, has constituted a change of the status quo, justified in the Chinese narrative as a response to the public purchase of three of the islands by the Japanese government in 2012. The regular paramilitary presence aims to create a shared administration.[6]

The construction of militarized artificial islands in the Spratlys is another example of how China employs its military to shift the balance of power. China has constructed port facilities and fighter jet hangars on Fiery Cross, Mischief, and Subi reefs, and it has deployed YJ-12B and YJ-62 antiship cruise missiles, HQ-9 surface-to-air missiles, radars, and sensor arrays on those islands.[7] This mix of force deployment and military infrastructure construction as an effort to support possible further deployment complicates the calculus of other claimants in the South China Sea. Despite their vulnerability to cruise missiles and other weapons, these structures have the potential to raise the costs for the United States of operating in the South China Sea in times of U.S.-China conflict before they are successfully neutralized.[8]

This pattern of enhancing presence to affect the military balance under Xi's leadership can also be observed in China's border conflict with India in the Himalayas. In 2017, the PLA's construction of a road in disputed Doklam, which would allow easier deployment of Chinese ground forces, led to a military standoff with India.[9] In the 2020–2021 Sino-Indian clashes along the LAC, China's perception that Indian construction activity to improve logistics support for military deployments and thus reduce the gap with China's more advanced network of roads and facilities was a key determinant of China's initiation of simultaneous incidents at several spots.[10]

In the Taiwan Strait, China's military deployments and force posture aim to gain comparative advantages over the Taiwan military and create options to impose costs on the United States. This goal has been the key determinant of China's military modernization and of many specific equipment choices, such as the programs of short- and medium-range ballistic missiles targeting Taiwan and the operational deployment of an antiship ballistic missile to deter U.S. aircraft carrier battle groups from approaching the area.

Expanding Administrative Control

Another of China's motivations is expanding de facto control over territory claimed by Beijing. This approach, in the context of the South China Sea, has been described as "salami slicing" or "the slow accumulation of small actions, none of which is a *casus belli*, but which add up over time to a major strategic change."[11] In the context of the East China Sea, the preferred term has been *gray zone coercion* to emphasize the difficulty for others to respond to Chinese law enforcement deployments.[12] The unifying theme between salami slicing and gray zone coercion is the outcome of such actions: expansion of China's control.

In unusually candid remarks in 2014, Rear Admiral Zhang Zhaoying, deputy commander of the South Sea Fleet, described China's strategy in the South China Sea as aimed at "continuously expanding the strength of Chinese administrative control" in order to achieve "effective administrative control" over the territories and waters claimed by China.[13] This approach has materialized in China's land reclamation work in the Spratlys and in the construction of military facilities to support the deployment of air and naval assets, as well as law enforcement operations. The PLA and the China coast guard have increased their maritime domain awareness through this infrastructure effort. The last step consistent with this approach of exerting effective administrative control is the adoption of the Coast Guard Law, which allows the China coast guard to open fire against foreign ships and to dismantle foreign structures built on islands and reefs in waters considered to be under Chinese jurisdiction.[14]

The East China Sea has witnessed a gradual increase in the pattern of China coast guard presence, playing on not only the frequency but also the duration of the navigation inside the 12-nautical-mile territorial sea and the contiguous zone and the number of ships being deployed. For example, Japanese figures show a jump in intrusions from 819 in 2013 to 1,097 in 2019, and in 2020, for the first time, China coast guard ships were deployed for more than 100 consecutive days.[15]

Expanding effective administrative control is less clear-cut in the border disputes with India. Some reports claim that India lost 300 square kilometers of land during the period of clashes with the Chinese military in 2020. However, there has been no official confirmation on either side, given the ambiguity both countries maintain regarding the delimitation of the LAC.[16] (In Doklam, however, the 2017 standoff in India was caused by road construction in an area unequivocally controlled by Bhutan.)

Under Xi, apart from the ongoing PLAAF campaign against Taiwan, this pattern of expanding China's effective administrative control over areas previously under the control of Taipei has never surfaced. On the contrary, during the 1958 Taiwan Strait Crisis, Mao Zedong opted not to seize Jinmen, despite the PLA's capability to complete the operation. Mao's thinking was that Jinmen and Matsu were Taiwan's link to the mainland and that cutting the link would diminish the prospects for cross-strait unification.

Punishment/Deterrence

A third motive is signaling China's dissatisfaction with those opposing its agenda and deterring others from taking contrary positions in territorial disputes. In the East and South China seas disputes, this approach has been described as "reactive assertiveness," by which the Chinese leadership frames actions taken by rival claimants as unilateral violations of the status quo to justify force deployments that tilt the balance in favor of China.[17] While the outcome is expansion of administrative control, elements of deterrence and punishment remain essential in Beijing's calculation. Of all the factors that explain Chinese military coercion under Xi, this is the only one stressed in the Chinese narrative of the various crises or moments of tension. In their analysis of the 2020–2021 clashes with India, for example, Chinese analysts place particular emphasis on the moves undertaken by the Narendra Modi government that signaled an Indian intention to gain the upper hand in the disputes.[18] The intention to stop a trend in the behavior of a rival claimant thus seems to be a strong determinant of China's behavior.

The punishment/deterrence element is particularly strong in China's Taiwan policy. It was a key determinant of Zhu Rongji's threats before the 2000 presidential elections in Taiwan and has been codified in article 8 of China's 2005 Anti-Secession Law on the employment of "non-peaceful means" against Taiwan. Moreover, the 1995–1996 Taiwan Strait Crisis provides a clear illustration of the use of coercive force to express Beijing's views of long-term trends in Taiwan's domestic politics and in U.S.-Taiwan relations.[19]

Testing U.S. Resolve

China has a strategic interest to obtain accurate intelligence on how the U.S. military would react to PLA moves in the Taiwan Strait, as well as to gradually erode the resolve of the United States to support China's rival claimants in all territorial disputes. Testing U.S. resolve affects the strategic calculus of all states in the region because deterrence relies on expected punishment, which considers "the perceived costs of the punishments the actor can inflict, and the perceived probability that he will inflict them."[20] For example, the Barack Obama administration's failure to stop China from seizing Scarborough Shoal in 2012 undermined many countries' confidence in U.S. determination to defend the status quo in East Asia. Conversely, clear statements by U.S. officials that the Senkaku Islands fall under the U.S.-Japan Mutual Defense Treaty, or the deployment of U.S. air assets over Scarborough Shoal in 2016, likely deterred China from further action toward Japan and from conducting land reclamation in Scarborough Shoal.

Testing U.S. resolve is especially valuable for China during the transition of U.S. Presidential administrations. For example, there seems to have been a moment of optimism in Beijing during the transition from the Donald Trump administration to the Joseph Biden administration in 2020–2021. Chinese media commentaries suggested that Biden would leave much less space to the Democratic Progressive Party (DPP) administration for "playing the U.S. against China."[21] The Trump administration was particularly supportive of Taiwan with strong and consequential measures, such as the change of the process for arms sales and allowing requests from Taiwan to be examined by Congress on a case-by-case basis.[22] Toward the end of Trump's term, the State Department lifted restrictions on political contacts between U.S. and Taiwan officials after a considerable easing on such restrictions led to visits of the U.S. Secretary of Health and Human Services and an Under Secretary of State.[23] Evaluating the continuity of such policies on arms exports and political contacts is an incentive for China to test a new U.S. administration. Beyond policies, China also needs to evaluate whether the discussion regarding Taiwan Strait security will continue moving in the direction of "strategic clarity," a concept initially advocated by U.S. defense experts such as Joseph Bosco that began to be adopted by foreign policy generalists toward the end of the Trump administration.[24]

Catering to Domestic Political Gains

China may also have domestic political incentives to expand military coercion against its rivals. The construction of artificial islands in the Spratlys figured prominently in the work report presented by Xi to the 19th Party Congress; it was mentioned on the second page, as part of the "major achievements in economic development" secured by the 18th Central Committee of the CCP.[25] Demonstrating the capacity to change the status quo to an internal audience is a logical incentive for the Party, albeit one that is difficult to measure given the nature of the Chinese political system. While public opinion matters, so does that of constituencies, including the PLA.

Risk Assessment

This section has analyzed China's possible perception of gains in military coercion of Taiwan. However, any Chinese decision to engage in coercion will also result from a careful assessment of the possible risks and costs. This assessment will likely involve several elements. First is the perceived impact on Taiwan's domestic politics. China is more likely to coerce if the outcome would be the weakening of the DPP, particularly the pro-independence "deep green" elements. Any action assessed to result in strengthening Taiwan's independence movement is likely to be rejected in Beijing—similar to the policy implemented by the Taiwan Affairs Office to "distribute benefits" [*rang li*, 让利] to segments of Taiwan's economy, which was pronounced a failure when Tsai and the DPP won the January 2016 presidential and legislative elections.

Second is the impact on U.S.-Taiwan relations. A crisis that is expected to end in a deepened U.S. commitment to Taiwan's security, through increased arms sales, greater strategic clarity, greater troop deployments in East Asia, or even a military presence in Taiwan through various forms (for example, port calls), is likely to be considered a failure in Beijing.

Third, the risk of escalation is a particularly important element in a decision that essentially rests on ensuring that no escalation occurs. A coercion strategy must include a realistic exit plan. China's assessment of the level of resistance of the people of Taiwan, the risk of targeted retaliation against Chinese military assets, the possibility of U.S. military intervention, and imposition of costs are all decisive factors in determining whether to initiate coercion. The calculation of possible human losses may also restrain a Chinese decision to launch an operation. In sum, the absence of confidence that escalation risks could be managed would make coercive options much less appealing to the Chinese leadership.

China's Air Campaign Against Taiwan

Since 2019, and more intensely since Tsai's January 2020 reelection, Chinese military pressure has taken center stage in the Taiwan Strait. In March 2019, two fighter jets from the PLAAF intruded into Taiwan's side of the median line. This was a major development because the PLAAF had not crossed the midline since 1999. In September 2020, a Chinese Foreign Ministry spokesman stated, "There is no so-called median line in the Strait," repeating the point made earlier by a PLAAF fighter pilot.[26] As a journal of the Central Committee of Fujian Province made clear, once the Foreign Ministry clarified China's official position, "the presence of the PLAAF's fighter jets is normalized, and they can come and go unconstrained inside the airspace of Taiwan."[27]

The PLAAF campaign against Taiwan may be a *new normal* [*xin changtai*, 新常态], to use one of Xi's signature terms. This section outlines the key facts and analyzes the political and operational aims of the air campaign. The ongoing operations against Taiwan demonstrate a clear search for military advantage gains, an attempt to expand Chinese military control over part of Taiwan's ADIZ, and an intention to deter Taiwan's pro-independence forces based on the assumption that they are encouraged by deepening U.S.-Taiwan ties. Given the timing, these activities might also be considered an effort to test the resolve of the new U.S. administration. However, aside from the intensification of the PLAAF presence in Taiwan's ADIZ itself, there is no strong open-source evidence to back that claim. Similarly, the search for domestic gains as part of the nationalistic mobilization of the Chinese population and intraparty politics is likely but appears to be a less solid explanation than the first three factors.

PLAAF Operations Against Taiwan Since 2019

Within an 18-month span, PLAAF operations against Taiwan reached such a threat level as to force the Taiwan Defense Ministry to change its public communication and choose transparency over its initial approach of selectively releasing information. Until September 2020, information released by the Defense Ministry indicated that the PLAAF had crossed the median line of the Taiwan Strait four times. The crossings occurred in February and August 2020, in operations designed to coincide with U.S. Health and Human Services Secretary Alex Azar's visit to Taiwan[28] and U.S. Under Secretary of State Keith Krach's visit in September 2020.[29]

This, however, was only the tip of the iceberg. This selective communication on specific operations was abandoned in September 2020 when the ministry began releasing daily updates on PLAAF activities inside Taiwan's ADIZ, including details regarding aircraft formations and itineraries.[30] The new information unveiled PLAAF operations in the southwestern corner of Taiwan's ADIZ, close to the Bashi Channel. The PLAAF has exerted pressure on Taiwan's air defense system by conducting circumnavigation flights around the island since Tsai's election in 2016.[31] Deployments of H-6K bomber formations escorted by fighter planes and KJ-500 early-warning or Y-8 electronic warfare aircraft aim to acquire the capacity to open an eastern front in a Taiwan scenario, as many Taiwan air and sea assets are based on the east coast of the island.

However, the PLA presence in Taiwan's southwestern ADIZ is a new and enduring reality for Taiwan's defense authorities. During the first months of 2021, PLAAF assets were continuously deployed in Taiwan's ADIZ, breaking new records. For example, the number of deployed aircraft reached a new height in April 2021 when 25 warplanes—including 14 Shenyang J-16 fighter jets, 4 Chengdu J-10 fighters, 4 Xian H-6 bombers, 2 Shaanxi Y-8 antisubmarine warfare planes, and 1 Shaanxi KJ-500 airborne early warning and control aircraft—were simultaneously present in Taiwan's ADIZ.[32] PLA presence is now so regular that the Taiwan Defense Ministry announced in March 2021 that it would no longer systematically send fighter jets on interception missions and would instead rely on monitoring the incoming flights with land-based missile forces.[33] This practice is similar to that of the Japan Air Self-Defense Force, which since March 2021 has mostly monitored Chinese intrusions with ground-based missile systems and radar planes.[34]

Altogether, the Defense Ministry announced that the Taiwan Air Force had scrambled 217 times for PLA aircraft intruding into the southwestern corner of Taiwan's ADIZ and 76 times against incoming aircraft crossing the median line of the strait. Taiwan's defense minister counted 49 cases of actual crossing of the line by the PLAAF between January and early October 2020.[35] For 2020, the consolidated number was 380 intrusions inside Taiwan's ADIZ.[36] In 2021, as of mid-April, the PLAAF had intruded on 92 days.[37]

Political and Military Goals of PLAAF Operations

From a military perspective, PLAAF operations test the reaction time of Taiwan's air defense. When the Taiwan air force scrambles and intercepts—which has been less the case since the March 2021 decision—it creates a risk of collision. Retired Air Force Lieutenant General Chang Yen-ting outlines two additional military motives for China: a short-term goal of collecting data on Taiwan's air defense and a longer term strategic goal of engaging the Taiwan air force "in a war of attrition by putting its frontline personnel under enough pressure to force military planners to divert attention and resources from other areas."[38] This dimension of gaining an advantage over Taiwan's air defense is illustrated by some specific operations of the PLAAF. For example, to test Taiwan's radar response, in April 2021, a Y-8 tactical reconnaissance aircraft entered Taiwan's ADIZ flying at an altitude as low as 30 meters.[39]

Such operations represent a marked shift from the 1990s, when the Taiwan air force enjoyed overwhelming superiority and was patrolling deep into the strait (there was no unofficial boundary in the median line of the Taiwan Strait until the 1995–1996 missile crisis). Building air superiority over Taiwan is a long-term PLA goal that requires investment in equipment as well as training exercises.[40] The military balance perspective is important for both sides and is reflected in the actual geographic operational space of the two air forces, which has changed continuously over time. Some Chinese military analysts, when arguing that there is no "stable median line," explain that there is only a changing balance of airpower between the two sides of the Taiwan Strait.[41]

Taiwan's Defense Ministry assesses that over the long term, the PLAAF intends to gradually establish a permanent presence in the strait because it allows access into the First Island Chain and is used by U.S. planes to conduct surveillance operations of Chinese maritime activities.[42] The regular presence of antisubmarine warfare (ASW) aircraft in Chinese formations strongly suggests a motive to exercise ASW capabilities in an area where U.S. and, in the future, Taiwan submarines could operate in wartime. Therefore, the second type of gain described in the analytical framework (expanding China's administrative control) cannot literally apply to the PLAAF's presence inside Taiwan's ADIZ, which is not territorial space under international law, but it still provides a useful explanation because one of its key elements is regular presence—as exemplified in the East and South China seas.

Punishment and deterrence are other factors. This was especially the case in 2020, when the Trump administration was still in office. Since 2020, China has conducted its Taiwan policy in an environment that has considerably deteriorated by the standards of its own unification goal. The Tsai administration enjoys a relatively high satisfaction rate in comparison with most Western democracies.[43] The Trump administration broke with past restraint in conducting military exchanges with Taiwan and pushing back in the South China Sea.[44] The 2018 Taiwan Travel Act has enabled high-level visits by senior U.S. administration officials to Taiwan. In the West, the COVID-19 pandemic has greatly enhanced Taiwan's image and seriously damaged China's.

A recent article in the *China Reunification Forum* captures this sense of vulnerability. The author lists the following negative trends facing China: Taiwan independence is now ideologically mainstream in Taiwan, pro-independence forces are now structurally stronger than pro-unification forces, and the door to cross-strait political consultations has been shut by the DPP. However, the main risk the author sees is U.S. behavior: "We should not rule out the possibility that the U.S. under certain circumstances might encourage Taiwan independence forces to go to the extreme, nor should we rule out the possibility that the U.S. could take the risk to initiate dangerous military operations against China."[45] In a reverse analysis of the lessons of the Korean War, the author concludes that the DPP government should learn from history and avoid the grave misperception regarding Chinese determination to defeat Taiwan independence, which would inadvertently lead to war.[46]

Such views suggest that military pressure constitutes an attempt to regain the initiative in the Taiwan Strait against trends that are highly unfavorable to China, at least in the short term. Indeed, retired Senior Colonel Wang Xiangsui, a professor at Beihang University and co-author of *Unrestricted Warfare*, describes the PLA's summer 2020 actions as "very clearly aimed at signaling to the United States that they should not take military risks."[47] He argues that this "kind of prevention is necessary" given Beijing's assessments that the U.S. election would lead to a period of confusion, which increases the risk of hostile U.S. action against China.

The PLAAF air campaign can also be explained as a form of signaling focused on Taiwan and the United States. Ma Xiaoguang, spokesperson of China's Taiwan Affairs Office, describes these patrols as a response to the Taiwan government's attempts to "use force to reject unification" [*yi wu ju tong*, 以武拒统].[48] The PLA's Eastern Theater Command communicates on operations aimed at defeating "Taiwan independence separatist activities."[49]

This resumption of PLAAF activity appears to result from greater U.S. military presence in the area and in the South China Sea in the later days of the Trump administration—a practice that was maintained early in the Biden administration. The U.S. factor also explains China's current focus on southwest Taiwan. Several exercises, including the PLAAF's first nighttime training mission, have taken place in that zone.[50] An air presence in the Bashi Channel, between Taiwan and the Philippines, sends political messages not only across the strait but also toward the South China Sea. Moreover, as Taiwan's military power is relatively concentrated in the north of the island, China's intention seems to be to stretch Taiwan's defense resources, which led to Taiwan's decision to abandon systematic interception in favor of monitoring with ground-based air defense missiles.

Air force patrols and other exercises are part of China's "cognitive domain warfare" [*renzhi yu zuozhan*, 认知域作战].[51] This message is captured by an editorial in the *Global Times*: "The paradox is that the more Taiwan authorities obtain from the United States, the closer they are to an unbearable turning point."[52] By saturating Taiwan's information space with the idea of a risk of war, these operations seek maximal psychological gains. Frequent PLAAF operations across the Taiwan Strait midline effectively convey that China does not fear the consequences of an accidental collision or a decision to take down an aircraft. Thus, the pressure to avoid escalation is on Taiwan, the defensive side. Indeed, during the February intrusion, one of the Chinese J-11 fighters locked its fire control radar on a Taiwan F-16 jet.[53]

Explaining China's political motives, Shen Ming-shih of Taiwan's National Defense University argues that PLAAF operations focus on "paralyzing Taiwan's psychology. Having the Taiwanese getting used to regular air operations by the Communist military would be equivalent to inviting the PLA fighters to cross the line and invade."[54] Lee Kuan-cheng, from the Institute of National Defense and Security Research, similarly concludes that China follows a two-pronged strategy: PLA exercises first create an environment of fear, and then the responsibility of causing tension is blamed on "Taiwan's ambitious politicians."[55] This strategy creates the impression that Taiwan faces a binary choice between being China-friendly and peaceful, or dangerously anti-China.

Several exercises conducted by the PLA in late 2020 are an effective reminder that psychological effects sometimes matter more than the actual demonstration of capabilities. First, in August, the Eastern Theater Command announced that live-fire exercises would be conducted simultaneously in the north and the south of Taiwan; however, in reality, only small-scale maneuvers took place, and very close to the coastline of the Chinese mainland.[56] Second, at the end of the month, the PLA Rocket Force test-fired DF-26B (intermediate-range) and DF-21D (medium-range) antiship ballistic missiles in the South China Sea.[57] The test generated confusion regarding the actual number of missiles tested and whether they had correctly reached their target. This, in turn, raised legitimate questions about the reliability of the guidance system of a capability that is still under development and needs high maneuverability to hit moving targets at sea. Third, in September, the Eastern Theater Command conducted missile drills and released a video titled "If War Broke Out Today." However, Taiwan military analysts were quick to question the video's authenticity and the actual location of the exercises, and they noted that the most important dimension of the PLA's action was taking place on its social media accounts.[58]

The line between deterring the deepening of U.S.-Taiwan ties and testing U.S. resolve to defend Taiwan is thin in practice and difficult to define because it depends on the extent to which air operations are conceived in Beijing as defensive or offensive—a question that cannot be satisfactorily answered based on any open-source material. However, China's decision to intensify its presence in Taiwan's ADIZ after Washington's change of administration is certainly aimed to assess the U.S. response at a moment when the new national security and East Asia teams were not entirely in place.

In sum, the ongoing air campaign against Taiwan, spanning two U.S. administrations, has clear operational and psychological objectives. The decisive factor appears to be the PLA's attempt to impose its superiority over a new geographic area of specific strategic value, especially for submarine operations. The intention to deter Taiwan's independence forces from being encouraged by favorable U.S. policies is another likely driver of Chinese actions, which also have a clear offensive component.

Looking Ahead: Three Scenarios of Military Coercion

At present, there is a contrast between the permanent presence established by the PLAAF inside Taiwan's ADIZ and the absence of a clear political signal to further turn the screws on Taiwan. The January 2021 Taiwan work conference of the CCP mentioned "turning our growing comprehensive strength and significant systemic advantages into greater efficiency in our Taiwan work."[59] The work report of the Chinese government to the National People's Congress restated "peaceful development of Cross-Strait relations" and China's "vigilance against" and intention to "resolutely deter any separatist activity seeking 'Taiwan Independence.'"[60] There is no sign in policy statements that China is warning of further coercive action in the short term.

Indeed, a full-scale invasion of Taiwan is not realistic in the coming years: China would risk losing, and a Tsai administration could seize the opportunity to formally declare independence. However, at the time of this writing—a year before the 20th Party Congress, a few months after the U.S. Presidential election, and the year of the centennial of the CCP's foundation in Shanghai—limited coercive actions to reach some of the gains described herein are not unrealistic. The next sections explore how the motives described thus far could play into three types of coercive campaigns against Taiwan: further incursions into Taiwan's territorial airspace and waters, seizure of an outlying island, or a major cyber offensive.

Military Operations Inside Taiwan's Airspace and/or Territorial Waters
Taiwan defense analysts must consider scenarios in which the PLAAF
penetrates Taiwan airspace or a PLA Navy ship enters Taiwan's territorial
seas.[61] Such actions would be highly escalatory. Recent operations have tak-
en place in Taiwan's ADIZ, which under international law is international
airspace and not above Taiwan's territory or within its territorial seas. Although Taiwan's rules of engagement are not public, it is likely that such
Chinese provocations would result in Taiwan forces opening fire, leading to
major risks of escalation. In April 2021, after Chinese drones were identified
circling the island, the Taiwan coast guard commented on the possibility
that a Chinese drone would enter Taiwan airspace over the Pratas Islands,
stating, "After it enters it will be handled under the rules. If we need to open
fire, we open fire."[62] The statement was intentionally vague about the conditions under which the Taiwan side would open fire, but it made clear that
the rules of engagement listed specific circumstances under which intrud-
ers would be shot down.

The *Global Times* has suggested that the deepening of U.S.-Taiwan political and defense ties might lead to such an outcome: "The PLA is still re-
strained. Every time a high-ranking U.S. official visits Taiwan, the fighter jets
of the PLA should be one step closer to the island. If the U.S. secretary of
state or secretary of defense comes to Taiwan, the PLA should fly its aircraft
over the island and conduct exercises above it."[63] In October 2020, *Global
Times* editor Hu Xijin argued that the PLA should "prepare a series of plans
that would punish the Taiwan authorities, including sending PLA jets on
missions over the island."[64]

A decision by China to enter Taiwan's airspace or territorial seas would
not simply be to signal or seek operational and political outcomes; it would
suggest that China does not fear the risks of escalation. Indeed, there would
be no administrative control gains in such a move, which could be a one-off
or the prelude to a war. If the escalation risks were managed, the deterrence/
punishment and the resolve-testing factors would be the most salient elements of such behavior. Domestic political gains would be uncertain; however, given the highly escalatory potential of such an action, CCP leadership
may gamble on its political value in terms of emotional mobilization in the
PLA or for the politicized segments of the Chinese population.

Seizing Dongsha Island or Other Outlying Islands

Rumors of a PLA operation to seize Dongsha Island made headlines in East Asia during the summer of 2020.[65] The "Four Sea exercises" carried out by the PLA in August triggered discussions in Taiwan regarding such a scenario.[66] These rumors were strengthened by an interview given by retired Major General Li Daguang in which he presented Dongsha as a possible "fortress" for the PLA Navy to facilitate access from Hainan to the Pacific Ocean and as a location that the PLA should avoid seeing leased by the Taiwan government to the United States.[67] Retired Lieutenant General Wang Hongguang, former deputy commander of the Nanjing Military Region, argued in December 2019 that occupying Dongsha and the Penghu Islands could suppress Taiwan strategically.[68] Asked about that opinion, the spokesperson of the Chinese Defense Ministry answered that the ministry did not comment on the personal views of experts and scholars.[69]

Aside from the above, there are very few Chinese sources on possible Dongsha operations—other than Internet and social media commentaries, which have limited value in assessing top-level policy debates. A Chinese commentator notes, for example, that seizing Dongsha is not a matter of China's capability but one of political choice: operationally, it is an easy task, but "just taking Dongsha Island has little significance." The only scenario in which seizing Dongsha would have perceived strategic value is as retaliation against actions undertaken by the Taiwan government; this thinking applies to all of Taiwan's outlying islands.[70] Similarly, author Alexander Cheung argues in a mainland Chinese publication that a single operation to capture Dongsha independent of a larger unification war is not a reasonable strategic choice.[71]

A capture of Dongsha Island could include gray zone elements, such as the use of coast guard and maritime militia assets. If successful, the maneuver would have some military value in expanding China's sea control and maritime domain awareness in the South China Sea and in supporting antisubmarine warfare operations. The seizure of Dongsha would be the quintessential scenario of expanding China's administrative control over an area under effective Taiwan jurisdiction. It could lead to an intense campaign of emotional mobilization in China, especially if Taiwan resists and China suffers casualties.

There are, however, two major risks for China. First is the risk that the Taiwan government does not respond and abandons Dongsha as part of a pro-independence project to revise the Taiwan constitution. After all, if Taiwan authorities lose control over territories that are historically theirs, this strengthens the argument to get rid of Taiwan's constitutional framework and to recenter the constitution on Taiwan island. Second is the risk of escalation, including through U.S. intervention. Taiwan and the United States are silent regarding their likely response to such an operation. Allowing Chinese decisionmakers to assess the possible costs based on almost no substantial information on likely responses is the current approach in Taipei and Washington. Some political figures in Taiwan's deep green camp argue that the loss of Dongsha may represent a major boost for the Taiwan independence movement but only a minor strategic cost for Taiwan—an outcome that would be a strong deterrent for Chinese actions. China may, however, calculate that forcing the status quo to change by using force in Dongsha could be represented as a major victorious development.

Cyber Attacks

Taiwan routinely faces cyber attacks from China. In 2018, Taiwan's Department of Cyber Security counted between 20 million and 40 million cyber attacks per month against targets on the island.[72] The Taiwan Foreign Ministry suffered an average of 2,100 cyber attacks per day in 2020.[73] The Taiwan government releases some information on infiltration operations. In August 2020, the Taiwan Investigation Bureau's Cyber Security Investigation Office accused China of a sustained infiltration campaign that over 2 years targeted 10 government agencies and succeeded in stealing data from 6,000 officials.[74]

In addition to such intrusions, which seem most likely to be motivated by intelligence-collection aims, Taiwan critical infrastructure companies have been targeted by cyber attacks. Taiwan's national companies China Petroleum Corporation and Formosa Petrochemical Group were hit during the spring of 2020.[75] National Taiwan University Hospital was also targeted around the same time. The sequence of operations led some analysts to speculate that these attacks were a test of Taiwan's cyber defenses in the lead-up to Tsai's second inauguration.[76] As is typical in such events—given that the attribution, the nature of the attack, and the extent of the damage are sensitive—not all information has been released. However, the PLA should be expected to train for cyber attacks resulting in physical damage to Taiwan's infrastructure on the model of reported Israeli and Russian cyber operations against Iran and Ukraine, respectively.

Cyber attacks could be standalone coercive operations, although they are sometimes described as initial steps in a larger Taiwan campaign. For example, retired Lieutenant General Wang Hongguang sees cyber attacks, in combination with electromagnetic pulse weapons, as a "necessary pre-battle step" to disrupt Taiwan's military command systems, Internet, and various local and transmission networks. He adds, "There are also more effective technical methods that can temporarily turn Taiwan into a state of mental disorder and the Taiwan military into [a] quadriplegic vegetative state. For reasons of confidentiality, these methods will not be discussed for the time being."[77]

A cyber attack damaging Taiwan's physical infrastructure would demonstrate Chinese capabilities and help China collect new intelligence regarding the level of Taiwan's defense, although China would run the risk of Taiwan's retaliation. The cross-strait offense-defense balance in cyberspace is one of the least understood elements of the military balance in the Taiwan Strait. States do not communicate about the level of their offensive and defensive capabilities, and crises reveal only some elements. Both sides would be able to use some plausible deniability, but if cyber attacks expand into physical infrastructure, analysis of attribution would point to the obvious source. Such an operation could be carried out with a goal of punishment/deterrence, although testing U.S. resolve could be another driver of the operation. It is not entirely out of the question that U.S. defensive capabilities could have a role in fending off an attack or that the United States could retaliate with an element of plausible deniability to reassert the credibility of its deterrence posture vis-à-vis China in the Taiwan Strait.

Conclusion

This chapter has constructed an analytical framework to assess the likelihood of further Chinese military coercion of Taiwan. It has highlighted the gains that China might seek from coercive operations: comparative military advantages, expanding China's administrative control, punishment/deterrence, testing U.S. resolve, and catering to domestic gains, especially the politicized public and groups/individuals within the CCP and the PLA.

The ongoing PLAAF campaign inside Taiwan's ADIZ and toward the median line in the Taiwan Strait is a case of coercion of Taiwan. China seeks to tilt the airpower balance with Taiwan further in its favor by collecting intelligence on Taiwan's air defenses and wearing down the Taiwan air force. These activities practically expand China's ability to operate and maintain a regular air presence within Taiwan's southwestern ADIZ and seek to nullify the concept of the median line in the Taiwan Strait as an air border. The activities also seek punishment and deterrence based on China's sense of vulnerability regarding public opinion trends in Taiwan and the deepening of U.S.-Taiwan relations. After the inauguration of Joe Biden, the deterrence goal has morphed to some extent into an attempt to test the resolve of the new U.S. leadership. Domestic gains are hard to measure and appear secondary to the other factors, but there is an element of emotional mobilization spurring cross-strait tensions during an intense U.S.-China strategic competition. The risks identified in the analytical framework—including risks of counterproductive effects on trends in Taiwan's domestic politics and on the deepening of U.S.-Taiwan ties, as well as risks of escalation not well planned or managed—appear under control from a Chinese perspective.

Is further coercion likely? The chapter has discussed three possible options, as summarized in the table. All options seek to achieve goals in terms of comparative military advantages, punishment/deterrence, and the testing of U.S. resolve. Only by seizing Dongsha would China's effective territorial control expand and generate a successful emotional mobilization of the Chinese population. All three scenarios carry high risks of escalation not being properly planned or managed, including through U.S. intervention. The seizing of Dongsha Island carries the highest political risk, as Taiwan's independence forces within and outside the DPP could advocate refraining from defending the island and announce that the Taiwan constitution is no longer valid since its territory has been altered. This scenario could have a powerful nonmilitary deterrent effect on Chinese thinking, but it could also be part of a long-term strategy in which seizing an outlying island of Taiwan pushes the two sides to confrontation—giving the PLA a pretext to launch a war. A cyber attack on physical infrastructure in Taiwan is also potentially highly escalatory given that Taiwan likely has credible offensive cyber capabilities that enable it to retaliate with some degree of plausible deniability.

Chinese sources tend to present the three operations described above either as punishment or part of a larger campaign against Taiwan. This chapter

Table. Possible Gains of Military Coercion

	Military Operations Inside Taiwan's Airspace or Territorial Sea	Seizing Dongsha Island	Cyber Attacks
Comparative Military Advantage Gains	X	X	X
Expanding Administrative Control		X	
Punishment/Deterrence	X	X	X
Testing U.S. Resolve	X	X	X
Catering to Domestic Political Gains	Secondary	X	Secondary

has analyzed the specific merits and risks of such operations by isolating them; however, it could be argued that coercive operations could contribute to achieving larger Chinese strategic goals over a longer time frame by sequencing hostilities against Taiwan in a series of crises that demonstrate China's determination to take risks. Therefore, the notion of possible gains is critical in planning policies that reduce the likelihood of coercive Chinese actions, a goal that could be achieved only by affecting China's perception of possible risks and costs.

Notes

[1] "Taiwan President Visits Air Defense Battery as China Tensions Rise," *Reuters*, September 11, 2020, available at <https://www.reuters.com/article/us-taiwan-china-security/taiwan-president-visits-air-defence-battery-as-china-tensions-rise-idUSKBN2620Y0>.

[2] See, for example, Suisheng Zhao, "Military Coercion and Peaceful Offence: Beijing's Strategy of National Reunification with Taiwan," *Pacific Affairs* 72, no. 4 (1999–2000), 495–512; Robert S. Ross, "The 1995–96 Taiwan Strait Confrontation: Coercion, Credibility, and the Use of Force," *International Security* 25, no. 2 (Fall 2000), 87–123.

[3] David E. Johnson, Karl P. Mueller, and William H. Taft, *Conventional Coercion Across the Spectrum of Operations: The Utility of U.S. Military Forces in the Emerging Security Environment* (Santa Monica, CA: RAND, 2003).

[4] Lyle J. Morris et al., *Gaining Competitive Advantage in the Gray Zone: Response Options for Coercive Aggression Below the Threshold of Major War* (Santa Monica, CA: RAND, 2019).

[5] Michael D. Swaine and M. Taylor Fravel, "China's Assertive Behavior Part II: The Maritime Periphery," *China Leadership Monitor*, no. 35 (2011), available at <https://taylorfravel.com/documents/research/fravel.2011.CLM.maritime.periphery.pdf>.

[6] Lyle J. Morris, "Blunt Defenders of Sovereignty—The Rise of Coast Guards in East and Southeast Asia," *Naval War College Review* 70, no. 2 (2017), 75–112.

[7] Derek Grossman, "Military Build-Up in the South China Sea," in *The South China Sea: From a Regional Maritime Dispute to a Geo-Strategic Competition*, ed. Leszek Buszynski and Do Thanh Hai (New York: Routledge, 2020).

[8] Gregory B. Poling, "The Conventional Wisdom on China's Island Bases Is Dangerously Wrong," *War on the Rocks*, January 10, 2020, available at <https://warontherocks.com/2020/01/the-conventional-wisdom-on-chinas-island-bases-is-dangerously-wrong/>.

[9] Harsh V. Pant, "China and India Pull Back on Doklam," Yale Global Online, September 14, 2017, available at <https://archive-yaleglobal.yale.edu/content/china-and-india-pull-back-doklam>.

[10] Ashley J. Tellis, "Hustling in the Himalayas: The Sino-Indian Border Confrontation," Carnegie Endowment for International Peace, June 2020, available at <https://carnegieendowment.org/files/Tellis_Himalayan_Border_Standoffs1.pdf>.

[11] Robert Haddick, "Salami Slicing in the South China Sea," *Foreign Policy*, August 3, 2012, available at <https://foreignpolicy.com/2012/08/03/salami-slicing-in-the-south-china-sea/>.

[12] Tetsuo Kotani, "The East China Sea: Chinese Efforts to Establish a 'New Normal' and Prospects for Peaceful Management," *Maritime Issues*, July 8, 2017, available at <http://www.maritimeissues.com/politics/the-east-china-sea-chinese-efforts-to-establish-a-new-normal-and-prospects-for-peaceful-management.html>.

[13] Ryan D. Martinson, "Panning for Gold: Assessing Chinese Maritime Strategy from Primary Sources," *Naval War College Review* 69, no. 3 (2016), 22–44.

[14] "China Set to Authorize Coast Guard to Remove Foreign Structures," *The Japanese News*, November 8, 2020.

[15] Alessio Patalano, "A Gathering Storm? The Chinese 'Attrition' Strategy for the Senkaku/Diaoyu Islands," *RUSI Newsbrief* 40, no. 7 (August 21, 2020), available at <https://rusi.org/explore-our-research/publications/rusi-newsbrief/gathering-storm-chinese-attrition-strategy-senkakudiaoyu-islands>.

[16] "China Gained Ground on India During Bloody Summer in Himalayas," *Bloomberg*, November 1, 2020, available at <https://www.bloomberg.com/news/features/2020-11-01/china-gained-ground-on-india-during-bloody-summer-in-himalayas>.

[17] *Reactive assertiveness* has been developed by the International Crisis Group's team in Beijing to analyze China's behavior in maritime disputes. See, for example, Stephanie Kleine-Ahlbrandt, "China: New Leaders, Same Assertive Foreign Policy," CNN, March 8, 2013, available at <https://www.crisisgroup.org/asia/north-east-asia/china/china-new-leaders-same-assertive-foreign-policy>.

[18] Mathieu Duchâtel, "The Border Clashes with India: In the Shadow of the U.S.," in *Military Options for Xi's Strategic Ambitions*, China Trends #8 (Paris: Institut Montaigne, February 2021), available at <https://www.institutmontaigne.org/en/publications/china-trends-8-military-options-xis-strategic-ambitions>.

[19] Thomas J. Christensen, "Windows and War: Trend Analysis and Beijing's Use of Force," in *New Directions in the Study of China's Foreign Policy*, ed. Alastair Iain Johnston and Robert S. Ross (Stanford: Stanford University Press, 2006).

[20] Robert Jervis, "Deterrence and Perception," *International Security* 7, no. 3 (1982–1983), 3–30.

[21] "The U.S. Election as a Turning Point? Will the DPP Be Able to Continue Following the Path of 'Playing the U.S. Against China'?" [美国大选是转机? 民进党是否会检讨"联美抗中"路线], *Cross Strait Commentary* [两岸快评], November 10, 2020, available at <http://www.taiwan.cn/plzhx/plyzl/202011/t20201110_12305977.htm>.

[22] "Trump's Ten Arms Sales to Taiwan, Military Rebalance in the Taiwan Strait," Institute for National Policy Research (Taiwan), n.d., available at <http://inpr.org.tw/m/405-1728-8533,c111.php?Lang=en>.

[23] "U.S. Lifts 'Self-Imposed Restrictions' on Taiwan Relationship: Pompeo," *Nikkei Asia*, January 10, 2021, available at <https://asia.nikkei.com/Politics/International-relations/US-lifts-self-imposed-restrictions-on-Taiwan-relationship-Pompeo>.

[24] Richard Haass and David Sacks, "American Support for Taiwan Must Be Unambiguous," *Foreign Affairs*, September 2, 2020, available at <https://www.foreignaffairs.com/articles/united-states/american-support-taiwan-must-be-unambiguous>.

[25] Xi Jinping, "Secure a Decisive Victory in Building a Moderately Prosperous Society in All Respects and Strive for the Great Success of Socialism with Chinese Characteristics for a New Era," speech delivered at the 19th National Congress of the Communist Party of China, Beijing, October 18, 2017, available at <http://www.xinhuanet.com/english/download/Xi_Jinping's_report_at_19th_CPC_National_Congress.pdf>.

[26] Kelvin Chen, "China Denies Existence of Median Line in Taiwan Strait," *Taiwan News*, September 22, 2020, available at <https://www.taiwannews.com.tw/en/news/4014231>.

[27] Cai Guoyan [蔡国烟], "There Is No 'Median Line' in the Strait" [海峡无"中线"], *Haixia Tongxun* [海峡通讯] 12 (2020), 60–61.

[28] "Chinese Military Planes Cross Median Line of Taiwan Strait," *CNA*, February 10, 2020, available at <https://focustaiwan.tw/politics/202002100016>; Keoni Everington, "Over 20 Chinese Fighter Jets Menaced Taiwan Strait's Median Line Monday," *Taiwan News*, August 14, 2020, available at <https://www.taiwannews.com.tw/en/news/3987348>.

[29] Chang Yan-ting, "Military Needs Reform to Counter PLA Threat," *Taipei Times*, September 27, 2020, available at <https://www.taipeitimes.com/News/editorials/archives/2020/09/27/2003744140/>.

[30] See Taiwan's Ministry of National Defense Web site, available at <https://www.mnd.gov.tw>.

[31] Nathan Beauchamp-Mustafaga, Derek Grossman, and Logan Ma, "Chinese Bomber Flights Around Taiwan, For What Purpose?" *War on the Rocks*, September 13, 2017, available at <https://warontherocks.com/2017/09/chinese-bomber-flights-around-taiwan-for-what-purpose/>.

[32] Eric Chang, "25 Chinese Military Aircraft Intrude into Taiwan's ADIZ," *Taiwan News*, April 13, 2021, available at <https://www.taiwannews.com.tw/en/news/4175573>.

[33] "Taiwan Says Tracks Intruding Chinese Aircraft with Missiles, Not Always Scrambling," Reuters, March 29, 2021, available at <https://www.reuters.com/article/us-taiwan-security-idUSKBN2BL0JS>.

[34] "Japan Scrambling Jets Less Against China as More F-35 Deployment Eyed," *Kyodo News*, March 3, 2021, available at <https://english.kyodonews.net/news/2021/03/ef1d2ba18bec-japan-scrambling-jets-less-against-china-as-more-f-35-deployment-eyed.html>.

35 Yu Kaixiang, "Yen De-fa: 49 Cases of Communist Aircraft Crossing the Median Line in the Taiwan Strait, the Largest Number in 30 Years" [嚴德發: 49架次共機逾越台海中線30年來最多], Central News Agency, October 7, 2020, available at <https://www.cna.com.tw/news/firstnews/202010070130.aspx>.

36 "Taiwan: 380 Communist Planes Harass Taiwan in 2020" [台灣: 共軍軍機2020年擾台逾380次], *Lienhebao* [聯合報], January 1, 2021.

37 "The PLA Air Force Intruded in Our Southwestern Air Space Almost Every Day in April" [解放軍4月幾乎天天侵我西南空域], *Apple Daily* [蘋果日報], April 19, 2021, available at <https://tw.appledaily.com/politics/20210419/DHRRFQ674ZBPBE4OXDQLUBYOOM/>.

38 Chang Yan-ting, "Outfoxing China's War of Attrition," *Taipei Times*, September 9, 2020, available at <https://www.taipeitimes.com/News/editorials/archives/2020/09/09/2003743059>.

39 Keoni Everington, "Taiwan Catches PLA Plane Trying to Sneak Below Radar at Only 30 Meters," *Taiwan News*, April 27, 2021, available at <https://www.taiwannews.com.tw/en/news/4188046>.

40 According to the figures of the U.S. Department of Defense, the People's Liberation Army Air Force (PLAAF) had 1,500 fighter jets in 2020, including 600 in its Eastern and Southern theaters, versus 400 for Taiwan. The PLAAF also operates 250 bombers in its Eastern and Southern theaters (450 in total), while the Taiwan air force does not operate bombers. See *Military and Security Developments Involving the People's Republic of China 2020: Annual Report to Congress* (Washington, DC: Office of the Secretary of Defense, 2020), available at <https://media.defense.gov/2020/sep/01/2002488689/-1/-1/1/2020-dod-china-military-power-report-final.pdf>.

41 Wu Peihuan, "The 'Median Line in the Taiwan Strait,' History of Taiwan Security's Most Sensitive Neurological Line" ["台海中线,"台湾安全最敏感的神经器史话], *Tanks and Armored Vehicles* [坦克装甲车辆] 5 (2019), 53–57.

42 Author's interview with a senior Defense Ministry official, September 2020.

43 "New Peak for Tsai Ing-wen's Satisfaction Rate" [蔡英文滿意度新高], *Tianxia* [天下], January 13, 2021, available at <https://news.cts.com.tw/cts/politics/202101/202101132027665.html>.

44 Mathieu Duchâtel, *Generally Stable? Facing U.S. Pushback in the South China Sea*, China Trends #6 (Paris: Institut Montaigne, August 6, 2020), available at <https://www.institutmontaigne.org/en/blog/china-trends-6-generally-stable-facing-us-pushback-south-china-sea>.

45 Pan Jiatang [潘佳瑭], "A Brief Assessment of the Security Situation in the Taiwan Strait, Part I" [略论台海安全局势及战略研判], *China Reunification Forum* [统一论谈], August 26, 2020, available at <http://www.zhongguotongcuhui.org.cn/tylt/202003/202008/t20200826_12292359.html>.

46 Pan Jiatang [潘佳瑭], "A Brief Assessment of the Security Situation in the Taiwan Strait, Part II" [略论台海安全局势及战略研判II], *China Reunification Forum* [统一论谈], August 27, 2020, available at <http://www.zhongguotongcuhui.org.cn/tylt/202004/202008/t20200827_12292539.html>.

47 Wang Xiangsui [王湘穗], "An In-Depth Analysis of U.S.-China Relations and Their Future" [深度解析中美关系及未来走向], speech delivered at the Moganshan Meeting, November 11, 2020, available at <http://www.aisixiang.com/data/123490.html>.

48 "PLA Conducts Training in Taiwan's Southwestern ADIZ for Two Consecutive Days, DPP Authorities Hold a Press Conference" [解放军连续2天在台西南空域演训 民进党当局紧急开记者会], *Taiwan.cn* [中国台湾网], September 11, 2020, available at <http://www.taiwan.cn/taiwan/jsxw/202009/t20200911_12295186.htm>.

⁴⁹ "China's Eastern Theater Command Says Recent Naval and Air Exercises in Taiwan Strait Are Necessary Measures to Deal with the Current Situation in the Taiwan Strait" [中国东部战区称近日海空兵力在台海演练是应对当前台海局势必要举措], Reuters, September 18, 2020, available at <https://www.reuters.com/article/china-mod-pla-tw-exercise-0918-idcnkbs2690bu>.

⁵⁰ "Chinese Warplanes Fly First Nighttime Mission Near Taiwan: MND," Central News Agency, March 17, 2020, available at <https://focustaiwan.tw/politics/202003170009>.

⁵¹ Elsa B. Kania, "Minds at War: China's Pursuit of Military Dominance Through the Cognitive Sciences and Biotechnology," *PRISM* 8, no. 3 (2019), 86–87.

⁵² "PLA Fighter Jets Send a Clear Signal to Taiwan and the United States" [解放军战机向台美发出明确信息], *Global Times*, August 11, 2020, available at <https://opinion.huanqiu.com/article/3zPlOiskJKq>.

⁵³ Lu Li-shih, "Changing the Rules of Engagement," *Taipei Times*, February 28, 2020, available at <http://taipeitimes.com/News/editorials/archives/2020/02/28/2003731740>.

⁵⁴ Shen Ming-shih [沈明室], "The Intent and Implication of PLA Air Force and Navy Circling Taiwan and Taiwan's Responses" [共軍機艦編隊繞臺意圖,影響及臺灣因應作為], *Prospect & Exploration* [展望與探索] 16, no. 7 (2018), 21–27.

⁵⁵ Kuan-Chen Lee [李冠成], "The CCP's Dual Strategies of Military Intimidation Against Taiwan and Calling for Restraint" [中共對台軍事恫嚇與呼籲克制的兩手策略], *National Defense Security Biweekly* [國防安全雙週報] 11 (2020), 19–25.

⁵⁶ "The Location of China's Taiwan Strait Exercises Is Revealed! Wang Ding-yu Highlights Three Characteristics" [中國台海軍演位置圖曝光! 王定宇曝3項特色], *Liberty Times* [自由時報], August 17, 2020, available at <https://news.ltn.com.tw/news/politics/breakingnews/3263115>.

⁵⁷ Joseph Trevithick, "China Tests Long-Range Anti-Ship Ballistic Missiles as U.S. Spy Plane Watches It All," *The Drive*, August 26, 2020, available at <https://www.thedrive.com/the-war-zone/36004/china-tests-long-range-anti-ship-ballistic-missiles-as-u-s-spy-plane-watches-it-all>.

⁵⁸ Kuan-Chen Lee [李冠成], "The Logic of PLA's Muscle-Flexing on Social Media: Observations on the Official Sina Weibo Account of the PLA Eastern Theater Command" [解放軍於社群媒體秀肌肉的邏輯: 以東部戰區微博為例], *National Defense Security Biweekly* [國防安全雙週報] 13 (2020), 13–18.

⁵⁹ "The Communist Party Holds Its 2021 Taiwan Work Conference, Wang Yang Mentions 'Four Musts'" [中共召開2021年對台工作會議 汪洋提出 "四要"], Central News Agency, January 18, 2021, available at <https://www.cna.com.tw/news/acn/202101180254.aspx>.

⁶⁰ Li Keqiang, "Report on the Work of the Government: Delivered at the Fourth Session of the 13ᵗʰ National People's Congress of the People's Republic of China on March 5, 2021," Xinhua, March 12, 2021, available at <http://www.xinhuanet.com/english/2021-03/12/c_139806315.htm>.

⁶¹ Author's interviews at the Institute for National Defense and Security Research, Taipei, September 2020.

⁶² Yimou Lee, "Taiwan Says It May Shoot Down Chinese Drones in the South China Sea," Reuters, April 7, 2021, available at <https://www.businessinsider.com/taiwan-may-shoot-down-chinese-drones-in-south-china-sea-2021-4?IR=T>.

⁶³ "PLA Friday Drills Not Warning, but Rehearsal for Taiwan Takeover," *Global Times*, September 18, 2020, available at <https://www.globaltimes.cn/content/1201338.shtml>.

⁶⁴ Hu Xijin, "PLA Could Send Jets over Taiwan to Defend Sovereignty if U.S. Military Jets Fly over Island," *Global Times*, October 24, 2020, available at <https://www.globaltimes.cn/content/1204487.shtml>.

65 "'Shock in Taiwan' as the PLA Exercise to Take Control over Dongsha Island" [解放军拟演练夺东沙 "震动台岛"], Ta Kung Pao [大公报], May 14, 2020, available at <http://www.takungpao.com/news/232110/2020/0514/448392.html>.

66 See, for example, Luo Tianbin, "Communist Military Confirms the August Island Seizing Exercise" [共軍證實8月模擬奪島演習], Liberty Times [自由時報], August 4, 2020, available at <https://news.ltn.com.tw/news/politics/breakingnews/3249054>.

67 Guo Yuandan and Sun Xiuping, "The PLA's 'Island Taking Exercises' in Dongsha Waters in August? Taiwanese Media Again Play a War Scenario" [解放军8月将在东沙岛海域进行"夺岛演习"? 台媒幻想的战争戏码又编好了], Huanqiu Shibao [环球时报], August 4, 2020, available at <https://www.sohu.com/a/411313221_162522>.

68 Leng Shumei and Liu Xin, "Forum Debates Taiwan Options," Global Times, December 22, 2019, available at <https://www.globaltimes.cn/content/1174433.shtml>.

69 "Why the Views of Wang Hongguang and Li Yi Are Not Advisable" [为啥李毅王洪光的这个观点均不可取], Voice of Xia Dynasty [夏朝之音], May 14, 2020, available at <https://user.guancha.cn/main/content?id=307334>.

70 "Should We Take Taiwan's Outlying Islands? Of Course!" [要不要拿下台湾外岛? 当然!], Wang Yi [网易], November 2, 2020, available at <https://3g.163.com/dy/article/FQEF2BO40534NARR.html>.

71 Alexander Cheung, "Simulation of a PLA Attack to Seize Control of Dongsha Island and Analysis" [解放军东沙岛夺岛作战兵棋推演及其分析], Zhihu [知乎], August 4, 2020, available at <https://zhuanlan.zhihu.com/p/163521290>.

72 Crystal D. Pryor, "Taiwan's Cybersecurity Landscape and Opportunities for Regional Partnership," in Perspectives on Taiwan: Insights from the 2018 Taiwan-U.S. Policy Program, ed. Bonnie S. Glaser and Matthew P. Funaiole (Washington, DC: Center for Strategic and International Studies, 2019), 10–15.

73 Matthew Strong, "Cyberattacks on Taiwan's Ministry of Foreign Affairs Increased 40-Fold in 2020," Taiwan News, March 30, 2021, available at <https://www.taiwannews.com.tw/en/news/4164261>.

74 Yimou Lee, "Taiwan Says China Behind Cyberattacks on Government Agencies, Emails," Reuters, August 19, 2020, available at <https://www.reuters.com/article/us-taiwan-cyber-china-idUSKCN25F0JK>.

75 "Taiwan Sees China as Likely Source of Coordinated Cyberattacks on Three Major Companies," Industrial Cyber, May 12, 2020, available at <https://industrialcyber.co/threats-attacks/industrial-cyber-attacks/taiwan-sees-china-as-likely-source-of-coordinated-cyberattacks-on-three-major-companies/>.

76 "Public Companies in Taiwan Target by Hackers, Officials Suggest This May Be Related to Tsai Ing-wen's Inauguration Ceremony" [台湾公营企业网络受黑客攻击, 官员声称是针对蔡英文就职典礼], Haixia Daobao She [海峡导报社], May 5, 2020, available at <https://www.sohu.com/a/393156049_120135071>.

77 Wang Hongguang [王洪光], "'Reunification by Force,' How to Do It? PLA Major General: Six Types of Operations for a Victory in Three Days" ["武统"台湾到底怎么打? 解放军中将: 六种战法, 三天拿下], Huanqiu Wang [环球网], March 27, 2018, available at <https://taiwan.huanqiu.com/article/9CaKrnK7519>.

CHAPTER 4

Firepower Strike, Blockade, Landing: PLA Campaigns for a Cross-Strait Conflict

By Michael Casey

Since the 1990s, the primary aim of China's defense modernization has been to provide Chinese leaders with credible options to deter Taiwan independence or compel unification by force. Indeed, military force has been a central component of Beijing's larger strategy to steer Taiwan toward unification—a goal Chinese President Xi Jinping explicitly linked in 2019 to his vision of realizing the "great rejuvenation of the Chinese nation" by midcentury.[1] The need to bolster the combat capabilities of the People's Liberation Army (PLA) was apparent after confrontations in the Taiwan Strait in 1995 and 1996, when Beijing's threats and PLA missile launches into the waters off Taiwan's coast prompted U.S. intervention. Taipei's defiance of Beijing's intimidation tactics and the deployment of the U.S. 7th Fleet revealed significant weaknesses in the PLA's ability to deter Taiwan independence. Chinese leaders subsequently pursued reforms to PLA doctrine, training, and force structure, placing priority on developing modern air, missile, and electronic warfare forces integral to deterring or defeating an advanced adversary such as the United States.[2]

The shift in China's national military strategy to a focus on Taiwan also prompted PLA planners to develop military campaigns for Taiwan-related contingencies, such as a firepower strike campaign intended to punish

Figure. Notional PLA Wartime C2 Structure for the Joint Island Landing Campaign

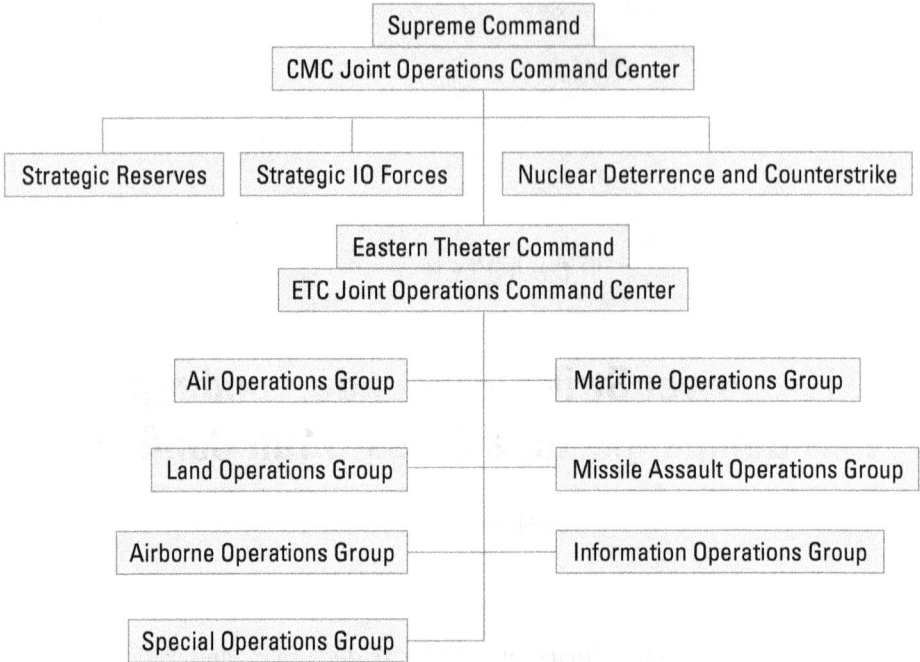

```
                    ┌─────────────────────────────────────┐
                    │          Supreme Command             │
                    │  CMC Joint Operations Command Center  │
                    └─────────────────────────────────────┘
   ┌──────────────────────┬──────────────────┬───────────────────────────────┐
┌──────────────┐   ┌──────────────────┐   ┌─────────────────────────────────┐
│  Strategic   │   │   Strategic IO   │   │ Nuclear Deterrence and          │
│  Reserves    │   │     Forces       │   │ Counterstrike                   │
└──────────────┘   └──────────────────┘   └─────────────────────────────────┘
                    ┌─────────────────────────────────────┐
                    │        Eastern Theater Command        │
                    │  ETC Joint Operations Command Center  │
                    └─────────────────────────────────────┘

      ┌───────────────────────┐          ┌───────────────────────────┐
      │  Air Operations Group │──────────│ Maritime Operations Group │
      └───────────────────────┘          └───────────────────────────┘

      ┌───────────────────────┐          ┌───────────────────────────────┐
      │  Land Operations Group│──────────│ Missile Assault Operations    │
      └───────────────────────┘          │ Group                         │
                                          └───────────────────────────────┘

      ┌─────────────────────────┐        ┌──────────────────────────────┐
      │ Airborne Operations Group│───────│ Information Operations Group  │
      └─────────────────────────┘        └──────────────────────────────┘

      ┌──────────────────────────┐
      │ Special Operations Group │
      └──────────────────────────┘
```

Sources: Adapted from Zhang Peigao, *Lectures on Joint Campaign Command* [联合作战指挥教程] (Beijing: Military Sciences Press, 2001), 12; Jiang Fanrang, ed., *Joint Operations Headquarters Work* [联合作战司令部工作] (Beijing: Military Sciences Press, 2004), 386.

Taiwan or support a blockade or invasion, a blockade campaign to coerce Taipei or lay the groundwork for an invasion, and an island-landing campaign meant to achieve unification.[3] Should Taipei declare independence, Chinese leaders may call on the PLA to threaten or apply violence to press Taiwan to reverse course and restore the status quo ante. Beijing may resort to force to compel Taiwan's leaders to the negotiating table in the event China no longer views peaceful unification as realistic. Chinese leaders may forgo limited military means, such as punitive missile strikes or a naval blockade, in favor of decisive military action—an amphibious invasion to seize control of the island—to accomplish their policy objectives.

Beijing's perception of the PLA's joint operational capabilities and its view of the risk of intervention by the United States and its allies and partners would be key factors in Beijing's decisionmaking calculus and the course of action Chinese leaders choose to take. Concern over the PLA's ability to engage in high-intensity combat could lead Chinese leaders to opt for less demanding missile or blockade campaigns and forgo an amphibious assault. Alternately, fear of foreign military intervention may motivate Beijing to risk an invasion of Taiwan rather than undertake a prolonged blockade, with the aim of securing China's objectives as quickly as possible and presenting its control of the island as a fait accompli to the international community.

This chapter provides an overview of three possible Chinese military campaigns for a cross-strait conflict outlined in PLA doctrinal writings over the past 20 years: a joint firepower strike campaign, joint blockade campaign, and joint island landing campaign. The chapter begins by summarizing PLA campaign planning and operational art, followed by reviewing the three major campaigns. Each overview includes a discussion of campaign phasing, the general military requirements to successfully execute them, and factors that would shape the campaign's ability to achieve China's strategic objectives. These include the campaign's expected duration and the threat of U.S. intervention on its outcome. The chapter concludes with a brief discussion of how new PLA capabilities could shape future campaign development.

PLA Campaign Planning and Operational Art

The PLA's approach to warfare at the operational level has been to develop a series of "campaigns" [zhanyi, 战役] that outline the types of activities required by "campaign large formations" [zhanyi juntuan, 战役军团] to achieve Beijing's strategic objectives across likely conflict scenarios. Falling between wars [zhanzheng, 战争] and battles [zhandou, 战斗], a *campaign* is defined as "combat operations consisting of a series of battles conducted by army corps-level units under a unified command to achieve a local or overall objective in a war."[4] Campaign scenarios span the spectrum of conflict, from border skirmishes to large-scale multinational wars.

Each PLA service has its own service campaigns [junzhong zhanyi, 军种战役] reflecting its capabilities, roles, and missions. PLA Navy (PLAN) campaigns, for example, include the sea blockade campaign and sea line of communications attack campaign,[5] while the PLA Air Force (PLAAF) must be able to execute air offensive, air defensive, and airborne campaigns.[6] The PLA has also developed joint campaigns [lianhe zhanyi, 联合战役] to harness the collective strength of multiple services for synergistic effects. These campaigns include the joint blockade, joint island landing, joint anti-air raid, and joint firepower strike campaigns.[7] In practice, the campaign commander adjusts, combines, and layers these service and joint campaigns to develop a war plan.[8] A summary of the PLA's doctrinal campaigns is included in the table.

In Chinese military science, PLA "war zone" [*zhanqu*, 战区] commanders develop joint operational plans or campaign plans consisting of a base order and supporting documents detailing the execution of the campaign's operational concept. Available PLA texts describe campaign plans as documents born of the PLA's tradition of top-down, detailed planning and operations research.[9] Historically, the size and scope of the war zone were shaped by the contingency at hand and China's wartime objectives. The PLA established an ad hoc joint war zone command in the lead-up to war—a potentially slow and cumbersome process driven by the PLA's ground force–centric military regions' lack of operational control over naval, air, and missile forces.[10] The creation of standing joint theater commands to replace the military regions in 2016 demonstrated a need to position the PLA to more rapidly respond to crises and conflicts, as well as more effectively train and plan as a joint force for specific missions.[11]

For a Taiwan conflict, the Eastern Theater commander and his staff in the theater joint operations command center (JOCC) would develop a campaign plan consisting of an activity plan [*xingdong jiahua*, 行动计划] and support plan [*baozhang jihua*, 保障计划]. According to the 2004 PLA book *Joint Operations Headquarters Work*, the activity plan includes the campaign's concept of operations, a situation assessment, the higher headquarters' intent, operational missions, the campaign's phasing and timelines, the organization of the commander's forces, and the missions of the campaign large formation's operations groups. During wartime, the PLA plans to organize its forces into functional and domain-specific "operations groups" [*jituan*, 集团], subordinate to the theater command, to lead forces in their areas or domains of responsibility. The activity plan also includes branch plans that, unlike U.S. military branch plans that detail operations for potential contingencies, lay out key campaign activities such as air, naval, and firepower operations. The second component of the campaign plan, the support plan, covers activities (for example, reconnaissance, communication support, transportation, logistics, meteorology and hydrology support, political work) needed for the campaign large formation to execute the actions described in the activity plan.[12]

The Eastern Theater Command and the Chinese high command will develop the Taiwan war plan—whether it is a missile, blockade, or invasion campaign—around the PLA's view of "informationized" [*xinxihua*, 信息化] warfare and systems theory. According to PLA strategists, the demands of modern warfare require Chinese forces to "fuse" the operational strengths of "all services and branches" by conducting "integrated joint operations" [*zonghe lianhe xingdong*, 综合联合行动].[13] The 2013 Academy of Military Science (AMS) textbook *Science of Strategy* defines *integrated joint operations* as multiservice operations that "rely on a networked military information system, employ digitized weapons and equipment, and employ corresponding operational methods in land, sea, air, outer space, and cyber space."[14] While Chinese forces will attempt to seize air, maritime, and information superiority—or what the PLA describes as the "three dominances" [*san quan*, 三权]—during a campaign against Taiwan, the volume's authors view information superiority as central to victory in modern wars.[15] The PLA considers modern warfare to be a confrontation between adversary "operational systems" [*zuozhan tixi*, 作战体系] and has developed an approach to warfare that PLA strategists term "system destruction warfare" [*tixi po ji zhan*, 体系破击战], in which one achieves victory by targeting the critical linkages and nodes that hold an adversary's operational system together.[16] As such, any PLA war plan would revolve around the need to successfully conduct joint operations, achieve information superiority—particularly at the outset of a campaign—and execute precision strikes against key strategic and operational targets such as command and control (C2) and logistics nodes. Additional characteristics of PLA operational art that would inform the Taiwan war plan include a heavy emphasis on deception, surprise, and seizing the initiative.[17]

Finally, one of the most important—if not the most important—planning considerations for the PLA would be the risk of U.S. military intervention. PLA strategists anticipate some form of intervention by the United States, or what PLA texts call a "strong" or "powerful enemy" [*qiang di*, 强敌], across most major contingencies. The PLA would dedicate much of its resources attempting to deter, degrade, or defeat U.S. military intervention should Washington decide to enter a Taiwan conflict.[18] Chinese leaders remain skeptical of the PLA's current ability to succeed in a major conflict against the United States, having set long-term modernization goals of developing the PLA into an informationized force by 2035 and a "world-class" military by 2049.[19] As a result, any PLA campaign against Taiwan would be accompanied by aggressive diplomatic, informational, and economic efforts to isolate Taiwan from the international community, justify Beijing's actions, erode support for the Taiwan government, and dissuade the United States from challenging China's use of force.

Should Chinese leaders come to view U.S. intervention as imminent, they may seek to balance the need to bolster China's deterrence efforts with a desire to avoid undue escalation into a wider war. The intensity of PLA activities directed at the United States would depend on what likely effects U.S. military operations were seen as having on the Taiwan campaign. That is not to say that Beijing intends to wait for strikes against its own forces before authorizing a response. PLA texts such as the 2013 AMS *Science of Strategy* and the 2015 National Defense University (NDU) *Science of Strategy* recommend aggressive, asymmetric attacks, particularly in the cyber and space domains, as a means to exploit a powerful adversary's weaknesses and compensate for PLA shortfalls.[20] The PLA principle of "active defense" [*jiji fangyu*, 积极防御] also allows for offensive action at the operational and tactical levels in response to an adversary's perceived first strike, suggesting the PLA may conduct attacks against U.S. forces or territory early in a crisis or conflict to both demonstrate Beijing's resolve and achieve operational effects.[21]

Joint Firepower Strike Campaign

The first campaign under consideration is the joint firepower strike campaign (JFSC). PLA sources describe joint firepower strikes as offensive operations with multiple services coordinating the planning, timing, and spacing of long-range precision strikes. According to the PLA textbook *Science of Joint Operations*, the purpose of the JFSC is to intimidate an adversary's leadership and population, break its will to resist, and force it to abandon or reverse its strategic intentions.[22] In a Taiwan contingency, the scale and scope of the JFSC would depend on China's strategic objectives. A limited strike against symbolic targets, for instance, could be used to demonstrate Beijing's disapproval of Taipei's actions, while more extensive strikes might be used to paralyze Taiwan's political, military, and economic systems. The PLA can execute the JFSC in isolation or in combination with other campaigns. As part of a joint blockade campaign, for example, the JFSC would attempt to annihilate antiblockade operations; in a joint island landing campaign, the JFSC would target Taiwan's defenses to prepare the way for amphibious forces to cross the Taiwan Strait. This section largely treats the JFSC in isolation, with the joint blockade and joint island landing campaigns addressed in the following sections.

Military Calculus

Chinese leaders may choose to execute a JFSC against Taiwan for two reasons. First, the flexibility of the JFSC affords Beijing opportunities to shape how the conflict unfolds. The PLA possesses a sizable and growing military advantage over the Taiwan military after decades of modernization efforts. In the event of conflict, Beijing would likely retain escalation dominance over Taipei, allowing the Chinese high command to calibrate the use of force for desired effects. Firepower strikes accompanied by operational pauses would allow room for political negotiations and for Taiwan's continued intransigence to be met with additional attacks. The JFSC can transition to a blockade or an amphibious invasion if necessary. Alternatively, such as in the face of imminent foreign military intervention, Chinese leaders can cease operations and pursue an end to the war with relatively few costs.

Second, Beijing is confident that it can accurately forecast the result of a JFSC. This confidence is based on extensive preconflict efforts to surveil Taiwan political, military, and economic targets, as well as reconnoiter Taiwan computer networks, which would support mission planning for the JFSC.[23] The military balance in the Taiwan Strait and the JFSC's relative chance of success compared with a blockade or invasion mean that, in many scenarios, the JFSC carries significantly less risk than do other courses of action.

Nevertheless, the JFSC may be insufficient to fulfill Beijing's objectives. PLA texts on joint firepower strike operations stress the need to tailor attacks to degrade an enemy's will; however, the history of modern airpower campaigns—from Vietnam to Afghanistan—is replete with examples of missile strikes proving unable to achieve desired effects on the battlefield. Bombing campaigns can spur local populations to rally around adversary leadership, while targeted governments, economies, and militaries find means to re-structure and survive in new, more resilient forms.[24] Therefore, the PLA's abil-ity to dismantle Taiwan's "operational system" may not translate to strategic success if the government in Taipei is left intact.[25] Images of Taiwan holding out against PLA attacks could also rally global public support around Taipei, leaving China susceptible to international sanctions or a military coalition coming to Taiwan's defense.

Campaign Phasing

The timing and phasing of the JFSC depends on its size and scope and whether the PLA conducts it in isolation or as part of a larger joint campaign, as well as on the terrain, disposition of forces, weather, and level of risk acceptable to the high command. An independent JFSC would likely be limited in scale and timed in relation to the reaction of Taiwan and the international community to PLA op-erations. Available PLA texts generally describe joint firepower strike operations as beginning with a preliminary phase characterized by mobilization activities; initial deployment of strike systems; and intelligence, surveillance, and recon-naissance (ISR) operations.[26] The campaign then moves to a primary phase fea-turing waves of kinetic and nonkinetic attacks sequenced according to target and munition type, and it concludes with ISR units conducting post-strike battle damage assessment.[27] A JFSC may feature only ballistic missiles employed by the PLA Rocket Force (PLARF) or a combination of ballistic and cruise missiles, artillery, electronic warfare systems, and offensive cyber activities.

Preliminary mobilization and ISR activities could take place days to weeks before the initiation of hostilities against Taiwan.[28] The PLA is likely to increase the readiness of its forces in the Eastern Theater, which would include recalling personnel, conducting equipment maintenance, stockpil-ing munitions, and organizing last-minute training, among other activities. Depending on the size of the JFSC, the PLAAF may forward-deploy special mission aircraft and unmanned aerial vehicles, as well as fighter and bomb-er aircraft, to airfields along the Taiwan Strait, while the PLAN may supple-ment the Eastern Theater's naval operations group with surface combatants, submarines, and support ships from the Northern and Southern theater navies, if needed. PLARF launch units would depart from garrison and, de-pending on the campaign's time requirements, deploy to hide sites or move

Table. Canonical PLA Campaigns

Army	Maneuver warfare campaign, mountain offensive campaign, positional offensive campaign, anti-terrorism maintaining stability operations campaign
Navy	Sea force–group campaign to eliminate the enemy, sealine of interdicting campaign, offensive campaign against coral island reefs, sea line guarding campaign, naval base defense campaign
Air Force	Air offensive campaign, air defensive campaign, airborne campaign
Rocket Force	Nuclear counterattack campaign, conventional missile assault campaign
Joint	Firepower strike campaign, blockade campaign, anti–air raid campaign, island-landing campaign

Source: Zhang Yuliang, ed., Science of Campaigns [战役学] (Beijing: National Defense University Press, 2006), vii–xii.

directly to launch locations.[29] Finally, ISR units would provide updates on enemy disposition and readiness and on environmental conditions relevant to the movement of PLA forces. The 2004 PLA textbook *Science of Second Artillery Campaigns* notes that conventional missile forces are most effective when Chinese forces can achieve surprise and the enemy is unprepared for the attack. This suggests that the PLA will mask its activities and quickly conclude preliminary operations.[30]

The main attack phase of the JFSC features waves of kinetic and nonkinetic attacks. PLA texts such as the *Science of Second Artillery Campaigns* and the 2006 *Science of Campaigns* identify adversary air bases, C2 centers, and logistics bases as key targets.[31] If the goal is to degrade Taiwan's warfighting ability, the PLA would likely target transportation infrastructure such as highways, bridges, and tunnels; energy infrastructure such as power stations and petroleum, oil, and lubricant (POL) storage sites; and intelligence collection facilities. Taiwan's air defenses and long-range strike systems, including coastal defense cruise missile launchers, fighter aircraft, and artillery, are also high-priority targets. *Science of Joint Operations* describes the sequencing of joint firepower operations as beginning with electronic attacks, followed by "preliminary-round strikes, follow-up strikes, and supplemental strikes."[32]

Electronic attack operations would be used to degrade adversary C2 and early warning systems, such as air defense radars, to facilitate subsequent missile strikes and ensure freedom of maneuver for manned aircraft. Preliminary-round kinetic strikes would then hit C2 nodes and communications infrastructure, with follow-up strikes targeting enemy surface-to-air missile systems, air defense artillery, and other strike systems that could be used to counterattack PLA forces. During an invasion, the PLA may also destroy tactical assets such as armored vehicles, fixed-gun emplacements, and artillery systems. Having eliminated Taiwan's immediate defensive capabilities, the JFSC would then move to destroy Taipei's war potential and ability to reconstitute its forces, including strikes on food, water, POL, and other economic targets.

Military Requirements

The JFSC's military requirements vary greatly depending on the size and complexity of the campaign. PLA texts, such as *Science of Campaigns* and *Joint Operations Headquarters Work*, emphasize the careful selection of targets, unified planning and command, concealment and surprise, coordination across services and combat arms, and sufficient logistics to sustain high-intensity combat operations. Accurate and timely ISR would be essential for target analysis and the efficient allocation of firepower, particularly for dynamic targets such as ships, aircraft, and armored vehicles. Each PLA service possesses its own organic ISR assets, while the Strategic Support Force, created in 2016, manages national platforms such as China's intelligence satellites.[33] More demanding joint firepower operations likely would require the PLA to quickly collect information from a wide number of ISR platforms, fuse that data into actionable intelligence, and disseminate it across services and command echelons. It remains unclear how effectively the theater commands would be able to task national assets normally subordinate to the Central Military Commission (CMC) joint operations command center, or whether interoperability between information systems used by different services would be adequate to support a common operating picture between strike platforms and command posts.

Similarly, to deconflict operations and synchronize attacks, the JFSC requires close coordination between PLA services and operations groups. PLA texts describe the PLAAF and Second Artillery Forces (now the PLARF) as taking the lead role in JSFC planning. *Science of Campaigns* identifies a firepower center within the campaign main command as responsible for planning and coordinating firepower strike operations. Following the 2016 reforms, this presumably means that there is a joint firepower center within the theater JOCC or that one would be established as part of the primary command post in the lead-up to war.[34] However, the proficiency of joint commanders and planners in the JOCC remains unclear, as do the command relationships and division of responsibility between the JOCC, its firepower center, and the various operations groups.

Finally, as with the joint blockade and joint island landing campaigns, preparation for third-party intervention is a key JFSC requirement. The PLA is likely to allocate some ISR resources to monitoring foreign military activities for indications of intervention, which could strain the bandwidth of its intelligence-collection and processing systems. A portion of the PLA's air, naval, and missile forces would probably remain postured to confront foreign military intervention if necessary. Limited C2 and ISR resources and the need to reserve key weapons systems for a war against a major adversary like the United States or Japan may also factor into JFSC planning during larger conflict scenarios.

Joint Blockade Campaign

The second doctrinal joint PLA campaign for cross-strait operations is the joint blockade campaign (JBC). PLA sources define the JBC as a "protracted campaign" that "aims to sever enemy economic conditions" to "compel the enemy to submit to campaign goals."[35] *Science of Campaigns* describes the JBC's primary mission as isolating the enemy island from the outside world and undermining the enemy's will and war potential.[36] The size and scope of the JBC depend on Beijing's strategic objectives. A scenario in which China aims to punish Taiwan could feature establishing a limited blockade with cyber operations used to degrade Taiwan's access to the global Internet or deploying the PLAN or China coast guard to inspect or detain commercial maritime traffic to and from the island. A goal to compel Taiwan's unification with the mainland would likely entail a larger campaign coupled with firepower strikes against Taiwan ports, airfields, and other military targets to seize air, maritime, and information superiority.

As with the JFSC, the PLA could execute the JBC in isolation or as part of a broader campaign, such as an amphibious invasion. The JBC could set the conditions for the joint island landing campaign by degrading Taiwan's defenses and war potential for subsequent amphibious operations. The Chinese high command may also wait to see the effects of the JBC, allowing time for negotiations and intensifying blockade operations or transitioning to an invasion should Taipei refuse to relent to Beijing's demands. Conversely, Chinese leadership could call off the JBC if foreign intervention threatened the blockade.

Military Calculus

Factors that could drive Beijing to order the JBC against Taiwan include political or military provocations by Taipei, a calculation that international circumstances are favorable to military operations, and a positive evaluation of the PLA's capability to execute the campaign. The 2015 NDU *Science of Strategy* states that a main characteristic of a strategic blockade is its "strong political quality, policy quality, and legal principle quality."[37] *Science of Campaigns* also notes that blockades by their very nature involve the interests of multiple countries, requiring commanders to pay heed to the "overall situation" and relevant international laws and norms that may restrict blockade activities.[38]

Before and during the JBC, China would conduct aggressive, whole-of-government public opinion, psychological, and legal efforts—or what PLA strategists describe as the "Three Warfares"—to justify its actions and limit international pushback. While Beijing almost certainly would hope for a quick resolution to the war, PLA texts acknowledge that the armed forces must be prepared for a protracted campaign, heightening the risk of an external enemy's military intervention.[39] The PLA's ability to simultaneously execute the blockade against Taiwan while deterring and defeating foreign intervention would prove central to Beijing's decisionmaking calculus. The broad scope of the battlefield, number of forces and combat methods involved, and ferocity of Taiwan resistance may tax PLA capabilities.

Doubts about PLA capabilities could drive the Chinese high command to choose a less risky course of action. The significant mobilization and sustainment requirements of the JBC, compared with the JFSC, mean that Chinese leaders have less political and military flexibility when committing to blockade. Those same requirements increase the risk that Taiwan or the international community identifies indicators of impending PLA action and organizes a response. Moreover, the allocation of sizable PLA air and naval forces to enforce the blockade and the need to prepare for foreign military intervention inherently obligate Beijing to assume risk in other regions, such as along the Sino-Indian border and South China Sea. PLA strategists are concerned with "chain reaction" warfare in which regional countries, domestic enemies, or the United States exploit a crisis, such as over Taiwan, to instigate conflicts around China's periphery while Chinese forces are preoccupied in the main theater of operations.[40]

Campaign Phasing

Science of Campaigns outlines a blockade campaign with four phases: an initial deployment phase, an offensive operations phase, a blockade sustainment phase, and a concluding phase.[41] Mobilization activities would presumably occur prior to the initial deployment phase, with military, government, and civilian sectors transitioning to a wartime footing. Under China's national defense system, mobilization could include requisitioning civilian vehicles to transport military equipment or civilian ships to support blockade enforcement. The initial deployment phase of the JBC would feature air and naval forces of the campaign large formation moving toward the operational area, which could include the discreet movement of aircraft to airfields along the Taiwan Strait, ships to at-sea staging areas, and missile units to concealed locations. Covert minelaying by air and naval units, particularly submarines, would also occur during this phase, as would the intensification of ISR activity to support blockade enforcement and firepower strike operations.

The offensive operations phase would begin with a public declaration that a blockade has been established, quickly followed by efforts to achieve information superiority over the adversary.[42] *Science of Campaigns* and other texts describe information dominance as a necessary precursor to establishing air and naval control for a blockade, recommending that the PLA conduct missile and electronic attacks against enemy observation, early warning, electronic warfare, and long-range precision strike systems.[43] With information dominance in hand, the PLA then would move to achieve air dominance, targeting air defenses, C2 facilities, airfields, and combat aircraft—preferably while they are on the ground.[44] The offensive operations phase would conclude with the PLAN establishing sea dominance around Taiwan and its outer islands. Primary targets would be enemy antisubmarine forces, surface combatants, mine clearing ships, and submarines.[45]

The blockade sustainment phase would involve the continuous disruption of Taiwan's air and sea lines of communication. Key activities would include blockading ports, inspecting maritime traffic, intercepting and expelling aircraft, and attacking adversary military forces as necessary.[46] Ground forces may occupy Taiwan's outer islands to eliminate threats to blockade enforcement operations. Because blockades normally cover a wide geographic area, the authors of *Joint Operations Headquarters Work* recommend that the campaign command identify main and secondary blockade directions, with stricter blockade enforcement occurring along the main direction. Taiwan's largest ports are Kaohsiung and Taichung, suggesting a main direction to the south and a secondary direction to the north.[47] For coordination and deconfliction purposes, *Science of Campaigns* and *Science of Second Artillery Campaigns* further divide the blockade area into blockade zones, air and maritime intercept zones, and firepower blockade zones.[48] The China coast guard, supported by maritime militia, would likely take the lead in conducting visit, board, search, and seizure operations, allowing the PLAN to focus on military forces attempting to break the blockade. Once the JBC achieves its objectives, the concluding phase would begin. In this phase, the PLA would withdraw participating forces; replenish air, naval, and missile systems; and prepare units for follow-on deployments.

Defensive operations occur across all phases of the JBC. Relevant service campaigns include the PLAN's naval base defense campaign and the PLAAF's air defensive campaign, which would entail deployment of coastal defense cruise missile and surface-to-air missile systems, as well as patrol craft, to key facilities and along the Taiwan Strait. As described in *Science of Campaigns*, the joint anti–air raid campaign provides the PLA with a template for how to conduct counterintervention operations during the JBC.[49] These activities would aim to deter Washington and its allies and partners from entering the conflict, as well as help sustain the blockade against air and missile attacks. If the United States did intervene, China's response would involve kinetic and nonkinetic attacks that would increase in intensity as the campaign progresses to signal Beijing's resolve. If the Chinese high command viewed the blockade as beginning to fail, it would likely expand the scope and scale of attacks against U.S. forces. Plausible offensive activities include antiship ballistic missile strikes against U.S. aircraft carriers or joint firepower strikes against U.S. bases in Japan and Guam. A significant escalation of the conflict could compel Chinese leaders to abandon the blockade and shift the PLA's primary effort to the joint anti–air raid campaign and major combat against the United States.

Military Requirements

The military requirements of the JBC depend on the campaign's objectives. *Joint Operations Headquarters Work* defines a blockade according to its intensity (closed, general, or relaxed) and level of isolation (complete, basic, or partial). A closed blockade or complete isolation requires that 80 percent of ships and aircraft be unable to pass through the blockade zone.[50] Sustainment is likely to be a primary requirement to meet those objectives during a protracted conflict. Ships and aircraft enforcement of the blockade would remain on station until they could be relieved and return to their home ports and airfields for resupply and maintenance (the PLAN's ability to reload weapons at sea remains unclear). Attrition would tax the PLA's ability to maintain the blockade around Taiwan, likely forcing difficult tradeoffs on where and how to allocate forces. Similar issues are likely to arise in the PLA's management of potential third-party intervention: some portion of the PLA, particularly long-range strike systems supported by ISR units, would be postured to deter or defeat U.S. forces instead of participating in the blockade. Given the PLAN's current logistics capabilities, sustaining a naval presence outside the First Island Chain as part of counterintervention operations would be challenging. Questions remain about the PLAN's ability to conduct antisubmarine and air defense operations far from the Chinese mainland and against the United States.

Additional JBC requirements highlighted in *Science of Campaigns* include preconflict preparations, seizing the initiative, unified command, and close coordination.[51] A JBC would probably feature significantly greater mobilization activities than would a JFSC in anticipation of a long-term blockade. Secrecy would also be of utmost importance for mobilization activities to ensure surprise and minimize the risk of foreign intervention. China's National Defense Mobilization Law stipulates that the State Council and CMC jointly lead mobilization through the National Defense Mobilization Committee (NDMC). Provincial governments also have their own NDMCs, and the effective sustainment of the JBC would likely require them to work closely with the Eastern Theater Command and Joint Logistic Support Force (JLSF). However, the post-reform command relationships between the theaters, JLSF, and NDMCs at various levels and their subordinate offices are unclear. Like the JFSC, the JBC is likely to require effective joint planning and close coordination between the services and other entities, such as the China coast guard. The need to intercept foreign civilian and military aircraft and ships while reducing the risk of inadvertent escalation would require strict adherence to approved rules of engagement, as well as devolving decisionmaking responsibilities to frontline units, which could prove troublesome for the PLA's centralized command structure.

Joint Island Landing Campaign

The third major joint campaign is the joint island landing campaign (JILC). According to PLA sources, the JILC is a large-scale joint offensive campaign to "break through the enemy's seacoast, and to seize and occupy landing fields or coastal airfields and harbors, so as to create favorable conditions for subsequent operational activities."[52] The JILC could be executed against the main island of Taiwan or against smaller islands, such as Jinmen or Matsu, held by Taiwan. The JILC, like the JFSC and JBC, would incorporate other campaigns, such as the joint anti–air raid campaign, as embedded or subordinate campaign activities.

The primary aim of the JILC is likely to secure the quick capitulation of Taiwan's political and military leadership and to ensure unification under Beijing's terms while deterring or, if necessary, defeating foreign military intervention. To accomplish these war aims, the PLA would likely attempt to occupy Taipei and isolate Taiwan politically, economically, and militarily; neutralize Taiwan's military capacity to resist; and prevent U.S. forces from interfering with PLA operations.[53] Beijing is also likely to try to minimize the conflict's effects on China's other national objectives, such as economic modernization and continued Chinese Communist Party rule, through continued access to international markets and increased domestic security measures. With Taipei under its control, the PLA would then move to secure the rest of the island, establish a new civilian government, eliminate any remaining resistance, and prepare for potential counter-landings by the United States and its allies and partners.[54]

Military Calculus

Key considerations for a decision to execute the JILC would likely include Chinese leaders' evaluation of the need for decisive military action, the strength of the PLA's joint operational capabilities, and the perceived risk of campaign failure. While both the JFSC and JBC would aim for a quick resolution to the fighting, both campaigns carry the risk of Taiwan refusing to accede to Beijing's demands, which would allow time for international resistance to coalesce. As a result, Beijing may view the JILC as the only viable means to achieve unification. Like the JFSC and JBC, the JILC would be accompanied by aggressive diplomatic, economic, and information efforts to isolate Taiwan, deter foreign intervention, and legitimize China's actions.

Chinese leaders would probably be wary of undertaking an invasion unless they were confident the PLA could successfully execute a campaign against Taiwan while fighting the United States. The political and military costs of a failed invasion would be high—possibly prohibitively so. Successive generations of Chinese leaders have defined unification with Taiwan as a key condition for national rejuvenation and thus as central to the Party's legitimacy.[55] However, high-intensity combat against Taiwan, and potentially the United States, could result in high attrition of PLA forces and set China's military modernization back decades. Consequently, Chinese leaders may view a failed invasion campaign as an existential threat to the regime. Chinese and Western scholars alike have raised the possibility that Beijing may consider using nuclear weapons under such conditions despite China's no-first-use nuclear pledge.[56] Regardless, the perceived costs of failure would probably motivate Beijing to conduct aggressive conventional deterrence activities against the United States, including offensive cyber and counterspace operations, across all phases of the conflict.[57]

Campaign Phasing

PLA texts describe the JILC as consisting of four phases: a preliminary stage featuring efforts to achieve air, maritime, and information superiority; a sea-crossing phase; a landing phase; and a concluding phase characterized by the expansion of landing sites and an initial push inland.[58] Similar to the JBC, mobilization activities would likely take place for several months before the onset of hostilities, based on the high logistics requirements and number of forces involved. Key mobilization efforts would likely include elevating units to higher states of readiness; forward-deploying air, missile, and ground forces; and positioning naval forces around Taiwan (and possibly deploying them to the western Pacific and South China Sea to counter U.S. intervention).[59] Covert mining of Taiwan's ports by aircraft and submarines and ISR activity directed against Taiwan, the United States, and regional powers such as Japan, would also occur prior to the conflict.

Once mobilization is complete, the JILC would move to a preliminary phase. According to *Science of Campaigns*, the goals of this phase include paralyzing the enemy's operational system and seizing the initiative to enable the amphibious assault. Here, the PLA would execute the JFSC as part of the invasion campaign, targeting air and naval bases, C2 nodes, and long-range strike systems, as well as the joint anti–air raid campaign to defend against Taiwan counterattacks and foreign military intervention.

The sea-crossing and landing phases of the JILC would feature the deployment of amphibious, air assault, and airborne forces across the Taiwan Strait in what the PLA describes as a "three-dimensional landing" [*liti denglu*, 立体登陆]. The Eastern Theater's amphibious combined-arms brigades would depart garrison to their embarkation points, load onto PLAN amphibious ships, maneuver to assembly areas off the Taiwan coast, disembark, and begin assault operations.[60] The amphibious force would be defended by naval screening groups and preceded by minesweeping vessels tasked with clearing assault lanes. PLA amphibious doctrine emphasizes landing at multiple sites and conducting flanking attacks with mobile units.[61] While the bulk of the invasion force would be delivered by sea, the standing up of army air assault units and fielding of new transport helicopters and the Y-20 heavy transport aircraft in recent years suggest that the PLA would also rely heavily on air delivery of forces for an invasion.[62] The key targets for these troops are likely to include Taiwan's major ports and airfields to facilitate the flow of second- and third-echelon forces and logistics supplies.[63] (For more on the airborne corps, see the chapter by Roderick Lee in this volume.)

The concluding phase of the JILC is the expansion and consolidation of established beachheads and initial push inland. How the PLA intends to consolidate its control over the rest of Taiwan is not readily apparent from available PLA texts, though, as Sale Lilly's chapter in this volume demonstrates, the PLA has increased urban warfare training that may be relevant to cross-strait operations. *Science of Campaigns* abruptly ends its discussion of the JILC's phases after PLA forces complete their landings. The PLA Army's maneuver warfare and mountain offensive campaigns would likely serve as templates for operations on Taiwan. Given the PLA's aim for speed and a quick victory, ground forces are likely to advance inland on Taipei, employing three-dimensional maneuvers to flank or bypass the remaining Taiwan defenders. Special operations forces would be the first into Taipei to neutralize Taiwan civilian and government leaders and seize key sites. People's Armed Police and other security forces would presumably backfill the PLA as conventional maneuver units advance across the rest of the island.[64]

Military Requirements

A major amphibious invasion is one of the most complex and difficult military operations. The Department of Defense publication *Military and Security Developments Involving the People's Republic of China 2020* notes that success "depends upon air and maritime superiority, the rapid buildup and sustainment of supplies onshore, and uninterrupted support."[65] Prior to the onset of the conflict, national defense mobilization would require preparing the Chinese economy and society for a protracted conflict, probably limiting China's ability to transition to a wartime footing without alerting Taiwan or the United States to its intentions. Nevertheless, the PLA may aim to achieve operational surprise through denial and deception efforts and through the normalization of PLA operations, such as through routine deployments and exercises around Taiwan, in the lead-up to war.

The campaign's logistics requirements would be immense. Execution of the JILC carries significant risk because of the PLAN's limited inventory of amphibious ships. Barring a major amphibious ship buildup, lift constraints may compel the PLA to focus its assault on a single region of Taiwan, such as the north, to quickly seize Taipei rather than conduct a multipronged invasion. Such a scenario would almost certainly impose additional requirements to seize or destroy key lines of communication, such as major highways connecting the north and south of the island, to limit Taiwan's ability to reinforce its defenses in the north. The question also remains of whether the PLA has been building amphibious lift optimized for a Taiwan scenario: *Military and Security Developments Involving the People's Republic of China 2020* points out that much of the PLAN's recent amphibious construction has focused on large multipurpose vessels such as helicopter landing docks, which would become high-value targets for enemy missiles and thus are more suited to expeditionary operations in places like the South China Sea.[66] (For further analysis of these issues, see the chapters by Conor Kennedy and Chieh Chung in this volume.)

Force preservation would also be a priority for PLA landing forces. Taiwan's ability to destroy or degrade elements of the initial invasion force would require second-echelon units to quickly land and secure critical infrastructure, particularly major ports, to ensure the timely flow of follow-on forces and supplies while defending against Taiwan counterattacks. Closely associated with this goal would be optimizing the campaign's joint firepower strikes for self-preservation: failure could expose landing forces to adversary air or missile strikes, thus jeopardizing the success of the entire campaign. *Joint Operations Headquarters Work* highlights securing the "three dominances" as critical to the campaign's success because of the vulnerability of amphibious forces to enemy long-range precision strikes.[67]

A final key campaign requirement would be to deter, degrade, or defeat foreign military intervention. According to the 2001 AMS *Science of Military Strategy*, key capabilities enabling success in the anti–air raid campaign include ISR and early warning, air and missile defenses, and long-range precision strikes.[68] *Joint Operations Headquarters Work* also describes effective C2 and campaign planning as essential requirements, given the number of forces involved and the size of the potential operating area.[69] These requirements would tax PLA capabilities even under the most ideal conditions. The worst-case scenario for PLA planners would be conducting high-intensity operations against Taiwan, the United States, Japan, and other U.S. allies and partners simultaneously. This type of fighting would require close coordination between all PLA services and multiple theaters, as well as overall campaign supervision by the PLA high command.[70]

Conclusion

This chapter has focused on the main doctrinal campaigns the PLA would use to build operational plans for wartime contingencies involving Taiwan: the JFSC, JBC, and JILC. The chapter outlined the political and military factors Chinese leaders would likely consider before deciding to undertake each campaign; how the overall campaign would unfold based on available PLA texts, operational constraints, and geographic realities; and the military requirements the PLA describes as necessary for their successful execution. Across all campaigns, the PLA highlights the need for logistics preparations and campaign planning, effective C2 and joint coordination across the services, situational awareness of the battlespace, and information operations.

While this chapter has not assessed the PLA's current capabilities to execute the above campaigns, it has identified certain limitations and vulnerabilities, such as immature command institutions and insufficient amphibious lift. A primary variable in each scenario is potential intervention by foreign military forces—specifically, those of the United States. Much of the PLA's campaign planning and resources would be spent preparing to deter intervention and limit escalation given this variable. Information operations in the form of cyber, electronic warfare, and counterspace activities appear to be key to deterring and defeating the "powerful adversary."[71]

New capabilities and missions almost certainly will drive the PLA to complete new doctrinal campaigns. *Military and Security Developments Involving the People's Republic of China 2020* notes in a special topic on emerging campaign concepts:

> *The People's Liberation Army . . . will likely need to update its existing doctrine, concepts, and campaigns to adapt to the long-term trends in global military affairs, meet the* [People's Republic of China] *evolving national security needs, and account for significant changes in the PLA's structural capabilities. Evolving campaign concepts will aim to advance the PLA's goal to become a fully modern and "informatized" force by 2035.*[72]

The report states that future campaigns will seek to integrate capabilities across all domains, particularly counterspace capabilities brought to bear by the Strategic Support Force, as well as potential forces stationed overseas. The PLA's long-term goal of increasing its long-range precision strike capabilities and air and naval presence outside the First Island Chain could lead to campaigns that emphasize control over distant-sea operational areas in support of the anti–air raid campaign. Any new campaigns or updates to existing campaigns would likely be in the form of a new generation of "operational regulations" [*zuozhan tiaoling*, 作战条令]. The regulations are roughly the equivalent to Western military doctrine, comprising "combat regulations" [*zhandou tiaoling*, 战斗条令] and "campaign outlines" [*zhanyi gangyao*, 战役纲要]. It appears the PLA delayed releasing its fifth generation of regulations (the fourth generation was published in 1999), perhaps due to bureaucratic infighting or because the PLA hoped to first complete the 2015 military reforms.[73] With the latest round of reforms completed or near completion, as well as the CMC's approval of a trial "Outline of Joint Operations for the People's Liberation Army" in November 2020, new regulations and associated campaigns likely should be expected within the next several years.[74]

Finally, future analysis must consider the range of available PLA sources given that much of the publicly available PLA literature is increasingly dated. Texts such as *Science of Campaigns* and *Joint Operations Headquarters Work* are now a decade and a half old. The most recent AMS versions of *Science of Strategy* is 8 years old.[75] That these latter sources mention campaigns discussed in older texts helps confirm that the broad contours of these campaigns continue to be relevant to contemporary PLA campaign planning. PLA writings on topics such as informationization and systems confrontation warfare are somewhat more recent. Future analysis on PLA doctrine must attempt to leverage texts researched and published by institutions such as AMS and NDU following PLA reforms launched in 2015. Translating these texts so they are accessible to a wider audience must also be prioritized.

Notes

[1] "Highlights of Xi's Speech at Gathering Marking 40th Anniversary of Message to Compatriots in Taiwan," Xinhua, January 2, 2019, available at <http://www.xinhuanet.com/english/2019-01/02/c_137715300.htm>.

[2] John Wilson Lewis and Xue Litai, *Imagined Enemies: China Prepares for Uncertain War* (Stanford: Stanford University Press, 2006), 10.

[3] M. Taylor Fravel, *Active Defense: China's Military Strategy Since 1949* (Princeton: Princeton University Press, 2019), 209–210.

[4] Zhang Yuliang, ed., *Science of Campaigns* [战役学] (Beijing: National Defense University Press, 2006), 19.

[5] Ibid., 500–522.

[6] Ibid., 557–574.

[7] Ibid., 271–291.

[8] Ibid., 217.

[9] Jiang Fanrang, ed., *Joint Operations Headquarters Work* [联合作战司令部工作] (Beijing: Military Sciences Press, 2004), 189–191; Dang Chongmin and Zhang Yu, eds., *Science of Joint Operations* [联合作战学] (Beijing: PLA Press, 2009), 205–312.

[10] Phillip C. Saunders et al., eds., *Chairman Xi Remakes the PLA: Assessing Chinese Military Reforms* (Washington, DC: NDU Press, 2019), 1–9.

[11] Ibid.

[12] Jiang, *Joint Operations Headquarters Work*, 189–191.

[13] Edmund J. Burke et al., *People's Liberation Army Operational Concepts* (Santa Monica, CA: RAND, 2020), 6.

[14] Shou Xiaosong, ed., *Science of Strategy* [战略学] (Beijing: Military Sciences Press, 2013), 124.

[15] Ibid., 130.

[16] Jeffrey Engstrom, *Systems Confrontation and System Destruction Warfare: How the Chinese People's Liberation Army Seeks to Wage Modern Warfare* (Santa Monica, CA: RAND, 2018), 1–3.

[17] Burke et al., *People's Liberation Army Operational Concepts*, 3.

[18] Shou, *Science of Strategy*, 100.

[19] Dennis J. Blasko, "The Chinese Military Speaks to Itself, Revealing Doubts," *War on the Rocks*, February 18, 2019, available at <https://warontherocks.com/2019/02/the-chinese-military-speaks-to-itself-revealing-doubts/>; *Military and Security Developments Involving the People's Republic of China 2020: Annual Report to Congress* (Washington, DC: Office of the Secretary of Defense, 2020), i–ii.

[20] Shou, *Science of Strategy*, 134–140; Xiao Tianliang, ed., *Science of Strategy* [战略学] (Beijing: National Defense University Press, 2015), 121–123.

[21] Alison A. Kaufman and Daniel M. Hartnett, *Managing Conflict: Examining Recent PLA Writings on Escalation Control* (Arlington, VA: CNA, 2016), 63–64; *Military and Security Developments Involving the People's Republic of China 2020*, 24.

[22] Dang and Zhang, *Science of Joint Operations*, 173–174.

[23] Peter Mattis, "A Guide to Chinese Intelligence Operations," *War on the Rocks*, August 18, 2015, available at <https://warontherocks.com/2015/08/a-guide-to-chinese-intelligence-operations/>.

[24] Robert A. Pape, "The True Worth of Air Power," *Foreign Affairs* (April–March 2004), available at <https://www.foreignaffairs.com/articles/2004-03-01/true-worth-air-power>.

[25] Engstrom, *Systems Confrontation and System Destruction Warfare*, 121; Matthew Adam Kocher, Thomas B. Pepinsky, and Stathis N. Kalyvas, "Aerial Bombing and Counterinsurgency in the Vietnam War," *American Journal of Political Science* 55, no. 2 (April 2011), 201–218.

[26] Jiang, *Joint Operations Headquarters Work*, 331–341.

[27] Zhang, *Science of Campaigns*, 84.

[28] Ian Easton, *The Chinese Invasion Threat: Taiwan's Defense and American Strategy in Asia* (Arlington, VA: Project 2049 Institute, 2017), 71–84.

²⁹ Yu Jixun, ed., *Science of Second Artillery Campaigns* [第二炮兵战役学] (Beijing: PLA Press, 2004), 336–338; Zhang, *Science of Campaigns*, 184.

³⁰ Yu, *Science of Second Artillery Campaigns*, 319–320.

³¹ Ibid., 314; Zhang, *Science of Campaigns*, 361.

³² Dang and Zhang, *Science of Joint Operations*, 218–219.

³³ Mark Stokes, Yang Kuang-shun, and Eric Lee, *Preparing for the Nightmare: Readiness and Ad Hoc Coalition Operations in the Taiwan Strait* (Arlington, VA: Project 2049 Institute, 2020), 7.

³⁴ Zhang, *Science of Campaigns*, 375.

³⁵ Ibid., 292.

³⁶ Ibid.

³⁷ Xiao, *Science of Strategy*, 204.

³⁸ Zhang, *Science of Campaigns*, 292.

³⁹ Jiang, *Joint Operations Headquarters Work*, 17.

⁴⁰ Joel Wuthnow, *System Overload: Can China's Military Be Distracted in a War over Taiwan?* China Strategic Perspectives No. 15 (Washington, DC: NDU Press, 2020), 10.

⁴¹ Zhang, *Science of Campaigns*, 297.

⁴² Jiang, *Joint Operations Headquarters Work*, 188.

⁴³ Zhang, *Science of Campaigns*, 39.

⁴⁴ Ibid., 340.

⁴⁵ Ibid., 342.

⁴⁶ Ibid., 304.

⁴⁷ Jiang, *Joint Operations Headquarters Work*, 176.

⁴⁸ Zhang, *Science of Campaigns*, 249, 349; Yu, *Science of Second Artillery Campaigns*, 140.

⁴⁹ Zhang, *Science of Campaigns*, 331–348.

⁵⁰ Jiang, *Joint Operations Headquarters Work*, 176.

⁵¹ Zhang, *Science of Campaigns*, 334.

⁵² Dang and Zhang, *Science of Joint Operations*, 226.

⁵³ Easton, *The Chinese Invasion Threat*, 93–113.

⁵⁴ Ibid., 110–113.

⁵⁵ Ministry of Foreign Affairs of the People's Republic of China, "Full Text of Jiang Zemin's Report at the 16ᵗʰ Party Congress on Nov. 8, 2002," November 18, 2002, available at < http://www.china.org.cn/english/2002/Nov/49107.htm>; "Full Text of Hu's Report at the 18ᵗʰ Party Congress," *China Daily*, November 18, 2012, available at <https://www.chinadaily.com.cn/china/19thcpcnationalcongress/2012-11/18/content_29578562.htm>.

⁵⁶ Fiona S. Cunningham and M. Taylor Fravel, "Dangerous Confidence? Chinese Views on Nuclear Escalation," *International Security* 44, no. 2 (2019), 79.

⁵⁷ Fiona S. Cunningham, "Maximizing Leverage: Explaining Strategic Force Postures in Limited Wars" (Ph.D. diss., Massachusetts Institute of Technology, 2018), 1–10.

⁵⁸ Zhang, *Science of Campaigns*, 316–330.

⁵⁹ Roderick Lee, "The PLA Navy's ZHANLAN Training Series: Supporting Offensive Strike on the High Seas," *China Brief*, April 13, 2020, available at <https://jamestown.org/program/the-pla-navys-zhanlan-training-series-supporting-offensive-strike-on-the-high-seas/>.

⁶⁰ The PLAN Marine Corps recently established two combined arms brigades in the Eastern Theater, but its role in a Taiwan invasion is uncertain. For the next several years, it likely will not be part of the main assault force, as the People's Liberation Army's Navy continues to outfit and train the new units. See *Military and Security Developments Involving the People's Republic of China 2020*, 48.

⁶¹ Ying-Yu Lin, "New Wine into New Wineskins: The Evolving Role of the PLA Navy Marine Corps in Amphibious Warfare and Other Mission Areas," *China Brief* 20, no. 2 (January 29, 2020), available at <https://jamestown.org/program/new-wine-into-new-wineskins-the-evolving-role-of-the-pla-navy-marine-corps-in-amphibious-warfare-and-other-mission-areas/>.

⁶² *Military and Security Developments Involving the People's Republic of China 2020*, 42.

⁶³ Zhang, *Science of Campaigns*, 372.

⁶⁴ Easton, *The Chinese Invasion Threat*, 134–141.

⁶⁵ *Military and Security Developments Involving the People's Republic of China 2020*, 114.

⁶⁶ Ibid., 47.

⁶⁷ Jiang, *Joint Operations Headquarters Work*, 213.

⁶⁸ Peng Guangqian and Yao Youzhi, eds., *Science of Military Strategy* [战略学] (Beijing: Military Science Publishing House, 2005 [English translation of 2001 publication]), 167.

⁶⁹ Jiang, *Joint Operations Headquarters Work*, 242.

⁷⁰ The Central Military Committee's joint operations command center would likely function as the command element representative of China's highest wartime authority—the Supreme Command consisting of senior-most political and military leaders.

⁷¹ Dennis J. Blasko, "China's Evolving Approach to Strategic Deterrence," in *China's Evolving Military Strategy*, ed. Joe McReynolds (Washington, DC: The Jamestown Foundation, 2016), 335–355.

⁷² *Military and Security Developments Involving the People's Republic of China 2020*, 163.

⁷³ Elsa Kania, "The PLA's Forthcoming Fifth-Generation Operational Regulations—The Latest 'Revolution in Doctrinal Affairs'?" *China Brief* 16, no. 7 (April 21, 2016), available at <https://jamestown.org/program/the-plas-forthcoming-fifth-generation-operational-regulations-the-latest-revolution-in-doctrinal-affairs/>.

⁷⁴ Ministry of National Defense of the People's Republic of China, "Approved by Xi Jinping, Chairman of the Central Military Commission, the Central Military Commission Issued the 'Outline of Joint Operations for the Chinese People's Liberation Army (Trial),'" November 13, 2020, available at <http://www.mod.gov.cn/topnews/2020-11/13/content_4874081.htm>.

⁷⁵ However, in 2020, the National Defense University issued a new, slightly updated version of this book. The last major overhaul of the NDU version came in 2015.

CHAPTER 5

"Killing Rats in a Porcelain Shop": PLA Urban Warfare in a Taiwan Campaign

By Sale Lilly

If China intends to complete a historic mission of recovering Taiwan, which Beijing regards as a renegade province, the People's Liberation Army (PLA) must cross the Taiwan Strait, land on hostile shores, and seize Taipei—the island's capital and political center. To date, military and academic scholarship on Taiwan contingency scenarios has emphasized PLA capabilities to gain superiority in the air, sea, and subsurface approaches in and around Taiwan before embarking on an amphibious assault force of the island's beaches.[1] However, Western scholarship, simulations, and wargames tend not to consider what happens next: how urban warfare and other types of post-landing operations might unfold.

Nevertheless, PLA views on operations following the initial assault may be highly influential in the decision to use force and in the outcome of an island landing. A PLA that believes successful decapitation strikes are sufficient to prevail in a Taiwan scenario may significantly overestimate its prospects for victory while underestimating the costs. U.S. leaders in 2003 and Russian leadership in 1996 both seriously misjudged the will of urban populations to resist external governance established by military force in Iraq and Chechnya, respectively. U.S. and Russian leaders also underestimated the

139

long timelines that accompanied stability operations in urban areas. If the past three decades of global combat operations on urban terrain are indicative of the kinds of wars the PLA could face in the future, combat operations could progress over months and years, not days and weeks.

It is telling that urban warfare is largely absent from the PLA literature, including even longer doctrinal writings that cover campaigns aimed at the conquest of Taiwan. While PLA sources acknowledge seizing cities as central to eventual victory in a Taiwan contingency, the same sources often dismiss the task of subduing a modern military and the 24 million people the PLA would have to govern or suppress in an urban occupation.[2] One PLA source blithely advises troops, following a successful amphibious landing, to "organize some force to thoroughly mop up the remnants of the enemy, particularly those in the hidden areas inside the buildings and the underground engineering facilities."[3] This may be easier said than done. If "some force" is an afterthought, then one would expect PLA thought, guidance, and training on urban warfare to be relatively limited. However, if "some force" is a more developed concept, then there should be evidence of PLA thought and training on the matter.

This chapter finds that the PLA has been strongly developing its urban warfare capabilities since at least 2009, but it may have reached some wrong conclusions about the prospects for a rapid victory in an urban conflict with Taiwan. PLA writings suggest a focus on foreign cases of rapid tactical success, especially U.S. experiences in Iraq and Syria. These writings also downplay the protracted insurgencies that followed those initial victories and ignore cases in which the offensive side suffered setbacks. And while the PLA has conducted extensive training and even oriented two of its three urban warfare training bases toward Taiwan scenarios, it has still focused on decapitation strikes rather than counterinsurgency. The evidence also suggests that the People's Armed Police (PAP), which has gained counterinsurgency experience in Xinjiang, would likely be employed in Taiwan only after a permissive environment was established.

This chapter is divided into four main parts. The first section provides an overview of PLA concepts of urban warfare and analyzes periods of heightened PLA interest in this topic over the past two decades. The second section utilizes official PLA publications to identify the foreign urban warfare examples the PLA has focused on, and the lessons drawn by PLA authors from those experiences. The third section reviews publicly disclosed PLA training events that have featured urban warfare components and considers the extent to which these scenarios have resembled the conditions the PLA might face in a cross-strait operation. This section also examines how PLA urban warfare exercises have matured since the establishment of a dedicated urban warfare exercise site in 2009. The final section summarizes the key findings and derives implications for PLA operations, U.S. policy, and further research.

PLA History and Definitions of Urban Warfare

When explaining the development of the PLA's recently built Military Operations on Urban Terrain (MOUT) facility and urban warfare doctrine review, Division Commander Wang Bin characterized the difficulties of contesting control of a city by reciting the idiom of "killing rats in a porcelain shop" [*ciqidian li da laoshu,* 瓷器店里打老鼠].[4] This expression captures both the brutality of urban warfare and the caution the "rat killer" should exercise in preserving the "porcelain." The phrase was reportedly coined by PLA 3rd Field Army Commander Chen Yi during the campaign to take Shanghai from the Nationalist Army in the spring of 1949.[5] In the 2-week battle, the PLA captured Shanghai while preventing the destruction of the city, effectively killing rats while not breaking too much porcelain in the process. Urban warfare, in short, is not a new concept for the PLA; similar caution would be warranted in trying to wrest control of Taiwan from urban defenders.

PLA publications use nuanced but somewhat inconsistent language when addressing urban warfare. A review of articles and news releases from 2000 to 2020 generated by the Ministry of National Defense, *PLA Daily*, the PLA's public-facing Web site 81.cn, and PLA authors publishing in journals indexed in the China National Knowledge Infrastructure database indicates that the PLA utilizes four terms as synonyms of *urban warfare* or *city warfare* [*chengshi zuozhan,* 城市作战]. PLA authors also include several subordinate but not mutually exclusive terms (for example, *underground warfare* in urban locations such as shopping centers and parking facilities). Some PLA discussions also include the terms *drone warfare, electro-magnetic warfare,* and *sniper warfare* in an urban warfare context. Figure 1 identifies the major terms that accompany PLA urban warfare texts, and table 1 provides brief definitions.

The frequency of PLA publications on urban warfare over time also offers clues as to when the Chinese military has paid special attention to this topic. Figure 2 illustrates the annual number of PLA mentions of four urban warfare terms between 2000 and 2020: *urban warfare, street fighting, urban offensive*, and *city offense-defense*. Two apparent spikes in attention occur in 2004–2005 and 2016–2019. It is tempting, given the timing, to attribute these spikes to negative trends in Taiwan; after all, the independence-leaning Democratic Progressive Party of Taiwan won major presidential victories in both periods.

However, analysis of primary source documents indicates that both spikes reflected increased PLA attention to U.S. operations in the Middle East and had little to do with developments across the Taiwan Strait. The first spike, in 2004–2005, can be attributed to PLA case studies of U.S. urban warfare experiences in the early stages of the Iraq War, in particular the battle of Baghdad and the first and second battles of Fallujah. The second spike, in 2016–2019, reflects a combination of Chinese observations of U.S. urban warfare during the multiyear battle of Aleppo in Syria and the battle of Mosul in Iraq. Moreover, a simple content review suggests a maturation of PLA thought on urban warfare, shifting from topical reporting to greater introspection on how PLA soldiers fight in urban spaces.

Figure 1. Select PLA Urban Warfare Terms and Hierarchy of Use

Urban Warfare [城市作战]	Street Fighting [巷战]	Urban Offense [城市进攻]	City Offense-Defense [城镇攻防]

Underground Warfare [地下战]
Megacity Warfare [超大城市战]
Night Warfare [夜战]
Tunnel Warfare [地道战]
Barricade Combat [街垒战斗]

Sources: 81.cn, mod.gov.cn, *PLA Daily*, and China National Knowledge Infrastructure publications sponsored by affiliated People's Liberation Army entities.

Table 1. PLA Urban Warfare Terms and Subordinate Concepts Defined

Terms
Urban warfare [*chengshi zuozhan*, 城市作战]. A doctrinal term, and the most generic term employed in PLA use, formally defined as combat operations in urban areas, and divided into urban offensive and urban defensive operations.[*] The term encompasses PLA foreign military experiences or study as well as counterterrorism scenarios on urban terrain.
Street fighting [*xiangzhan*, 巷战]. Not a doctrinal term but formally acknowledged in some PLA publications as depicting "tenacious resistance."[†] In the context of PLA and pro-PLA military blogs, the term helps cue the audience toward the brutality required to achieve capture of an urban target, often in describing Russian, Israeli, or American experiences in urban warfare.[‡]
Urban offense [*chengshi jingong*, 城市进攻]. A doctrinal term, formally defined as "an offensive campaign against enemies who rely on the defense of the city and its periphery."[§] Often used in lieu of the term urban warfare (even though the general term includes a category of defensive operations), when PLA publications are describing a PLA training evolution or study emphasis. Does not cover foreign military experiences in urban warfare, and the term most likely to be employed in discussing the capture of Taipei or other Taiwan cities.
City offense-defense [*chengzhen gongfang*, 城镇攻防]. Not a doctrinal term, although often used interchangeably with *urban offense*. Nuanced use includes publications on PLA training evolutions where a dedicated opposition force provides a defensive opposition to the PLA unit practicing Military Operations on Urban Terrain, presumably because both units benefit from training on urban terrain. Not employed to describe foreign militaries or counterterrorism on urban terrain.

Subordinate Concepts
Underground warfare [*dixia zhan*, 地下战]. Distinct from tunnel warfare and military constructed underground facilities (UGF), this term encompasses commercial, civilian, and local government facilities, such as subway lines and underground shopping centers.[¶]
Megacity warfare [*chaoda chengshi zhan*, 超大城市战]. Urban warfare that takes place in sprawling city metropolises that include populations of 10 million or more. PLA authors often cite U.S. Army publications in attempting to define this term and treat megacity warfare as a special case of urban warfare and as a general global trend.[**]
Night warfare [*ye zhan*, 夜战]. Combat in darkness and highlighted by use of night-vision equipment, infrared, and lasers.[††] PLA urban warfare publications also identify the city as an artificial cause of darkness, including the interior of powerless buildings, underground shopping facilities, and so forth, and as perhaps a necessary but undesirable consequence of having launched "paralyzing" attacks against an enemy.[‡‡]

> **Tunnel warfare** [*didao zhan*, 地道战]. Used in conjunction with more traditional concepts of military bunkers, tunnels, and UGF. Term also used to describe urban combat environments such as Stalingrad and Aleppo where combatants excavate tunnels to facilitate combat resupply.

> **Barricade combat** [*jielei zhandou*, 街垒战斗]. Combat through and on obstacles in urban pathways to "create conditions for the development of offensives along the streets."[§§]

Notes:

[*] Academy of Military Sciences [军事科学院] (AMS), *PLA Dictionary of Military Terminology* [中国人民解放军军语] (Beijing: Military Sciences Press, 2011), 73.

[†] Ibid., 135.

[‡] Ren Ruijuan [任瑞娟], "The Chinese Army Must Attach Great Importance to the Study of Urban Warfare" [中国军队须高度重视城市战研究], *PLA Daily* [解放军报], January 15, 2008, available at <http://military.china.com.cn/txt/2008-01/15/content_9534439.htm>.

[§] AMS, *PLA Dictionary of Military Terminology*, 110.

[¶] Shi Chunmin [石纯民] and Dong Jianmin [董建敏], "Underground Space: A Key Battlefield for Future Wars" [地下空间:未来战争的关键战场], *China National Defense News* [中国国防报], October 18, 2018, available at <http://www.mod.gov.cn/jmsd/2018-10/18/content_4826976.htm>.

[**] Huang Anwei [皇安伟], Xiao Huixin [肖慧鑫], and Xin Juntao [辛军涛], "Megacity Subway System Defense" [超大城市地铁系统防护研究], *National Defense* [国防], No. 9 (2019), 77.

[††] AMS, *PLA Dictionary of Military Terminology*, 77.

[‡‡] Wang Wang [王王] and Wang Hangdong [王航东], "A Preliminary Study on Physical and Mental Adaptability Training in Urban Underground Space Combat Environment" [城市地下空间作战环境身心适应性训练初探], *Journal of Military Physical Education and Sports* [军事体育学报] 36, no. 3 (2017), 8.

[§§] AMS, *PLA Dictionary of Military Terminology*, 676.

The PLA's (Misguided) Lessons from Iraq

What has the PLA learned from the U.S. urban warfare experience? While Western scholars widely acknowledge that U.S. conduct in the 1991 Gulf War heavily influenced PLA strategic thinking on joint and systems warfare, less well known is the impact of the 2003 battle of Baghdad and the 2004 second battle of Fallujah on PLA strategic thought.[6] Nevertheless, as discussed already, PLA authors have been preoccupied with these two battles.[7] Evidence suggests that PLA urban warfare analysts believe the battle of Baghdad demonstrated that a mechanized force can quickly seize an opponent's capital with relatively few casualties. There is also evidence that the PLA interpreted the outcome of the second battle of Fallujah, which occurred only 1 year after the fall of Baghdad, as proof that an active urban insurgency can be quickly isolated and crushed.[8] Chinese authors describe that battle as "the

Figure 2. Open-Source PLA Citations of Urban Warfare Themes

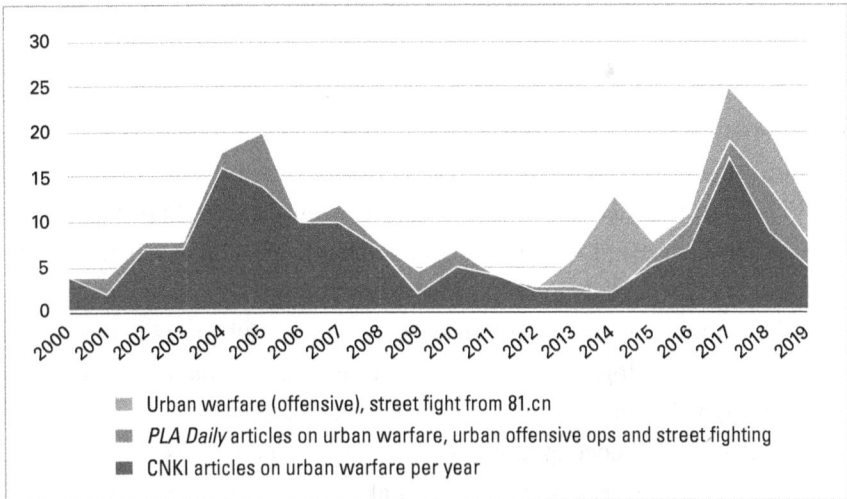

Urban warfare (offensive), street fight from 81.cn

PLA Daily articles on urban warfare, urban offensive ops and street fighting

CNKI articles on urban warfare per year

Sources: 81.cn, mod.gov.cn, *PLA Daily*, and China National Knowledge Infrastructure publications sponsored by affiliated People's Liberation Army entities.

largest, shortest, and most effective urban combat operation carried out by the U.S. military after the Vietnam War."[9]

PLA authors correctly observed the near-term tactical success of these U.S. operations; however, they failed to grasp their aftermath. The second battle of Fallujah points to success for the offensive side, but only in contrast to the first battle of Fallujah, in which U.S. forces attempted and failed to secure the city with an economy of force operation. PLA interpretations of the battle of Baghdad are also rose-colored, in that various authors assess the collapse of the sitting government as a mechanized game of "capture the flag," with campaign victory conditions equivalent to reaching a destination. These interpretations ignore that the U.S. war experience in Iraq from 2003 to 2011 was without a clear victory, with resistance intensifying over time, increasing casualties in occupation to stabilization forces, and a worrying tactical trend wherein mechanized armor was exposed to asymmetric threats such as improvised explosive devices.[10] PLA authors similarly describe Saddam Hussein's rapid fall in 2003 as an example of "beheading" via special forces, allowing an aggressor to "cut off the head of a snake" [*qieduan shetou*, 切断蛇头].[11] That the 2003 fall of Baghdad ended only one brief phase of the war and opened an almost decade-long second phase seems to be of negligible interest to PLA authors.

Read differently, PLA writers' perceptions of successful U.S. urban warfare experiences in Iraq could represent the style of campaign the PLA hopes to execute following an amphibious landing on Taiwan. If the PLA leadership has absorbed similar lessons from recent U.S. urban contests, then they almost certainly know that these conflicts can last months, if not years. Based on the available PLA literature, one can conclude that the only urban warfare the PLA intends to fight is the kind that lasts a few days. Perhaps that is why one author urges the PLA to view the second battle of Fallujah, a battle fought in the span of 2 weeks, as an urban warfare archetype.[12] PLA scholars, by contrast, focus much less on the lessons from less successful, protracted conflicts in places such as Mogadishu, Grozny, and Vietnam—signaling that they do not believe the PLA intends to face such situations.

Yet the PLA's preoccupation with the "quick victory" cases of Baghdad and Fallujah ignores realities that could make a battle for Taipei more complicated. Both the battle of Baghdad and the second battle of Fallujah occurred in relatively permissive environments where the U.S. military used time to its favor to build friendly forces, execute information operations to gain the support of local civilians, and, in the case of Fallujah, conduct blocking movements to halt defender resupply.[13] There is no reason to believe that, in a scenario in which time is of the essence—either to counter U.S. intervention or to minimize the window during which the international community might rally to the cause of the defender—the PLA would have the same time advantages credited to the U.S. military in Baghdad and Fallujah.

The differences in campaign scale between Taipei and the two coalition urban warfare battles in Iraq are also significant. The larger Taipei urban region encompasses Taipei, New Taipei City, and Taoyuan, including a population of around 10 million as of 2021. This region meets one of the common thresholds for the term *megacity* and is approximately twice the size of Baghdad's population in 2003 and perhaps 20 times the size of Fallujah's population in 2004. Problems such as refugee flows and insurgencies may intensify as the base population increases.

Taiwan's manmade vertical expanses above and below sea level place even more demands on those planning for urban warfare. For the Syrian and Iraqi urban battlefields, the multilevel buildings that dominated the cities could still be characterized as "low-rise."[14] As average building height increases, a range of urban combat considerations may become relevant, such as tank barrel azimuth suitability and helicopter vulnerability. In addition to the height of Taipei's skyscrapers, subterranean commercial structures, including parking garages, underground shopping centers, and metros, greatly expand the combat areas for urban warfare, posing unique challenges to an invader and providing substantial space for a defender to resist aggression.[15] In sum, a review of PLA writings indicates that the Chinese military has closely observed urban conflicts across the globe but may have drawn incomplete findings or the wrong lessons for an urban conflict specific to Taiwan.

PLA Urban Warfare Training: An Incipient Focus on Taiwan

While there are relatively few explicit mentions of a Taiwan urban warfare scenario in PLA sources, evidence suggests this scenario has influenced recent Military Operations on Urban Terrain training. Analysis of PLA urban warfare publications provides details on urban warfare exercise tempo and sometimes on specific MOUT facility locations. Since at least 2009, the PLA has used dedicated MOUT spaces in at least three locations: the main MOUT facility within the greater Zhurihe Training Base [*zhurihe xunlian jidi*, 朱日和训练基地] in Inner Mongolia, which has been used since 2009; a potential pilot or legacy facility at Yanshan [*yanshan*, 燕山] that may still be available for smaller scale MOUT exercises in mountainous terrains; and, perhaps most relevant for a Taiwan scenario, a mock city complete with "a library, coffee shop, and power plant" located at a "certain training field in Northern Jiangsu" mentioned in a PLA video distributed on JS7TV and Zhihu.com in 2020.[16]

The MOUT training calendar seems to have annual exercises incorporated into the larger Stride series of exercises located at Zhurihe. Outside of these exercises, which receive annual pro forma reporting, typically during the summer months, there are mentions of urban warfare–focused training exercises, sometimes directly associated with "urban offense." MOUT exercises are sometimes carried out during multinational training events focused on counterterrorism, such as the Shanghai Cooperation Organization Peace Mission exercises.[17] Based on the exercises the PLA chose to publicize, there is a clear evolution in terms of size, as well as a geographic expansion of military units that receive priority training beyond the Beijing-based brigades that seemed to receive early emphasis from 2008 to 2015. A summary of these exercises is provided in table 2.

It is unclear if the 2020 exercise at the Jiangsu MOUT facility represents a to-be-determined exercise slate and whether any additional facilities were developed. A possible motive is that Jiangsu is better situated by military region, climate, and unit needs to support MOUT operations in Taiwan compared with the MOUT facilities at Zhurihe. (Inner Mongolia sits in the Central Asia Plateau, is mainly grassland and desert, and is subject to at least 3 months of snow and freezing temperatures.[18] The location is thus ideal for artillery drills but cannot simulate Taiwan's subtropical climate and mountainous geography.) The Jiangsu MOUT facility also reflects a focus on realistic training for a Taiwan scenario. Limited reporting indicates that the PLA

Table 2. Select PLA Urban Warfare Training Exercises, 2008–2020

Training Evolution*	Participating Units (Theater Command)	Location	Urban Warfare Term(s) Employed
2008: Urban Warfare Study Group, Pilot†	Mountain Warfare Brigade–Tongbai Mountain Guerrillas‡	Yanshan	Urban warfare, street fighting, urban offense
2009: Zhurihe MOUT Inauguration	Unnamed Beijing motorized infantry brigade, with PLAAF, PLARF, and PAP units of unmentioned sizes	Zhurihe Training Base	Urban warfare, urban offense
Peace Mission 2014	Multinational-Shanghai Cooperation Organization partners, SOF detachment	Zhurihe Training Base	Urban warfare, street fighting
Stride 2015-B, C§	Unnamed Beijing motorized infantry brigade with subordinate army aviation and SOF detachment	Zhurihe Training Base	Urban warfare, street fighting
Stride 2017¶	80th Army Group–"Storm Group" (Northern); 81st Army Group–"Prairie Wolves" (Central); both motorized infantry brigades	Zhurihe Training Base	Urban offense

Training Evolution*	Participating Units (Theater Command)	Location	Urban Warfare Term(s) Employed
2018: Unnamed**	79th Army Group (Northern) Aviation Brigade	Liaoning Province	Urban warfare
Stride 2018††	81st Army Group (Central)	Zhurihe Training Base	Urban offense
Stride 2019-A‡‡	Unnamed brigade-size unit	Zhurihe Training Base	Urban offense
2020: Unnamed	73rd Army Group (Eastern)	Jiangsu Province MOUT Facility	City offense-defense

Key: MOUT: Military Operations on Urban Terrain; PAP: People's Armed Police; PLAAF: PLA Air Force; PLARF: PLA Rocket Force; SOF: special operations forces.

Notes:

 * Only some evolutions were mentioned by exercise iteration in a calendar year: 2019-A, 2015-C, and so forth.

 † "The Beijing Military Region Group Army Organized Modern Urban Offensive Combat Exercises" [北京军区集团军组织现代城市进攻作战演练], *PLA Daily* [解放军报], August 23, 2009, available at <http://mil.news.sina.com.cn/2009-08-23/0627563459.html>.

 ‡ Division Commander Wang Bin stated that he had repurposed a mountain warfare unit to fulfill a March 2008 request by the Beijing Military Region to simulate realistic urban warfare scenarios. The unit was identified as the Tongbai Mountain Guerrillas [*tongbaishan youji dui*, 桐柏山游击队]. The location Yanshan may have been intentional or incidental to the exercise based on the units' parent command.

 § Wu Yuanjin [武元晋], "Urban Combat, New Combat Forces Are Emerging: Review of the Exercise 'Stride-2015 Zhurihe C' by a Motorized Infantry Brigade of the Beijing Military Region" [城市作战, 新型作战力量初露锋芒-北京军区某摩步旅"跨越-2015·朱日和C"演习复盘见闻], *PLA Daily* [解放军报], July 21, 2015, available at <http://news.mod.gov.cn/action/2015-07/21/content_4601789.htm>.

 ¶ Li Tianpeng [李天鹏], "'Stride–2017 Zhurihe': A Thousand-Word Summary of the 'Storm Force' Battalion Commander" ["跨越—2017·朱日和"-"暴风雨部队" 营长的千字总结], *China Military Online* [中国军网], September 21, 2017, available at <http://www.81.cn/syjdt/2017-09/21/content_7765024.htm>.

 ** Hao Hailong [郝海龙], "The Iron Wings Whirl, the 'Battlefield' Goes from the Wilderness to the City" [铁翼飞旋 "战场" 由荒原到城区], *PLA Daily* [解放军报], February 25, 2018, available at <http://www.81.cn/jfjbmap/content/2018-02/25/content_200236.htm>.

 †† "'Stride–2018 Zhurihe' Exercise Begins" ["跨越-2018·朱日和"演习拉开战幕], *PLA Daily* [解放军], July 23, 2018, available at <http://www.xinhuanet.com/mil/2018-07/23/c_129918673.htm>.

 ‡‡ "'Stride-2019 Zhurihe A' A Certain Army Brigade Accepts Battlefield Inspection for the First Time as a Red and Blue Dual Identity" ["跨越-2019·朱日和A" 陆军某旅首次以红蓝双重身份接受战场检验], *PLA Daily* [解放军报], July 12, 2019, available at <http://www.81.cn/jmywyl/2019-07/12>.

has adopted more realistic urban warfare features, using many of the urban battlefield debris training aids initially employed by the U.S. Army's Zussman Urban Combat Training Center at Fort Knox, Kentucky.[19]

Despite its dissimilarities with Taiwan, Zhurihe remains valuable due to the presence of mock-ups of key Taipei sites, including Taiwan's Presidential Office Building and possibly the Legislative Yuan.[20] These buildings will likely have special relevance for practicing the decapitation strikes the PLA believes are critical in replicating the initial U.S. successes in Baghdad.[21] If strategic signaling were Beijing's only goal, it would seem unnecessary for the PLA to upgrade what already appears to be a credible reproduction of the "head of the snake," though some have cast these developments as potential evidence of an entrepreneurial service (the PLA) proving its relevance amid competition for funds and significance.[22] PLA leadership, which has often been urged by Xi Jinping to make military training more combat-realistic, may have been moved to make further urban warfare investments.[23] In total, the Taipei urban replicas can be viewed as one element of a multipart urban warfare training capability that is required to authentically develop urban warfare capabilities.

China's PAP has also prepared for urban warfare scenarios, but its role in a Taiwan contingency is less clear than that of the PLA. The PAP has gained experience in urban operations in Xinjiang and Hong Kong.[24] These operations have similarities in mission profiles that could include counterterrorism operations, special operations forces or SWAT-like police capabilities, riot or crowd control, and other broadly defined force protection measures.[25] At a March 2021 inspection of the 2nd Mobile Contingent Headquarters—a unit that might have support responsibilities for a PLA invasion of Taiwan[26]— in Fuzhou City, Fujian Province, Xi and Central Military Commission Vice Chairman Xu Qiliang observed a demonstration of the PAP performing many tactical pieces of urban combat.[27]

While Xi's visit emphasizes the importance placed on the PAP in supporting the PLA, it is the latter's job to fight and win wars. Notably, in the 200 PLA sources reviewed for this chapter, the PAP was not mentioned once as a contributing force. Additionally, analogous reasoning from the PLA's preferred case studies—Baghdad and Fallujah—does not mention the U.S. military's use of National Guard units. The National Guard's role is not identical to that of the PAP within China's armed forces. However, the concept of relief in place for urban operations, which has been explored extensively in the U.S. experiences in Iraq and Afghanistan, goes unmentioned in existing PLA coverage of the battles.[28] If the PAP is to be relevant in Taiwan, its utility and experience, drawn from places such as Xinjiang and Tibet, would seem to be most useful after the PLA has secured a victory and is anticipating a long occupation. The PAP appears less relevant during, and immediately after, the initial assault on Taiwan. The PLA reckoning on the likelihood of either of those scenarios may be driving this relative silence on the PAP and urban warfare.

Conclusion

This chapter has identified three key findings from a review of the PLA's scholarly reflection on urban combat and its public record of urban warfare exercises. First, PLA scholarship suggests a preoccupation with conflicts that were relatively short and successful for the attacker. Yet drawing lessons from cases such as Baghdad and Fallujah does not accurately represent the vast majority of urban warfare experiences in the 20th and 21st centuries. The experience of offensive armies in multiple urban warfare conflicts, such as the first and second battles of Grozny, Hue City, and Aleppo, suggests that battles occur over weeks, if not months. In addition, the PLA's emphasis on U.S. tactical success in these cases ignores that U.S. and coalition forces fought for years afterward to secure these cities despite material and technological advantages. In one conflict (Baghdad), successful decapitation strikes seemed to play little or no role in preventing a multiyear conflict.

Second, the PLA is building a dedicated urban warfare capability. Developing training facilities specifically for this purpose began with a pilot or test capability MOUT facility and expanded to include a designated space at the PLA's Inner Mongolia training facility and an urban warfare mock-up in Jiangsu Province. PLA urban combat capabilities are nurtured by at least annual training exercises that include elements of decapitation strikes and block-to-block fighting with armored and dismounted infantry forces.

Third, the PLA's urban warfare capability appears increasingly directed at Taiwan. At least two of the PLA's three MOUT facilities could be associated with simulating conditions on Taiwan. The Zhurihe facility possesses credible replicas of Taipei's key political sites (reflecting the focus on quick decapitation strikes), and the Northern Jiangsu facility is situated in the PLA's Eastern Theater Command and bears resemblance to the island in terms of topology and climate. While the PLA might need to conduct additional urban warfare scenarios, including noncombatant evacuation operations in a far-flung location, stability operations in a possible Korean Peninsula crisis, and urban operations in locations such as Xinjiang, evidence indicates that PLA urban combat training is increasingly oriented toward Taiwan.

These findings have implications for wargaming, policy, PLA studies, and Taiwan's military readiness. First, Taiwan scenario wargaming should take urban conflict settings into account. Many publicly available wargame discussions include multiphase Taiwan contingencies that model conflict in the land, sea, and air domains. However, these studies usually treat the land as synonymous with Taiwan's beaches. As the PLA builds a credible urban warfare combat capability, it will be increasingly important to examine how defenders can repulse an aggressor force attempting to transition through warfare disciplines (for example, amphibious to urban, jungle to urban) to test assumptions about PLA actions and defender responses. Modeling urban combat for unclassified discussions may be difficult, but commercially available systems have already been used by the U.S. military to introduce urban warfare mechanics as a part of professional military education.[29] These games could also examine the propensity for Taiwan's population to resist an occupying force and include sensitivity analysis for comprehensive, partial, or scant support for starting and sustaining armed resistance.

Second, PLA attempts to modernize its urban warfare capabilities have implications for U.S. scientific and technological cooperation with China. As one example, this chapter's literature review found mention of PLA urban warfare requirements for a tactical method to employ radar "that can penetrate brick walls, wooden doors, rubble and other non-metal obstacles to detect human life characteristics" to better identify and defeat embedded defenders.[30] In that light, discussions on China's efforts to acquire foreign technologies might be viewed differently. China's military research institutes have participated in four iterations of the International Radar Conference, which has been held in China and to which Western and Japanese academics have been invited to present research findings on such topics as "Radars for Non-Contact Vital Sign Detection," a call for papers that included an interest in "Thru-Wall Detection Radar," and a demonstration night titled "Human Activity Classification with Radar."[31] There are certainly nonmilitary uses for wall-penetrating radar in humanitarian and disaster relief. However, considering a stated PLA military need and the PLA's participation at these types of events, increased professional caution should be exercised when sharing findings that could provide a technological solution to kill a Taiwanese defender.[32]

Third, future research should address several questions about the PLA's ability to integrate urban warfare into larger plans for cross-strait operations. For instance, what force and unit structure could the PLA employ to conduct urban warfare operations in Taiwan? Identifying these forces is important for two reasons. First, the identified unit and echelon could illuminate the equipment, firepower, and doctrine these soldiers bring to the fight. Second, there is an opportunity to compare PLA depictions of an amphibious landing package with the units the PLA intends to use to seize Taiwan's cities. Do the force compositions match? If not, what could explain the lack of urban warfare forces in the amphibious group? The answers have implications for predicting whether protracted on-island operations may unfold in ways that are not beneficial for a force hoping to achieve a fait accompli or quick recognition of the People's Republic of China's sovereignty over Taiwan.

Another set of questions concerns the fungibility of PLA forces. If Beijing has identified battalion-size landing units as optimal for Taiwan invasion scenarios, with "three infantry companies, three amphibious assault vehicle/tank companies, one air defense company, and one anti-tank company,"[33] then a key question for the PLA is how effectively these units could be reconstituted into ones capable of conducting urban operations. Due to the weight and size restrictions for amphibious vehicles moving on sand and gravel, there are inherent limitations in the mobile protected firepower assets identified as "necessary" to win modern urban warfare battles.[34] Given recent evidence from Syria and eastern Ukraine, standoff infantry weapons and light armored vehicles—the exact type mentioned in a potential PLA amphibious landing package—are insufficient to succeed in modern urban warfare.[35] Will these lessons be something the PLA learns only in defeat, or can it adapt to this feature of urban warfare prior to the onset of hostilities? This is only one issue that will determine whether the PLA can realize its vision of rapid urban operations to subdue the enemy.

Fourth, those responsible for ensuring Taiwan's military readiness could take PLA urban warfare preparations as an opportunity to rethink the capacity in which the island's military and civilian populations are prepared for national defense. Conformal military design—the concept of integrating sensor and weapons functionality into the natural contours of military ships and aircraft—could be extended to urban landscape design. Much the same way that modern or aesthetically designed heavy-base cement pots or planters have become standard antiterrorism force protection barriers in the U.S. Capitol region and other sensitive areas, Taiwan's urban design could (or may already) contain design features that complicate an invading force's mobility. For example, the 2018 unnamed PLA urban aviation exercise near Liaoning specifically mentioned attempts to land rotary aircraft on high-rise buildings, suggesting that hazards to rotors, perhaps conformal to urban needs, could represent an approach to making urban warfare more hazardous to an invader.

Another consideration for Taiwan's military readiness is the extent to which the population could readily adopt conventional munitions and commercial technology to resist an invader. As coalition forces in Iraq experienced from 2004 to 2011, conventional military ordnance, dispersed in the early days of conflict, combined with modern retail electronics and ingenuity, helped create a lethal and effective improvised explosive device campaign to harass, ambush, and assault coalition vehicle movements. The hundreds of motorcycle and scooter repair shops that abound on the streets of Taipei today serve a relevant commercial function. But the same metal crimpers, spooled copper wire, batteries, and multitools that serve repair work today are not all that different from the materials used in the improvised explosive device workshops of Fallujah or Kandahar. Providing Taiwan's military or military reservists with basic insurgency techniques and training may also be a way to signal the island's resolve to complicate and extend any invasion time frame well beyond a few days of conflict. In a test of wills, the Chinese Communist Party may need to ask itself if the PLA is able and willing to begin such a fight in which the enemy may be willing to destroy the "porcelain shop."

Notes

[1] David A. Shlapak, David T. Orletsky, and Barry A. Wilson, *Dire Strait? Military Aspects of the China-Taiwan Confrontation and Options for U.S. Policy* (Santa Monica, CA: RAND, 2000), 12; Steve Tsang, *If China Attacks Taiwan: Military Strategy, Politics, and Economics* (London: Routledge, 2006); Timothy R. Heath, *Chinese Political and Military Thinking Regarding Taiwan and the East and South China Seas* (Santa Monica, CA: RAND, 2017), available at <https://www.rand.org/pubs/testimonies/CT470.html>.

[2] Sun Longhai [孙龙海], Cao Zhengrong [曹正荣], and Yang Ying [杨颖], *Informatized Army Operations* [信息化陆军作战] (Beijing: National Defense University Press, 2014), 173, 179, 191.

[3] Ibid., 205, 206.

[4] "The Beijing Military Region Group Army Organized Modern Urban Offensive Combat Exercises" [北京军区集团军组织现代城市进攻作战演练], *PLA Daily* [解放军报], August 23, 2009, available at <http://mil.news.sina.com.cn/2009-08-23/0627563459.html>.

[5] "Chen Yi: Liberation of Shanghai Was Like 'Killing Rats in a Porcelain Shop'" [陈毅: 解放上海就像 '瓷器店里打老鼠'], *People's Daily*, May 27, 2009, available at <http://cpc.people.com.cn/GB/64162/64172/85037/85039/5991763.html>.

[6] Dean Cheng, "Chinese Lessons from the Gulf Wars," in *Chinese Lessons from Other Peoples' Wars*, ed. Andrew Scobell, David Lai, and Roy Kamphausen (Carlisle, PA: Strategic Studies Institute, 2011), 153, 168–170.

[7] See Li Jiufeng [李久峰], "A Classic of City-Siege Warfare: A Perspective on Fallujah's Operation 'Phantom Fury'" [城市攻坚战的不老经典—费卢杰 "幻影愤怒" 行动透视], *Military Digest* [军事文摘] (2019), 55.

[8] See Liu Peng [刘鹏], "Stones of Other Mountains—Fierce Battle of Fallujah: Classic Cases of U.S. Army Urban Warfare" [他山之石- 激战费卢杰: 美军城市作战经典战例], *Sina Military Affairs*, May 28, 2018, available at <http://mil.news.sina.com.cn/2018-05-28/doc-ihcaquev4225234.shtml>.

[9] Li, "A Classic of City-Siege Warfare," 55.

[10] Andrew J. Bacevich, *The Limits of Power: The End of American Exceptionalism* (New York: Henry Holt and Company, 2008), 157.

[11] Ren Ruijuan [任瑞娟], "The Chinese Army Must Attach Great Importance to the Study of Urban Warfare" [中国军队须高度重视城市战研究], *PLA Daily* [解放军报], January 15, 2008, available at <http://military.china.com.cn/txt/2008-01/15/content_9534439.htm>.

[12] Xia Wei [夏维] et al., "Using the Second Battle of Fallujah as a Blueprint to Promote Modern Urban Warfare Research" [以第二次费卢杰战役为蓝本推动现代城市作战研究], *Conmilit* [现代军事], November 5, 2016, 86.

[13] Gian Gentile et al., *Reimagining the Character of Urban Operations for the U.S. Army* (Santa Monica, CA: RAND, 2017), 65–67.

[14] Haider J.E. Al-Saaidy and Dhirgham Alobaydi, "Studying Street Centrality and Human Density in Different Urban Forms in Baghdad, Iraq," *Ain Shams Engineering Journal* 12, no. 1 (March 2021), 1111, 1113.

[15] Public polling in Taiwan over the past 20 years has indicated a range of assessments on its citizens' will to fight in the event of an invasion by the People's Republic of China. See Russell Hsiao, "What Would Taiwan Do If China Invaded?" *National Interest*, April 24, 2018, available at <https://nationalinterest.org/feature/what-would-taiwan-do-if-china-invaded-25542>.

16   Video from a September 2020 posting used the phrase *certain training field in Northern Jiangsu* [苏北某训练] 地基. "Red and Blue Confrontation Tests the Offensive and Defensive Capabilities of the Combined Forces in Cities and Towns" [陆军第73集团军某合成旅: 红蓝对抗检验合成部队城镇攻防能力], PLA TV Web [中国军视网], video, 3:36, September 24, 2020, available at <http://www.js7tv.cn/video/202009_230306.html>.

17   "Chinese Special Operation Members in Urban Anti-Terrorism Training," *China Military Online*, August 26, 2014, available at <http://www.ecns.cn/visual/2014/08-26/131543.shtml>.

18   Yongfei Bai et al., "Primary Production and Rain Use Efficiency Across a Precipitation Gradient on the Mongolia Plateau," *Ecology* 89, no. 8 (August 2008), 2140–2153.

19   Feng Fei [冯非] et al., "A Combined Brigade of the 73rd Army Group"; Michael Behlin, 3rd Sustainment Command (Expeditionary) Public Affairs, "19th Engineers Conduct Platoon Certification Exercise," *Army.mil*, June 14, 2011, available at <https://www.army.mil/article/59574/19th_engineers_conduct_platoon_certification_exercise>.

20   Victor Robert Lee, "Satellite Imagery: China Staging Mock Invasion of Taiwan?" *The Diplomat*, August 9, 2015, available at <https://thediplomat.com/2015/08/satellite-imagery-from-china-suggests-mock-invasion-of-taiwan/>. Comparisons of Zhurihe public overhead imagery between August 9, 2015, when *The Diplomat* reported on the mock attack on the presidential office, and 2020 indicate a possible expansion of fabrications that might include a building representing the size and general orientation of the Legislative Yuan.

21   Ren, "The Chinese Army Must Attach Great Importance to the Study of Urban Warfare."

22   Greg Austin, "China's Military Trains for Taiwan Invasion with Mock-Ups," *The Diplomat*, August 11, 2015, available at <https://thediplomat.com/2015/08/chinas-military-trains-for-taiwan-invasion-with-mock-ups/>.

23   Dennis J. Blasko, "The Chinese Military Speaks to Itself, Revealing Doubts," *War on the Rocks*, February 18, 2019, available at <https://warontherocks.com/2019/02/the-chinese-military-speaks-to-itself-revealing-doubts/>.

24   Greg Torode, "Exclusive: China's Internal Security Force on Frontlines of Hong Kong Protests," Reuters, March 18, 2020, available at <https://www.reuters.com/article/us-hongkong-protests-military-exclusive/exclusive-chinas-internal-security-force-on-frontlines-of-hong-kong-protests-idUSKBN2150JZ>.

25   Joel Wuthnow, *China's Other Army: The People's Armed Police in an Era of Reform*, China Strategic Perspectives No. 14 (Washington, DC: NDU Press, 2019), 21.

26   Ibid., 13.

27   China Global Television Network, "Xi Instructs Armed Police to Enhance Military Training, Combat Readiness," CCTV, March 26, 2021, available at <https://www.cctvplus.com/news/20210326/8183713.shtml>.

28   Larry Minear, "The U.S. Citizen-Soldier and the Global War on Terror: The National Guard Experience" (master's thesis, Tufts University, 2007), 13–15.

29   James Lacey, "How Does the Next Great Power Conflict Play Out? Lessons from a Wargame," *War on the Rocks*, April 22, 2019, available at <https://warontherocks.com/2019/04/how-does-the-next-great-power-conflict-play-out-lessons-from-a-wargame/>.

30   Han Qinggui, "Adapt to the Characteristics of Urban Operations and Continuously Improve the Level of Weaponry and Equipment" [适应城市作战特点不断提升武器装备能力建设水平], *National Defense* [国防], no. 1 (2018), 78.

31   See Institute of Engineering and Technology International Radar Conference 2020 "Call for Papers," available at <http://www.ietradar.org/down/CFP.pdf>.

[32] The 2015 International Radar Conference held in Hangzhou, China, supported nine papers on wall-penetrating radar, four of which included authors affiliated with the People's Liberation Army. All are available at <https://digital-library.theiet.org/content/conferences/cp677>.

[33] Ian Easton, *The Chinese Invasion Threat: Taiwan's Defense and American Strategy in Asia* (Manchester: Eastbridge Books, 2019), 337.

[34] Gentile et al., *Reimagining the Character of Urban Operations for the U.S. Army*, xi.

[35] Ibid., 60–62.

III

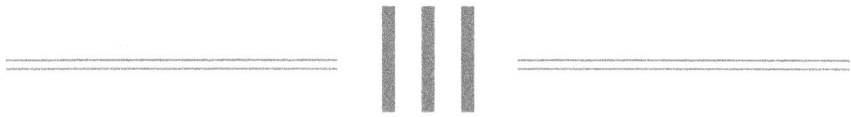

Chinese Forces and the Impact of Reform

CHAPTER 6

PLA Army and Marine Corps Amphibious Brigades in a Post-Reform Military

Joshua Arostegui

There is much speculation about a potential Chinese invasion of Taiwan, but whether the People's Liberation Army (PLA) can achieve victory will ultimately depend on the quantity and quality of its amphibious forces. The difference between PLA Army (PLAA) and PLA Navy Marine Corps (PLANMC) amphibious units has become increasingly clear following the 2017 reforms to PLA organizations at the corps level and below. While much analytic attention has been paid to the expanded and more expeditionary-focused PLANMC, the transition of two PLAA amphibious mechanized infantry divisions and a single amphibious armor brigade into six amphibious combined arms brigades demonstrates renewed emphasis on Taiwan and lays the foundation for actual warfighting capabilities. Although each service now maintains six amphibious-capable brigades, the differences in organization, command structure, equipment, and training represent the varying directions the PLAA and PLA Navy (PLAN) are taking in preparing for future landing operations.

According to the U.S. Department of Defense report *Military and Security Developments Involving the People's Republic of China 2020*, the PLA has 12 brigades available to conduct amphibious operations in a joint island landing campaign against Taiwan.[1] The PLANMC, however, has far fewer amphibious heavy combined arms battalions than those within the PLAA's six amphibious brigades. This disparity does not represent a lack of PLANMC combat power but exemplifies a force designed and equipped for securing Chinese overseas interests in a wide range of environments beyond the Taiwan Strait. To enable such planned operations, the PLANMC added lighter and more mobile battalions as part of a transition from amphibious to multidimensional brigades.[2]

In contrast, the PLAA remains focused on cross-strait operations. The 2017 reforms pushed enough combat power down to the 24 PLAA amphibious combined arms battalions so that each battalion now has nearly as much combat support capacity as its mechanized infantry regiment predecessor. The six PLAA amphibious brigades are fully standardized and similarly equipped and designed to execute opposed landings using previous division-regiment doctrine at smaller scales. Thus, the transformation from the division-regiment to the brigade-battalion construct does not signify changes at the strategic campaign level as much as at the operational and tactical levels. According to the PLA, the flattened chain of command enables lower echelon leaders to execute landing operations with more initiative and independence.[3] However, the PLAA amphibious brigades' size and heavy equipment require adequate naval transport that currently exists in limited numbers and a robust logistics capability that remains untested. Without sufficient PLAN medium and heavy lift, the PLAA amphibious brigades are at best a tool for deterrence, enabling China to influence the outlook of Taiwan and regional competitors with increased publicity of amphibious brigades' training operations tempo.

This chapter develops these arguments in four main sections. The first discusses the restructure of PLAA and PLANMC amphibious units following the 2017 force-wide reform. The second section outlines the possible roles of the PLA's amphibious units in a Taiwan island-landing campaign. The third details how PLA amphibious unit exercises and training have become more extensive and complex following the 2017 reform. The fourth section provides insight into the potential challenges that PLA amphibious units face in carrying out landing operations because of the restructure. Each section is based on a foundation of official PLA media sources, military texts, and journal articles, while materials from the U.S. Government and professional corporations such as Jane's Information Group (Janes) assist with in-depth understanding of system and force capabilities.

PLAA and PLANMC Brigade Reorganization

Following decades of both successful and unsuccessful island landings, the PLA has long recognized the need to maintain capable amphibious forces. Successful near-shore island-landing operations in 1955, along with the seizure of the Vietnam-occupied Paracel Islands in 1974, demonstrated the PLA's willingness to execute joint landing operations under relatively favorable conditions. However, the PLA's inability to cross the Taiwan Strait to defeat Chiang Kai-shek's Nationalists in and after 1949 remains the ultimate reminder that Beijing requires a competent and sizable amphibious capability to achieve reunification by force.[4] This mission resulted in the establishment of permanent PLA amphibious forces that have been restructured multiple times. This section details the latest reforms to both the PLAA and PLANMC amphibious units.

The New PLAA Amphibious Brigade

The PLA's first fully amphibious unit was a short-lived marine division established in 1954. After its disbanding in 1957, the PLA lacked dedicated amphibious units until 1980, when the PLAN's 1st Marine Brigade was established.[5] Nearly 20 years later, the PLAN created the 164th Marine Brigade from an army division, while around the same time the PLAA transitioned the historic 1st Motorized Infantry Division, 1st Group Army,[6] Nanjing Military Region, into the 1st Amphibious Mechanized Infantry Division (hereafter referred to as amphibious division). The 124th Amphibious Division, 42nd Group Army, Guangzhou Military Region, appeared not long after. These two divisions, along with the existing 14th Armor Brigade, 31st Group Army, Nanjing Military Region, constituted the only mechanized amphibious forces in the PLAA.[7] Figure 1 provides an organizational overview of the former PLAA amphibious division.

Following the 2017 PLA "below the neck" reforms, the two amphibious divisions split into four amphibious combined arms brigades, while the amphibious armor brigade and elements from motorized infantry units transitioned into another two amphibious combined arms brigades. Each of the new brigades, like its division predecessors, fell under group armies within the PLA Eastern Theater Command (located across from Taiwan) and the adjacent Southern Theater

Figure 1. Former PLAA Amphibious Mechanized Infantry Division

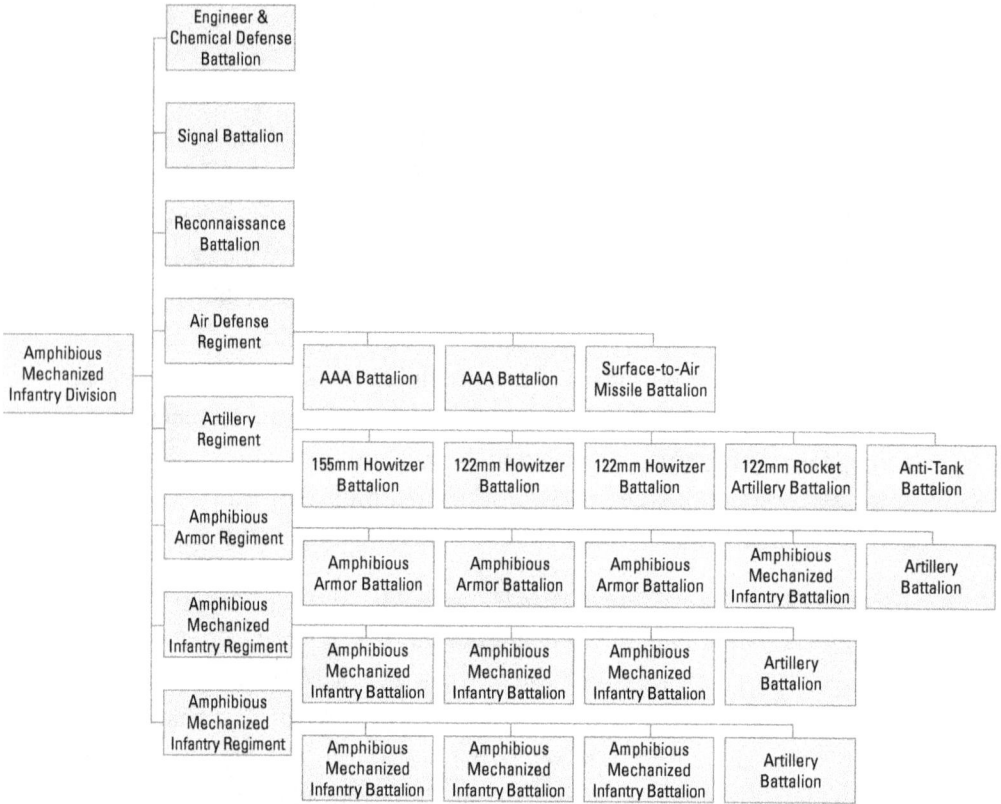

Command.[8] The new amphibious brigades pushed most of the same capabilities that existed in the earlier construct down to the battalion level, allowing the PLAA to retain its amphibious doctrine and tactics, techniques, and procedures (TTPs).[9] Table 1 and figure 2 outline the theater command and group army organization of the amphibious brigades according to Janes.[10]

The new PLAA amphibious brigade, made up of approximately 5,000 soldiers, is a variant of the new heavy combined arms brigade modeled after the U.S. Army's Armored Brigade Combat Team.[11] Table 2 and figure 3 detail the organization, equipment, and elements of the new amphibious brigade.[12]

The new PLAA combined arms brigade is a modular formation that provides the commander interchangeable combat and functional support battalions and companies to build mission-specific operational units. The amphibious brigade's battalions also mirror the group army's organization, improving its ability to call on corps-level fires, intelligence and reconnaissance, and other capabilities. The plug-and-play modularity of the PLAA amphibious brigade- and corps-level force structure is also reflected in its four amphibious combined arms battalions, which improves tactical combat power generation.[13]

Table 1. Post-2017 PLAA Amphibious Brigades

Theater Command	Group Army	Amphibious Brigade	Garrison
Eastern	72nd	5th Combined Arms	Hangzhou
		124th Combined Arms	
	73rd	14th Combined Arms	Zhangzhou
		91st Combined Arms	
Southern	74th	1st Combined Arms	Guangzhou
		125th Combined Arms	

Figure 2. Post-2017 PLAA Group Army Structure

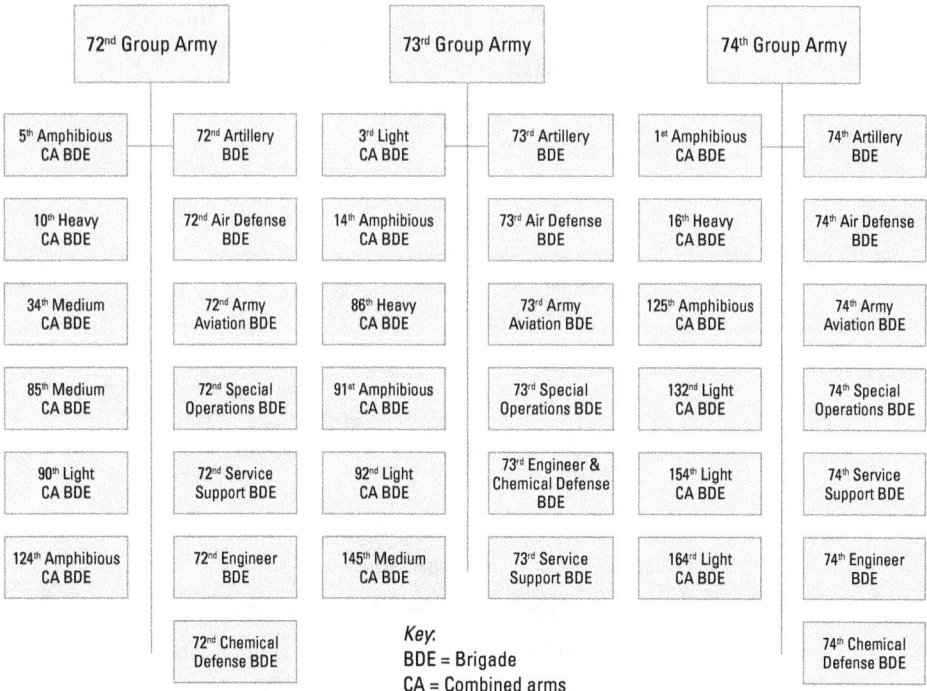

72nd Group Army		73rd Group Army		74th Group Army	
5th Amphibious CA BDE	72nd Artillery BDE	3rd Light CA BDE	73rd Artillery BDE	1st Amphibious CA BDE	74th Artillery BDE
10th Heavy CA BDE	72nd Air Defense BDE	14th Amphibious CA BDE	73rd Air Defense BDE	16th Heavy CA BDE	74th Air Defense BDE
34th Medium CA BDE	72nd Army Aviation BDE	86th Heavy CA BDE	73rd Army Aviation BDE	125th Amphibious CA BDE	74th Army Aviation BDE
85th Medium CA BDE	72nd Special Operations BDE	91st Amphibious CA BDE	73rd Special Operations BDE	132nd Light CA BDE	74th Special Operations BDE
90th Light CA BDE	72nd Service Support BDE	92nd Light CA BDE	73rd Engineer & Chemical Defense BDE	154th Light CA BDE	74th Service Support BDE
124th Amphibious CA BDE	72nd Engineer BDE	145th Medium CA BDE	73rd Service Support BDE	164rd Light CA BDE	74th Engineer BDE
	72nd Chemical Defense BDE				74th Chemical Defense BDE

Key:
BDE = Brigade
CA = Combined arms

Table 2. PLAA Amphibious Brigade Equipment/Elements

Battalion	Equipment/Elements
Combined Arms BN x 4	Amphibious 105mm assault guns Amphibious IFVs Amphibious APCs Amphibious engineering vehicles Heavy mortar elements Air defense elements with MANPADS Reconnaissance elements
Reconnaissance BN	Amphibious reconnaissance vehicles with UAVs Technical reconnaissance troops
Artillery BN	Amphibious 122mm howitzers Tracked 122mm rocket artillery Tracked anti-tank guided missile systems
Air Defense BN	Tracked AAA systems Tracked short-range SAM systems MANPADS
Operational Support BN	Command and control systems Electronic warfare systems Engineering platforms Chemical defense platforms Security elements
Service Support BN	Logistics elements Medical support elements Equipment repair and maintenance elements

Key. APC: armored personnel carrier; BN: battalion; IFV: infantry fighting vehicle; MANPADS: man-portable air-defense system; SAM: surface-to-air missile: UAV: unmanned aerial vehicle.

In PLAA island-landing operations, the brigade is responsible for a landing section [*denglu diduan*, 登陆地段] with multiple battalion landing points [*denglu dian*, 登陆点].[14] The new amphibious combined arms battalion is better equipped and organized to execute the mission against a landing point compared with its single service arm battalion predecessor, which required the

Figure 3. PLAA Amphibious Combined Arms Battalion Organization

Amphibious 105mm Assault Gun Company
Amphibious 105mm Assault Gun Company
Amphibious Mechanized Infantry Company
Amphibious Mechanized Infantry Company
Firepower Company
Service Support Company

creation of temporary combined arms formations. Table 3 contrasts the new amphibious combined arms battalion with its pre-restructure equivalents.[15]

The New PLANMC Brigade

At the same time as the new PLAA structure became clear, the PLANMC expanded from two to six marine brigades, in addition to a new special operations forces (SOF) brigade and an aviation brigade. Along with establishing a PLANMC headquarters and removing the first two brigades from the command of the PLAN South Sea Fleet, the four new brigades were constructed from PLAA coastal defense units and an infantry brigade, providing the PLAN's naval infantry with troops trained in littoral combat, while the SOF and aviation brigades were built from standing PLAN units.[16]

Table 3. Pre- and Post-Reform Amphibious Battalion Structure

Amphibious Maneuver Battalion Type	Amphibious Assault Vehicles	Amphibious IFVs	Organic Artillery and Air Defense	Organic Engineering	Organic Reconnais-sance
Pre-reform Amphibious Mechanized Infantry Battalion	Task-assigned	31 IFVs (3 companies)	6 100mm mortars (2 platoons)	Task-assigned from regiment	
Pre-reform Amphibious Armor Battalion	31 assault guns (3 companies)	Task-assigned	Task-assigned		
Current Amphibious Combined Arms Battalion	28 assault guns (2 companies)	28 IFVs (2 companies)	6 100mm mortars (2 platoons); 4 MANPADS (1 platoon)	1 platoon	1 platoon

Key: IFV: infantry fighting vehicle; MANPADS: man-portable air-defense system.

Before 2017, the two original PLANMC brigades shared the same structure and were both primarily focused on South China Sea and conventional
amphibious operations.[17] Each PLANMC brigade included four light infantry
battalions and combat support battalions, as well as an organic amphibious
armor regiment that included an amphibious tank battalion, two amphibious
armored infantry battalions, and a self-propelled howitzer battalion.[18] After
the restructure, all PLANMC brigades took on organizations similar to their
PLAA combined arms brigade counterparts.

The PLANMC chain of command, nevertheless, is different from a PLAA
group army. The PLANMC headquarters, a corps-level command located
in Guangdong Province, falls directly under the PLAN headquarters rather
than a theater command. The PLANMC's unique chain of command, with
garrisons along the entire Chinese coast, indicates that it is a national-level
strategic asset like the PLA Air Force (PLAAF) Airborne Corps. Based on this
command structure, it is unlikely that the PLANMC or PLAAF Airborne Corps
will ever be deployed as a complete unit like a PLAA group army, but rather in
reinforced brigades or smaller elements.[19]

Following the 2017 expansion and the deployment of PLANMC units to
the PLA's base in Djibouti, the PLAN's naval infantry component appears to
be Beijing's choice for joint expeditionary operations abroad, while maintaining some capability for small reef and island operations in the South
China Sea and expanding its training to additional regions and climates. The
PLANMC is moving toward a lighter force structure that would also optimize
its capacity for nonwar military activities, especially those that protect China's overseas interests, but would limit its use to small island operations or
auxiliary roles in a large-scale campaign against Taiwan.[20]

Unlike the PLAA amphibious brigades, the six new PLANMC brigades
are neither standardized nor designed to fit into a group army–centric island-landing group. Little is known about some of the newest PLANMC
brigades, particularly those that transitioned from PLAA coastal defense
units. Although the 1st and 2nd brigades remain fully equipped with the
Type-05 tracked amphibious series of vehicles and smaller numbers of
wheeled mechanized chassis, three of the four new brigades appear to be
equipped differently.[21] Table 4 details the known equipment holdings for
each PLANMC brigade.[22]

Table 4. PLANMC Equipment

Brigade	Known Equipment
1st	Type-05 heavy amphibious tracked chassis; Type-09 8x8 wheeled chassis[*]
2nd	Type-05 heavy amphibious tracked chassis; Type-09 8x8 wheeled chassis[†]
3rd	Type-09 8x8 wheeled chassis[‡]
4th	Type-09 8x8 wheeled chassis[§]
5th	Type-09 8x8 wheeled chassis[¶]
6th	Type-05 amphibious tracked chassis; Type-09 8x8 wheeled chassis; Lynx 8x8 all-terrain vehicle

Notes:

[*] "Under the Guidance of Xi Jinping's Thoughts on Socialism with Chinese Characteristics—New Era, New Methods, New Chapter—Forging a Powerful Force that Can Quickly Respond to All Areas" [在习近平新时代中国特色社会主义思想指引下一新时代新作为新篇章 锻造合成多能快速反应全域运用的精兵劲旅], CCTV [央视网], October 14, 2020, available at <https://tv.cctv.com/2020/10/14/VIDEJa9VkX29qsf5U1agxiHG201014.shtml>. The video shows elements of a PLA Navy Marine Corps Tiger Brigade, an honorific for the 1st PLANMC Brigade. The brigade in Djibouti operates Type-09 wheeled vehicles. It is unclear if those vehicles are also found in the brigade's table of equipment in China.

[†] Song Xin [宋歆], "'Blade Warriors': Always Following Orders and Waiting for Peace" ["刀锋战士": 时刻听从号令, 为和平而守候], *China Military Online* [中国军网], September 9, 2019, available at <http://www.81.cn/tzjy/2019-09/09/content_9615797.htm>. The 2nd PLANMC Brigade showed a mechanized infantry company with Type-09 platforms participating in peacekeeping training.

[‡] "A Certain PLANMC Brigade: Implement the Spirit of the Plenary Session and Strive to be a Pioneer in Transformation" [海军陆战队某旅: 贯彻全会精神 争做转型先锋], *China Military TV Online* [中国军视网], November 23, 2020, available at <http://www.js7tv.cn/video/202011_234913.html>.

[§] "Direct Fire Training Range—The Marine Corps Kicked off with a 'Good Start' with Live Firing and New Equipment" [直击演训场海军陆战队实弹射击新装备打响 "开门红"], CCTV [央视网], July 12, 2020, available at <https://tv.cctv.com/2020/07/12/VIDEw5Cg3mFAHPCKwmcvRCoi200712.shtml>.

[¶] People's Navy Official WeChat Microblog [人民海军官方微信], "Marine Corps, You're So Handsome!" [海军陆战队, 你真帅!], WeChat [微信], October 17, 2020, available at <https://mp.weixin.qq.com/s/vSJZCcNaZcjkp2iisvwaEQ>.

The 6th PLANMC Brigade appears to have at least three different types of battalions: heavy amphibious, medium wheeled, and light air assault. If the 6th Brigade is a model for the other brigades, the PLANMC would be able to field a future force package equipped for both amphibious operations and nonwar military activities. However, based on existing amphibious operations doctrine, the brigade's limited number of heavy armored amphibious platforms would make a PLANMC brigade unsuitable as a first echelon main landing force during an opposed Taiwan landing.

The PLAA and PLANMC's primary amphibious armored vehicle, the Type-05 series, has no parallel in foreign military forces. The Type-05 vehicle series, which was developed solely for amphibious landing operations, provides a PLA landing force with a universal armored combat platform able to swim long distances. The Type-05 series consists of three primary maneuver and fires platforms, detailed in table 5.[23]

According to Janes, the following variants of the Type-05 are also fielded in the PLAA and PLANMC: armored personnel carrier, armored recovery vehicle, command and control vehicle, artillery command vehicle, communications vehicle, armored breaching vehicle, and reconnaissance vehicle.[24] Although the Type-05 series has been fielded to most of the PLAA amphibious brigades, some units are still equipped with first-generation equipment, such as the Type-63A light amphibious tank.[25] The Type-09 8x8 wheeled vehicles— including the ZBL-09 infantry fighting vehicle and the ZTL-11 105-millimeter

Table 5. PLAA and PLANMC Vehicles

Platform	Type	Weapons	Crew Capacity
ZBD-05	IFV	30mm cannon; 7.62mm MG; HJ-73 ATGM	3 crew + 8 infantry
ZLT-05 (also called ZTD-05)	Assault gun	105mm gun; 12.7mm MG; 7.62mm MG	4
PLZ-07B	Howitzer	122mm gun; 12.7mm MG	5

Key: ATGM: anti-tank guided missile; IFV: infantry fighting vehicle; MG: machine gun.

assault gun, found in nonamphibious PLAA brigades and in each PLANMC brigade—are designed to be capable of amphibious operations, though their afloat speed is significantly slower than that of the Type-05.[26] With the unique capabilities each type of amphibious vehicle brings to the force, the post-restructure PLAA and PLANMC amphibious brigades are equipped to carry out a wide range of similar missions differing in scale and force projection.

PLA Amphibious Unit Role in Joint Blockade and Island Landing Campaigns

The PLA's 2013 *Science of Military Strategy* lists participation in large-scale operations to preserve national unity in the "main strategic direction" [*zhuyao zhanlüe fangxiang*, 主要战略方向], a reference to the Taiwan Strait, as the first of several strategic missions for the PLAA.[27] As the primary ground component in a large-scale joint operation, the text specifies that the PLAA would need to participate in blockade and control operations, firepower strikes, island-landing operations, and defensive operations (for a description of the primary cross-strait campaigns, see Michael Casey's chapter in this volume). Most important, the document clarifies that the PLAA will assault beaches, conduct on-island assaults, assault fortified positions in urban areas, and participate in postconflict stabilization operations in joint island-landing operations.

Various pre-reform PLAA operational art texts assessed that the PLANMC brigades would play roles in opening up sea lines and securing landing points for the PLAA amphibious division breakthrough as an initial landing force.[28] While the original two PLANMC brigades were adequately outfitted with heavy amphibious platforms to perform these roles, the structure of the new PLANMC brigades indicates that the PLAN does not intend to use its naval infantry as an initial landing force in a joint island landing campaign against Taiwan. The new brigades, however, do provide the PLAN with some capabilities to participate in island-blockade operations and small-scale actions that support a landing campaign. The following sections describe how PLAA and PLANMC units would participate in both a joint island blockade and joint island landing campaign.

Joint Island Blockade Campaign

The PLA's 2009 *Science of Army Operations* describes island blockade and control operations implicitly targeting Taiwan as a high-priority mission for the PLAA.[29] PLAA contributions to an island blockade include not only kinetic and nonkinetic fires to assist the PLAN and PLAAF but also maneuver forces to land on key offshore islands. The army's role in a joint island blockade campaign is to help cut off Taiwan's economic and military ties with the outside world, thereby isolating and intimidating the government into submission and creating favorable conditions for follow-on landing operations.[30]

The new PLAA amphibious brigades and the more established PLANMC brigades are well suited for island blockade operations. *Science of Army Operations* notes that ground forces participate in four phases of island blockade operations: deploying forces and posturing for combat, paralyzing the enemy and seizing control over the blockaded area, implementing a sustainable blockade to gradually weaken and exhaust the enemy, and combining strikes and defensive actions to defeat the enemy's counterblockade offensives.[31]

In the deployment phase, PLAA amphibious brigades in the 72nd and 73rd group armies are already garrisoned in locations that enable rapid maneuver to Chinese coastlines adjacent to the Taiwan Strait.[32] While the PLAN, PLAAF, PLA Rocket Force, and PLA Strategic Support Force focus long-range and strategic capabilities against Taiwan, the firepower and amphibious landing assets of the PLAA and PLANMC could deliver landing forces to Taiwan's offshore islands such as Jinmen and Matsu. The PLAA amphibious brigades, once in place, could use their organic reconnaissance and electronic warfare systems to maintain situational awareness on these islands, while the air defense battalion could provide point defense of key command and control hubs for PLAA units participating in the blockade operations.

In the paralysis phase, the PLAA amphibious brigades are also configured to participate in a joint firepower strike. PLAA amphibious brigades have a strong advantage over PLANMC brigades in this respect. PLAA amphibious brigade howitzers and rocket artillery have the range and accuracy to suppress tactical defensive targets on Jinmen and much of the Matsu Islands.[33] While all PLANMC brigades maintain fire support battalions, not all are equipped with self-propelled chassis. It is unclear if PLANMC brigades have rocket artillery, which would limit their organic fires to tube artillery. The new PLAA amphibious brigades could also play a role in information dominance in this phase through their new organic electronic warfare company, a capability the PLANMC apparently lacks.[34]

The paralysis phase also includes seizure of Taiwan's smaller offshore islands to disrupt counterblockade operations and confine the movement of enemy ships and planes.[35] The PLAA views near-shore island offensive operations as "three-dimensional" missions to capture a portion of large islands or entire smaller islands. These operations would likely be PLAA-centric and require minimal participation of the other services. Near-shore operations would allow PLAA amphibious brigades to land without the need for transport vessels because PLAA amphibious brigade assets, such as the Type-05 series vehicles, are able to swim from coast to island in suitable weather and sea states. PLAA small island-landing doctrine also calls for air assault units to secure key positions.[36] Because PLAA SOF brigades and light combined arms brigades train for air mobility operations with army aviation brigades, units from the same group army could be used for rear area landings and close air support. The PLANMC would almost certainly rely on joint support for similar operations despite some brigades maintaining organic air assault assets.

Joint Island Landing Campaign

If given the order to reunify Taiwan through military means, the PLAA would take the lead in breaking through the enemy's coastal defenses, establishing a beachhead, destroying and repelling entrenched defenders, and creating favorable conditions for second-echelon forces. *Science of Army Operations* notes that this large-scale campaign would occur only after political and diplomatic efforts were exhausted and would be used to devastate separatist forces while attempting to limit unnecessary civilian casualties and preserving civilian infrastructure. According to the text, based on the Taiwan Strait's monsoon and typhoon seasons, a period between late March and late April or late September to mid-October would be most suitable for a landing operation.[37] *Science of Campaigns* notes that a landing campaign could normally be divided into three major phases: advance operations, embarkation and sea-crossing, and assault onto land to establish a landing site; however, passages from the PLA's *Army Combined Arms Tactics Under Informationized Conditions* provide more specific details about the sea-crossing and landing phases.[38]

Advance Operations. A joint firepower strike, as part of the advance operations phase of the landing campaign, is carried out concurrently with attempts to gain information, sea, and air dominance.[39] Neither PLAA amphibious brigades nor PLANMC brigades are designed and equipped for participation in this phase of operations, except for providing limited point air defense capabilities. Both brigade types lack long-range firepower and electronic warfare systems capable of reaching Taiwan's shores, and they are not designed to carry out antiship fires.

Embarkation and Sea-Crossing. The PLAA's capability to participate in the embarkation and sea-crossing phase of the island-landing campaign was greatly improved with the conversion of amphibious divisions into amphibious brigades. Following the 2017 restructure, the amphibious brigades centralized all their subordinate battalions into one location, allowing for improved mobilization timelines. The PLAA amphibious brigades are now strategically garrisoned near ports of embarkation to facilitate rapid movement to their assembly areas and loading onto amphibious-capable vessels. This positioning limits their exposure to enemy fires during the pivotal loading and transport phases, especially if executed during nighttime.[40]

The PLAA amphibious brigade is equipped to provide its own point air defense system at loading zones. The amphibious brigade's air defense battalion and combined arms battalion assets could provide short-range protection for the embarkation area and at sea, complementing PLAN, PLAAF, and PLAA medium- to long-range air defense systems.[41]

PLANMC brigades are also located near major ports of embarkation, which ensures minimal difficulty in moving the units to their loading zones. Although PLANMC brigades have air defense battalions, they appear to be primarily equipped with older towed anti-aircraft artillery guns. These weapons could serve as close-range point air defense but lack the range, accuracy, and mobility of equipment currently fielded in PLAA amphibious brigades. This deficiency would leave these PLANMC brigades reliant on higher echelon PLAN and PLAAF air defense systems.

Selection of Landing Sections and Points. Modern PLAA amphibious brigades are equipped to assault a wider landing section compared with their smaller regimental predecessors. An amphibious brigade commander could assign 2 amphibious combined arms battalions (56 amphibious assault guns and 56 amphibious infantry fighting vehicles) to defeat 2 defending companies on a 2- to 4-kilometer (km) front—an objective previously assigned to a reinforced amphibious infantry regiment (93 amphibious infantry fighting vehicles and at least 1 company of task-assigned amphibious assault guns).[42]

In the pre-reform PLAA, amphibious landing battalions concentrated on landing points with a width of 0.5 to 1 km.[43] Now, an amphibious brigade commander can transfer brigade-echelon elements down to the combined arms battalions to increase combat power against the main landing point while ensuring that the secondary landing point and reserve combined arms battalions remain in close enough proximity for mutual support within the landing section.[44] An individual amphibious combined arms battalion now likely has an expanded landing point width of 1.5 to 2 km, which would make the brigade landing section an approximately 3- to 4-km front. If accurate, two amphibious brigades could land in an area roughly the same as a division.

Troop Allocation and Deployment. According to the PLA's *Army Combined Arms Tactics Under Informationized Conditions*, the commander of one of the PLAA's former amphibious divisions would utilize 10 primary groups in 3 to 5 assault waves.[45] The new amphibious brigade's modular structure enables the same operational group structure as its division predecessor (see table 6). New PLANMC brigades lack many of the self-propelled weapons systems and access to corps-level aviation assets required for a similar organization.

Table 6. PLAA Amphibious Brigade Landing Groups

Group	Mission	Amphibious Division Unit Assigned	Amphibious Brigade Equivalent
Advance Landing Group	Get ashore first to seize key points; provide reconnaissance to landing units	Task-assigned: one SOF BN or two PLANMC BNs	Reconnaissance BN and combined arms BN reconnaissance platoons
Air Assault Group	Seize enemy frontline positions and key points in-depth; stop enemy combat reserve from counterattacking	Task-assigned: one air assault BN	Task-assigned: one air assault BN

Group	Mission	Amphibious Division Unit Assigned	Amphibious Brigade Equivalent
Assault Landing Group	Land on main and secondary directions; seize and control landing section; ensure deep assault group can enter combat	Two amphibious infantry regiments; task-assigned amphibious tank, artillery, air defense, engineer, and chemical defense elements	Two amphibious combined arms BNs
Deep Assault Group	Attack and occupy defensive in-depth positions; expand and consolidate landing section; ensure follow-up landing troops get ashore	Amphibious armor regiment; task-assigned amphibious infantry, artillery, and engineer elements	One amphibious combined arms BN
Fire-power Assault Group	Destroy enemy artillery, C2, EW, ISR locations; strike enemy armored targets and fortified defense works; attack enemy helicopters and assist air assault group	Artillery regiment (with organic anti-tank BN); task-assigned army aviation platforms	Artillery BN; task-assigned army aviation platforms
Combat Reserve Group	Go ashore immediately after deep assault group; carry out mobile combat tasks to deal with unexpected scenarios	One task-assigned combined arms BN with anti-tank, engineer, and chemical defense elements	One amphibious combined arms BN
Air Defense Group	Go ashore with deep assault group or firepower assault group; conduct aerial reconnaissance, prevent enemy reconnaissance, defeat enemy aviation and airborne weapons over the combat area	Air defense regiment	Air defense BN

Group	Mission	Amphibious Division Unit Assigned	Amphibious Brigade Equivalent
Electronic Warfare Group	Conduct communications and radar jamming; intercept enemy radio communications and radar signals	EW BN (if organic) or group army task-assigned EW elements	Operational support BN EW company
Obstacle Clearing Group	Open passageways at the water's edge and through beach barriers to ensure assault units get ashore	Engineer and chemical defense BN elements	Combined arms BN engineer platoons
Combat Engineer Reserve Group	Construct command posts, open temporary piers, enable follow-up troops get ashore	Engineer and chemical defense BN elements	Operational support BN engineer company

Key: BN: battalion; C2: command and control; EW: electronic warfare; ISR: intelligence, surveillance, and reconnaissance; PLANMC: PLA Navy Marine Corps; SOF: special operations forces.

Opening of Landing Pathways. The new amphibious brigade structure provides each amphibious combined arms battalion with its own reconnaissance and engineering platoons that could be supplemented with brigade-level elements to open up landing pathways, a role that previously required regimental assets.[46] The combined arms battalion staff enables coordination with supporting aviation units to provide cover fire for these initial landing teams. Additionally, evidence suggests that at least one amphibious brigade could use a new unmanned system to destroy water obstacles near the shore prior to engineering troops landing.[47] PLA media indicate that the 1st and 2nd PLANMC brigades, and likely the 6th Brigade, have similar engineering and reconnaissance capabilities at the brigade and battalion levels; however, it is unknown whether the new brigades also have their own support elements at the same echelons.[48]

Debarkation, Swimming, and Direct Fires. According to PLA doctrine, amphibious armor typically debarks transport vessels 4 to 8 km from shore to begin their swim. The initial waves include obstacle removal elements as described above, followed by assaulting infantry and armor and finally by artillery and supporting forces.[49] While the restructure likely had minimal effect on debarkation TTPs, the inclusion of 28 amphibious assault guns in each combined arms battalion increased the amount of direct fire support for the assaulting waves. New units equipped with ZLT-05 105-millimeter assault guns and Type-05 reconnaissance vehicles improve the commander's capability, in optimal conditions, to direct fires against important enemy targets, especially fortifications, firing points, and armored vehicles up to 2 km from shore.[50]

In addition, the PLAA combined arms battalion staff often includes an integrated PLAA aviation officer. Theoretically, this arrangement means that the participating combined arms battalions could request attack helicopter support, allowing them to achieve superior effects on landing points compared with their predecessors. However, the proficiency level of PLAA close air support during the landing phase remains questionable. The PLAN does not have attack helicopters, which forces the PLANMC brigades to rely on joint land-based aviation support. This situation could change as the PLANMC Aviation Brigade develops.

Beachhead Landing and Expansion. The PLA expects the landing of amphibious combined arms battalions on the enemy shore to remain the most violent operation in a joint island landing campaign, even after the joint firepower strike. PLA scholars believe that Taiwan military defenders would concentrate all firepower on landing armored vehicles and that destroyed vehicles could block the number of available pathways onto the beach.[51]

The 2017 reforms flattened the PLAA's command structure, enabling the amphibious brigade's subordinate combined arms battalion to replace the amphibious regiment as the basic ground unit in a joint island landing campaign. As a result, the amphibious combined arms battalion could now independently react to situations on the shore and request higher echelon PLAA and joint support when required. This arrangement allows joint commanders to respond to successes and failures at different landing points and to pass down orders more quickly through digital communications and a reduced number of command echelons.[52] The arrangement also ensures that PLAA air assault units and PLAAF Airborne Corps brigades landing farther inland would be better prepared to connect with troops coming from the beachhead.

The new amphibious brigades and amphibious combined arms battalions also have advantages in combat support compared with their predecessors. Previously, the regiment controlled functions such as material support, equipment recovery, and medical rescue. The establishment of amphibious brigade service support battalions and combined arms battalion service support companies enables lower echelon units to independently execute these functions.[53] For instance, the amphibious combined arms battalion is equipped with armored recovery and medical vehicles to manage casualties and is able to request support from nearby amphibious brigades and other services. New combat information systems also allow combined arms battalion staff members to monitor ammunition and fuel consumption to better react to logistics requirements.[54]

After successfully destroying enemy defenses, securing a beachhead, and establishing on-site command posts, amphibious brigades would be used to defeat enemy counterattacks and expand the area of control. This would enable nonamphibious platforms to come ashore via landing craft to relieve the first echelon landing troops and connect with air assault units landing 2 to 4 km away from the shoreline. These follow-on units could also participate in operations to connect with PLAAF Airborne Corps units dropped farther to the rear (for more on the Airborne Corps, see the chapter by Roderick Lee in this volume).[55]

The two original PLANMC brigades could conduct similar assaults, though their capacity to call on higher echelon ground component and joint support remains unclear. The level of protection required for assaulting amphibious armored vehicles leaves the remaining four PLANMC brigades incapable of executing this type of large-scale landing operation. The transfer of landing point control to follow-on forces would also be more difficult for a PLANMC brigade than it would be for a PLAA amphibious brigade in the same group army as its relief.

Training and Exercises

Due to the complex nature of opposed amphibious landings, the PLA has always placed a premium on amphibious training. Prior to and after the 2017 restructure, PLAA amphibious units maintained regular training cycles focused on amphibious landing throughout the year, with most exercises occurring between May and September.[56] By contrast, even before the reforms, the two PLANMC brigades had begun to train for operations in a wide spectrum of environments, including arctic, forest, plateau, and desert conditions.[57]

Despite the expanded focus on operational environments, the PLANMC has continued to dedicate much of its training to amphibious landings.

PLAA Amphibious Brigade Training: 2017–2020

PLAA amphibious training became gradually more complex after the April 2017 reorganization, with brigades initially focused on training at smaller echelons. Although the amphibious brigades were newly established, they all came from former amphibious divisions or an amphibious-capable armor brigade, ensuring that training could continue without a major disruption and that doctrine would remain roughly consistent. Thus, during the remainder of 2017 and all of 2018, PLAA amphibious brigade training events appeared to concentrate on improving the capabilities of the new amphibious combined arms battalions and their staffs.[58] Beginning in 2019, more emphasis was placed on multibattalion amphibious exercises, while also ramping up training on complex TTPs such as loading and unloading at sea and conducting nighttime operations.[59] By 2020, PLAA amphibious brigades were more confident in publicizing brigade-level exercises and the capabilities of their new operational support and reconnaissance battalions.[60]

An amphibious brigade of the 73rd Group Army became a focal point in 2020 as the PLA published videos and articles throughout the May to September training cycle demonstrating the unit's capabilities. In October 2020, official PLA media sources posted a series of videos detailing the final brigade-level multibattalion exercise that took place in September. The videos described the landing operation in full and included footage of the amphibious brigade loading onto PLAN vessels under the cover of darkness and brigade electronic warfare vehicles setting up for combat. The PLA also used the exercise to demonstrate the capabilities of new seaborne unmanned obstacle destruction systems and load-carrying unmanned ground vehicles. This type of landing exercise, however, serves more than simply training PLAA troops in amphibious operations.[61]

As referenced in *Military and Security Developments Involving the People's Republic of China 2020*, a large-scale amphibious invasion is one of the most complicated and difficult military operations and would likely strain the PLA's capabilities. The report acknowledges that the PLA is better suited for small island-landing operations, such as those against Matsu or Jinmen; however, even those missions include significant political risk.[62] Despite the recognized challenges in executing large-scale landing operations, PLA media frequently display the amphibious brigades landing in opposed force exercises. The existence and high-profile training of these units serve a purpose in Chinese deterrence: to intimidate Taiwan and demonstrate to other regional powers the PLA's resolve to execute complex amphibious operations against Taiwan if ordered. According to a 2019 RAND study, China uses large-scale military exercises as a form of gray zone operations, with military intimidation used to threaten potential military attack or military escalation.[63]

During periods of strained relations between China and Taiwan, such as during a U.S. Cabinet member's visit to Taiwan for Lee Teng-hui's memorial service in September 2020, a heavy focus is placed on publicizing detailed landing operations to signal both to Taiwan and to U.S. audiences. Chinese media services such as *Global Times*, considered a propaganda outlet by the U.S. Government, often describe those exercises as warnings against Taiwan independence and demonstrations to the United States that the PLA has the capability to execute a reunification-by-force operation.[64] This is an example of how normal PLA amphibious training events could be repurposed for strategic effect as part of China's "Three Warfares" [*san zhan*, 三战]. Along with Beijing's use of legal warfare, PLA media outlets use videos and images of the amphibious training events as forms of media warfare to shape global opinion and psychological warfare to influence foreign decisionmakers.[65]

PLANMC Brigade Training: 2017–2020

Because the first two PLANMC brigades remained mostly intact, a clear reduction in training events did not occur after the 2017 restructure. Several small-scale exercises during 2017 continued to demonstrate the capability of the 1st and 2nd brigades to execute small island and reef seizures.[66] The four new PLANMC brigades, as they transitioned from PLAA light infantry forces to naval infantry, were understandably absent from known training events throughout 2017. However, the 6th Brigade became a regular fixture in PLA media beginning in 2018, and by 2020, the 1st, 2nd, and 6th brigades were observed executing larger landing exercises with an emphasis on the inclusion of multiple service arms. However, the events appeared mostly in line with the traditional PLANMC South China Sea mission set.[67] In addition, the 4th and 5th brigades appeared in PLA videos and articles with new wheeled Type-09 vehicles, although their training was limited to driving and firing events, such as those the PLANMC publicizes about its forces in Djibouti, where complex amphibious landings are not required.[68]

The PLANMC, unlike PLAA amphibious brigades, uses its naval infantry to engage with international partners abroad and at home. Although most training events appeared to use PLANMC SOF brigade elements, the PLANMC's conventional forces were also playing larger roles in international exercises. During the May 2019 Sino-Thai joint naval exercise Blue Commando–2019, elements of a PLANMC heavy combined arms battalion executed a landing in southern Guangdong Province.[69] In January 2020, PLANMC elements participated in joint landing drills with Pakistan's marine forces.[70] PLANMC armored vehicle elements also continuously participated in Russia's International Army Games "Seaborne Assault" event from 2015 to 2019, even hosting the program in 2018.[71] The PLA likely uses these exercises to demonstrate its prowess to regional competitors and the capabilities of its amphibious vehicles to potential buyers of Chinese weaponry and systems.

Post-Reform Disadvantages and Challenges

Although the 2017 restructure improved the ability of PLAA amphibious brigades to carry out amphibious landings against Taiwan, the large number of changes to structure, staffs, and equipment types resulted in new challenges for commanders. Similarly, PLANMC brigade commanders lack a full table of equipment and adequate training in amphibious operations. Most important, lack of adequate amphibious transport limits the ability of units from both services to participate in a joint island landing campaign.

The establishment of PLAA amphibious brigades to replace the former amphibious divisions improved the independence of action and speed of information flow. However, the increase in combat power at the amphibious brigade and amphibious combined arms battalion levels included a new set of problems for tactical commanders. The overall size of combined arms battalions increased with the move from a single service arm to more than 10 in each battalion. Amphibious combined arms battalion commanders no longer command only infantry companies but gained responsibility for armor, artillery, air defense, reconnaissance, signal, engineering, chemical defense, and other service arms that were formerly found only at the brigade and division levels. According to *PLA Daily*, a new amphibious combined arms battalion staff enables the commander to lead more than twice the number of amphibious platforms compared with before the restructure. It also enables the commander to use real-time battalion reconnaissance capabilities to adjust operations before landing the troops.[72] Even with a small combined arms battalion staff, however, tactical commanders would be faced with vulnerabilities resulting from networked command and information systems; competing requirements from subordinate, lateral, and higher units; and operations in a complex electromagnetic environment. These new requirements could lead to accidents and poor combat decisions during a landing operation.[73]

The small number of large-scale amphibious landing exercises may also reduce the effectiveness of the amphibious brigades. Because brigade-size landing events became common only in 2020, the PLA will likely need several more years before it is comfortable executing larger training events with multiple amphibious brigades landing simultaneously. Although recent smaller scale exercises utilized joint capabilities, with PLAN vessels delivering PLAA landing forces and PLAAF aircraft providing fire support, the limited scale is not representative of the realistic requirements expected during a joint island landing campaign.[74]

Limited opposing force training also reduces the combat potential of the amphibious units. The army's amphibious brigades, unlike other PLAA combined arms brigades, have not made the cross-theater trip to the PLA's Joint Training Base at Zhurihe in Inner Mongolia, which plays a role like that of the U.S. Army's National Training Center. As a result, the amphibious brigades have not had the opportunity to train against that base's dedicated limited opposing force unit in large exercises such as Stride. Without such experience, the PLAA amphibious brigades likely train against themselves or theoretical opponents. Because much of the amphibious force, like most other army units, is filled with 2-year conscripts, the lack of realistic training leaves it unprepared for the high-intensity confrontation expected during a Taiwan landing. This factor, compounded by the need for troops to operate modern digitized systems, could lead to failure up and down the chain of command during the landing.[75]

Logistics support is another challenge for PLAA amphibious brigades. The PLAA established group army service support brigades, combined arms brigade service support battalions, and combined arms battalion service support companies to form a continuous campaign- to tactical-level supply chain during wartime. However, the PLAA's service support brigades are primarily responsible for supporting group army command posts. This arrangement leaves the amphibious brigades and battalions reliant on their own logistics capacity and on support from the PLA Joint Logistic Support Force.[76] The PLA expects the rapid consumption of fuel, ammunition, and other materials to challenge landing forces because they can carry only their own loadouts during the initial assault.[77] Although tactical support forces within the amphibious brigades participate in landing exercises, it remains unclear how closely, if at all, the Joint Logistic Support Force participates in these events. Without a robust relationship with the Joint Logistic Support Force prior to a landing campaign, the amphibious brigades could struggle to remain ready for combat after the battle begins.

The primary disadvantage facing the new PLANMC brigades is the slow pace of equipment fielding.[78] Although the 1st and 2nd brigades maintain their pre-reform equipment holdings, three of the four new brigades lack sufficient mechanized forces to enable the full spectrum of overseas operations for which they must prepare, such as humanitarian assistance and disaster relief, and other nonwar military activities. The new 6th Brigade, transitioned from the former PLAA 77th Motorized Infantry Brigade, appears to be the only other combat-ready unit based on equipment fielding and training operations tempo.[79] The 4th and 5th brigades both field at least one battalion of medium-wheeled Type-08 chassis, but this leaves them relatively combat-ineffective for any kind of amphibious landing or overseas deployment except supplying troops to the PLAN base in Djibouti.

The new PLANMC brigades, like the PLAA amphibious brigades, also suffer from a lack of realistic training and exercises. Although the 1st and 2nd brigades have trained for operations in different environments, and the 6th Brigade is seemingly testing a new organizational construct, the remaining brigades appear only to train on the use of newly fielded systems. While the PLA often portrays the PLANMC as operationally ready for unique reconnaissance and shipboard operations, many of these media reports and videos focus on PLANMC SOF brigade capabilities rather than those of the amphibious brigades.

Finally, the most serious challenge facing PLA amphibious brigades is the lack of available PLAN amphibious transport (for further detail, see the chapter by Conor Kennedy in this volume). In island-landing training, both services rely on the limited number of modern PLAN vessels, such as the *Yuzhao* Type-071 dock landing ship allocated to the PLAN South and East sea fleets and smaller vessels such as the Type-072 tank landing ships.[80] Although the PLAN continues to build new amphibious vessels, notably the two new *Yushen* Type-075 helicopter assault ships, the numbers remain modest.[81] PLAA coastal defense brigades also maintain small transport squadrons with old Type-271 landing craft that could be used in near-island operations, but they rarely participate in large-scale amphibious training.[82] According to the U.S. Department of Defense, the limited increase in large oceangoing amphibious ships indicates a near-term focus on regional and eventually global expeditionary missions rather than preparation for a beach assault on Taiwan.[83]

Although the PLA has trained to transport forces using civilian shipping such as ferries and roll-on/roll-off vessels, use of those unprotected ships would be unsuitable for a Taiwan beach landing (although they could deliver forces if a port or harbor were captured).[84] Without adequate PLAN medium and heavy lift for the PLAA amphibious brigades, PLA overall effectiveness in a joint island landing campaign would be questionable. Moreover, if PLANMC brigades were tasked with smaller independent operations during the campaign, uncertainties might arise over which service's amphibious units would get transport priority. Because the joint island landing campaign relies so heavily on the PLAA's amphibious beach landing to shape conditions for victory, the PLAA would likely win that competition.[85] However, whether the PLAN is willing to place its expensive new amphibious transport vessels near a landing zone and potential Taiwan antiship fires is another question that remains unanswered.

Conclusion

The 2017 PLA force-wide restructure expanded the size of the PLANMC's amphibious force while concurrently turning the PLAA's existing amphibious divisions into more modular combined arms brigades. As a result, both PLA services improved their capabilities to execute different future missions. The PLANMC amphibious brigades appear to be turning into potential "first responders" for a wide range of contingencies throughout Asia, while PLAA amphibious brigades have become increasingly focused on the sole mission of a Taiwan landing campaign. Indeed, holding onto this mission was critical for a PLAA that otherwise faced steep cuts under the recent reforms.[86]

However, that heavy PLAA force may not adequately represent the future of Chinese amphibious operations. According to an October 2018 *PLA Daily* article, the future of amphibious operations is changing from one of "large-scale amphibious landings" to "small-scale special operations."[87] These changes would adjust combat requirements from using amphibious armored vehicles to "seize a beachhead and establish a zone" to "attacking a point to control an area" using a full-spectrum approach that includes all the operational domains. The article also mentions amphibious equipment requirements changing from the capability to "break through beach defenses" to "ensuring ships reach targets." There is also a specific focus in the article on adjusting from "last-minute urgent deployment" to "routine forward deployment" and adjusting combat support from the "beachhead on land" to the "floating base at sea." Each factor indicates that some thinkers in the PLA believe the future of amphibious operations lies in the PLANMC and its potential ability to carry out full-spectrum operations abroad.

The *PLA Daily* article also details how future amphibious operations could require dynamic and precise command as well as a transition from large numbers and scale to "streamlined and highly capable." The new PLAA amphibious brigades have already started implementing these concepts. The authors conclude that future amphibious operations could change from "manned and informationized" to "unmanned and intelligentized."[88] There is already evidence that the PLAA amphibious brigades are in the initial stages of incorporating new unmanned technologies for obstacle destruction and load-carrying equipment.[89] These developments indicate that the amphibious brigades are at the forefront of technological advancement in the service, signaling that their level of importance to the PLAA remains high despite future amphibious goals better suited to their PLANMC counterparts.

The article does not, however, address the future of amphibious operations in a joint island landing campaign against Taiwan. The PLA's campaign requirements for timely mobilization, rapid transport, and complex landings to establish beachheads in a heavily opposed assault demand more than small-scale special operations to attack key points and gain support from floating bases. The campaign would require well-trained heavy amphibious mechanized units that could land in multiple locations to overrun Taiwan's defenders on shore.[90] The PLA's most powerful amphibious landing units remain in the hands of the PLAA, whose brigades regularly demonstrate their proficiency in island-landing operations. Yet, without a dedicated approach to building sufficient naval lift, these forces remain heavily deterrent in nature.

The author thanks Dennis Blasko for his review of the draft.

Notes

[1] *Military and Security Developments Involving the People's Republic of China 2020: Annual Report to Congress* (Washington, DC: Office of the Secretary of Defense, 2020), 118.

[2] Chen Guoquan [陈国全] and Wu Haoyu [吴浩宇], "The Marine Corps Builds a Multi-Dimensional Integrated New-Type Combat Force" [海军陆战队打造多维一体新型作战力量], Xinhua, May 5, 2020, available at <http://www.xinhuanet.com/2020-05/05/c_1210604164.htm>.

[3] Zhang Xuhang [张旭航], Wang Weiqing [王伟庆], and Qiu Ruiqing [邱瑞清], "From Establishing Combined Arms to Combat Power Integration—The Combined Arms Battalion 'Asks for Directions' to the Beachhead" [从编制合成到战斗力合成 营 "问路" 水际滩头], *China Military Online* [中国军网], December 18, 2019, available at <http://www.chinamil.com.cn/lj/2019-12/18/content_9699027.htm>.

[4] Kevin McCauley, "Amphibious Operations: Lessons of Past Campaigns for Today's PLA," *China Brief* 18, no. 3 (February 26, 2018), available at <https://jamestown.org/program/amphibious-operations-lessons-past-campaigns-todays-pla/>; David Simpler, "Saigon Says Chinese Control Islands, But Refuses to Admit Complete Defeat," *New York Times*, January 21, 1974, available at <https://www.nytimes.com/1974/01/21/archives/saigon-says-chinese-control-islands-but-refuses-to-admit-complete.html>.

[5] Li Faxin [李发新], *The Chinese PLA Navy Marine Corps* [中国人民解放军海军陆战队] (Beijing: Wuzhou Communications, 2013), 1–5.

[6] The PLA Army (PLAA) group army is roughly equivalent to a U.S. Army corps.

[7] Dennis J. Blasko, "PLA Amphibious Capabilities: Structured for Deterrence," *China Brief* 10, no. 17 (August 19, 2010), available at <https://jamestown.org/program/pla-amphibious-capabilities-structured-for-deterrence/>.

[8] *Jane's Sentinel Security Assessment—China and Northeast Asia: China—Army*, September 22, 2020, available at <https://customer.janes.com/Janes/Display/JWARA133-CNA>; *Military and Security Developments Involving the People's Republic of China 2019: Annual Report to Congress* (Washington, DC: Office of the Secretary of Defense, 2019), 86–89.

9 Dennis J. Blasko, "The PLA Army After 'Below the Neck' Reforms: Contributing to China's Joint Warfighting, Deterrence, and MOOTW Posture," *Journal of Strategic Studies* 44, no. 2 (2021), 14–16; Ping Zhiwei [平志伟] and Wang Lijie [王立杰], *Army Combined Arms Tactics Under Informationized Conditions* [信息化条件下陆军合同战术] (Beijing: PLA Press, 2009), 133–134; Xu Ping [徐平], "What Is the Combined Arms Battalion? Do You Understand the Organization of the Battalion in the Service?" [什么是合成营? 你了解军队中营的编制吗], *China Military Online* [中国军网], March 23, 2020, available at <http://www.chinamil.com.cn/theory/2020-03/23/content_9775313.htm>. The article does not specifically reference amphibious combined arms battalions, but it discusses how the PLAA combined arms battalion replaced the regiment as the basic combat unit.

10 *Jane's Sentinel Security Assessment: China—Army*. The 72nd and 74th Group Armies either split their Engineer and Chemical Defense Brigade into two separate brigades. See "A 72nd Group Army Engineer Brigade Took the Initiative to Solve Grassroots Problems" [第72集团军某工兵旅主动为基层排忧解难], *China Military Online* [中国军网], January 16, 2019, available at <http://www.81.cn/jfjbmap/content/2019-01/16/content_225391.htm>; Zhao Shuoyang [臧朔阳] and Yang Huihuang [杨辉煌], "A 72nd Group Army Chemical Defense Brigade Conducts Actual Realistic Combat Training" [陆军第72集团军某防化旅开展实战化训练], *China Military Online* [中国军网], February 26, 2019, available at <http://www.81.cn/jwgz/2019-02/26/content_9434416.htm>; Peng Xi [彭希], "China's 18th Batch of Peacekeeping Construction Engineer Elements Set Off to Lebanon" [中国第十八批赴黎巴嫩维和建筑工兵分队出征]], *China Military Online* [中国军网], May 19, 2019, available at <http://www.81.cn/jwgz/2019-05/19/content_9507014.htm>; Zhang Shishui [张石水], "Energetic Barracks: Our New Way of Doing Things Between Classes" [活力军营 我们的课间新花样], *China Military Online* [中国军网], March 17, 2019, available at <http://www.81.cn/jfjbmap/content/2019-03/17/content_229430.htm>.

11 Blasko, "The PLA Army After 'Below the Neck' Reforms," 16.

12 All the equipment and elements listed here have been viewed or referenced in multiple PLA videos and articles. Nonamphibious variants of each system are also common to the PLAA's conventional heavy combined arms battalions.

13 Liu Xuanzun, "Combined Arms Battalion Becomes Basic Combat Unit of PLA," *Global Times*, March 22, 2020, available at <https://www.globaltimes.cn/content/1183390.shtml>; Liu Jianwei [刘建伟] and Zhang Ning [张宁], "Pay Attention to the Construction of the Army Combined Arms Battalion: 1 + 1 > 2, Combat Power Integration Is the Ultimate Goal!" [关注陆军合成营建设: 1+1>2, 战斗力合成才是最终目标!], *China Youth Daily Online* [中国青年网], May 11, 2020, available at <http://military.china.com.cn/2020-05/11/content_76029419.htm>.

14 Ping and Wang, *Army Combined Arms Tactics Under Informationized Conditions*, 152.

15 "In Depth: China Built the World's Strongest Amphibious Assault Units with over 1,000 Combat Vehicles," *Sina Military* [新浪军事], September 2, 2016, available at <https://mil.sina.cn/sd/2016-09-02/detail-ifxvqcts9244954.d.html>; "112 Tanks + 112 IFVs, the PLA's Heavy Combined Arms Brigade Crushes Similar Elements in the U.S. and Russia" [112辆坦克+112辆步战车, 我军重型合成旅碾压美俄同级别], *Sohu* [搜狐], July 18, 2019, available at <https://new.qq.com/omn/20190718/20190718A0MBHH00.html>.

16 Dennis J. Blasko and Roderick Lee, "The Chinese Navy's Marine Corps, Part 1: Expansion and Reorganization," *China Brief* 19, no. 3 (February 1, 2019), available at <https://jamestown.org/program/the-chinese-navys-marine-corps-part-1-expansion-and-reorganization/>.

17 *Military and Security Developments Involving the People's Republic of China 2020*, 48.

18 Dennis J. Blasko, *The Chinese Army Today*, 2nd ed. (New York: Routledge, 2012), 103.

[19] Dennis J. Blasko and Roderick Lee, "The Chinese Navy's Marine Corps, Part 2: Chain-of-Command Reforms and Evolving Training," *China Brief* 19, no. 4 (February 15, 2019), available at <https://jamestown.org/program/the-chinese-navys-marine-corps-part-2-chain-of-command-reforms-and-evolving-training/>.

[20] *Military and Security Developments Involving the People's Republic of China 2020*, 48.

[21] Blasko and Lee, "The Chinese Navy's Marine Corps, Part 1."

[22] *Jane's Sentinel Security Assessment—China and Northeast Asia: China—Navy*, October 19, 2020, available at <https://customer.janes.com/Janes/Display/JWNA0034-CNA>.

[23] *Jane's Land Warfare Platforms: Armoured Fighting Vehicles—Type 05, ZBD-05, ZTD-05, PLZ-07B*, October 8, 2020, available at <https://customer.janes.com/Janes/Display/JAA_A071-JAFV>.

[24] Ibid.

[25] *Jane's Land Warfare Platforms: Armoured Fighting Vehicles—Type 63, Type 77*, August 26, 2020, available at <https://customer.janes.com/Janes/Display/JAA_1272-JAFV>.

[26] *Jane's Land Warfare Platforms: Armoured Fighting Vehicles—Type 09; ZBL-09, VN1*, October 20, 2020, available at <https://customer.janes.com/Janes/Display/JAA_A095-JAFV>.

[27] Shou Xiaosong [寿晓松], ed., *Science of Military Strategy* [战略学] (Beijing: Military Science Press, 2013), 199.

[28] Ping and Wang, *Army Combined Arms Tactics Under Informationized Conditions*, 155.

[29] Cui Yafeng [崔亚峰], *Science of Army Operations* [陆军作战学] (Beijing: PLA Press, 2009), 186.

[30] Ibid., 186–187; Zhang Yuliang [张玉良], ed., *Science of Campaigns* [战役学] (Beijing: National Defense University Press, 2006), 292.

[31] Cui, *Science of Army Operations*, 188–190.

[32] *Jane's Sentinel Security Assessment: China—Army*.

[33] *Military and Security Developments Involving the People's Republic of China 2019*, 81; *Jane's Land Warfare Platforms: Artillery and Air Defence—Type 89 (40 Round) 122mm*, September 7, 2020, available at <https://customer.janes.com/Janes/Display/JAA_0588-JAAD>.

[34] "Multiple Combat Arms Held a Joint Three-Dimensional Cross-Sea Landing on China's Southeastern Coast" [中国东南沿海多兵种举行联合立体渡海登陆], CCTV [央视网], October 11, 2020, available at <https://tv.cctv.com/2020/10/11/VIDEmdsVKMslVAmB4dmBdDfk201011.shtml>.

[35] Cui, *Science of Army Operations*, 188–189.

[36] Ping and Wang, *Army Combined Arms Tactics Under Informationized Conditions*, 189.

[37] Cui, *Science of Army Operations*, 190.

[38] Zhang, *Science of Campaigns*, 316; Ping and Wang, *Army Combined Arms Tactics Under Informationized Conditions*, 167.

[39] Zhang, *Science of Campaigns*, 316.

[40] Ping and Wang, *Army Combined Arms Tactics Under Informationized Conditions*, 166.

[41] "The Amphibious Armored Vehicle Carries a MANPADS Operator for Mobile Surface-to-Air Firing" [两栖装甲输送车搭载单兵便携式防空导弹操作手进行机动对空射击], *Sina News*, September 20, 2019.

[42] Ping and Wang, *Army Combined Arms Tactics Under Informationized Conditions*, 142.

[43] Ibid., 152.

[44] Ibid., 145–146.

[45] Ibid., 154–156.

46 "Amphibious Armored Unit" [两栖装甲部队], CCTV [央视网], November 23, 2019, available at <http://tv.cctv.com/2019/11/23/VIDEdRpPB5An13Wx2GN2EECM191123.shtml>; Ping and Wang, *Army Combined Arms Tactics Under Informationized Conditions*, 174–175.

47 "Multiple Combat Arms Held a Joint Three-Dimensional Cross-Sea Landing on China's Southeastern Coast."

48 *Jane's Land Warfare Platforms: Armoured Fighting Vehicles—Type 05, ZBD-05, ZTD-05, PLZ-07B.*

49 Ping and Wang, *Army Combined Arms Tactics Under Informationized Conditions*, 171–172.

50 Ibid., 177; Lin Wei [林炜], Qu Yang [屈洋], and Liu Hongkun [刘洪坤], "The Analysis of the Amphibious Tank Company's Aquatic Thermodynamic Power Support Action on the System Dynamics" [基于SD的两栖坦克连水上火力支援行动分析], *Fire Control and Command Control* [火力与指挥控制] 37, no. 2 (2012), 6; Zhu Yinggui [朱英贵], Li Su [李苏], and Zhao Jianjiang [赵建江], "Application of Fire to the Amphibious Tank Elements in the Phase of Assault Landing" [水陆坦克分队突击上陆阶段火力运用], *Fire Control and Command Control* [火力与指挥控制] 33, no. 2 (2008), 57–58.

51 Weng Hui [翁辉], Liu Jun [柳俊], and Jiang Guanghe [姜广贺], "Research on Landing Operations Amphibious Armored Equipment Combat Damage" [登陆作战两栖装甲装备战损研究], *Journal of Military Transportation University* [军事交通学院学报] 21, no. 10 (2019), 45.

52 Zhu Feng [朱峰], Guan Qunsheng [管群生], and Chen Zijian [陈子建], "Research on the Construction of Army Force Projection Capability" [陆军兵力投送能力建设研究], *Journal of Military Transportation University* [军事交通学院学报] 20, no. 5 (2018), 4; Zhang, Wang, and Qiu, "From Establishing Combined Arms to Combat Power Integration."

53 Zhong Chongling [仲崇岭], "More than 800 Days After Birth: The Growth of the Service Support Battalion" [诞生800余天：勤务保障营成长记], *China Military Online* [中国军网], November 7, 2019, available at <http://www.81.cn/lj/2019-11/07/content_9670563.htm>.

54 Huang Qian [黄谦] and Wang Hongqi [王红旗], "Amphibious Heavy Combined Arms Brigade Landing Operations Logistics Support" [两栖重型合成旅登陆作战后勤保障], *National Defense Technology* [国防科技], 40, no. 3 (2019), 91–92.

55 Ping and Wang, *Army Combined Arms Tactics Under Informationized Conditions*, 177–181.

56 Blasko, *The Chinese Army Today*, 188.

57 Blasko and Lee, "The Chinese Navy's Marine Corps, Part 2."

58 "A Certain Brigade of the 73rd GA: Amphibious Armored Forces Landed on the Beach" [第73集团军某旅: 两栖装甲部队抢滩登陆], CCTV [央视网], August 16, 2017, available at <http://tv.cctv.com/2017/08/16/VIDEvueFwKEGYsl7XPqQXrwN170816.shtml>; "How Is the Amphibious Steel Powerhouse Forged? It's Blown from a Trumpet" [两栖钢铁劲旅如何锻造? 从一把小号说起], *PLA Daily* [解放军报], September 26, 2017, available at <http://81.cn/lj/2017-09/26/content_7769137_2.htm>; "A Certain Brigade of the 74th GA: Amphibious Combat Vehicles Float and Fire on the Waves" [第74集团军某合成旅: 泛水编波 两栖战车海上浮渡射击], CCTV [央视网], April 20, 2018, available at <http://tv.cctv.com/2018/04/20/VIDE3EEV6vHkzlUPU2O1X8zI180420.shtml>.

59 Eastern Theater Command Official WeChat Microblog [人民前线], "Day and Night: External Training, the Smell of Soldiers!" [昼夜不停: 外训, 最有 "兵味"!], WeChat [微信], July 9, 2019; Zhang, Wang, and Qiu, "From Establishing Combined Arms to Combat Power Integration."

⁶⁰ Peng Zhuowu [彭卓武], Sheng Yangdi [盛洋迪], and Li Huaikun [李怀坤], "Integrated into the System, Open Up the Channels, This Operational Support Battalion Makes a Fist" [融入体系, 打通 "经脉", 这个作战支援营做到攥指成拳], *PLA Daily* [解放军报], August 16, 2020, available at <http://www.81.cn/jmywyl/2020-08/16/content_9882860.htm>; "Amphibious Reconnaissance Vehicle Launches First Drone at Sea" [两栖侦察车首次海上发射无人机], *China Military TV Online* [中国军网八一电视], September 18, 2020, available at <http://tv.81.cn/jbmdm/2020-09/18/content_9875313.htm>; "Service Arms Coordinate a Three-Dimensional Offense and Defense to Forge an Amphibious Combat Force" [兵种协同立体攻防 锻造两栖作战劲旅], *China Military TV Online* [中国军视网], August 8, 2020.

⁶¹ "A Certain Heavy Amphibious Combined Arms Brigade of the 73ʳᵈ Group Army Organized a Live Fire Test at Sea" [陆军第73集团军某两栖重型合成旅组织海上实弹考核], *China Military TV Online* [中国军视网], June 2, 2020, available at <http://www.js7tv.cn/video/202006_218933.html>; "Multiple Combat Arms Held a Joint Three-Dimensional Cross-Sea Landing on China's Southeastern Coast." The artillery battalion rocket artillery may have been simulating a joint firepower strike.

⁶² *Military and Security Developments Involving the People's Republic of China 2020*, 114.

⁶³ Lyle J. Morris et al., *Gaining Competitive Advantage in the Gray Zone* (Santa Monica, CA: RAND, 2019), 8, 30–31. According to this study, the *gray zone* is defined as an "operational space between peace and war, involving coercive actions to change the status quo below a threshold that, in most cases, would prompt a conventional military response, often by blurring the line between military and nonmilitary actions and the attribution for events."

⁶⁴ Liu Xuanzun, "PLA Holds Amphibious Landing Drills to 'Show Firm Will Against Taiwan Secessionists,'" *Global Times*, October 12, 2020, available at <https://www.globaltimes.cn/content/1203126.shtml>; Mark Magnier, "U.S. Sending State Department Official Keith Krach to Taiwan for Lee Teng-hui Memorial Service," *South China Morning Post*, September 17, 2020, available at <https://www.scmp.com/news/world/united-states-canada/article/3101848/senior-us-state-department-official-keith-krach>; David Brunnstrom and Humeyra Pamuk, "U.S. Designates Four Major Chinese Media Outlets as Foreign Missions," Reuters, June 22, 2020, available at <https://www.reuters.com/article/us-usa-china-media-restrictions/u-s-designates-four-major-chinese-media-outlets-as-foreign-missions-idUSKBN23T2Y8>.

⁶⁵ *Military and Security Developments Involving the People's Republic of China 2020*, 130.

⁶⁶ Huang Panyue, "Marines Rush Enemy Positions in Amphibious Raid Rehearsal," *China Military Online*, August 29, 2017.

⁶⁷ Zhang Yan [张彦], Shang Wenbin [尚文斌], and Pan Ruichen [潘瑞晨], "Transformation: How Did a Certain Marine Brigade Start This Must-Win Battle Without Gunpowder?" [转型: 海军陆战某旅如何打响这场没有硝烟的必赢战], *China Military Online* [中国军网], June 7, 2018, available at <http://www.81.cn/syjdt/2018-06/07/content_8055360.htm>; PLAN Official Weibo Microblog [中国人民解放军海军官方微博], "Amphibious Elite South China Sea Three-Dimensional Assault" [两栖精锐南海滩涂立体突击], *Sina Weibo* [新浪微博], October 14, 2020, available at <https://m.weibo.cn/detail/4559944038222402>; "Amphibious Armored Equipment Is Full of Firepower—A Live Fire Drill Afloat at Sea" [两栖装甲装备火力十足 直击海上浮渡实弹射击演练], *China Military TV Online* [中国军视网], August 29, 2020, available at <http://www.js7tv.cn/video/202008_227937.html>.

68 Zhao Lei and Zhou Jin, "Live-Fire Exercises Conducted by PLA Base in Djibouti," *China Daily*, November 25, 2017, available at <https://www.chinadaily.com.cn/china/2017-11/25/content_34966883.htm>; "Direct Fire Training Range—The Marine Corps Kicked Off with a 'Good Start' with Live Firing and New Equipment" [直击演训场 海军陆战队实弹射击 新装备打响 "开门红"], CCTV [央视网], July 12, 2020, available at <https://tv.cctv.com/2020/07/12/VIDEw5Cg3mFAHPCKwmcvRCoi200712.shtml>; "Marine Corps, You're So Handsome!" [海军陆战队, 你真帅!], WeChat [微信], October 17, 2020, available at <https://mp.weixin.qq.com/s/vSJZCcNaZcjkp2iisvwaEQ>.

69 Huang Panyue, "Chinese-Thai Marines Conduct Joint Beach-Landing Operation," *China Military Online*, May 13, 2019, available at <http://eng.chinamil.com.cn/view/2019-05/13/content_9502155.htm>.

70 "China-Pakistan 'Sea Guardian-2020' Maritime Exercise: Fighting Side-by-Side, Chinese and Pakistani Marines Train Together" [中巴 "海洋卫士-2020" 海上联合演习并肩战斗中巴海军陆战队员混编同训], CCTV, January 8, 2020, available at <http://tv.cctv.com/2020/01/08/VIDEZ6xPH4OgIs3phJHWIqqJ200108.shtml>.

71 Xu Yi, "PLA Teams Complete Preparations for IAG 2019," *China Military Online*, July 25, 2019, available at <http://eng.chinamil.com.cn/view/2019-07/25/content_9567870.htm>; Liang Yu, "'Seaborne Assault' Concluded in China," Xinhua, August 11, 2018, available at <http://www.xinhuanet.com/english/2018-08/11/c_137383614.htm>.

72 Zhang, Wang, and Qiu, "From Establishing Combined Arms to Combat Power Integration."

73 Weng, Liu, and Jiang, "Research on Landing Operations Amphibious Armored Equipment Combat Damage," 44; Wang Delin [王德林], Fan Xu [范旭], and Zhao Junye [赵俊业], "Army Combined Arms Battalion Staff Officer Training" [陆军合成营参谋训练], *National Defense Technology* [国防科技] 40, no. 2 (2019), 104.

74 Weng, Liu, and Jiang, "Research on Landing Operations Amphibious Armored Equipment Combat Damage," 44–45.

75 Ibid., 45.

76 Li Zihao [李子豪], "Research on Problems with Army Combined Arms Brigade Logistics Support" [陆军合成旅后勤保障问题研究], *National Defense Technology* [国防科技] 40, no. 1 (2019), 115–117.

77 Huang and Wang, "Amphibious Heavy Combined Arms Brigade Landing Operations Logistics Support," 90.

78 *Military and Security Developments Involving the People's Republic of China 2020*, 48.

79 Blasko, "The PLA Army After 'Below the Neck' Reforms," 22.

80 *Jane's Sentinel Security Assessment—China and Northeast Asia: China—Navy*, September 22, 2020, available at <https://customer.janes.com/Janes/Display/JWNA0034-CNA>.

81 Rick Joe, "The Future of China's Amphibious Assault Fleet," *The Diplomat*, July 17, 2019, available at <https://thediplomat.com/2019/07/the-future-of-chinas-amphibious-assault-fleet/>.

82 Wang Shichun [王世纯], "The Maritime Transport Squadron of an Eastern Theater Army Coastal Defense Brigade Recently Launched a Landing Training Event with the Army" [东部战区陆军海防旅船艇大队近日联合陆军开展了海上登陆训练], *The Observer Online* [观察者网], August 18, 2018, available at <https://www.guancha.cn/military-affairs/2018_08_18_468639.shtml?web>.

83 *Military and Security Developments Involving the People's Republic of China 2020*, 117.

84 Zhao Jiaqing [赵佳庆], Zhang Xu [张旭], and Zhang Shaokai [张劭锴], "'Raptors' Cross the Sea—A Record of the Shenyang Joint Logistic Support Center's Cross-Sea Projection Exercise Jointly Held with a Shipping Company" ["猛龙" 过海—沈阳联勤保障中心联合航运船企开展跨海投送 演练纪实], *PLA Pictorial* [解放军画报], no. 8 (2019), 84–87.

85 Zhang, *Science of Campaigns*, 355.

86 For more information on cuts the PLAA faced during the reform, see John Chen, "Choosing the 'Least Bad Option': Organizational Interests and Change in the PLA Ground Forces," in *Chairman Xi Remakes the PLA: Assessing Chinese Military Reforms*, ed. Phillip C. Saunders et al. (Washington, DC: National Defense University Press), 85–124.

87 "Amphibious Operations, No Longer the Way You Think" [两栖作战, 早已不是你以为的那种打法], *PLA Daily* [解放军报], October 2, 2018, available at <http://www.81.cn/jmywyl/2018-10/02/content_9302793.htm>.

88 Ibid.

89 "Multiple Combat Arms Held a Joint Three-Dimensional Cross-Sea Landing on China's Southeastern Coast."

90 Zhang, *Science of Campaigns*, 371.

CHAPTER 7

The PLA Airborne Corps in a Taiwan Scenario

Roderick Lee

Air-delivered People's Liberation Army (PLA) forces will be a crucial component of a joint island landing campaign (JILC) directed toward Taiwan, yet Western scholars have paid limited attention to these forces. A nested airborne campaign is critical to the larger JILC, as airborne forces are expected to land in conjunction with amphibious forces and improve the overall chance of success during the landing phase. This chapter provides a detailed understanding of the PLA Air Force (PLAAF) Airborne Corps and associated forces needed to execute an airborne campaign vis-à-vis Taiwan.

This chapter finds that the PLAAF Airborne Corps has evolved into a capable and modern combined arms force and that the PLA has gradually improved its ability to load and deliver these forces to landing areas in Taiwan. However, four major limitations could complicate the PLA's ability to execute an airborne campaign as part of a JILC: insufficient transport capacity to support airborne operations, insufficient capacity for aerial ports of embarkation, lack of combined arms and joint training (specifically in conducting formation escort and joint fires), and limited options for offensive and defensive ground operations.

The chapter first discusses the PLAAF Airborne Corps' organization, equipment, and training. It then identifies airlift capabilities that could support an airborne campaign. The next section discusses the aerial ports of embarkation (APOEs) that could be used to load airborne forces. Next, the limiting factors that would hamper PLA airborne operations are identified. The chapter concludes with a discussion of how the PLA is attempting to overcome some of these weaknesses, along with further complicating factors that Taiwan could introduce through its own defensive operations.

Structure, Organization, and Training

To understand the potential unfolding of an airborne campaign and the capability limitations that might frustrate those operations, one must first understand the basic characteristics of the PLAAF Airborne Corps. This section discusses the structure, organization, and training of the corps and other PLA airborne and air assault forces.

Basic Structure

The PLAAF Airborne Corps constitutes the bulk of the PLA's air-deliverable ground forces and is the most likely force to be used in an airborne campaign. The People's Republic of China (PRC)'s 2019 Defense White Paper suggests that the PLAAF Airborne Corps is administratively and operationally subordinate to PLAAF Headquarters. A limited body of PLA command and control literature suggests that, in wartime, a theater ground operations group command [*lu shang zuozhan jituan zhihui bu*, 陆上作战集团指挥部] may have an operational control relationship [*jizhong zhikong guanxi*, 集中指控关系] with airborne units.[1] However, besides PLAAF-specific media outlets, the Central Theater Command appears to be the primary outlet for peacetime reports on PLAAF Airborne Corps training. This line of reporting makes sense geographically, as all PLAAF Airborne Corps units are based within the Central Theater Command area of responsibility. However, this arrangement may pose challenges in a Taiwan scenario, where the Eastern Theater Command is likely the primary command.

Prior to 2017, the PLAAF Airborne Corps was called the 15th Airborne Corps.[2] The 15th Airborne Corps oversaw the 43rd, 44th, and 45th Airborne divisions, which in turn oversaw subordinate regiments and battalions that, for administrative purposes, were typically organized around troop type.[3] Although this arrangement worked from a management perspective, it was not ideal from an operational perspective. This division-regiment structure meant that only a full division-sized formation could execute combined arms operations. This arrangement lacked operational flexibility and was further hampered by the PLA's inability to deliver a full division using its conventional fixed-wing transport aircraft fleet.

During the 2017 "below the neck" reform, the PLA rearranged the structure of its airborne force by renaming the 15th Airborne Corps the PLAAF Airborne Corps and breaking up the airborne divisions into more flexible and easier-to-deploy brigades. This corps-level command now oversees six identified combined arms brigades, a special operations brigade, an operational support brigade, an aviation transport brigade, a training base, and a new training brigade (see figure 1).[4] However, the tables of organization and equipment for these six combined arms brigades vary greatly, which in turn defines the types of operations each unit can conduct.

Figure 1. General Organizational Structure of the PLAAF Airborne Corps

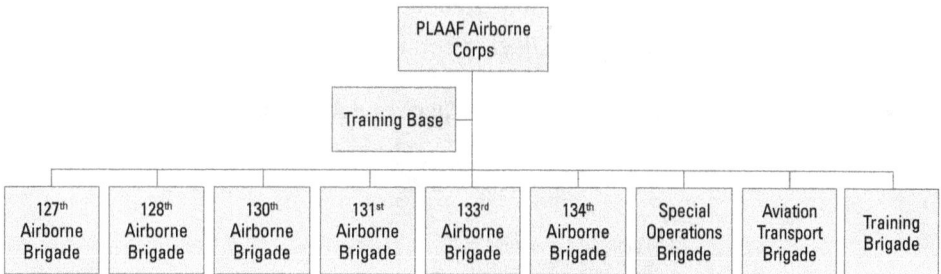

In general, a PLAAF Airborne Corps combined arms brigade consists of four combined arms battalions (see figure 2).[5] The PLAAF may designate an airborne combined arms battalion as a mechanized battalion, motorized battalion, or assault battalion depending on the battalion's table of organization and equipment.[6] Each combined arms brigade also has an artillery battalion, reconnaissance and pathfinder battalion, operations support battalion, service support battalion, and possibly a transportation battalion.[7]

Some, if not all, PLAAF Airborne Corps brigades also maintain reserve personnel to supplement active-duty personnel in wartime. Both the 128th

Figure 2. Standard PLAAF Airborne Corps Combined Arms Brigade Structure

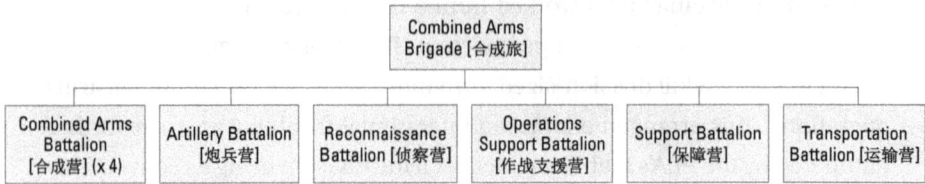

and 131ˢᵗ Combined Arms brigades have at least 100 reserve personnel.[8] Assuming that all units have such reserve elements and that the observed batches of reserve personnel conducting training represent only a fraction of the total, each brigade likely has anywhere between one company to one battalion's worth of additional reserve personnel available.

The combined arms battalion is the basic maneuver unit for the PLAAF Airborne Corps, just as it is for other parts of the PLA, including the ground force amphibious units (see the chapter by Joshua Arostegui in this volume for details). Although the size of a combined arms battalion varies across brigades, most battalions consist of roughly 500 soldiers and officers.[9] Each combined arms battalion typically has three infantry companies, which may be designated as mechanized, motorized, or assault (based on the battalion type); a weapons company; and likely a command company (see figure 3).[10]

Figure 3. Standard PLAAF Airborne Corps Combined Arms Battalion Structure

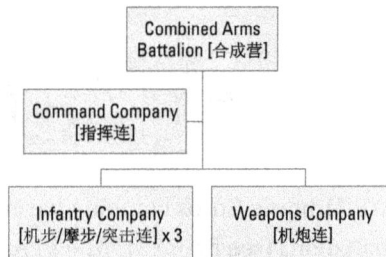

The artillery battalion provides most of a combined arms brigade's indirect fire support. For nonmechanized units, these battalions could also provide direct fire options if howitzers and anti-aircraft artillery are used in a direct fire role. Although available information is insufficient to provide a full table of organization and equipment breakdown, each battalion likely operates the following elements (see figure 4):

Figure 4. Assessed PLAAF Airborne Corps Artillery Battalion Structure

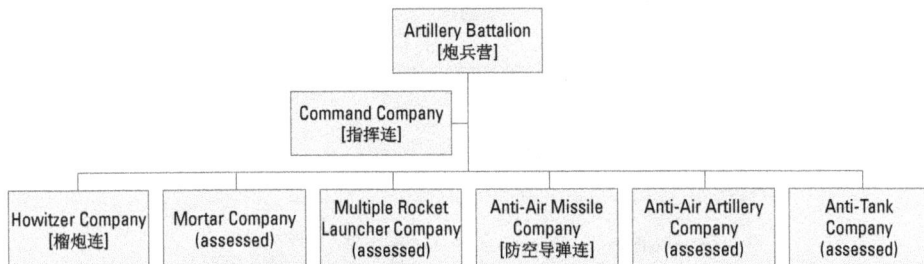

- at least one howitzer company equipped with roughly five PL-96 122-millimeter (mm) howitzers[11]

- a mortar element equipped with an unidentified number of 82mm mortars[12]

- at least one multiple rocket launcher element equipped with roughly six Type 63 107mm multiple rocket launchers[13]

- an anti-air missile company equipped with man-portable air defense systems[14]

- an anti-aircraft artillery element[15]

- an anti-tank guided missile element.[16]

A combined arms brigade's reconnaissance and pathfinder battalion provides an advanced echelon unit that marks landing zones, provides transport pilots with navigational aids, assists with securing the landing zone, and provides organic surveillance systems (including small unmanned aerial vehicles) for the brigade. This battalion consists at least of a pathfinder company, armed reconnaissance company, and instrument reconnaissance company (see figure 5).[17] Although this unit is lightly equipped and provides limited firepower, widespread issuance of night-vision devices means that these units are among the best equipped to conduct night operations.

Operational support, service support, and transportation battalions provide additional support services to the combined arms brigade. Key functions include communications; intelligence, surveillance, and reconnaissance; logistics; engineering; and transportation. These battalions include a communications company, parachute service company, and logistics service company.[18]

Figure 5. Assessed Organization of a PLAAF Airborne Corps Reconnaissance and Pathfinder Battalion

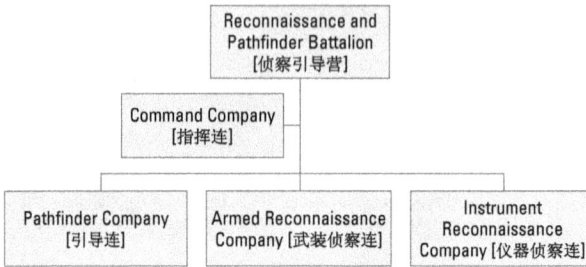

```
                      ┌─────────────────────┐
                      │  Reconnaissance and │
                      │  Pathfinder Battalion│
                      │      [侦察引导营]     │
                      └─────────────────────┘
           ┌──────────────────┐
           │ Command Company  │
           │     [指挥连]      │
           └──────────────────┘
  ┌──────────────┐  ┌──────────────────────┐  ┌──────────────────┐
  │ Pathfinder   │  │ Armed Reconnaissance │  │   Instrument     │
  │ Company      │  │ Company [武装侦察连]   │  │ Reconnaissance   │
  │  [引导连]     │  │                      │  │ Company [仪器侦察连]│
  └──────────────┘  └──────────────────────┘  └──────────────────┘
```

Subordinate Units

Despite their similar organizational structure, the airborne combined arms brigades differ widely in their weapons and equipment. Half the brigades are likely light motorized units, which are easiest to deliver via fixed-wing aircraft but lack heavy vehicles often needed for ground maneuver operations outside of urban environments. Two brigades are mechanized brigades equipped with light armored combat vehicles, which enables these units to engage in maneuver operations. The final brigade is an air assault brigade with its own organic rotary-wing assets to provide vertical lift and direct fire support. The subsequent sections discuss the six combined arms brigades in greater detail.

Light Motorized Combined Arms Brigades. The 127th, 128th, and 131st Combined Arms brigades are the PLAAF Airborne Corps' light motorized units. Based on PRC press and video reporting, these units appear to be equipped with a mix of Mengshi 4x4 vehicles and Bobcat 8x8 all-terrain vehicles.[19] Given their garrison size, it is unlikely that these brigades are fully motorized. Instead, they operate a mix of motorized and light infantry battalions.

These brigades are likely the fastest and most deployable within the PLAAF Airborne Corps. Given their lack of heavy equipment, they can be easily loaded and deployed by a wide range of aircraft, as well as from a range of airfields. These brigades thus provide the PLAAF with a flexible force to be used against lower end threat targets, including assaulting fortifications, seizing targets in restrictive terrain, and defending areas against light and mechanized forces. However, the lack of heavy equipment and mobility means these units are ill-suited for offensive operations in open terrain.

Air Assault Brigade. The 130th Combined Arms Brigade is the PLAAF's only known dedicated air assault unit. The unit can execute both airborne (troops delivered to the battlefield via parachute) and air assault (troops delivered directly to the battlefield by rotary-wing aircraft) operations.[20] The 130th Brigade's distinguishing feature is its subordinate helicopter regiment, which operates three flight groups.[21] Based on identified helicopter tail numbers, one flight group operates roughly 12 Z-9WZ utility helicopters, another operates roughly 12 Z-8KA transport helicopters, and a third operates at least 17 Z-10 attack helicopters. This regiment provides the brigade with a wide array of transport, reconnaissance, and fire support options. However, capability is limited to the helicopters' on-station time. If the rotary-wing component is unavailable, the 130th essentially becomes an understrength light combined arms brigade.

Compared with other combined arms brigades, the 130th Brigade likely consists of a much smaller ground combat element. Like other brigades, the unit's major ground combat element resides within its four assault battalions.[22] The probable first battalion is likely a roughly full-size assault battalion consisting of more than 400 soldiers and officers. However, the brigade's second, third, and fourth assault battalions appear to be understrength "half battalions" consisting of roughly 260 personnel each.[23] The PLAAF may intend to deliver these smaller half battalions using the brigade's transport helicopters, while the larger 400-person battalion is delivered by fixed-wing aircraft.

This brigade is partially motorized, with each platoon equipped with at least 14 CS/VP11 4x4 small all-terrain vehicles.[24] Roughly two vehicles per platoon have 12.7mm heavy machine guns affixed to the roof, with another two fitted with an unidentified crew-served weapon (possibly QLZ04 35mm grenade launchers or Type 88 general purpose machine guns). Although the vehicles are designed to accommodate four soldiers—two seated in the front and two in the rear—they can carry at least seven soldiers over short distances.[25] These vehicles provide a limited amount of tactical mobility and firepower to air assault platoons. Beginning in 2020, the PLAAF began issuing night-vision devices to select assault companies.[26] This makes the 130th Brigade the only known PLAAF Airborne Corps combined arms brigade with relatively widespread availability of personal night-vision devices.

Mechanized Brigades. The 133rd Combined Arms Brigade is one of two mechanized combined arms brigades in the PLAAF Airborne Corps.[27] In the spring of 2020, this unit began receiving a Norinco-produced 4x4 light tactical armored vehicle.[28] A standard mechanized infantry company under this brigade likely includes 10 to 14 standard vehicles equipped with 12.7mm heavy machine guns and 5 vehicles fitted with a 30mm cannon.[29] With 3 such companies per battalion, a full combined arms battalion under the 133rd Brigade operates at least 56 vehicles. The artillery battalion likely operates several additional vehicles as prime movers.

The other mechanized brigade is the 134th.[30] As of 2020, it is likely the only PLAAF Airborne Corps brigade that operates the air-droppable ZBD-03 infantry fighting vehicle and PCP001 82mm rapid fire mortar system. Based on observed vehicle numbers, handheld photography of these systems, and available vehicle storage at the 134th Brigade's garrison, each battalion likely operates between 40 and 50 ZBD-03s allocated across 3 mechanized infantry companies, along with 6 PCP001s in a firepower company.[31] This brigade may also operate an unknown number of multiple rocket launch systems mounted to a Mengshi chassis.[32]

Il-76s and Y-20s are the only aircraft capable of delivering the ZBD-03 infantry fighting vehicle. Although a ZBD-03 might fit into the cargo hold of a Y-9, the need to deploy extensive cushioning to prevent the vehicle from being damaged on landing and the lack of reporting on Y-9s paradropping ZBD-03s suggest that the PLA is currently unable to paradrop a ZBD-03 from a Y-9. The PLAAF has demonstrated the ability to airdrop three ZBD-03s, although most training typically involves dropping only one or two.[33] Thus, delivering a full mechanized infantry battalion would require between 13 and 16 Y-20s or Il-76s along with at least 12 Y-8s or Y-9s.

Airborne Training

PLAAF Airborne Corps brigades have trained to execute all four major airborne campaign ground operations activities: capturing landing sites, establishing a landing base, conducting ground offensives, and transitioning into defensive operations.[34] Most training appears to have been held at the battalion level, with only a few events consisting of a brigade-size element.[35] Airborne training often occurs at night, although most units lack night-vision devices.[36] Units also train to drop into a variety of environments, including regions with possible water hazards.[37] The maximum acceptable wind speed for training is 8 meters per second with gusts of 10 meters per second.[38] Personnel train to drop in roughly 1-second intervals per column and use both the ramp and side doors to egress the aircraft.[39]

A typical PLAAF Airborne Corps training event involves pathfinder and reconnaissance elements to guide aircraft to drop zones, an initial assault echelon that secures the immediate area, subsequent assault once firepower and other support elements are available, and a transition to defensive operations.[40] Notional blue—that is, enemy—targets in these training events include airports, fortified positions, and other unidentified strategic points.[41] Although PLA press typically does not identify the size of the blue force, on at least one occasion a 76th Group Army 12th Heavy Armor Combined Arms Brigade combined arms battalion acted as the blue force against a PLAAF Airborne battalion-size element acting as the red force.[42] This example suggests that PLAAF Airborne units do train to operate against mechanized and armored formations.

PLAAF Airborne Corps units train regularly with select PLAAF transport units as well as local civilian elements involved in transportation. However, no observed training event in 2019 or 2020 involved cooperative joint training with PLAAF fixed-wing combat aircraft or any other PLA service.

PLA Army and Navy Units
In addition to the PLAAF Airborne Corps, several other PLA units train to be delivered by air. Although most of these units will likely be allocated to special operations missions for other campaigns during a Taiwan scenario and therefore would be unavailable to support an airborne campaign, they train to conduct airborne or air assault operations and thus provide nonconventional options to supplement the PLAAF Airborne Corps.

The PLA Army maintains two air assault brigades that could support an airborne campaign. Both of their home garrisons are out of range of Taiwan, and thus both units would have to redeploy to prepared or ad hoc airfields closer to Taiwan before conducting island operations.[43] However, these units are likely allocated to support other island-landing campaign groups and not an airborne campaign that is part of the main invasion effort. Some, if not all, PLA Army special operations force brigades, PLA Army combined arms brigade reconnaissance battalions, and PLAN Marine Corps elements also train to jump from fixed-wing or rotary-wing aircraft.[44] However, much like the PLA Army air assault units, these units would likely be assigned to other missions rather than an airborne campaign.

Air Transport

The PLA maintains a growing fleet of transport aircraft to deliver its array of PLA airborne and air assault units. This section summarizes the PLA's available airlift that can support an airborne campaign directed toward Taiwan. Although any PLA unit equipped with transport aircraft can participate in an airborne campaign, only certain PLAAF transport units train regularly to conduct such operations. Thus, this section does not discuss theater air force transport and rescue brigades, training units, or any other PLA aviation units that may operate transport aircraft but that have no training experience in airborne operations. Although the PLA would also have access to many civilian aircraft mobilized for wartime operations, the PLA could not use these aircraft during the initial airborne campaign, as they are not designed to support static line jumps.

The PLAAF's 4th and 13th Transport divisions as well as the Airborne Corps' aviation transport brigade provide the bulk of the PLA's fixed-wing airlift capability. PLA press has widely recognized these three units for providing airlift in support of the COVID-19 pandemic relief efforts in Wuhan in early 2020. This suggests that these units are the preferred means of air transport.[45] Reporting on PLAAF Airborne Corps training also suggests that these three units are the primary providers of airlift.[46]

The 4th Transport Division, which is subordinate to the Western Theater Command Air Force, oversees three transport regiments.[47] Based on handheld photography of known airframes associated with the 4th Transport Division and high-count values for active probable Y-20s and Y-8s or Y-9s at known 4th Transport Division operating areas, this unit actively operates approximately 13 Y-20s and 24 Y-9s.[48] There are several older Y-8s and Y-7s at probable 4th Transport Division facilities, but the lack of activity from 2019 to 2020 suggests these are inactive airframes. Although this unit is nearly 1,000 kilometers (km) away from most PLAAF Airborne Corps units, its relative proximity to the airborne training area near Golmud means it regularly trains with the Airborne Corps.[49]

The 13th Transport Division, which is subordinate to the Central Theater Command Air Force, also oversees three transport regiments.[50] Based on handheld photography of known airframes associated with the 13th Transport Division and high-count values for active probable aircraft at known 13th Division operating areas, this unit likely operates approximately 10 Y-20s, 22 Il-76s, and 20 Y-8s or Y-9s.[51]

The Airborne Corps also operates its own organic aviation transport brigade.[52] This unit is equipped with a mix of Y-8s, Y-12s, and An-2s. Although the Airborne Corps frequently uses this unit to conduct jump training, it operates only roughly six Y-8s.[53] In an airborne campaign, Y-12s and An-2s could be pressed into service, but the limited passenger and cargo capacity of these aircraft means that they could deliver only sabotage detachments or pathfinders. Furthermore, the limited range of these aircraft would force them to operate from airfields relatively close to Taiwan. Therefore, only Y-8s under this brigade are considered when tallying the PLA's total fixed-wing lift capacity in the discussion below.

In addition to the 130th Brigade's helicopter regiment, the PLA has several rotary-wing units that could be used in either an air assault or airdrop role during an airborne campaign. The PLA Army operates a total of 15 aviation or air assault brigades, while the PLAN Marine Corps operates an additional aviation brigade.[54] Although these brigades vary in composition, each brigade can transport between two and four companies, depending on the number and types of transport helicopters available. As such, the PLA rotary-wing fleet can transport roughly two to five light infantry brigade equivalents.

Aerial Ports of Embarkation

The 2006 *Science of Campaigns* states that the concentration and assembly of the airborne force must be conducted in secret and that the commander must select unexposed areas in the rear, while also carrying out deceptive activities. Since the PLA emphasizes denial and deception to obfuscate the early stages of an airborne campaign, this section identifies the viable APOEs that the PLA can use in a Taiwan invasion scenario. These include current transport unit bases and any other PLA or civilian airfield capable of accommodating Y-8 or larger transport aircraft.[55]

The PLA maintains 59 airfields capable of accommodating and loading a Shaanxi Y-8 or Y-9 transport aircraft on an apron (see table 1). Thirty-six of those airfields are also capable of accommodating a Xi'an Y-20 transport aircraft. Only

33 can accommodate 15 or more Y-8 or Y-9 transport aircraft. At least 13 of these 33 airfields host another unit, and thus the resident unit would have to vacate the airfield for it to be used by transports. Qionglai Air Base is the only airfield that has two runways to allow for a higher volume of takeoffs and landings.

Given China's military-civil fusion strategy's emphasis on increasing resource-sharing between the military and civilian sectors, the PLA can expect greater access to civilian airfields in the coming years.[56] There are approximately 89 civilian airfields in the PRC with an International Civil Aviation Organization (ICAO) aerodrome reference code of 4D or higher (referring to airfields with the longest runways and capable of handling

Table 1. PLA Airfields Capable of Accommodating Y-8/Y-9 Transport Aircraft

Name on Wikipedia	Y-8/9 Max	Y-20 Max
Qionglai Air Base	82	63
Beijing Nanjiao Air Base	67	52
Changzhou Benniu Air Base	38	29
Kaifeng Air Base	34	26
Leizhuang Airfield	30	23
Yangluo Airfield	30	23
Nanning Wuxu Air Base	43	22
Lhasa Gonggar Airport	48	20
Guiping Mengshu Air Base	24	16
Dangyang Air Base	20	15
Mahuiling Air Base	19	14
Tuchengzi Air Base	18	13
Laiyang Air Base	16	12
Lalin Air Base	37	11
Yantai Southwest Air Base	15	11
Leiyang Air Base	30	10
Golmud Air Base	26	9

Name on Wikipedia	Y-8/9 Max	Y-20 Max
Qihe Air Base	19	9
Shanhaiguan Air Base	17	8
Qingyang Air Base	22	7
Dehong Mangshi Airport	23	6
Shadi Air Base	18	6
Yinchuan/Xincheng Air Base	20	6
Lintong Air Base	26	5
Liancheng/Lianfeng Air Base	18	3
Taihe Air Base	20	3
Luzhou Airfield	16	2
Anqing Airport	32	0
Beijing Shahezhen Air Base	18	0
Nanjing Luhe Airport	44	0
Shanghai Dachang Air Base	15	0
Shaoyang Wugang Airport	20	0
Shenyang Yu Hung Tun Air Base	16	0

planes with relatively long wingspans).[57] However, airfields rated as 4D often have very limited apron space and thus would be able to accommodate fewer than five large military transport aircraft. Airfields rated 4E or 4F are more likely to accommodate more than five Y-8 or Y-9s and thus are the minimum threshold used in this section. The PRC has roughly 55 civilian airfields with an ICAO aerodrome reference code of 4E or 4F. Although this chapter does not provide a breakdown of apron space for these airfields, 20 of the 55 4E or 4F airfields have 2 or more runways. These 20 airfields can accommodate a higher volume of air traffic relative to military airfields that are predominantly single-runway facilities. Figure 6 provides a map with applicable military and civilian airfields.

Figure 6. Airfields Capable of Supporting Large-Scale Airborne Operations

Legend: Icons in yellow are civilian airfields capable of supporting large-scale airborne operations. Icons in red are military airfields capable of supporting large-scale airborne operations.

The PLA maintains only two dedicated rotary-wing airfields within 400 km of Taiwan: Hui'an Air Base and an unidentified site in Zhangpu County, both located in Fujian Province. Hui'an is the home garrison of the 73rd Group Army's aviation brigade.[58] The PLA began construction on the unidentified Zhangpu site in 2020. PLA rotary-wing assets could also utilize seven other PLA airfield stations within 400 km of Taiwan; however, using these facilities for rotary-wing lift across the strait would mean temporarily halting fixed-wing operations. As of 2020, there are an additional seven civilian airports (with two more under construction) within 400 km of Taiwan that could be used for cross-strait operations. PLA Army aviation units also occasionally train to operate from prepared forward-operating bases along the coast.[59] These sites consist of a large clearing and several small concrete pads for takeoff and landing. The PLA may have several such sites within 400 km of Taiwan already prepared and could easily establish more with a few weeks' notice.

Limiting Factors

Despite the PLA's efforts to reform and modernize its airborne and fixed-wing transport forces and their supporting infrastructure, several potential challenges could limit the size of an airborne campaign or reduce its chances of success. Given the current size and equipment of the PLAAF Airborne Corps, available airlift, and infrastructure, this section identifies four limitations in an airborne campaign: available airlift, available ports of embarkation, joint training, and deployable ground forces. These factors are based predominantly on the constraints posed by available physical assets and observed standard tactics, techniques, and procedures.

Limited Airlift

The first challenge in any airborne campaign concerns available airlift. Although the PLA has more than 100 medium-size transport aircraft in its inventory, only some units train to support airborne operations. Specifically, only 3 division-level units, with 47 heavy and 63 medium-sized transports at their disposal, train to conduct airborne operations. Assuming a 90 percent readiness level, this number would be further reduced to roughly 40 heavy and 57 medium-sized transports. A related issue is aircraft load capacity. Some Western and Chinese sources state that a Y-9 can carry upward of 100 paratroopers, and an Il-76 or Y-20 can carry more than 125 paratroopers.[60] However, footage of PLAAF Airborne Corps training indicates that those figures are actually only 65 and 90, respectively.[61] There are also clear constraints on the vehicles that can be transported by fixed-wing aircraft: for example, an officer assigned to a brigade's support department, likely referencing the Y-20s and Il-76s, stated that "two types of our large transport aircraft can drop three of these vehicles [referring to tactical 4x4 vehicles] at a time."[62]

Based on these lower figures, table 2 shows three lift configurations if the entire available transport fleet is used. The table reveals that the PLA could deliver either 1 mechanized brigade combat element consisting of 2,300 combat personnel and 120 ZBD-03 armored fighting vehicles or 2 light brigade combat elements consisting of 5,240 combat personnel and limited fire support. These numbers indicate the PLA would need to double the size of its current airlift fleet to transport the majority of the PLAAF Airborne Corps in two trips. The PLA would likely also require even more aircraft to sustain

Table 2. Notional Lift Configurations

Heavy Mechanized Deployment (134th Brigade)							
Payload	Personnel	ZBD-03	Tactical 4x4	Mengshi	Bobcat	Howitzers	MLRs
IL-76/Y-20	120						
Y-8/Y-9	2,300			30		10	6

Mechanized Deployment (133rd Brigade)							
Payload	Personnel	ZBD-03	Tactical 4x4	Mengshi	Bobcat	Howitzers	MLRs
IL-76/Y-20			104			10	12
Y-8/Y-9	3,700						

Light Infantry Deployment (127th, 128th, 131st, or 130th Brigades)							
Payload	Personnel	ZBD-03	Tactical 4x4	Mengshi	Bobcat	Howitzers	MLRs
IL-76/Y-20	1,540		28	22		10	12
Y-8/Y-9	3,700						

airborne forces beyond the initial 24 to 48 hours of combat operations. Given that the PLA is continuing production of Y-20s and Y-9s, and assuming the PLA will acquire sufficient airframes to deliver a full brigade combat element, one could expect the PLA's airlift inventory to grow by at least 50 percent to address this challenge.

Rotary-wing transport can supplement the PLAAF's fixed-wing fleet; however, there will likely be competing requirements for these units. As such, an airborne campaign commander may not be able to rely on such forces to move troops across the Taiwan Strait.

Limited Aerial Ports of Embarkation

The second constraint is limited availability of APOE hubs able to support large-scale air transport operations. Wuhan and Kaifeng/Zhengzhou are the most convenient hubs because they are near PLAAF Airborne Corps garrisons (see table 3). However, both hubs are suboptimal for loading the entire fleet of Y-20s or Il-76s with heavy equipment because the combined apron

Table 3. Likely Aerial Port of Embarkation Hubs for Airborne Operations

APOE Hub	Constituent APOEs	Number of Runways
Wuhan	Yangluo Airfield, ZHHH	3
Kaifeng/Zhengzhou	Kaifeng Air Base, ZHCC	3
Beijing	Beijing Nanjiao Air Base, Beijing Shahezhen Air Base, ZBAA, ZBAD	9
Chengdu	Qionglai Air Base, ZUUU, ZUTF	6

space at these hubs is insufficient to land and load the entire airlift fleet and would require the PLA to split its loading phase across two or more hubs. Furthermore, each hub features only three runways (one at a military APOE and two at a civilian APOE). The PLAAF would thus take roughly an hour to get an entire aviation transport group of 110 aircraft into the air given a very generous 1.5-minute takeoff interval at each APOE.[63]

Chengdu and Beijing provide much better options as APOE hubs given the large number of airfields in proximity, which would cut the total time to get an entire aviation transport group of 110 aircraft into the air to under 30 minutes. However, these facilities are relatively far from PLAAF Airborne Corps garrisons and would require units to first transport equipment by rail, likely adding at least a day of transit time.[64] Table 4 shows a notional transit breakdown for the 134th Brigade to travel from Wuhan to Beijing using Department of Defense *Standardization of Work Measurement* times as guidelines.

Inadequate Combined Arms and Joint Training
Despite the growing importance of joint operations in PLA operational thought, PLA airborne forces only have limited experience with them. This limitation becomes apparent when examining how the PLA envisions organizing an airborne operation. An airborne campaign has clear groupings that in turn reveal locations for joint training requirements.[65] As table 5 shows, many of the campaign groupings involve other PLAAF forces or forces from other PLA services. However, the PLA appears to be deficient in training to execute the expected missions for some of these groupings.

Although the Airborne Corps regularly trains with fixed-wing transport aircraft, other elements needed to execute the airborne component of a JILC

Table 4. Notional Travel Times from PLAAF Garrison (Wuhan) to Aerial Port of Embarkation Hub (Beijing)

Wuhan to Beijing Rail Transit	
Load and Secure Vehicles on Flatbed Trucks	30 min
Transit from 134th Garrison to Wuhan Station	50 min
Unload Vehicles from Flatbed Trucks	15 min
Load Vehicles onto Rail Flatbed Cars	60 min
Rail Transit from Wuhan to Beijing	270 min
Unload Vehicles from Rail Flatbed Cars	30 min
Load Vehicles onto Flatbed Trucks	30 min
Transit to Beijing Daxing	60 min
Flatbed Truck Unload at Beijing Daxing	15 min
Total Time	9 hr 20 min

have not been incorporated into these exercises. Specifically, based on observations from 2019 and 2020, the PLA lacks training in three areas relevant to airborne campaigns. First, no observed training events involved PLAAF fixed-wing combat aircraft providing cover for fixed-wing transport aircraft. The only known instances of such coordination involved a few cases of fighters providing ceremonial escorts for PLAAF transport aircraft returning the remains of PLA soldiers found in North Korea. Second, the PLA did not publicize any training events involving fixed-wing aircraft providing fire support for PLAAF Airborne Corps units on the ground. Third, no known training involved supporting fires from PLA Army, Navy, or Rocket Force units. Given the importance of escorts in ensuring the survivability of transport aircraft while transiting the air corridor and joint fires to support PLAAF airborne units on the ground, the lack of training in these areas may prove to be major challenges during an airborne campaign.

There may be several reasons behind this lack of combined arms or joint training. The current PLA training schedule might not allow for such training due to a prioritization of other training subjects. Another possibility is that the PLA no longer envisions the need to provide significant joint fires in

Table 5. Airborne Campaign Groupings

Campaign Grouping	Eligible Units
Air Assault Group [空中突击集团]	PLAAF brigades equipped with 4.5-generation fighters or JH-7 fighter bombers
Air Cover Group [空中掩护集团]	Most PLAAF fighter brigades
Missile Assault Group [导弹突击集团]	PLARF SRBM and LACM-equipped brigades, some PLA Army artillery elements if within range
Reconnaissance Group [侦察编队]	Ground-based meteorology support elements, PLAAF or PLAN special mission aircraft divisions
Jamming Group [干扰编队]	PLAAF special mission aircraft divisions, other PLAAF aviation brigades fitted with ECM pods
Suppression Formation [压制编队]	Most PLAAF fighter brigades
Air Transport Group [空中运输集团]	4th and 13th Transport divisions, Airborne Aviation Transport Brigade, rotary wing units
Sabotage Detachment [破袭分队]	Special operations force units
Advanced Echelon [先遣梯队]	Airborne pathfinder and reconnaissance battalions, combined arms battalions
Assault Echelon [突击梯队]	Airborne combined arms battalions, operational support engineering elements
Rear Echelon [后方梯队]	Airborne combined arms battalions, artillery battalions, and support elements
Follow-On Echelon [后续梯队]	Additional airborne elements as needed

Key: ECM: electronic countermeasures; LACM: land attack cruise missiles; PLAAF: PLA Air Force; PLAN: PLA Navy; PLARF: PLA Rocket Force; SRBM: short range ballistic missiles.

support of an airborne campaign once forces have landed due to improvements in an airborne brigade's organic fire support. The PLA might also believe that it will not have to provide significant fighter cover because of having greater confidence in achieving air superiority prior to an airborne campaign. A final possibility is that the PLA simply does not perceive the need to spend training resources preparing today's warfighters for a mission they do not envision executing soon.

Limited Ground Operations

Although the current PLAAF combined arms brigades are much more capable than airborne formations a decade ago, current constraints on deliverable forces limit operations on the ground. Using the notional lift configurations of a single-wave heavy mechanized, light mechanized, and light infantry deployment depicted in table 2, one can establish the upper bounds of what types of ground operations might be possible in an airborne campaign. The PLA, in short, would have to make key tradeoffs in each of these scenarios.

A heavy mechanized brigade-level formation consisting of three mechanized combined arms battalions, one light combined arms battalion, and an augmented artillery battalion likely represents the high end of an air-delivered force intended to conduct maneuver warfare against a mechanized, armored, or heavily entrenched adversary. This configuration, however, does not allow for more than one primary brigade-level objective because the single light combined arms battalion is the only element capable of acting as the advanced echelon. For example, if the Republic of China (ROC) Army defended Taoyuan Airport and air base with a battalion-size element, this PLA airborne mechanized brigade formation is likely suited to seize the airport and air base.[66] However, should additional ROC Army elements counterattack, the formation may be unable to secure its own base of operations during the ground offensive phase. In this scenario, the single light combined arms battalion that initially seized the landing area would be the sole defending PLA unit. Also, the PLA formation would be unable to simultaneously seize another objective due to all available forces being committed to the Taoyuan Airport offensive. The PLA would likely deploy several additional airborne battalion-sized elements to better secure the initial base of operations in the area, as well as to seize secondary objectives of interest.

A light mechanized formation of two light mechanized combined arms battalions, four light combined arms battalions, and two artillery battalions provides a campaign commander greater flexibility to assault or defend multiple points. This configuration can be divided into two brigade-level formations capable of conducting independent operations, each including one mechanized combined arms battalion, two light combined arms battalions, and an artillery battalion. Such a configuration would be adequate to seize two lightly defended points, such as communications stations, radar sites, or even air defense sites, so long as they are defended by a company-size or smaller ROC Army element. However, such lightly defended points are unlikely to be of significant campaign value unless ROC forces failed to recognize a target's importance.

Should an airborne campaign commander focus on seizing undefended or lightly defended points and holding them against counterattacks, the commander could opt to deploy a light infantry configuration consisting of eight light combined arms battalions, two artillery battalions, and only enough prime movers to support the artillery battalions. This option allows for essentially two nearly full-size brigade formations that could defend two separate sectors with four combined arms battalions and an artillery battalion assigned to each sector. The commander may, alternatively, opt to defend four to eight smaller points with one to two battalions each while assigning the artillery battalions as the situation evolves. This configuration requires landing in a lightly defended or undefended area to allow the initially dispersed forces to consolidate into a defensible position. The central areas of Taiwan between Taichung and Chiayi would be ideal for such a deployment. However, deploying to this area has little campaign value besides blocking ROC Army forces in southern Taiwan from deploying north to defend Taipei.

Conclusion

The PLA's ability to successfully execute an airborne campaign has improved dramatically since 2010. The reorganization of the PLAAF Airborne Corps into a brigade-centric force has made it a more flexible, maneuverable, and lethal force. Introduction of the new 4x4 tactical vehicle also improves the mobility and lethality of those units equipped with it. Not only have these airborne units been reorganized and better equipped, but they also are continuously improving their training quality. The extensive improvements to China's military and civilian airfields have simplified the logistics of loading airborne forces into fixed- and rotary-wing aircraft. Finally, the introduction of large airlift assets such as the Y-20 and Y-9 has improved the PLA's overall airlift capacity.

These reforms and modernization achievements have led to a PLAAF Airborne Corps with a reasonable chance of seizing a key target defended by up to a battalion-size ROC Army element or seizing an undefended area and subsequently defending it against one or more ROC Army brigade-size elements. However, the PLA's ability to execute more extensive operations is hampered by several limitations, most of which it is actively trying to overcome. The lack of sufficient airlift is the most important limitation for an airborne campaign, but it is not the only challenge. The relatively small size of the PLA's current transport aircraft fleet is one of the easiest limitations to resolve given additional Y-20 and Y-9 production. Although it is hard to determine the exact production rates for either aircraft, the PLA could likely double its current airlift capacity by 2030, should it choose to do so.

Harder to address are other limitations, such as the challenge of loading brigade-size airborne elements onto aircraft. Although the PLAAF Airborne Corps occasionally trains to conduct up to a brigade-sized drop, it does not appear to train to execute a multibrigade deployment. Moving two brigade-size airborne elements, transport forces, and support units to the right location under wartime conditions with little to no training would almost certainly be a tall order. Similarly, while the PLA emphasizes joint training overall, the PLAAF Airborne Corps does not appear to be following suit. Escorting large transport formations and conducting joint fires are unique and challenging mission sets that the PLA has not yet developed for airborne operations. The PLA must allocate training time to the pertinent units, despite what is almost certainly a busy training schedule.

Two crucial factors not addressed in this chapter merit additional evaluation. First, this chapter has focused entirely on a "first wave" and did not explore follow-on personnel and materiel requirements for airborne forces deployed on the ground. This subject demands an entirely separate study, given the complexities associated with projecting force-on-force engagements and the materiel consumption associated with those engagements. However, the foundational data on airlift and APOEs presented here may be of use for such research.

Second, the adversary always has a say. This chapter did not account for the ROC military's and greater Taiwan's response to an airborne campaign. For instance, the air transport group is inevitably a slow and vulnerable target, while air and ground force echelons are highly reliant on continued supplies and joint fire support. ROC military forces have a geographic and comparative advantage when contesting these capabilities. Current capabilities that Taipei is acquiring under the Overall Defense Concept are very much in line with contesting an airborne landing (for details, see the chapters by Drew Thompson and Alexander Chieh-cheng Huang in this volume). Short-range air defense systems, whether vehicle-mounted or man-portable, are extremely effective against slow aircraft such as Y-20s and Y-9s. They would also be extremely resilient in the face of PLA suppression of enemy air defense missions due to their small physical and emissions signature. Further exploration of what exactly would be needed to neutralize PLAAF Airborne units once on the ground is another topic that deserves additional study.

Notes

[1] Liu Wei [刘伟], *Theater Joint Operations Command* [战区联合作战指挥] (Beijing: National Defense University Press, 2016).

[2] Kevin Pollpeter and Kenneth W. Allen, eds., *The PLA as Organization v2.0* (Vienna, VA: Defense Group, Inc., 2015), 368.

[3] Ibid.

[4] Guo Qing [郭庆] and Jiang Long [蒋龙], "Airborne Troops Accelerate Their Transformation into a Synthetic 'Flying Army'" [空降兵加速转型成为合成 "飞行军"], *China Youth Daily* [中国青年报], May 7, 2020, available at <http://www.xinhuanet.com/politics/2020-05/07/c_1125950453.htm>; Xu Xiongshi [徐雄师] and Deng Huiwen [邓惠文], "90 Minutes to Test 11 Subjects for a Special Operations Brigade of Airborne Troops for Integrated Assessment" [90分钟考11个科目空降兵某特种作战旅进行融合式考核], CCTV Military Channel [央广军事], April 8, 2019, available at <http://www.mod.gov.cn/power/2019-04/08/content_4839012.htm>; "Military Mission: Reappearing 'The Most Beautiful Retrograde' in the New Year" [军人使命新春再现 "最美逆行"], *Air Force Reporter* [空军记者], February 14, 2018, available at <https://xw.qq.com/amphtml/20180214A05LSY00>; CCTV-7 Military Report [军事报道], video, 24:59, July 10, 2019, available at <https://tv.cctv.com/v/v1/VIDExFTHmF57h2YxEBiQvSXN190710.html>; Chen Xi [陈曦], "A Training Base for Airborne Troops Organizes Comprehensive Drills Across Regions for Graduates" [空降兵某训练基地组织毕业学员千里跨区综合演练], Xinhua, July 10, 2018, available at <https://www.xinhuanet.com/mil/2018-07/10/c_129910871.htm>; CCTV-7 Military Report [军事报道], video, 6:49, January 30, 2019, available at <https://tv.cctv.com/2019/01/30/VIDEMNEV3O1tZNYt23UAsqbl190130.shtml>.

⁵ "Hundreds of Paratroopers Are Fully Equipped for Airborne Combat" [实拍数百伞兵全副武装空降战斗空中绽放密集集伞花], CCTV News [央视新闻], August 13, 2018, available at <http://m.news.cctv.com/2018/08/13/ARTI3u9o4Rfc7oJnIf33GHkA180813.shtml>; Liu Kang [刘康] and Li Dongdong [李冬冬], "An Interview with Li Xiangdong, the Commander of the 3ʳᵈ Mechanized Infantry Battalion of an Airborne Corps Brigade," *Air Force News* [空军报], April 13, 2018, 1; Xiong Hao [熊浩] and Jiang Long [蒋龙], "Zhou Liwen, Commander of the Fourth Battalion of a Brigade of Paratroopers: 'Steel Piles' on the Dam" [空降兵某旅四营营长周立文: 堤坝上不倒的"钢桩"], *PLA Daily* [解放军报], August 17, 2020, available at <http://www.81.cn/tzjy/2020-08/17/content_9883267.htm>.

⁶ Xiong and Jiang, "Zhou Liwen, Commander of the Fourth Battalion of a Brigade of Paratroopers"; Liu and Li, "An Interview with Li Xiangdong"; CCTV-7 Military Report, February 27, 2019.

⁷ Xie Chengyu [谢程宇], "Go to the Next Company to Listen to Class. . . ." [走, 去隔壁连队听听课], *Air Force News* [空军新闻], May 14, 2020, available at <https://mp.weixin.qq.com/s/_BdFMDMyRZfAYanxnrjr_Q>; CCTV-7 Military Report [军事报道], video, 25:29, March 10, 2019, available at <https://www.youtube.com/watch?v=Y7tRqcFUXr0>; Tang Zhiqiang [汤志强], "Hard Fight ≠ Actual Combat" [苦战化≠实战化], *PLA Daily* [解放军报], October 19, 2020, available at <http://m.yunnan.cn/system/2020/10/19/031049310.shtml>; Tang Jiajun [唐家军] and Jiang Long [蒋龙], "Airborne Support Battalion Improves Military Skills," *Air Force News* [空军报], May 21, 2019, 2; CCTV-7 Military Report, June 12, 2019.

⁸ Zhang Hongbing [张洪兵] and Xiong Huaming [熊华明], "Veterans Return to Camp to Restore 'Muscle Memory'" [退伍老兵回营恢复 "肌肉记忆"], *China National Defense News* [中国国防报], November 25, 2018, available at <https://mp.weixin.qq.com/s/6CVSV8PN7SsuD1uVhHJMbg>; Chen Qian [陈倩], "One Hundred Pre-Regimented Reserve Soldiers of a Certain Brigade of Airborne Troops Stationed in Hubei Obtained 'Certificates' on the Battlefield" [驻汉空降兵某旅百名预编预备役士兵取得战场 "合格证"], *Chutian City Daily News* [楚天都市报], November 12, 2018, available at <https://k.sina.cn/article_1720962692_6693ce8402000ji51.html%3Ffrom%3Dmil+&cd=3&hl=en&ct=clnk&gl=us>.

⁹ Liu Kang [刘康], "Join Force as Elite Soldiers and Strike Out" [合力成势精兵出击], *Air Force News* [空军报], September 11, 2018, 1.

¹⁰ Xiao Yanfei [肖艳飞], "Fighting Fiercely in the Northwest Desert, 'Post-00' Recruits Join the Battle Sequence!" [鏖战西北大漠, "00后" 新兵加入战斗序列!], *Air Force News* [空军新闻], June 4, 2020, available at <https://mp.weixin.qq.com/s/Mz8oNNj_z-8NQWI_BdCQLQ>; Xie, "Go to the Next Company to Listen to Class."

¹¹ "Directly Attack the Front Line of the Training Exercise" [进驻就打检验部队远程机动作战能力], CCTV-7 Noon National Defense [正午国防军事], video, 1:36, June 15, 2020, available at <https://tv.cctv.com/2020/06/15/VIDESJqbFEFhyeO9ezRxSiAi200615.shtml>;   CCTV-7 Military Report, April 14, 2019.

¹² "Directly Attack the Front Line of the Training Exercise."

¹³ Ibid.

¹⁴ CCTV-7 Military Report, February 27, 2019.

¹⁵ CCTV-7 Military Report, April 14, 2019.

¹⁶ CCTV-7 Military Report [军事报道], June 22, 2020, available at <https://v.cctv.com/2020/06/22/VIDE6Rb3HoW2kCJnIyUrDHuA200622.shtml>.

17   Huang Linying [黄琳颖], "The Battle Begins at 4:30 in the Morning—A Glimpse of the Tactical Operations of a Certain Brigade of Airborne Troops with Live Ammunition for Seven Days and Nights" [战斗，从凌晨四点半开始—空降兵某旅七昼夜实兵实装实弹战术行动一瞥], *Air Force Online* [空军在线], February 4, 2019, available at <https://mp.weixin.qq.com/s/FYIVImKZl5UKEJZ8NfIGDg>; Xiao Yanfei, "Scouts Are Going to Fight" [侦察兵就要拼], *China Youth Daily* [中国青年报], March 26, 2020, available at <https://tech.sina.cn/2020-03-26/detail-iimxyqwa3209103.d.html>; "Directly Attack the Front Line of the Training Exercise."

18   "The Same Paratrooper, She Fought for the Country, But She Fought for the Nationality, Which One Is More Beautiful?" [同样是空降兵，她为国而战，而她却为国籍而战，哪个更美], *Military Discipline House* [军纪之家], April 13, 2019, available at <https://kknews.cc/military/eypgmxy.html>; Zeng Yanfeng [曾艳峰] and Tang Jiajun [唐家军], "Newly Formed Airborne Brigade Emphasizes Safety and Stability Work," *Air Force News* [空军报], May 29, 2018, 1; CCTV-7 Military Report, July 19, 2019.

19   CCTV-7 Military Report, October 29, 2020.

20   CCTV-7 Military Report, September 5, 2020.

21   Yang Xuan [杨璇], Zuo Lixiang [左礼响], and Xuan Shihao [宣世豪], "Air Assault, Bravely Strive for the First! He Is the First Batch of Direct 10K Instructors and Captain Liu Dongliang!!" [空中突击，勇争第一!他就是第一批直-10K教员，机长刘栋梁!!], *Our Sky* [我们的天空], April 9, 2020, available at <https://zhuanlan.zhihu.com/p/128450591>.

22   CCTV-7 Military Report, July 29, 2019.

23   Source available from the CASI Media Archive, May 1, 2019.

24   CCTV-7 Military Report, October 28, 2020.

25   CCTV-7 Military Report, September 17, 2020.

26   CCTV-7 Military Report, September 5, 2020.

27   "The Municipal Bureau of Commerce Launches Party Day Activities on the Theme of 'July 1ˢᵗ, Do Not Forget the Original Heart, Keep in Mind the Mission'" [市商务局开展迎 "七一不忘初心，牢记使命" 主题党日活动], Wuhan Bureau of Commerce [武汉市商务局], July 3, 2019, available at <http://sw.wuhan.gov.cn/ztzl_26/jgjs/bwcxljsmztjyhd/202001/t20200106_570569.shtml>; CCTV-7 Military Report, November 2, 2020.

28   Guo Qing [郭庆] et al., "New Equipment Lined Up with Paratroopers! 'Aerial Combined Force' Is Taking Shape" [新装备列装空降兵! "空中合成部队" 正在形成], *Air Force News* [空军新闻], May 27, 2020, available at <https://mp.weixin.qq.com/s/-I3DF9A2BKiNwOclX2DQ-w>.

29   CCTV-7 Military Report, November 2, 2020.

30   Zhao Ke [赵克], "The Veteran of the Shangganling Campaign Seeks to Realize the Dream of the Troops: I Finally Met My Family" [上甘岭战役老兵寻当年部队终圆梦: 我终于见到家人了], *Engineering Machinery Daka* [工程机械大咖], October 19, 2020, available at <https://mp.weixin.qq.com/s/siDhBqZNtJmGNzr7YlXTxQ>.

31   "When Will The 'One Hero and Three Gangs' Be Realized as the Only Main Tank of Our Airborne Troops?" [我军空降兵唯一主力战车,何时实现 "一个好汉三个帮"?], *Frame Spot* [帧察], December 15, 2019; Yao Jianing, "Vehicle-Mounted Rapid Fire Mortars in Live-Fire Test," *China Military Online*, June 12, 2016, available at <http://english.chinamil.com.cn/news-channels/photo-reports/2016-06/12/content_7096660.htm>;   CCTV-7 Military Report [军事报道], June 7, 2020, available at <https://v.cctv.com/2020/06/07/VIDE68n1Yyg2gr33CGSteq7u200607.shtml>; Yao, "Vehicle-Mounted Rapid Fire Mortars In Live-Fire Test."

32   CCTV-7 Military Report, September 17, 2020.

[33] CCTV-7 Military Report, September 25, 2020; Volga Dnepr Airlines, "Volga Dnepr Airlines Il-76TD-90VD," available at <https://www.volga-dnepr.com/files/booklet/il-76e_final.pdf>.

[34] Zhang Yuliang [张玉良], ed., *Science of Campaigns* [战役学] (Beijing: NDU Press, 2006), 589–599.

[35] Liu, "Join Force as Elite Soldiers and Strike Out," 1; Zhang Xiangfeng [张祥锋], "Airborne Troops on Central Media: Cross-Regional Assault, Airborne Troops Will Be Delivered in an Integrated System!" [央媒上的空降兵: 跨区域突击, 空降兵整建制投送!], *Our Sky* [我们的天空], September 25, 2020, available at <https://mp.weixin.qq.com/s/EoDKOnLMoc8vFqkMvCwL8w>.

[36] Zhang Pengbei [张朋倍] and Zhang Zhe [张哲], "Airborne Troops on the Central Media: Shocked, Let's Watch the Parachuting Training of Airborne Troops on the Water!" [央媒上的空降兵: 震撼, 一起来看空降兵水上集群伞降训练!], *Our Sky* [我们的天空], August 6, 2020, available at <https://mp.weixin.qq.com/s/GSM1djw_M8GrNT2X3Q-XMA>.

[37] Ibid.

[38] Liu Kang [刘康], "Paratroopers" [空降神兵], *China Armed Forces* [中国军队], August 1, 2018, 103.

[39] CCTV-7 Military Report, June 30, 2019.

[40] Fang Chao [方超], He Yonghui [贺勇辉], and Xia Peng [夏澎], "The Central Part of the Sword, Fierce Soldiers Tempering the 'Iron Fist' in the Desert" [中部论剑, 鏖兵大漠淬炼 "铁拳"], *Central Theater Trumpet* [中部战区号角], June 11, 2020, available at <https://mp.weixin.qq.com/s/KRWDquLaE-C7WqRjBQuC4A>; Xiao, "Fighting Fiercely in the Northwest Desert"; Zhang, "Airborne Troops Will Be Delivered in an Integrated System!"

[41] Huang, "The Battle Begins at 4:30 in the Morning"; CASI, "3ndTCEd," CASI Periodical Archive, November 25, 2019; Fang et al., "The Central Part of the Sword."

[42] Li Zhongyuan [李忠元] and Sun Yufei [孙玉飞], "Synthetic Battalion vs. Paratroopers, Land and Air Rivals Each Other!" [合成营VS空降兵, 陆空互为对手!], *Western Army Strong Military* [西陆强军号], August 17, 2020, available at <https://mp.weixin.qq.com/s/fp49lxK6ZU7P-0oTvTJziw>.

[43] *Military and Security Developments Involving the People's Republic of China 2020: Annual Report to Congress* (Washington, DC: Office of the Secretary of Defense, 2020), 77.

[44] Mao Shichuan [毛世川], Zhang Di [张迪], and Xiang Jialiang [向家良], "The First Big Plane Jump, Parachute Blossoms in Snowy Plateau" [首次大飞机实跳, 伞花绽放雪域高原], *Western Army Strong Military* [西陆强军号], September 24, 2020, available at <https://mp.weixin.qq.com/s/eESSbXTc-Ik9nV1k2eMIUg>; CCTV-7 Military Report, October 30, 2020; CCTV-7 Military Express, October 14, 2020, available at <http://www.js7tv.cn/video/202010_231825.html>.

[45] Zhao Wenhan [赵文涵], "Urgent Air Freight! The High-Definition Big Picture Is Here!" [紧急大空运! 高清大图来了!], *Our Sky* [我们的天空], February 14, 2020, available at <http://www.xinhuanet.com/politics/2020-02/14/c_1125573788.htm>.

[46] CCTV-7 Military Express, September 28, 2020; CCTV-7 Military Report, October 23, 2020; CCTV-7 Military Report, July 25, 2020.

[47] "China: Air Force," *Janes World Air Forces*, October 5, 2020.

[48] European Space Agency (ESA), Sentinel Hub EO, January 1, 2020, available at <https://apps.sentinel-hub.com/eo-browser/>.

[49] CCTV-7 Military Express, September 28, 2020.

[50] *Military and Security Developments Involving the People's Republic of China 2020*, 111; Janes, "China: Air Force."

51 ESA, Sentinel Hub EO.

52 *Janes*, "China: Air Force."

53 ESA, Sentinel Hub EO.

54 *Military and Security Developments Involving the People's Republic of China 2020*, 48.

55 The estimates for fixed-wing airfields below are based on the following requirements:

- minimum ICAO aerodrome reference code equivalent of 4D or better
- a 5-meter (m) buffer at each end of each apron
- apron depth of at least 70 m to accommodate and load a Shaanxi Y-8 or Y-9 transport aircraft
- apron width of at least 50 m per Y-8 or Y-9 to accommodate the wingspan of the aircraft as well as space between an adjacent aircraft's wingtip
- apron depth of at least 100 m to accommodate and load a Xi'an Y-20 transport aircraft
- apron width of at least 65 m per Y-20 to accommodate the wingspan of the aircraft as well as space between an adjacent aircraft's wingtip
- within roughly 2,000 km of Taiwan.

56 Alex Stone and Peter Wood, *China's Military-Civil Fusion Strategy* (Montgomery, AL: China Aerospace Studies Institute, 2020), 57.

57 An International Civil Aviation Organization aerodrome reference code is a two-part designation that indicates an airfield's overall length and width. This in turn informs users whether a particular aircraft can land at a particular airfield.

58 *Military and Security Developments Involving the People's Republic of China 2020*, 98.

59 CCTV-7 Military Report [军事报道], April 27, 2020, available at <http://www.js7tv.cn/video/202004_214931.html>; CCTV-7 Military Report, November 6, 2020.

60 Andrew Tate, "China Mass Producing Y-9 Surveillance Aircraft," *Janes*, December 9, 2019, available at <https://www.janes.com/defence-news/news-detail/china-mass-producing-y-9-surveillance-aircraft>; "Il-76 CANDID: Status and Outlook for the Soviets' Major Transportation Aircraft Program," Central Intelligence Agency Directorate of Intelligence Research Paper, December 1, 1985.

61 Liu, "Join Forces as Elite Soldiers and Strike Out," 1; CCTV-7 Military Report [军事报道], October 16, 2018, available at <http://tv.cctv.com/2018/10/16/VIDEy3WrkiLCbgXPQzdEdoGG181016.shtml>.

62 Liu Kun [刘坤], "My Country's First Batch of Certain Wheeled Armored Vehicles Developed and Produced by the Ordnance Industry Group Was Officially Installed" [由兵器工业集团研制生产的我国首批某型轮式装甲车正式列装], China North Industries Group [中国兵器工业集团], May 8, 2020, available at <https://mp.weixin.qq.com/s/4Hb29CoyTahN_9Co_YoDkQ>.

63 Federal Aviation Administration, "Federal Aviation Administration Airport Traffic Control—Terminal Departure Procedures and Separation," FAA Order JO 7110.65Y, July 16, 2020, available at <https://www.faa.gov/documentLibrary/media/Order/7110.65Y.pdf>.

64 *Standardization of Work Measurement Volume IX: Miscellaneous Occupations* (Washington, DC: Defense Industrial Resources Support Office, January 1977), 345.

65 Zhang, *Science of Campaigns*, 597.

66 This and all subsequent speculative scenarios assume a 3:1 attacker-to-defender ratio is needed.

CHAPTER 8

Getting There: Chinese Military and Civilian Sealift in a Cross-Strait Invasion

Conor M. Kennedy

I n mid-October 2020, the People's Liberation Army (PLA) held amphibious exercises off Fujian and Guangdong provinces involving multiple arms of the 73rd Group Army. Video coverage of the event showed an impressive number of capabilities clearly intended as a message for Taiwan.[1] The exercise was also of practical significance: despite advancements in fixed- and rotary-wing transport aircraft, sealift remains the primary means for transporting heavy equipment, as well as personnel, fuel, and cargo, across the Taiwan Strait. This primacy reflects both the proximity of the mainland to Taiwan and the large capacity of ships.

Due to the hostile combat environment, initial assault waves by the People's Republic of China (PRC) on Taiwan would be embarked primarily on PLA Navy (PLAN) and PLA Army (PLAA) amphibious ships. The amphibious assault would comprise the PLAA's amphibious combined arms brigades and units from the PLAN Marine Corps (PLANMC). However, a current weakness of a cross-strait invasion is the lack of a sufficient number of PLA landing ships. As this chapter discusses, new and old PLAN and PLAA platforms still make up the core amphibious lift capabilities for the landing force, but PLAN construction has largely focused on developing large ocean-going amphibious ships.

As a potential workaround, a PLA study on reactivating mothballed PLAN landing ships for entry into PLAA watercraft units raised the possibility of a short-term surge in amphibious lift capacity.[2] Even with this solution, however, the likely attrition in the amphibious fleet during the opening salvos of the conflict would mean the PLA drawing on China's civilian merchant fleet to get follow-on forces ashore. The PRC has the legal authority to assume control over its large civilian shipping fleets and to mobilize them for military use. Recent developments—such as implementing national defense requirements in merchant fleet construction and modification, organization, and military training, along with other logistics solutions—indicate that the PLA is actively working to resolve problems within the merchant fleet to make up for shortcomings in organic PLA sealift. The PLA is also making efforts to ensure successful debarkation operations in a variety of situations, such as exploring the use of artificial harbors to help establish landing bases. Also, large numbers of China Coast Guard (CCG) and maritime militia forces are available to supplement PLA transportation operations in a cross-strait landing.

This chapter explores such problems and developments in amphibious lift in three main sections. The first assesses PLAN and PLAA organic amphibious lift capacity. The second discusses the role of the civilian merchant fleet in transporting PLA forces across the strait and explains two scenarios on the debarkation of those forces. The third briefly examines how the CCG and the maritime militia fleets might support amphibious landing operations in a Taiwan invasion. Each section draws from Chinese-language and PLA-affiliated sources to inform its analysis.

A caveat: this chapter does not attempt to predict which landing sites PLA planners could select. Rather, it focuses on the PLA's ability to get forces across the strait and commence landing and debarkation operations. This discussion omits several critical factors, including phases of bombardment, the battle for air superiority, the struggle for sea control, mine and obstacle clearance, U.S. intervention, and countless other variables that could each influence the outcome of a PLA landing operation.

The PLAN Amphibious Fleet

Although PLAN ships would form the core of the amphibious fleet, they would be supplemented and supported by PLAA landing vessels. Consisting of both new and old classes of ships, this combined fleet would be tasked with delivering combat troops onto Taiwan's coastline and sustaining them until landing zones are built up or a suitable port is secured and made operable. The PLAN fleet is organized into several landing ship *zhidui* [支队] and *dadui* [大队] units in the Southern, Eastern, and Northern theater command navies.[3] Table 1 details the number of ships in each of the theater command navies and their total capacity in troops and amphibious armored vehicles, based on the author's assessment from Chinese open-source reporting. In the aggregate, the PLAN can generate enough lift for up to 19,080 combat troops and approximately 666 ZTD-05 amphibious assault vehicles. Table 2 lists the capacities of individual types of PLAN and PLAA landing ships.

Overall, amphibious shipping is limited compared with PLA amphibious combat forces. In addition to 8 Type-071 amphibious transport docks (also known as landing platform docks [LPDs]), the landing ship, tank (LST)/landing ship medium (LSM) fleet stands at about 29 and 32, respectively, assigned unevenly to the Northern, Eastern, and Southern theater commands.[4] This capacity is sufficient to land the PLANMC's 1st and 2nd brigades with their amphibious armor and possibly some of the newly created marine brigades, provided they are equipped for the fight.[5] However, PLAN landing ships will not exclusively transport PLANMC forces. Southern Theater navy landing ship units primarily train with the 1st and 2nd Marine brigades, while the Eastern and Northern theater navies' landing ship units frequently train with army units.[6] Table 1 demonstrates that the Eastern and Southern theater commands' landing ships have the capacity to transport more than a single brigade each. Additionally, the initial landing units would comprise reconnaissance and obstacle clearance elements and assaulting infantry and armor units under naval fire support. Artillery and support units would come ashore in later waves.[7] Capable offshore transfer and lighterage systems could free up landing ship vehicle decks to maximize the number of amphibious assault units from multiple brigades in the initial waves. Nonetheless, PLAN amphibious ships alone would be insufficient to get all six PLAA amphibious combined arms brigades of the 72nd, 73rd, and 74th group armies across the strait in the first assault. These brigades likely total somewhere between 30,000 to 36,000 personnel and thousands of vehicles and armor—significantly more than the PLAN landing ship capacity displayed in table 1.[8] Those forces would have to embark on a mix of PLAN and PLAA watercraft landing ships.

225

Table 1. PLAN Landing Ships by Assignment and Total Lift Capacity

	Northern Theater Navy	Southern Theater Navy	Eastern Theater Navy	Hong Kong Garrison	Assignment Unknown	Total
Type-071 LPD	0	4	2	0	2	8
Type-072B LST	0	0	6	0	0	6
Type-072A LST	3	5	1	0	0	9
Type-072III LST	0	4	6	0	0	10
Type-072II LST	0	1	3	0	0	4
Type-073A LSM	0	6	4	0	0	10
Type-073III LSM	0	1	0	0	0	1
Type-074A LSM	3	4	3	0	0	10
Type-074 LSM	8	0	0	3	0	11
Type-958 LCAC	0	2	0	0	3	5
Total Capacity	2,960 troops; 66 ZTD-05s	7,190 troops; 276 ZTD-05s	6,300 troops; 252 ZTD-05s	750 troops; 9 ZTD-05s	1,880 troops; 63 ZTD-05s	19,080 troops; 666 ZTD-05s

Key: LCAC: landing craft air cushion; LPD: amphibious transport dock; LSM: landing ship medium; LST: landing ship, tank.

Sources: Various People's Liberation Army and People's Republic of China Web sites and news reports.

Notes: These figures use the ZTD-05 amphibious assault vehicle due to its large size (length: 31 feet; weight: 29 tons) and common assignment to both PLA Navy Marine Corps and PLA Army amphibious units. ZBD-05 amphibious infantry fighting vehicles are similar in size but weigh slightly lighter. Ship capacity has been adjusted as many are listed according to their ability to transport 40-ton main battle tanks, while accounting for well-deck spatial dimensions where possible. Type-958 LCAC, also known as the *Zubr*-class, is included due to its size and likely role in shore-to-shore missions. This craft does not embark on a parent ship, unless carried by a semi-submersible platform. An eighth LPD is included due to progress on the ship as of fall 2020, which could potentially press it into service early. This table also assumes the complete retirement of the Type-079 LSM class. Any inaccuracies in total lift capacity are the author's own. The eighth LPD *Qilianshan* (祁连山) was launched in June 2019. See "After the 8th Type-071 Amphibious Dock Landing Ship Is Launched, Hudong Shipyard Will Fully Build the Type-075 Amphibious Assault Ship" [第8艘071登陆舰下水后 沪东船厂将全力建造075两栖舰], *Sina Military* [新浪军事], June 11, 2019, available at <https://mil.news.sina.com.cn/jssd/2019-06-11/doc-ihvhiews8037051.shtml>.

Table 2. Landing Ship Capacity

	Capacity
Type-075 LHA	1,200 troops, potentially 50–60 ZTD-05s, 30 helicopters, 3 Type-726 LCACs
Type-071 LPD	730 troops, 24 ZTD-05s, 2–4 helicopters, up to 4 Type-726 LCACs
Type-072B LST	260 troops, 10 ZTD-05s, 1 helipad
Type-072A LST	250 troops, 10 ZTD-05s, 1 helipad
Type-072III LST	250 troops, 10 ZTD-05s, 1 helipad
Type-072II LST	200 troops, 10–11 ZTD-05s
Type-073A LSM	180 troops, 8–10 ZTD-05s
Type-073III LSM	180 troops, 6–7 ZTD-05s
Type-074A LSM	70 troops, 4 ZTD-05s
Type-074 LSM	250 troops or 2–3 ZTD-05s
Type-958 LCAC	360 troops or 3 main battle tanks
Type-271IIIA	200 troops or 3 main battle tanks
Type-271III	200 troops or 3 main battle tanks
Type-271II	200 troops or 2 main battle tanks

Key: LCAC: landing craft air cushion; LHA: landing helicopter assault; LPD: amphibious transport dock; LSM: landing ship medium; LST: landing ship, tank.

Sources: Xuan Ya [悬崖], "Discussion on China's Landing Ships" [漫谈中国登陆舰艇], *Ordnance Knowledge* [兵器知识], No. 5 (2016), 18; Wu Ge [吴戈] and Che Fude [车福德], "The Type-071 Amphibious Dock Landing Ship is Far from Enough" [071型两栖船坞登陆舰是远远不够的], *Modern Ships* [现代舰船], No. 9A, (2013), 11. The numbers used in this assessment are based on a Republic of China Ministry of National Defense report. See Jian Yijian [簡一建], "Research and Analysis of the Development of the Communist Army's 'Amphibious Combat Capabilities'" [共軍"兩棲作戰能力" 發展之研析], *Army Academic Bimonthly* [陸軍學術雙月刊], December 2017, 58. For Type-075: "Type-075 Amphibious Assault Ship" [075型两栖攻击舰], *Shipborne Weapons* [舰载武器], March 2020, 15. The Type-075 is frequently compared to the U.S. Navy's *Wasp*-class LHDs, which can carry up to 61 amphibious assault vehicles (AAVs): 40 stowed in the well deck and 21 in the upper vehicle storage area. While the total vehicle stowage area is unavailable, the AAV occupies slightly less space than the Type-05, which could impact total vehicle stowage. See "LHD-1 Wasp Class," Federation of American Scientists Military Analysis Network, May 9, 2000, available at <https://fas.org/man/dod-101/sys/ship/lhd-1.htm>. See also Chen Yize [陈弋泽], "The Historic Mission of a Domestically-Built Amphibious Assault Ship" [国产两栖攻击舰的历史使命], *Modern Ships* [现代舰船], No. 24 (2019), 30. For Type-071: *The PLA Navy—New Capabilities and Missions for the 21ˢᵗ Century* (Suitland, MD: Office of Naval Intelligence, 2015), 18; Liao Zhiyong [廖志勇] and Chen Ran [陈冉], "Move When You Hear the Order, Move Like the Wind: A Marine Corps Brigade War Vehicle Spits the Waves [闻令而

动, 动若风发: 海军陆战队某旅-战车劈开万重浪], *People's Navy* [人民海军], January 9, 2018, 2.
Type-072B: Xuan, "Discussion on China's Landing Ships," 17; Dennis J. Blasko, "The PLA Navy's Yin
and Yang: China's Advancing Amphibious Force and Missile Craft," in *China's Evolving Surface Fleet*,
China Maritime Studies Institute Report No. 14, ed. Peter A. Dutton and Ryan D. Martinson (Newport,
RI: U.S. Naval War College, 2017), 6. For Type-072A, Type-072III, and Type-072II, Type-073A, Type-
073III, Type-074A, and Type-074: Jian, "Research and Analysis of the Development of the Communist
Army's 'Amphibious Combat Capabilities,'" 58–61; Blasko, "The PLA Navy's Yin and Yang," 6. For
Type-958: "The PLAN Bison Hovercraft Is Defective and Cannot Be Used During the Day" [中国海军
野牛气垫船有缺陷1年有上白天不能全速使用], *Sina Military* [新浪军事], May 15, 2019, available
at <https://mil.news.sina.com.cn/jssd/2019-05-15/doc-ihvhiqax8857206.shtml>. For Type-271II, Type-
271III, and Type-271IIIA: "Graphics: 271-Series Landing Craft (*Yulian* class)" [图文资料: 271系列登陆
艇 (玉连级)], *News.ifeng.com* [凤凰资讯], January 31, 2008, available at <http://news.ifeng.com/mil/
special/planland/doc/200801/0131_2720_386505.shtml>; Zhao Xing [赵星], "A Half Century's Journey:
A Record of the Development of PLAN Amphibious Ships" [半个世纪的征程: 记中国海军两栖舰艇
的发展], *Shipborne Weapons* [舰载武器], No. 5 (2006), 11–12.

Notes: Chinese estimates of the capacity of landing ships can sometimes be exaggerated. For
example, one analyst states that the six Type-072B LSTs in the Eastern Theater Navy can satisfy the
transport requirements of a PLAA brigade at one reinforced battalion of troops and equipment per
ship. This is unlikely even with the stowing of vehicles on the top decks of some LSTs. Other analysts
claim that the Type-071 LPD has a capacity between 500 and 800 troops and 24-35 ZBD-05 vehicles, the
equivalent of a PLAN Marine Corps battalion. This could be true depending on the operation. A leaner
complement of amphibious forces would be embarked in missions to distant areas due to sustainment
and berthing limitations. However, in a cross-strait landing mission, larger numbers of troops can be
loaded since ships would not be required to provide extensive support for the short trip.

Secondary PLA amphibious landing capability would come from the
PLAA coastal defense force's watercraft units [*chuanting budui*, 船艇部队].
Recently placed under the PLAA and reorganized into brigade-level units,
coastal defense brigades [*haifang lü*, 海防旅] reportedly contain a total of 10
watercraft *dadui*.[9] Each *dadui* has several landing craft assigned to subordi-
nate *zhongdui* [中队], made up primarily of older Type-271II, Type-271III, and
Type-271IIIA landing craft.[10] These more numerous but smaller displacement
craft played a notable role during the major amphibious exercises held in the
Taiwan Strait during the 1995–1996 crisis and remain an essential resource for
PLAA amphibious training and operations.[11] Each Type-271 can carry up to 5
ZTD-05 assault vehicles or 200 combat troops.[12] Estimates of this fleet range
from 80 Type-271 series up to 200 ships when counting older classes of vessels still potentially in the force.[13] Although estimating the total forces that
PLAA watercraft units could transport is difficult, they are widely considered
a sizable supplement to the PLAN's amphibious fleet. While older, smaller,
and slower than PLAN landing ships, they do have the range to reach landing

zones if weather conditions are not too severe. That said, watercraft units must modernize to provide more reliable cross-strait lift options to the PLA.

As part of the larger PLA reforms, the PLAA watercraft units are undergoing a shift to better support a "projection-type army" [*tousongxing lujun*, 投送型陆军]. This revised focus is intended to enhance watercraft units' ability to work jointly with the PLAN, expand operations in the "near seas," and improve support for a cross-sea landing.[14] To meet these requirements, the PLAA appears to be developing new landing craft to replace its aging fleet of Type-271s. A new landing craft developed by the PLAA, revealed in late 2015, displaces less than 500 tons, though it is unclear if larger scale production has commenced or whether the landing craft is intended as a replacement platform.[15]

In a significant development, experts from the PLAA's Military Transportation University sought to identify and evaluate decommissioned PLAN ships for reassignment to the PLAA's coastal defense watercraft force. These experts state that this effort would rapidly fill the gap in current transportation capacity while the PLAA develops new classes of watercraft vessels. They identify 5,000-ton class LSTs and 2,000-ton class LSMs built between 1960 and 1980 as a considerable resource to utilize while addressing challenges in balancing suitability, technical issues, costs, and infrastructure. They note that the PLAN's strict equipment management practices have left many vessels in good working condition with many years of service remaining. Furthermore, these decommissioned ships should be deployed with the watercraft units of the Eastern and Southern theater commands and become a main force in large-scale maritime transport of operational forces.[16] Although many hurdles must likely be overcome to bring numerous mothballed PLAN landing ships back into service, this plan does raise the possibility of a short-term surge in lift capacity.

Growth in the PLAN amphibious fleet has mainly been concentrated in large blue water platforms such as LPDs and landing helicopter dock (LHD) amphibious assault ships, with relatively little change in more traditional amphibious platforms such as LSMs and LSTs.[17] The PLAN's eighth LPD was launched in June 2019 and close to commissioning in mid-2021; its first Type-075 LHD was launched in September 2019, followed by a second and third hull in April 2020 and February 2021, respectively.[18] The Type-075 is unlikely be fully operational for some time. With the first hull commissioned in April 2021, the Type-075 LHD class would add modest capacity for a Taiwan invasion, but its real strength lies in its aerial delivery capabilities.[19] Each ship has a capacity of about 1,200 troops, 30 helicopters, and a large number of vehicles.[20] One Chinese observer argues that the Type-075 could put an entire PLANMC infantry battalion ashore in a single trip if equipped with up to 20 Z-18 transport helicopters.[21] This arrangement may not be possible if the goal is also to bring light vehicles and other equipment to bolster maneuverability and firepower. Rapid vertical envelopment operations by the PLANMC's new "air assault battalions" [*kongzhong tuji ying*, 空中突击营] from dozens of miles off Taiwan's coast would add a useful, but relatively limited near-term capability for the amphibious assault.[22] Together, the Type-071 and Type-075 platforms would eventually provide large-scale multidimensional landing capabilities, but the Taiwan Strait presents a constrained battlespace that may reward volume over range.

First-wave amphibious assault units would depend mainly on PLAN and PLAA landing ships to get to their landing zones. Protected by screens and supported by naval gunfire, numerous swimming vehicles and assault craft would depart their ships and head toward Taiwan's beaches. Once ashore, they would get to work on establishing and expanding beachheads in their respective landing sectors. Large numbers of PLAA ground combat forces would likely be near staging areas or already embarked in numerous transport ships in offshore areas to prevent clutter in the amphibious area of operations. These follow-on forces would most likely contain main battle tanks, artillery systems, and other heavy equipment that could not join the amphibious assault waves. To be sure, several variables could determine the effectiveness of the joint island landing campaign (for a description, see Michael Casey's chapter in this volume). For example, air defense of amphibious task forces provided by land-based aircraft or by PLAN surface ships would have to be robust. Although beyond the scope of this chapter, this concern is present in PLAN writings.[23] The next section addresses China's merchant fleet and outcomes when the PLA does and does not secure a usable port.

Civilian Merchant Fleets

Given likely attrition during a landing, PLAN and PLAA landing ships are currently insufficient to deliver successive assault waves. Absent dedicated PLA or government-owned squadrons of merchant ships such as those operated by the U.S. Military Sealift Command, the ship-to-shore movement of the entire assault force and follow-on echelons must continue using ships drawn from the civilian merchant fleet. This section first discusses the interaction of merchant shipping with the PLA before exploring two scenarios: first, when the PLA can secure and use a port, and second, when it must offload troops across Taiwan's beaches. It then considers new shipboard ramp technologies that may enable a unique amphibious role for some types of merchant shipping.

Merchant Fleet–PLA Integration

As of 2019, China ranked third in ownership, by tonnage, of the world's fleet. This includes 3,987 PRC-flagged ships of 1,000 tons or greater, totaling 90,930,376 deadweight tons. These figures more than double when PRC-owned but foreign-flagged ships are counted.[24] When PRC-flagged seagoing ships over 100 tons, excluding inland waterway and fishing ships, are considered, this number rises to 6,197 total ships—including 1,515 bulk carriers, 862 general cargo ships, 322 container ships, and 2,530 other types of ships.[25] Furthermore, China has the most registered mariners in the world; at the end of 2017, the total was 1,483,247 personnel, with 52.2 percent working in inland waters and the rest in coastal and international routes.[26] In 2018, the licensed merchant marine reached 363,281 personnel, including 34,652 captains, 24,152 first mates, and 32,192 chief engineers.[27] Although most of China's merchant fleets have little experience working with the military, some are involved in supporting PLA transport requirements.

The PRC government has the legal authority to assume control over civilian shipping carriers and make them available for military purposes. This power stems from several laws and regulations governing mobilization of civil transport, including the 1995 Regulation on National Defense Transportation, the 2003 Regulations on National Defense Mobilization of Civil Transport Resources, the 2010 National Defense Mobilization Law, and, most recently, the 2016 National Defense Transportation Law. These rules allowed for the creation of National Defense Transportation Support Forces [*guofang jiaotong baozhang duiwu*, 国防交通保障队伍] in civilian transportation enterprises that would carry out a range of supporting functions, including transportation support.[28] The 2016 law expanded what was largely a domestic-focused transportation support force, obligating medium and large transport companies operating overseas to support PLA operations. It also established new "strategic projection support forces" [*zhanlüe tousong zhi-yuan liliang*, 战略投送支援力量] focused on providing "rapid, long-distance, and large-scale national defense transportation support."[29] Although the exact numbers of organized units are difficult to assess, these forces represent a vast resource pool of domestic and long-range transportation support forces for a cross-strait landing.

Incorporation of defense requirements into merchant shipping construction and training would greatly amplify their use in cross-strait transport. Ship registries and capacity are reported to the military, while governments support the implementation of defense requirements by ship operators and in shipbuilding.[30] The approval of Technical Standards for New Civilian Ships to Implement National Defense Requirements provides significant guidance for ensuring that newly built ships are technically ready for military service, reducing the time needed for modification.[31] Nevertheless, obstacles such as cost and burdensome oversight appear to have kept many current ships from implementing these requirements. In 2017, a deputy commander of the Northern Theater Command Army explained that fewer than 2,000 transport vessels are suited for "direct mobilization."[32]

Organizing transport units and providing relevant training could empower civilian shipping to better coordinate with the military. Starting in 2012, the PLA began establishing "strategic projection support ship fleets" in major shipping companies. These units included roll-on/roll-off (RO-RO) ships, container vessels, bulk carriers, tankers, auxiliary crane ships, barges, and semi-submersible ships.[33] These civilian support fleets are organized into transport *zongdui*, *dadui*, and *zhongdui* [*haiyun zongdui/dadui/zhongdui*, 海运总队/大队/中队] for unit, fuel, and cargo transport.[34] Organization into transport units will help ready vessels and their crews for future tasking.

Maintaining operationally ready transportation support forces that could coordinate with the PLAN also requires effective training. In 2015, the National Transportation War Readiness Office released the first formal "Outline for Training and Evaluation of National Defense Transportation Specialized Support Forces" to guide and standardize instruction of the strategic projection support ships and other national defense transportation support units.[35]

Training is conducted at each of the strategic projection support fleet's three levels. *Zongdui* establish annual training plans for the *dadui* to implement, while coordinating shipping activities with support for PLA unit–training activities. Exercises include formation maneuvers, command and control, communications, and lifesaving with PLAN ships.[36]

Yet problems in the implementation of training exist. Local Transportation War Readiness offices monitor only training, leaving regular planning and implementation up to the enterprises themselves.[37] This arrangement has resulted in mixed outcomes for crew instruction. One 2017 PLA study, for instance, found that many enterprises neglected training implementation.[38] That said, some units have performed well, actively training with the PLA on numerous occasions.[39] Even limited training and PLA involvement in vessel operations could be enough for effective transportation support.

Offloading from Merchant Ships: Two Scenarios

With enemy forces approaching, Taiwan defenders would likely attempt to render their own ports inoperable through demolition or channel obstruction. Repairing these port terminals would require significant manpower and materials and would take far too long.[40] The next two sections focus on when Taiwan fails to prevent the PLA from accessing its ports and when it succeeds in forcing alternative means of debarking forces.

Port Secured. China's extensive merchant shipping capacity could be utilized only if those ships could effectively offload troops and equipment. This capability would depend heavily on operable port terminals in Taiwan and unobstructed channels. Early PLA amphibious operations would thus prioritize the capture of a port and airfield, while clearance teams and repair units would rush to bring damaged and degraded ports back online. This section examines the role of RO-RO ships, which are widely recognized by the PLA as essential to the transport of follow-on forces in a cross-strait landing.[41]

The first ships in port would urgently unload combat reinforcements and critical munitions for ground operations on Taiwan. With the proper requirements or modifications, fast RO-RO ships are a key enabler for this mission, capable of rapidly transporting PLAA Group Army motorized and mechanized units that can offload under their own power. This transport mode also allows units to quickly organize for combat after completing transit and debarkation operations. According to PLA experts, 63 civilian RO-RO ships are currently suitable for use by military units, totaling 140,000 deadweight tons.[42] It is unknown if all these ships have the necessary modifications for carrying heavy equipment, such as high-strength ramps and deck structures. If so, the RO-RO fleet could carry a significant number of units, including heavy combat forces sorely needed to reinforce the lightly armored amphibious forces.

The following list identifies companies with "transport *dadui*" operating large RO-RO ships; the number of ships in each company is also given. However, it is unclear how many of these ships are part of the strategic projection support ship fleet.

- Fifth Transport *Dadui* [海运五大队], CSC RORO Logistics Co., Ltd. [深圳长航滚装物流有限公司]: 25 car carriers of varying sizes[43]

- Eighth Transport *Dadui* [海运八大队], Bohai Ferry Group [渤海轮渡股份有限公司]: 17 RO-RO ferries (20,000- to 45,000-ton ships)

- Ninth Transport *Dadui* [海运九大队], Hainan Strait Shipping Co., Ltd. [海南海峡航运股份有限公司]: 18 RO-RO ferries (6,000- to 11,000-ton ships)[44]

- Unidentified Transport *Dadui*, Zhoushan Strait Ferry Group Co., Ltd. [舟山海峡轮渡集团有限公司]: 45 various types of small to medium coastal ferries (passenger, high-speed passenger, passenger-vehicle, cargo, hazardous materials, etc.).[45]

The Bohai Ferry Group merits close examination. This company runs quick routes daily from ports in Shandong Province to Dalian and Lüshun in Liaoning Province, as well as some regional international routes. Over the years, the PLA has repeatedly recognized company leadership for its commitment to constructing ships that implement national defense requirements. The company invested a considerable sum of money on 7 large RO-RO ships with modifications and reinforced deck structures for PLA transport and regularly participates in large-scale military exercises and maritime transportation support, completing more than 40 transport missions for the PLA to date. This cooperation has proved so successful that the former PLA Logistics Academy named the company a professional education training base for personnel majoring in military transportation.[46]

Overall, the company operates 17 large RO-RO ships, displacing 460,000 tons.[47] The company began implementing national defense requirements when the former Jinan Military Region Military Transportation Department joined in the design process for the *Bohai Cuizhu* [渤海翠珠] in 2010. This 35,000-ton RO-RO ship would be the company's first to include various designs for PLA support, such as improved communications and command systems, stronger ramps, space reserved for medical facilities, and a helipad. Its maiden voyage was marked with a PLA embarkation exercise of armored vehicles, artillery pieces, and transport trucks.[48]

These requirements were implemented in the company's following ships, including three additional 35,000-ton models.[49] In September 2020, an improved 45,000-ton class RO-RO passenger ship, *Zhonghua Fuxing* [中华复兴], entered operation, with three more of this class planned.[50] The company also launched two new multipurpose 25,000-ton RO-RO ships in October 2020. These new classes feature improvements such as quarter-stern ramps in addition to their straight stern and bow ramps, which enable more flexible options for loading and unloading at terminals not configured for RO-RO.[51] It is also likely that several of the 20,000-ton-class ships built prior to 2012 would also be available to provide rapid terminal-to-terminal transport support, either as part of the strategic projection support fleet or through requisitioning mechanisms. Chinese media hails a 20,000-ton car carrier built to national defense specifications for a separate company, CSC RORO Logistics Co., Ltd., as another model example. This ship is reportedly able to transport two mechanized infantry battalions and contains additional supporting spaces for forces embarked for longer durations.[52] Assuming similar capabilities in Bohai Ferry Group's seven ferries built after the *Bohai Cuizhu*, some of which are significantly larger, this company alone could easily transport entire brigades.

Securing a port would not directly allow many of these RO-RO ships to debark their forces. Many Chinese RO-RO ships use straight stern and bow ramps to load and unload at terminals equipped with approach walls, breasting dolphins, and adjustable shore ramps to match the height of the ships' freight decks and ramps. Such terminals can be found in Yantai, Dalian, and Haikou. At conventional quay wall terminals, the RO-RO ships would have to execute a Mediterranean mooring in unfamiliar harbors, a challenging maneuver complicated by currents and wind. Before the delivery of a large, brand-new

RO-RO terminal nearby, the Hainan Strait Shipping Company's ferries used this method of mooring regularly in their operations at Hai'an Port. These ferries typically drop a stern anchor and land on sloped steps of varying heights along the quay wall.[53] However, a variety of tugboats and pushing craft would likely be available to assist due to the importance of their cargoes in a cross-strait operation. Additionally, the Bohai Ferry Group has conducted this form of mooring at conventional docks with its 35,000-ton-class ships to comply with military requirements.[54] One advantage of this procedure is that it occupies less quay frontage, allowing multiple RO-RO ships to debark simultaneously. Should a terminal be partially damaged, only several meters would be needed to accommodate ship ramps and an unobstructed approach.[55]

More challenging than executing a Mediterranean mooring in Taiwan would be uncontrollable variables at debarkation sites. Apart from currents and wind, accounting for vessel freight deck height relative to the vertical height of the dock surface at varying tidal states would determine the window of time for these ships to successfully unload cargo. If the slope of ramps is too extreme at low or high tide, many vehicles could have trouble debarking. Tracked and wheeled armored vehicles may be more flexible, and military trucks often have high undercarriage clearance to prevent bottoming out. Dealing with the variable slope of ramps and measures to ensure smooth unloading could slow down operations. Lightening these vessels during unloading could also influence the operation of ramps. The task becomes even more complex when factoring in the varying sizes and ramp configurations of the RO-RO fleet. PLA transportation experts who have carefully examined these operations recognize that RO-RO unloading operations would have to be carefully timed and have thus constructed models to predict dockside operational windows.[56] Should a port terminal become secure enough to enable RO-RO operations, planners could use the destination terminal's quay wall height and available tidal data to predict the volume of reinforcements and cargo that could be delivered in a given time.

To mitigate these problems, the PLA has highlighted embark-debark operations at conventional docks in recent exercises. Though there is a focus on supporting the transport of combined arms maneuver units, other services are also prepared for RO-RO transport. For example, the PLA Air Force transported air defense units in 2014 by embarking them at general cargo terminals and debarking at container terminals.[57] Open sources indicate several

PLA Air Force exercises utilizing RO-RO ships for long-distance transport in recent years.[58] Gaining proficiency in moving units onto RO-RO ships may be a decisive factor influencing the speed and volume at which the PLA could use these ships to reinforce combat units already ashore. Additionally, PLA military transportation personnel may be directly involved in training RO-RO crews or supervising operations on board vessels.[59] The extent of this direct involvement in large-scale operations, however, is unclear.

PLA scholars recognize that logistic fixed targets and transportation forces, even at their embarkation sites, would be under pressure from enemy attacks.[60] RO-RO ships may afford some cover for the massing of force by allowing PLA forces to embark at ports far away from the expected crossing. Changes to the regular ferry services of the Bohai Ferry Group or Hainan Strait Shipping Company could potentially serve as an early-warning indicator. At the same time, covert preparations would leave little room for preinvasion rehearsals on any significant scale, as doing so would alert adversaries.

Over the Beaches. Without an operating terminal, the PLA would struggle to get its forces ashore quickly and in large numbers, placing the entire invasion in jeopardy. This challenge requires the PLA to bring the temporary infrastructure needed to facilitate the offloading and marshaling of follow-on forces. Once a landing area is secured, PLA sources would advise that a landing base [*denglu jidi*, 登陆基地] be established that includes piers, medical stations, depots, and repair sites. Apart from command, logistics, and equipment elements, debarkation components would be set up to assemble the lightering and transfer equipment, clear obstacles, prepare beach areas for vehicle movement, and coordinate joint forces going ashore. According to one estimate, afloat offloading systems would begin assembling at sea 2 hours after forces capture the beach. Shore-based landing bases would begin assembly no later than 6 hours after.[61] Also, landing bases would establish helicopter landing zones for vertical lift movement.[62]

PLA experts note that artificial harbors like those used during the Normandy landings during World War II would be a critical requirement for a large-scale landing operation. Despite the changes in amphibious warfare toward sea and air integrated landing operations, these scholars argue that artificial harbors would play a key role throughout an entire campaign.[63] According to PLAN experts, the scale of the battlespace, highly transparent operations, and the threat of long-range precision strikes present major challenges for support operations at degraded conventional ports. Many PLA texts urge the development of modern artificial port systems that utilize floating wave attenuators, modular mobile berthing and transfer platforms, transfer platforms for RO-RO ships, assembled trestle wharves, floating causeway systems for crossing tidal mudflats, amphibious materials transfer platforms, and mat systems for moving vehicles across beaches.[64] Extensive floating systems would solve the problem of unloading operations with RO-RO and other ship types, as both ship and platform would ride the tides.

For close to 20 years, the PLA has developed and experimented with equipment for offloading personnel and supplies without access to port facilities; however, experts note that obstacles remain for RO-RO ship operations, offshore lightering, amphibious unloading, container handling in coastal areas and at sea, and general low efficiency across many systems.[65] For instance, much of the PLA's current "pier-less" unloading equipment is in prototype, not in production. These experts argue for limited allocation of core equipment for training exercises and a concurrent investment in the storage and maintenance of such equipment.[66]

Nevertheless, China has demonstrated the engineering capacity to build and deploy artificial harbor and landing bases. Its major construction and engineering companies regularly generate news reports around the world with the scale of their projects, whether large-scale artificial land reclamation and construction in the Spratly Islands or massive port infrastructure projects overseas. The PLA would seek to leverage these companies to achieve large-scale offshore debarkation. These activities include bringing along numerous commercial platforms, such as deck barges onto which cargo ships would offload, semi-submersible barges, floating storage equipment, and even mobile harbor platforms used in the fishing industry.[67] Two PLAN engineers discussing pier-less unloading noted that some platforms are currently introducing offshore platform leg stabilization and suction anchor technologies used in commercial industries to enhance wind and wave resistance of debarkation structures.[68] Stronger mooring systems could help prevent damage from severe weather conditions, such as when the U.S. artificial harbor Mulberry "A" was destroyed by an unforeseen storm during the Normandy landings.[69] Nonetheless, these structures would need to span from deep water to the surf zones and across exposed areas at low tide—putting them under significant stress. One 2010 Chinese source stated that most of the PLA's existing platforms for heavy equipment can operate in sea state three (1.6- to 4-foot swells) and survive in sea states four to five (8- to 13-foot swells).[70]

The PLA is also developing civilian semi-submersible ships to support amphibious and transfer operations when conventional facilities are unavailable. Part of the strategic projection support fleet, these ships could carry amphibious forces and various landing craft or serve as a transfer platform from larger cargo or RO-RO ships with the requisite modifications for transfer operations.[71] This ability provides additional offshore capacity to support the amphibious assault. Some of these vessels are built as dual civilian and military use platforms, fulfilling intermediate support roles such as fueling and rearming platforms for helicopter operations. Such tasks were publicized in an August 2020 Eastern Theater Command exercise involving the 40,000-ton *Zhenhua*-28 and an aviation brigade of the 71st Group Army.[72] These operations require the civilian vessel to have munitions storage compartments, fueling containers, hose connections, and other features to support multiple types of helicopters.[73]

Semi-submersible ships could also greatly enhance the construction of landing bases. Many ships have large open decks and could deliver the key components for afloat mobile port equipment, including mobile loading equipment, barges, pontoon wharves, ramp systems, and other equipment used in the debarkation and transfer process.[74] Crane barges, deck barges, mooring systems, concrete structures, and various other equipment could also be delivered into offshore positions. These systems could be floated off once in position and, if capable, assembled under their own power or by tugs and other pushing craft to help form artificial harbors and causeways to reach the beaches.

Significant amounts of equipment could be delivered through the semi-submersible fleet. The PLAN's only semi-submersible ship, the mobile landing platform *Donghaidao* delivered in July 2015, displaces 20,000 tons.[75] However, the largest vessels are found in the commercial sector. Of the 34 large open-deck commercial semi-submersible ships built globally over the past 25 years, 27 are owned by Chinese companies.[76] An unknown number have already joined the strategic projection support ship fleet and could be readily mobilized and modified for PLA use.[77] These large vessels, many with

dynamic positioning systems, could prove valuable in fleet operational maneuvers during a cross-strait landing.

COSCO Shipping Specialized Carriers Company, Ltd., operates eight
vessels, the largest of which was launched in 2016 and is capable of carrying 98,000 metric tons.[78] Shanghai Zhenhua Heavy Industries Company, Ltd.,
has seven vessels with capacities from over 30,000 to 50,000 tons.[79] Its latest
semi-submersible, the *Zhenhua*-33, is a 50,000-ton civil-military dual-use
ship launched in 2016 and built with oversight by the PLAN and the Wuxi
Joint Logistic Support Center.[80] The *Zhenhua*-33's main deck covers 7,700
square meters.[81] It was publicly shown sporting four designated helicopter
landing pads and marked areas for fuel and ammunition support. This large
deck could also transport numerous landing craft or dozens of amphibious
vehicles pre-staged for launch.[82] The ship would need to simply submerge its
stern to allow vehicles to easily drive off into the sea. Several of these ships
could provide a significant boost for the PLAN's amphibious fleet.

Augmenting Ship-to-Shore Movement

China's RO-RO vessels also have a potential role in directly supporting the
ship-to-shore movement of landing forces. In 2016, PLA reports described
a RO-RO ferry equipped with ramps that could launch amphibious armor.[83]
This new ramp system was demonstrated during PLANMC exercises in July
2020 with a 15,560-ton RO-RO ferry owned and operated by COSCO Shipping
Ferry Co., Ltd.[84] During the drill, Type-05 armor embarked aboard the RO-RO
ship at the Southern Theater Navy 6th Landing Ship *Zhidui* facility and were
launched from its modified stern ramp offshore at the amphibious training
area. The new ramp system was directly driven by large hydraulic rams and
support arms connecting the top of the freight deck to mounting assemblies
installed on an elongated stern ramp. Additional hydraulic rams on the back-
side of the ramp connecting to the ramp flap may also articulate further to
assist vehicle recovery.[85] The system keeps the ramp rigid while deployed into
the water, whereas normal ramps with preventer stays could be snapped off
by the dynamic stress caused by currents.

Given the number of RO-RO ships available and their carrying capacity,
this new capability, when combined with PLAN landing ships, could significantly increase estimates of China's total amphibious lift capacity. Surging

construction of the PLA's landing ships would logically precede a preinvasion buildup, taking months or years of preparation and remaining easily visible to overhead imagery or ship spotters. However, this ramp system may allow the PLA a faster and cheaper means of surging amphibious lift, raising the question of how early such ramp conversions could be detected. Large RO-RO ships also allow units to load well ahead of a planned invasion, supporting personnel with shipboard amenities normally enjoyed by the public. They could load during optimal periods, such as on low-visibility nights with cloud cover, easing pressure on assembly and embarkation timelines.

The CCG and Maritime Militia

A cross-strait invasion would also involve the China Coast Guard and maritime militia forces, both of which are the world's largest.[86] These paramilitary forces would be available to PLA commanders during wartime and represent significant volume in the number of ships China could generate during a cross-strait landing.

The CCG operates a fleet of more than 130 ships larger than 1,000 tons, including 2 cutters displacing 12,000 tons—by far a larger force than that of any other coast guard.[87] Using these capabilities, the CCG would mobilize to provide a variety of support functions to the joint island landing campaign, including evacuating casualties, replacing PLAN attrition in manpower and possibly some platforms, performing escort duties, potentially engaging in some antisubmarine warfare, and participating in both direct and indirect combat.[88] While the cutter fleet lacks significant organic amphibious capabilities, its sheer size cannot be ignored. With limited armaments, CCG ships are fast and require fewer sensors and exquisite combat systems, likely leaving ample shipboard space to support rapid transits of personnel to and from Taiwan.

The maritime militia constitutes another important supplement to a cross-strait landing.[89] These forces, as a subset of a nationwide militia system, are managed through the provincial military district system. The militias have a deep history supporting PLA landings against Nationalist-held offshore islands in the 1950s. Between April and May 1950, maritime militias from the provinces of Zhejiang, Fujian, Guangdong, and Guangxi contributed more than 16,700 vessels and 48,000 personnel to support the PLA's capture of Hainan Island, the Zhoushan Archipelago, the Wanshan Archipelago, and other coastal islands.[90] Although maritime militia missions have expanded in recent years with the emphasis on maritime rights protection in peacetime, their wartime support functions have not changed. Maritime militia transport units today leverage faster and larger tonnage merchant and fishing fleets as well as modern technologies to enhance support performance and coordination.[91] These upgrades mean that maritime militias in coastal provinces still represent a vast pool of manpower and vessels—and a range of capabilities.

Like the strategic projection support ship fleets, maritime militias train with active-duty forces and are familiar with the types of modifications required to accelerate their activation and readiness. Militias organized for transport support are formed with PLA units in mind, designating vessels based on unit requirements. Larger transport ships are allocated for artillery, air defense, and armored units, and smaller vessels for lighter motorized units. PLA units coordinate their requirements in terms of ships, missions, armaments, modifications, and support with transport units to generate plans, measures, and solutions for problems in delivering these capabilities, which are then submitted to the relevant provincial military and government authorities to resolve. Maritime militia transport units were previously organized based on PLA ship transport units into "militia ship transport regiments" [*minbing chuanyuntuan*, 民兵船运团], with several subordinate "transport *zhongdui*" and "supporting *fendui*."[92] These units comprised a mix of merchant cargo and fishing vessels and conducted training with PLA units for cross-strait transport operations.[93] They have likely been reorganized into "maritime militia transport *dadui*" [*haishang minbing yunshu dadui*, 海上民兵运输大队].[94] For example, the militia transport *dadui* formed in the Nanjing Twin Rivers Shipping Co., Ltd., operates large bulk carriers forming smaller *zhongdui* units.[95]

In a cross-strait landing, maritime militias could be mobilized to provide numerous supporting missions. These include minelaying, reconnaissance, deception, logistics support, and various other functions.[96] For instance, maritime militia units could utilize civilian covers to support a variety of PLA operations. Under the guise of fishing, they could potentially insert special operations forces and PLANMC frogmen to begin the critical mine and obstacle clearance operations for approaching amphibious units. The maritime militia might also carry PLA personnel to conduct coastal and beach reconnaissance ahead of a landing, including the use of unmanned aerial and surface vehicles.[97]

Maritime militia ships may provide additional capacity to transport troops and equipment across the strait. Nationwide, likely thousands of vessels could be mobilized for this mission. Coastal provinces would have at least several dozen units at their disposal, but estimating the number and type of units, as well as their ships, is difficult.[98] Their readiness, capacity, and coordination are also difficult to assess, though PLA texts stress continued efforts at leveraging the maritime militia. One 2004 source, for instance, suggests that some maritime militia transport units would deliver combat troops directly onto beachheads.[99] These units would likely contain smaller draft fishing vessels operating in greater numbers and would probably not be with the first waves. Larger militia transport ships would remain in rear transport anchorage areas, transferring their cargoes to vessels going ashore.

Conclusion

The organic PLAN and PLAA amphibious landing ships most relevant to a cross-strait landing have not increased tremendously but remain a robust core capability. Although challenges remain in assessing these forces, such as quantifying the number of landing craft in the PLAA's watercraft forces and estimating the potential to reactivate decommissioned ships, this chapter has explored the possibility that commercial ships such as RO-RO, semi-submersible, and maritime militia ships could fill some of the gaps in overall sealift. Speed would be crucial, as demonstrated by the development of a robust RO-RO ship-based transport fleet. In his chapter in this volume, Chieh Chung notes the importance of faster and more efficient PLA logistics support, which gives Taiwan less time to transition to a wartime footing and mobilize its forces. His chapter provides extensive detail on an improving logistics and mobilization system throughout China that connects all the critical links in moving PLA forces into operational areas and supporting them. Such work highlights the importance of examining China's progress in the civilian sector in addition to PLA lift capacity. Some activities, such as changes in regular ferry services across the Bohai Gulf or the Qiongzhou Strait, could provide early indicators of mobilization efforts. They deserve close attention. The potential ability of modified RO-RO ships in delivering landing forces using modified ramp systems also raises new concerns on the overall estimate of total landing forces crossing the strait.

Greater use of civilian ships in an island-landing scenario would also require the PLA to overcome technical challenges. For instance, one important problem is the PLA's approach to using numerous PRC-owned foreign flag of convenience ships—and whether the PLA could maintain a registry of these ships and their capabilities. Some experts are confident that these vessels would be called up if needed.[100] How the PLA would organize shipping for large-scale transport is another problem. One study by the Naval Research Institute focuses on vessel requisition planning in large-scale transport operations and seeks to optimize vessel selection and assignment when loading forces at numerous embarkation sites. The authors describe the problem set:

> *National Transportation War Readiness Departments select and config-*
> *ure the various types of mobilized civilian vessels of shipping companies*
> *according to the scale and types of equipment and materials required of*
> *a maritime strategic projection mission. The number of various types of*
> *ships are determined to minimize the transport time and cost to com-*
> *plete a projection mission.*

This study builds a model to simulate various means of disposition that satisfy overall transport volume, time, and cost requirements and is predicated on the PLAN's reliance on a multitude of mobilized civilian ships to increase capacity in current and future operations, including future island-landing operations.[101]

Current PLA amphibious lift capacity leaves little room for error or attrition in a joint island landing campaign. Attrition levels may worsen if Taiwan makes significant progress implementing many of the measures of the Overall Defense Concept (for details, see the chapters by Alexander Chieh-cheng Huang and Drew Thompson in this volume). Losses to the limited PLAN/PLAA amphibious fleet by Taiwan's antiship missiles could prove catastrophic to the entire endeavor, halting the movement of numerous PLA follow-on units onboard civil transports transiting toward the island. That said, the PLA continues to demonstrate careful study and planning of logistics operations to deliver essential follow-on heavy forces with or without an intact port terminal—a factor that could determine how long amphibious and airborne combat units must hold Taiwan's beaches and key areas and the degree of attrition those forces could expect to suffer.

Notes

[1] For a video of this exercise, see "Projecting Real Combat! People's Liberation Army Landing Exercises on the Southeast Coast" [突出实战 解放军在东南沿海登陆演练], CCTV–Asia Today [CCTV今日亚洲], video, 24:18, October 17, 2020, available at <https://www.youtube.com/watch?v=lCDcAg9ItGk>.

[2] Gu Yin [顾因] et al., "Research on Improving Shipping Ability Structure with Decommissioned Vessels" [利用退役舰艇改善船艇部队运力结构研究], *Journal of Military Transportation University* [军事交通学院学报], no. 1 (2018), 19–22.

[3] The terms *zhidui* and *dadui* are often translated as "ship detachment" and "ship group," respectively, but they are not consistently translated in various sources. For accuracy, it is often best to use the original Chinese terms. In this chapter, the terms *zongdui* [总队], *zhidui* [支队], *dadui* [大队], and *zhongdui* [中队] are used from highest to lowest levels of unit organization. For a superior explanation of this translation issue, see Kevin Pollpeter and Kenneth W. Allen, eds., *The PLA as Organization v2.0* (Vienna, VA: Defense Group, Inc., 2015), 50, available at <https://www.airuniversity.af.edu/CASI/Display/Article/1586201/pla-as-organization-20/>.

[4] This chapter's assessment of landing ships differs from the Department of Defense 2020 China Military Power Report's count of 21 landing ships medium and 31 landing ships, tank, in the Northern, Eastern, and Southern theater navies.

[5] New PLA Navy Marine Corps brigades in the Northern Theater Command likely conduct training with landing ships of the Northern Theater Navy. See Pan Ruichen [潘瑞晨] and Li Jinxing [李金星], "Combined Strike" [合同打击], *People's Navy* [人民海军], July 2, 2018, 3.

[6] Dennis J. Blasko, "The PLA Navy's Yin and Yang: China's Advancing Amphibious Force and Missile Craft," in *China's Evolving Surface Fleet*, China Maritime Studies Institute (CMSI) China Maritime Report No. 14, ed. Peter A. Dutton and Ryan D. Martinson (Newport, RI: Naval War College Press, July 2017), 8.

[7] See the chapter by Joshua Arostegui in this volume.

[8] Estimates of PLA Army (PLAA) combined arms brigade personnel range from 5,000 to 6,000 but may vary by brigade type. See Dennis J. Blasko, "The PLA Army After 'Below the Neck' Reforms: Contributing to China's Joint Warfighting, Deterrence and MOOTW Posture," *Journal of Strategic Studies* 44, no. 2 (December 2019), 164–165.

[9] Coastal defense units were previously the responsibility of the provincial military district system. Recent reforms have consolidated many coastal defense regiments into brigades. It is unclear how this consolidation has affected the watercraft units. See "Coastal Defense, Reserve, and Experimental Troops Transferred to the Army to Aid Ground Force Transformation" [海防、预备役及实验部队转隶陆军 助推陆军转型], *The Observer* [观察者网], May 17, 2017, available at <https://www.guancha.cn/military-affairs/2017_05_17_408788.shtml>.

[10] Blasko, "The PLA Navy's Yin and Yang," 8.

[11] Despite their age, these craft are still valued for their versatility in PLAA coastal operations. See "The Eastern Theater Command Army Coastal Defense Brigade Ship *Dadui* Recently Conducted Maritime Landing Training with the Army" [东部战区陆军海防旅船艇大队近日联合陆军开展了海上登陆训练], *The Observer* [观察者网], August 18, 2018, available at <https://www.guancha.cn/military-affairs/2018_08_18_468639.shtml?s=zwyxgtjbt>.

[12] "Graphics: 271-Series Landing Craft (*Yulian* class)" [图文资料: 271系列登陆艇 (玉连级)], *Ifeng.com* [凤凰资讯], January 31, 2008, available at <http://news.ifeng.com/mil/special/planland/doc/200801/0131_2720_386505.shtml>.

[13] Rick Joe, "The Future of China's Amphibious Assault Fleet," *The Diplomat*, July 17, 2019, available at <https://thediplomat.com/2019/07/the-future-of-chinas-amphibious-assault-fleet/>; Blasko, "The PLA Navy's Yin and Yang," 8.

[14] Other new missions include greater support to forces garrisoned on coastal islands, protection of underwater cables, patrols in the near seas, and reconnaissance and security functions at sea. See Chen Zhengfei [陈正飞] et al., "Crises and Opportunity in Construction of Frontier and Coastal Defense Watercraft Forces in New Period" [新时期边海防船艇部队建设的危与机], *Journal of Military Transportation University* [军事交通学院学报], no. 9 (2019), 39–40.

[15] "High Resolution: Army Special-Use Through Deck Landing Ship Unveiled" [高清: 陆军专用直通甲板登陆舰亮相], *Global Times* [环球网], November 11, 2015, available at <http://military.people.com.cn/n/2015/1111/c1011-27803829.html>; Xuan Ya [悬崖], "Discussion on China's Landing Ships" [漫谈中国登陆舰艇], *Ordnance Knowledge* [兵器知识], no. 5 (2016), 18.

[16] Gu et al., "Improving Shipping Ability Structure with Decommissioned Vessels," 19–22.

[17] *Annual Report to Congress: Military and Security Developments Involving the People's Republic of China 2020* (Washington, DC: Office of the Secretary of Defense, 2020), 117.

[18] Wang Shichun [王世纯], "Third 075 Launched and May Have Sea Trial Within the Year" [075三号舰下水 或于年内试航], *The Observer* [观察者网], January 29, 2021, available at <https://cj.sina.com.cn/articles/view/1887344341/707e96d5020010r39>.

[19] Xavier Vavasseur, "China Commissions a Type-055 DDG, a Type-075 LHD and a Type-094 SSBN in a Single Day," *Naval News*, April 24, 2021, available at <https://www.navalnews.com/naval-news/2021/04/china-commissions-a-type-055-ddg-a-type-075-lhd-and-a-type-094-ssbn-in-a-single-day/>.

[20] "Type-075 Amphibious Assault Ship" [075型两栖攻击舰], *Shipborne Weapons* [舰载武器], March 2020, 15.

[21] Ibid., 19.

[22] Niu Tao [牛涛] and Fan Xudong [范旭东], "A Certain Marine Corps Brigade Improves the Quality and Effectiveness of Training and Preparation: Heng Ge Will Soon Write a New Chapter" [海军陆战队某旅提升练兵备战质效: 横戈马上再写新篇], *People's Navy* [人民海军], July 24, 2018, 3.

[23] For an example from the 4th Landing Ship *Dadui* in Haikou, see Yin Fengmin [尹凤敏], "Interaction Analysis About Air-Defense Firepower's Conjunction Use in the Amphibious Ship Formation" [两栖作战编队防空火力协同的交互性分析], *Ship Electronic Engineering* [舰船电子工程] 30, no. 9 (2010), 45.

[24] These figures comprise vessels more than 1,000 tons. When compared, the United States has 822 national flag vessels totaling 9.5 million in deadweight tonnage. Refer to table 2.6 in United Nations Conference on Trade and Development, Geneva, "Review of Maritime Transport 2019," January 31, 2020, 37, available at <https://unctad.org/system/files/official-document/rmt2019_en.pdf>.

[25] United Nations Conference on Trade and Development, "Merchant Fleet by Flag of Registration and by Type of Ship, Annual," available at <https://unctadstat.unctad.org/wds/TableViewer/tableView.aspx?ReportId=93>.

[26] "2017 China Crew Development Report" [2017年中国船员发展报告], Ministry of Transport of the People's Republic of China [中华人民共和国交通运输部新闻办公室], June 2018, 5.

[27] Duan Zunlei [段尊雷], Li Ye [李烨], and Liu Jinjing [刘金晶], "Team-Building Characteristics and Countermeasures of Our Seamen in the New Situation [新形势下中国海员队伍发展的特点与对策], *Maritime Education Research* [航海教育研究], no. 4 (2018), 1–2.

[28] See chapter 6 in *National Defense Transportation Regulations* [国防交通条例], February 24, 1995, available at <https://baike.baidu.com/item/%E5%9B%BD%E9%98%B2%E4%BA%A4%E9%80%9A%E6%9D%A1%E4%BE%8B>; article 2 of *National Defense Mobilization of Civil Transport Resources Regulations* [民用运力国防动员条例], 2003, available at <http://en.pkulaw.cn/display.aspx?cgid=f121bea40b0cb4a6bdfb&lib=law>; chapter 10 of the *National Defense Mobilization Law* [国防动员法], 2010, available at <http://www.gov.cn/flfg/2010-02/26/content_1544415.htm>; the *PRC National Defense Transportation Law* [中华人民共和国国防交通法], September 3, 2016.

[29] See articles 36–38 of the *PRC National Defense Transportation Law*. For more details on the organization and national authorities involved in constructing civil transport forces, see Conor M. Kennedy, *Civil Transport in PLA Power Projection*, CMSI China Maritime Report No. 4 (Newport, RI: Naval War College Press, December 2019), available at <https://digital-commons.usnwc.edu/cmsi-maritime-reports/>.

[30] Article 31, *PRC National Defense Transportation Law*.

[31] These standards covered five categories of vessels, including container, roll-on/roll-off (RO-RO), multipurpose, bulk carriers, and break bulk. See Zhao Lei, "New Rules Mean Ships Can Be Used by Military," *China Daily*, June 18, 2015, available at <http://www.chinadaily.com.cn/china/2015-06/18/content_21036944.htm>; Liu Hang [刘航], "China's 'Technical Standards for New Civilian Ships to Implement National Defense Requirements' Formally Promulgated" [我国 "新造民船贯彻国防要求技术标准" 正式颁布实施], *China Military Online* [中国军网], June 5, 2015.

[32] "Hu Xiubin: 'Four Insufficients' Present in the Construction of China's Maritime Strategic Projection Reserve Forces" [胡修斌: 我国海上战略投送后备力量建设存在 "四个不足"], China National Radio [央广网], March 9, 2017, available at <http://news.cnr.cn/zt2017/2017h/ppzb/lhzkzyt/zkzythxb/zbkx/20170309/t20170309_523647186.shtml>.

[33] Cao Wuge [曹吴戈] and Ye Haolong [叶皓龙], "Merchant Ships Join the Military: Chinese Version of Expeditionary Landing Ship Dock Emerge" [民船参军: 中国版远征船坞登陆舰浮出水面], *Transportation of Guangdong* [广东交通], no. 2 (2017), 17; Liu Gang [刘刚] and Yu Pengcheng [虞鹏程], "Our Reflection on the Quick Organization of Military Sealift Reserve Forces" [关于组建快速动员海运力量的思考], *National Defense Transportation Engineering and Technology* [国防交通工程与技术], no. 3 (2014), 3.

[34] Ibid.

[35] Zhou Jixiao [周济晓] and Zhang Ge [张歌], "National Defense Transportation Specialized Support Forces Now Have Their First Training and Evaluation Outline" [国防交通专业保障队伍有了首部训考大纲], *PLA Daily* [解放军报], February 7, 2015.

[36] He Guoben [何国本] et al., "Current Situation and Countermeasures of Strategic Projection Support Fleet Training" [战略投送支援船队训练现状及对策], *Journal of Military Transportation University* [军事交通学院学报], no. 5 (2017), 2.

[37] Ibid., 2.

[38] Ibid., 1–4.

[39] Several examples can be found in Kennedy, *Civil Transport in PLA Power Projection*.

[40] Jiang Kaihui [蒋凯辉] and Han Shuang [韩爽], "Development in Support Technology for Sea-Shore Handling Heavy Equipment" [重装备岸海转运保障技术与发展], *National Defense Transportation Engineering and Technology* [国防交通工程与技术], no. 1 (2010), 2.

[41] Other ships, such as oilers, cargo, and container carriers, merit attention as the primary movers of PLA war materiel and fuel but are omitted to bring attention to the key capabilities enabling combat units to get to their operational areas.

⁴² Li Peng [李鹏], Sun Hao [孙浩], and Zhao Xiqing [赵喜庆], "Impact of National Strategic Delivery Capability Development on Construction of Combined Arms Forces and Countermeasures" [国家战略投送能力发展对合成部队建设的影响与对策], *Journal of Military Transportation University* [军事交通学院学报], no. 8 (2019), 3.

⁴³ CSC RORO Logistics Co., Ltd. [深圳长航滚装物流有限公司], "Red Research Promotes the Spirit of the Long March: Reviewing History to Strengthen National Defense Awareness" [红色研学弘扬长征精神: 重温历史增强国防意识].

⁴⁴ Li Yuanxing [李远星] and Wang Bing [王丙], "Research on Construction and Use of Strategic Projection Support Forces in the New Era" [新时代战略投送支援力量建设运用研究], *National Defense* [国防], no. 12 (2017), 20–23; Hainan Strait Shipping Co., Ltd. [海南海峡航运股份有限公司], "Business Scope" [业务范围], available at <http://www.hnss.net.cn/col/col17598/index.html>.

⁴⁵ "Zhejiang Civil Transport Ferries Active in Military Exercise" [浙江民运航渡活跃演兵场], *PLA Daily* [解放军报], February 22, 2017, available at <http://military.people.com.cn/n1/2017/0222/c1011-29099602.html>; "Straits Ferry to Invest 200 Million Yuan to Create a New Landscape of 'Blue Highways'" [海峡轮渡将投入2亿元 打造 "蓝色公路" 新风景], *Zhoushan Daily* [舟山日报], January 21, 2018, available at <https://zj.zjol.com.cn/news.html?id=854956>; "Strait Ferry's First Hazardous Chemical RO-RO Ship 'Zhou-20' Commences Operations" [海峡轮渡首艘危化品滚装船 "舟渡20" 投入运营], *Eworldship.com* [国际船舶网], August 18, 2019, available at <http://www.eworldship.com/html/2019/OperatingShip_0818/151959.html>.

⁴⁶ Bohai Ferry Group Co., Ltd. [渤海轮渡集团股份有限公司], "National Defense Mobilization Work Advanced Individual Award Ceremony Held in Yantai" [全国国防动员工作先进个人颁奖仪式在烟台举行], July 4, 2020, available at <http://www.bhferry.com/e/action/ShowInfo.php?classid=11&id=81>.

⁴⁷ Bohai Ferry Group Co., Ltd. [渤海轮渡集团股份有限公司], "Who We Are" [我们是谁], available at <http://www.bhferry.com/brief.html>.

⁴⁸ Li Xiang [李响], "Record of a Successful Practice in Civil-Military Fusion: the RO-RO Ship 'Bohai Cuizhu' Enhances Our Military's Maritime Strategic Projection Capabilities" [军民融合领域的一次成功实践: "渤海翠珠" 滚装船提升我军海上战略投送能力纪实], *National Defense Science and Technology Industry* [国防科技工业], no. 1 (2012), 53.

⁴⁹ Bohai Ferry Group Co., Ltd. [渤海轮渡集团股份有限公司], "Bohai Zuanzhu" [渤海钻珠], available at <http://www.bhferry.com/zuanzhu.html>.

⁵⁰ Bohai Ferry Group Co., Ltd. [渤海轮渡集团股份有限公司], "'Zhonghua Fuxing' Officially Entered Operations in the Bohai Gulf" ["中华复兴" 轮正式投入渤海湾营运], September 25, 2020, available at <http://www.bhferry.com/e/action/ShowInfo.php?classid=11&id=96>.

⁵¹ Bohai Ferry Group Co., Ltd. [渤海轮渡集团股份有限公司], "Multipurpose RO-RO Ship 'Bohai Hengda' Launched" [多用途滚装船 "渤海恒达" 轮下水], October 19, 2020, available at <http://www.bhferry.com/e/action/ShowInfo.php?classid=11&id=99>.

⁵² "Five Years of Endurance: Exhibition of Grand Achievement, Various Types of Naval Equipment Lay a Foundation to Compete for Sea Power" [砥砺奋进的五年: 大型成就展 海军多种装备为争夺制海权打下基础], *China.org* [中国网], October 19, 2017, available at <http://mil.qianlong.com/2017/1019/2107258_8.shtml>.

53   Ferry terminals are used to handle annual surges in transport volume. For example, RO-RO ferry and rail ferry services across the Qiongzhou Strait during the weeklong travel period for National Day in October 2019 were able to move 365,025 passengers and 78,498 vehicles. New and old ferry terminals are in operation. See "48 RO-RO Passenger Ships Put into Use on the Qiongzhou Strait Route from Zhanjiang to Haikou to Deal with Peak Passenger Flow of 'October 1ˢᵗ'" [琼州海峡湛江至海口航线投入48艘客滚船迎战 "十一" 客流高峰], *CNR* [央广网], September 30, 2020, available at <http://news.cnr.cn/native/city/20200930/t20200930_525284389.shtml>.

54   Bohai Ferry Group Co., Ltd., "National Defense Mobilization Work Advanced Individual Award Ceremony Held in Yantai."

55   Jiang and Han, "Development in Support Technology for Sea-Shore Handling Heavy Equipment," 2.

56   For two examples citing actual PLA cases, see Zhao Junguo [赵俊国] and Liu Baoxin [刘宝新], "Loading and Unloading Support of RO-RO Ship with Stern Straight Type Springboard T-Type Berthing at Vertical Lifting Wharf" [艉直式跳板滚装船丁靠直立式码头装卸载保障], *Port & Waterway Engineering* [水运工程], no. 6 (2017), 77–80; Yao Yuan [姚远] et al., "Study on Loading and Unloading Times of RO-RO Ship Berthing at Vertical Wharf" [滚装船靠泊直立式码头卸载时间研究"], *Journal of Military Transportation University* [军事交通学院学报], no. 5 (2019), 91–95.

57   Liu Baoxin [刘宝新], Zhao Junguo [赵俊国], and Hu Weiping [胡维平], "Research on Loading and Unloading Support of RO-RO Ship Mooring Alongside Vertical Lifting Wharf" [滚装船靠泊直立式吊装码头装卸载保障研究], *Journal of Military Transportation University* [军事交通学院学报], no. 12 (2016), 26.

58   Kennedy, *Civil Transport in PLA Power Projection.*

59   One such example can be seen in a June 2014 Guangzhou Military Region exercise in which military transportation department personnel were present on the bridge of a RO-RO ferry carrying an unidentified PLAA mechanized infantry company. This training event could be a one-off experiment. See "Guangzhou Military Region's First Exercise Using a Civilian Ship to Load and Unload Live Troops" [广州军区首次民船成建制实兵装卸演练], CCTV [央视网], video, 2:35, June 20, 2014, available at <https://news.cctv.com/2014/06/20/VIDE1403241489289947.shtml>.

60   Chen Xuanyu [陈炫宇], Ren Cong [任聪], and Wang Fengzhong [王凤忠], "Problems to Countermeasures in Logistical Support in Cross-Strait and Beach Landing Transportation" [渡海登岛运输勤务保障面临的问题和对策], *Logistics Technology* [物流技术], no. 10 (2016), 166–169.

61   For an official definition of the term *landing base*, see Academy of Military Sciences [军事科学院], *PLA Directory of Military Terminology* [中国人民解放军军语] (Beijing: Military Sciences Press, 2011), 94; Wang Xin [汪欣] and Wang Guangdong [王广东], "Research on the Application of Transportation and Projection Forces in the Establishment of Landing Bases for Cross-Sea Landing Operations" [运输投送力量在跨海登岛作战登陆基地开设中的运用研究], *National Defense Transportation Engineering and Technology* [国防交通工程与技术], no. 5 (2019), 12–13.

62   Zhao Delong [赵德龙] et al., "Study on Base Support for Mechanized Infantry Brigade's Landing Operation" [机械化步兵旅登陆作战基地保障研究], *Journal of Military Transportation University* [军事交通学院学报], no. 9 (2014), 46.

63   Luo Lei [罗雷] et al., "Construction and Enlightenment of Normandy Landing Artificial Port" [诺曼底登陆人工港的建设与启示], *Journal of Military Transportation University* [军事交通学院学报], no. 1 (2020), 15–18.

⁶⁴ Cai Jingtao [蔡惊涛], Diao Jinghua [刁景华], and Li Zengzhi [李增志], "Review and Revelation of Artificial Harbor Construction in Normandy Landing" [诺曼底登陆战役人工港建设的回顾和启示], *Value Engineering* [价值工程], no. 6 (2014), 327–328; Zhao et al., "Study on Base Support for Mechanized Infantry Brigade's Landing Operation," 45.

⁶⁵ These developments can be compared to U.S. military (joint) logistics over the shore operations.

⁶⁶ Luo et al., "Construction and Enlightenment of Normandy Landing Artificial Port," 15–18.

⁶⁷ Yang Maoduo [杨茂铎], "Efforts to Solve Difficult Problems to Improve Aviation Military Traffic and Transportation Support Capabilities" [着力破解难题，提升航务军交运输保障能力], *National Defense* [国防], no. 4 (2017), 75–77.

⁶⁸ Lin Wei [林伟] and Liu Lijie [刘立洁], "Research on the Replenishment Mode of Island Transportation" [岛礁运输补给方式研究], *China Storage & Transport* [中国储运], no. 8 (2016), 133.

⁶⁹ Luo et al., "Construction and Enlightenment of Normandy Landing Artificial Port," 18; Jiang and Han, "Development in Support Technology for Sea-Shore Handling Heavy Equipment," 2.

⁷⁰ For the official description of sea states by the National Marine Environmental Forecasting Center, see National Marine Environmental Forecasting Center [国家海洋环境预报中心], "Table of Sea State Levels" [海况等级表], available at <http://www.nmefc.cn/nr/cont.aspx?itemid=301&id=3726>; Jiang and Han, "Development in Support Technology for Sea-Shore Handling Heavy Equipment," 2.

⁷¹ Liu Gang [刘刚], "On the Needs for the Mobilization of Civilian Semi-Submersible Vessels in China and the Prospects of their Potentialities" [我国半潜式运输船动员需求及能力展望], *National Defense Transportation Engineering and Technology* [国防交通工程与技术], no. 3 (2015), 1–2.

⁷² "Eastern Theater Command Army Aviation Multi-Type Helicopter Trains with a Maritime Civilian Platform for Take Off and Landing" [东部战区陆航多型直升机训练海上民用平台起降], CCTV-7 Military Report [军事报道], August 20, 2020, available at <https://www.guancha.cn/military-affairs/2020_08_20_562254.shtml>.

⁷³ Cao and Ye, "Merchant Ships Join the Military," 17.

⁷⁴ Gao Jie [高洁] and Lai Yuhong [赖瑜鸿], "Another Merchant Ship 'Joins the Military': Damaged Chinese Warships Have an Exclusive Vehicle" [又一艘民船 "参军," 中国战损舰船有了专属座驾], PLA Press Department [解放军记者部], April 16, 2017, available at <http://inews.ifeng.com/50948428/news.shtml?&back>.

⁷⁵ Mike Yeo, "China Commissions First MLP-Like Logistics Ship, Headed for South Sea Fleet," *USNI News*, July 14, 2015, available at <https://news.usni.org/2015/07/14/chinas-commissions-first-mlp-like-logistics-ship-headed-for-south-sea-fleet>.

⁷⁶ Chen Chuli [陈矗立], "Strategic Analysis of the Semi-Submersible Transport Market Based on the 'Porter's Five Forces' Model" [基于 "波特五力" 模型的半潜船运输市场战略分析], *World Shipping* [世界海运], no. 8 (2019), 12–13.

⁷⁷ Gao and Lai, "Another Merchant Ship 'Joins the Military.'"

⁷⁸ Yang Hongsuo [杨洪所], Zhang Qun [张群], and Hu Shuang [胡双], "Competition and Prospects of the Global Semi-Submersible Vessel Transport Industry" [全球半潜船运输行业竞争格局与前景], *Plant Maintenance and Engineering* [设备管理与维修], no. 12 (2018), 116; "China's Largest Semi-Submersible Ship 'Xin Guanghua' Begins Operations" [我国最大半潜船 "新光华" 轮投入运营], *China Ocean News* [中国海洋报], December 9, 2016, available at <http://www.oceanol.com/keji/kjdt/2016-12-09/65182.html>.

[79] Yang, Zhang, and Hu, "Competition and Prospects of the Global Semi-Submersible Vessel Transport Industry," 116.

[80] "China's First Dual Use Semi-Submersible Ship Completed and Enters Use in Nantong" [中国首艘军民两用半潜船在南通启动建成投入使用], CCTV [央广网], March 15, 2017, available at <http://www.ntjoy.com/news/yw/2017/03/2017-03-15554678.html>.

[81] Wang Xin, "China's First Dual-Use Semi-Submersible Put into Operation," *China Plus*, March 15, 2017, available at <http://chinaplus.cri.cn/news/china/9/20170315/1540.html>.

[82] Potential amphibious vehicle lift assuming vehicle spacing of 1.2 meters fore and aft and 0.5 meters starboard and port, as well as sufficient flush-deck fastening points or appropriate modification; this means the *Zhenhua-33* could handle up to 150 ZTD-05 vehicles. This assumption is based on a total of 51 square meters per vehicle using one PLA author's estimates for RO-RO loading and spacing of tracked equipment and artillery, which accounts for vehicle movement while at sea as well as space for proper fastening. Spacing is only slightly different for fore-and-aft wheeled vehicles. See Chen Yiping [陈益平], "Research on Issues Related to Military Use RO-RO Transportation" [军用车辆船舶滚装运输有关问题研究], *National Defense Transportation Engineering and Technology* [国防交通工程与技术], no. 5 (2018), 5.

[83] Li Hong [李宏] and Gao Jie [高洁], "Strategic Delivery Support Fleet Enters the Joint Exercise Field" [战略投送支援船队开进联合演练场], *PLA Daily* [解放军报], September 11, 2016.

[84] COSCO Shipping Ferry Co., Ltd. [中远海运客运有限公司], "Bang Chui Dao" [棒棰岛].

[85] "China's Navy: Landing Combat Exercise Develops Amphibious Combat Capabilities" [中国海军: 渡海登陆作战演练锤炼两栖作战能力], CCTV [央视网], video, 1:38, August 3, 2020, available at <https://tv.cctv.com/2020/08/03/VIDEf15KuSr28oMmGTNd63Nz200803.shtml>.

[86] Andrew S. Erickson, "Maritime Numbers Game: Understanding and Responding to China's Three Sea Forces," *Indo-Pacific Defense Forum*, January 28, 2019, available at <https://ipdefenseforum.com/2019/01/maritime-numbers-game/>.

[87] *Military and Security Developments Involving the People's Republic of China 2020*, 71; Kyle Mizokami, "China Launches Another Monster Coast Guard Cutter," *Popular Mechanics*, January 14, 2016, available at <https://www.popularmechanics.com/military/navy-ships/a18990/china-launches-second-monster-coast-guard-cutter/>.

[88] Ye Jun [叶军], "On Building China Coast Guard as Supporting Force for China Navy in Time of War" [海警在战时对海军进行支援的问题探讨], *Journal of China Maritime Police* [公安海警学院报], no. 1 (2012), 6–8; Liu Zhangren [刘章仁], "Strengthening Coordination Between Navy and Coast Guard to Improve Marine Control Ability" [论海警海军协同配合提高海洋管控能力], *Journal of China Maritime Police Academy* [公安海警学院学报], no. 3 (2014), 53–54. For an in-depth examination of the growth and militarization of the China Coast Guard, see Ryan D. Martinson, *The Arming of China's Maritime Frontier*, CMSI China Maritime Report No. 2 (Newport, RI: Naval War College Press, June 2017), 2.

[89] Wu Pingxiang [吴品祥], "Vigorously Strengthen the Construction of Militia Shipping Regiments" [大力加强民兵船运团建设], *National Defense* [国防], no. 2 (2004), 42. For a more recent inclusion of the maritime militia in a cross-strait joint landing campaign, see Zhao et al., "Study on Base Support for Mechanized Infantry Brigade's Landing Operation," 45.

[90] Han Huaizhi [韩怀智], ed., *Contemporary Chinese Militia* [当代中国民兵] (Beijing: China Social Sciences Press, 1989), 234.

[91] Kou Zhenyun [寇振云] and Feng Shi [冯时], "'Four Requirements' in Strengthening Maritime Militia Construction" [加强海上民兵建设 "四要"], *National Defense* [国防], no. 5 (2016), 41–42.

92 Guo Suqing [郭苏青], "Creating Militia Ship Transport Regiments to Support Units in a Cross-Sea Landing Operation" [组建民兵船运团保障部队渡海登陆作战], *National Defense* [国防], no. 12 (2004), 35.

93 For two examples in Zhejiang Province, see "Xiangshan County Militia Shipping Regiment Assists PLA Amphibious Landing Training" [象山县民兵船运团助力解放军两栖登陆训练], Xinhua [新华网], September 25, 2013, available at <http://www.chinanews.com/mil/2013/09-25/5319125.shtml>; "Zhoushan City Formed a Militia Shipping Group" [舟山市组建成立民兵船运团], *PLA Daily* [解放军报], October 24, 2003, available at <http://news.sina.com.cn/c/2003-10-24/1547984589s.shtml>. The 1st Militia Ship Transport Regiment in Taizhou Has Several Subordinate "Fishing *Zhongdui*" and "Transport *Zhongdui*." See "Taizhou City Establishes a Militia Ship Transport Regiment" [台州市组建民兵船运团], *Zhejiang Online News* [浙江在线新闻网站], July 14, 2004, available at <http://zjnews.zjol.com.cn/05zjnews/system/2004/07/14/003047058.shtml>.

94 Wang Haitao [王海涛], "Implement the Overall National Security Concept and Actively Promote the Transformation of Coastal Defense Construction" [贯彻总体国家安全观, 积极推进海防建设转型], *National Defense* [国防], no. 10 (2014), 54.

95 Nanjing Twin Rivers Shipping Co., Ltd. [南京两江海运股份有限公司], "Company Conducts Maritime Militia Training" [公司开展海上民兵训练], September 2, 2019.

96 Liu Zili [刘自力] and Chen Qingsong [陈青宋], "Tasks and Operations of the Maritime Militia When Participating in Maritime Combat" [海上民兵参加海战的任务与行动], *National Defense* [国防], no. 11 (2018), 50–51.

97 In wartime, contingents of special operations forces and marine corps reconnaissance units could likely form special operations detachments centered on the maritime militia. See ibid., 51.

98 The author found 63 individual maritime militia units in the various counties of Zhejiang Province; however, there are likely more, particularly in major port areas. It should be noted that not all are units organized for transport missions, but they could serve in this role through some degree of modification. See exhibits 0-3 and 0-5 in Andrew S. Erickson and Ryan D. Martinson, eds., *China's Maritime Gray Zone Operations* (Annapolis: Naval Institute Press, 2019).

99 Guo, "Creating Militia Ship Transport Regiments to Support Units in a Cross-Sea Landing Operation," 37.

100 Chinese national defense mobilization laws allow for requisition of Chinese-owned vessels despite being foreign flagged. See Liu Baoxin [刘宝新] and Liu Jiasheng [刘嘉生], "Research on National Defense Mobilization of Chinese-Funded Ship with Flag of Convenience" [中资方便旗船国防动员问题研究], *Journal of Military Transportation University* [军事交通学院学报], no. 1 (2018), 15–18.

101 Li Zhouqing [李周清] et al., "Selection, Deployment and Optimization of Merchant Ships for Maritime Strategic Projection" [海上战略投送动员民船多点选型配置优化], *Journal of Military Transportation University* [军事交通学院学报], no. 3 (2019), 4–7.

CHAPTER 9

PLA Logistics and Mobilization Capacity in a Taiwan Invasion

Chieh Chung

M ainland Chinese analysts often use the term *large-scale joint operations* [*da guimo lianhe zuozhan*, 大规模联合作战] to describe taking Taiwan by force. Given the People's Liberation Army (PLA)'s perception that Chinese military actions against Taiwan will invite foreign intervention, fighting "a quick battle for a quick result" [*suzhan sujue*, 速战速决] has become exceedingly important for PLA doctrine.[1] However, the PLA has not yet acquired the capability to fight a quick battle in the Taiwan Strait. A key reason is the limited capacity of its joint logistics support and national defense mobilization systems. The PLA has recently made efforts to improve its logistics mobilization capabilities; some of these were put to the test in the fight against the COVID-19 pandemic in 2020, when the PLA needed to move resources across the country in an accelerated time frame.[2] Yet there are still indications that the PLA would face challenges in transporting and sustaining forces across the strait.

This chapter analyzes recent improvements in Chinese military logistics as well as continuing challenges in providing logistics support for cross-strait operations. It finds that the 2015–2016 reforms led to progress in the structure of the logistics and national defense mobilization system. The chapter also surveys the estimated requirements and perceived shortages in the logistics arena during wartime and analyzes possible follow-on improvements. The chapter finds that, due to the complexity and scale of the operations and the remaining weaknesses and limitations, it will take the PLA considerable time to improve these systems to the point that a quick battle for a quick result could be attained. Taiwan must take advantage of this window of opportunity to strengthen its own ability to counter China's logistics operations.

The chapter is divided into four sections. The first section reviews the PLA's post-reform joint logistics structure, including the relationships between the logistics system and the theater commands. The second section details the PLA's perceived logistics requirements for a cross-strait invasion in three areas—materiel support, medical support, and transportation—and documents weaknesses in each area. The third section describes the structure of, and weaknesses in, the PLA's mobilization system, which would also be called on to contribute logistics support in wartime. The fourth section considers improvements to infrastructure, personnel, and information systems that might be pursued in the coming years to support both systems. This analysis establishes a framework for further research on the PLA's efforts to upgrade its logistics mobilization capabilities for an invasion of Taiwan.

The chapter draws on underutilized research published in PLA periodicals including the *Journal of Military Transportation University* and *National Defense*, as well as books published by the PLA National Defense University and the PLA Logistics Academic Research Center. Most authors of these papers and publications are active-duty PLA commanders and staff officers directly involved in logistics or mobilization systems, military academics who specialize in these subjects, or officers enrolled at PLA academies. Their writings provide diverse perspectives on key topics and are more thorough and informative than articles in PLA propaganda outlets such as *PLA Daily*.

The PLA's Post-Reform Logistics System

At the end of 2012, Central Military Commission (CMC) Chairman Xi Jinping instructed the military to "build a logistics system that ensures victory in modern warfare, serves the needs of the military in its move toward modernization, and enables a transformation into an informatized mode of operation." Collectively, these admonitions composed the "three major tasks in the construction of modern logistics."[3] Acting on Xi's instructions, the PLA drew up plans for restructuring the logistics system between 2013 and 2015. In late 2015, the CMC, as part of its general outline for military reform, decided to do the following:

> Adjust and reform the logistics support system's leadership and management on the basis of the current system, to optimize the relationship between logistics support forces and their leaders, and to build a logistics support system that is compatible with the joint operations command mechanism and that incorporates and combines general and specialized logistics support.[4]

To better understand how the new joint logistics system will contribute to PLA operations against Taiwan, this section first reviews key organizational changes and then identifies the relationship between the joint logistics and command systems.

Basic Organization

The new organizational structure consists of a CMC Logistic Support Department (LSD) responsible for logistics management, a Joint Logistic Support Force (JLSF) responsible for operational support, and logistics departments in each of the services.[5] At the CMC level, the previous General Logistics Department was reorganized and renamed the LSD. This organization serves as the CMC's "staff, service, and executive unit" for logistics affairs, including "executing plans for the logistics support system across the services, conducting policy research, setting standards, checking, and supervising."[6] The LSD is also the primary agent for providing logistics support to the CMC Joint Operations Command Center (JOCC), which would serve as the PLA's top command post in wartime.[7]

On September 13, 2016, the CMC inaugurated the JLSF as the main force to execute joint logistics support as well as strategic and campaign support missions.[8] The JLSF is the strategic and campaign support's "fist force" [quantou liliang, 拳头力量] directly subordinate to the CMC and will thus play a key role in logistics support for joint operations.[9] It is headquartered at the Wuhan Joint Logistics Support Base, formerly known as the General Logistics Department Wuhan Rear Area Base, which, according to one PLA article, takes orders directly from the CMC JOCC.[10] In early 2018, the Wuhan base was upgraded from corps to theater deputy leader grade, symbolizing its important status within the PLA's joint operations system. Exercising power equivalent to a major PLA component, the JLSF has nearly acquired the status of an independent service.[11] In addition to hosting the JLSF command staff, the base maintains strategic reserves that may be allocated to any theater in a contingency.[12]

The JLSF headquarters in turn oversees five Joint Logistic Support Centers (JLSCs), each based in one of the five PLA theater commands. The JLSC headquarters are in Wuxi (Eastern Theater), Guilin (Southern Theater), Zhengzhou (Central Theater), Xining (Western Theater), and Shenyang (Northern Theater). Their mission is to provide support—including materiel supply, medical, transportation and delivery, and military facility support—to units based in these theaters.[13] Below this level, dedicated logistics units and other units with relevant equipment have been combined into new logistics support departments. They are responsible for unit-specific logistics and equipment buildup, logistics and equipment support, and joint logistics support missions for designated areas.[14]

While the PLA has strengthened its joint logistics capabilities, a division of labor remains between joint and service logistics. The PLA describes "joint logistics forces as the backbone and elements of all the PLA's services as auxiliary forces, with a combination of centralized and decentralized modes of operation and a separate treatment of general-purpose and service-specific hardware."[15] Based on this distinction, the PLA Army has built up its LSD, while the PLA Navy, Air Force, and Rocket Force have consolidated their respective logistics support departments to guide "service-specific logistics" [*junzhong zhuanyong houqin*, 军中专用后勤] construction projects and organize service logistics support.[16] One exception is the Strategic Support Force, which has directed its Operational Logistics Planning Bureau [*zhanqin jihua ju*, 战种计划局] to take responsibility for both general logistics support and coordination of general-purpose equipment support.[17]

Through the structural adjustments mentioned above, a "peacetime administrative chain of command" and a "wartime operational chain of command" have been formed within the logistics support system of the PLA. According to one PLA analyst, an "administrative chain of command" extends from the CMC to the Wuhan Joint Logistics Support Base and service logistics departments to the JLSCs and theater service logistics forces to joint logistics support forces. This system is responsible for the construction and management of joint logistics support at all levels.[18] Its focus is on transportation and delivery; emergency logistics; logistics support base construction; and "military-civil fusion" [*junmin ronghe*, 军民融合], which refers to the use of civilian resources to boost logistics support capacity and quality.[19]

PLA sources describe a "wartime operational chain of command" separate from the logistics support department under the CMC JOCC and the CMC LSD to the theater service logistics departments and JLSCs to joint logistics support forces. This logistics support mechanism is integrated into the joint operations command system centered on the five theater commands.[20] It features a shallow depth and a broad width, meeting the requirements of modern information warfare for a flat organization.[21]

Integration into the Joint Operations Command System

The relationship between the new logistics system and the theaters varies between peacetime and wartime conditions. In peacetime, operational units submit requests for general materiel to theater-based JLSCs and requests for service-specific materiel to theater service logistics support departments. After reviewing the requests, these two authorities send the requested materiel to subordinate rear warehouses. The materiel is then delivered by the warehouses and their materiel support departments (or detachments) via local transportation means to the requesting units.[22]

There would be a stronger integration of joint logistics forces into the theater structure during wartime compared with during peacetime arrangements. Specifically, operational planning bureaus within the theater joint staff departments would direct both the JLSCs and the theater service logistics support departments. These joint logistics commands would coordinate the distribution of resources to operational units.[23] In particular, PLA sources indicate that materiel requested by operational units would be distributed via relevant operational planning departments and delivery forces to theater JLSCs (general materiel) and theater service logistics support departments (service-specific materiel).[24] The two distribution channels would then deliver materiel to designated destinations. Guidance would also be offered to these requesting units to teach them how to use the materiel.[25]

If a specific theater command cannot meet the requirements based on its internal capabilities, the theater commander would likely submit requests to the LSD through the CMC JOCC. That organization, managed by the CMC Joint Staff Department, would generate replenishment plans and order theater commanders in other regions to provide support to the main theater. If more than two theaters are involved in a joint campaign, the LSD would likely coordinate the distribution of logistics resources to enable cross-theater joint operations through the CMC JOCC.

Logistics Requirements for an Invasion of Taiwan

PLA publications on logistics support often refer to the use of force against Taiwan as "large-scale joint operations" to "achieve the goal of unifying the country."[26] The aim of such operations has changed from "anti-Taiwan independence" to "promoting unification." The modes of operations have also changed from warning strikes and partial blockades to a wider variety of means, including strategic deterrence, a general blockade, paralysis with large-scale firepower strikes, and an amphibious landing on parts of the island (for a discussion of the primary campaigns, see the chapter by Michael Casey in this volume).[27] Potential theaters of operations have also expanded to encompass eastern Taiwan and its coastal waters.[28]

If the PLA launches large-scale joint operations against Taiwan, such operations would surely involve troops from multiple theater commands and services. The number of troops involved, the scale and extent of the operations, the intensity of the conflict, and the amount of materiel consumed would be enormous. The logistics support capacity needed for such a campaign would likely surpass that for any previous campaigns that the PLA has ever launched.

More important, the PLA must be prepared for a possible intervention by the "strong enemy"—that is, the United States—and a "chain reaction in other strategic directions,"[29] meaning the expansion of the conflict to other theaters. The PLA thus hopes that it can bring the campaign against Taiwan to a conclusion within a short time frame and that the strategic goal of "the first engagement as the final engagement" [*shouzhan ji juezhan*, 首战即决战] can be achieved through quick and decisive tactical operations.[30]

To satisfy this objective, large-scale joint operations will require an increase in materiel consumption and a surge in the demand for mobilization within a short period of time.[31] The PLA would need to manage logistics tasks including materiel supply support, medical service support, and transportation and delivery support. The following sections review PLA estimates of these logistics requirements and offer an analysis of current deficiencies in each area.

Materiel Supply Support

According to a study by the PLA Logistics Academic Research Center, the materials necessary for an amphibious landing would total more than 30 million metric tons, with 5.6 million metric tons of oil consumed.[32] Amphibious landing operations by a single combined arms brigade consume an estimated 625,457 kilograms of petrol and diesel per day.[33] Compounding the sheer scale of the effort, PLA sources suggest that materiel supply faces several problems. First, logistics support is described as "being relatively small in scale, having a low degree of materialization, a low level of mechanization, and sub-standard professionalism on the part of reserve logistics support forces, and being weak in specific logistics support (especially for maritime forces and airborne troops)."[34] This system cannot meet the requirements for large-scale joint operations.

Second, regarding military warehousing capacity, the PLA's land-based logistics support bases are well developed, but large and comprehensive modernized logistics support bases that can provide support for all the PLA's services to conduct joint operations remain unsatisfactory. Also, there are currently no prepositioned and forward-deployed logistics support bases.[35] In terms of the amount of materiel stored, the PLA had by 2016 stockpiled enough materials and equipment to meet the requirements for a medium-sized campaign. However, current stores—especially military rations and reserve equipment—are insufficient to satisfy the logistics support demands of large-scale joint operations.[36]

Third, with respect to the distribution of materiel, there is a self-assessed problem of "first-line units low in their stocks, second-line units weak in their capabilities, and third-line units faraway in their locations." First-line units, with relatively few military warehouses and large military wharves at their disposal, have limited materiel storage and cargo-handling capacity, and their distribution and comprehensive logistics support capabilities are relatively weak.[37] Given that the PLA lacks sufficient supplies for a major campaign, additional supplies that can be obtained through the national defense mobilization system are crucial. The efficiency of the mobilization system, as discussed below, plays a key role in this respect.

Medical Service Support

According to estimates from the PLA Logistics Academic Research Center, considering the "enemy's capability to conduct surveillance and reconnaissance and precision strikes with deadly weapons" and the difficulty in launching cross-strait operations, the PLA would suffer a high "combat attrition rate." The specific rate cited for the ground combat force is about 7 percent, maritime combat force about 15 percent, air combat force about 10 percent, and Rocket Force about 5 percent. The total estimated number of injured PLA personnel is about 120,000.[38] Nearly 48,000 beds would be needed to take care of the wounded troops.[39]

In the 2020 fight against the coronavirus pandemic, the PLA tested its medical service capacity as it mobilized personnel and materials in large numbers and delivered them to Wuhan. By February 25, a total of 150,000 beds were available in designated hospitals, mobile cabin hospitals, isolation care points, and medical observation points. This experience demonstrates that the PLA's emergency medical response capacity could quantitatively meet the basic requirements for future large-scale joint operations. Meanwhile, the "mobile cabin hospitals, designated hospitals, and hospitals for critical and serious illnesses and conditions" that the PLA jointly established with the private medical sector won recognition from PLA leaders.[40] This type of cooperation is likely to continue to provide support to theaters in large-scale military actions.

Several other signs indicate that the PLA has improved its medical service support capacity. First, the completion rate of military medical service facility construction projects has been over 86 percent.[41] Second, the land-based mobile medical service support system can now set up 46 field hospitals and an additional 43 army division-level first aid stations within a short period of time, and has the capacity to treat 36,000 patients daily.[42] Third, the PLA owns rear hospitals that, once expanded, can treat 70,000 patients daily.[43] This figure may further increase with a boost in the treatment capacity of the private medical sector in coastal provinces in southeast China. Fourth, stocks of medicine for use by individual soldiers are enough to support 600,000 servicemembers. Stocks of commonly used medicines for wartime needs can support 500,000 soldiers for a duration of 30 days.[44]

Although the PLA does not seem to have a serious problem with the quantity of readily available resources, it appears to lack the capability to reach the goal of fighting a quick battle for a quick result. Its current speed in transporting and delivering medical service personnel and materiel, as well as its ability to make prior preparations, are insufficient to achieve the PLA's goals in a large-scale operation. In the fight against COVID-19, for instance, despite an all-out effort to provide medical service support to Wuhan, it still took 10 days for the PLA to complete the construction of a single makeshift hospital and a host of mobile cabin hospitals.

Moreover, since large-scale joint operations against Taiwan will cover parts of mainland China, maritime areas, and Taiwan proper, PLA troops will be greatly exhausted after the long journey, not to mention the prior movement to assembly points and preparations for war.[45] Various types of warfare and counter-warfare will be launched at the same time. Campaigns will unfold on the ground, at sea, and in the air simultaneously, resulting in a surge in casualties within a short time that will be scattered unevenly in different regions.[46] Such casualties will include soldiers who fall overboard, especially in waters east of Taiwan, and those injured while executing "multiple-point simultaneous parachuting" missions over Taiwan. None of these casualties will be easily located and evacuated.[47] This situation makes the overall logistics support plan for the campaign even more difficult.

Transportation and Delivery Support

To invade Taiwan, the PLA needs to launch large-scale joint operations by sea and air. The number of troops to be projected to medium- and long-range destinations would be in the "hundreds of thousands."[48] As studies by the PLA Logistics Academic Research Center point out, advance troops are estimated to be in the tens of thousands, roughly the main strength of six combined arms brigades.[49] Some of these troops must be projected by air, including about two brigades projected by helicopters to perform air maneuver operations.[50] Seaborne delivery requires the capacity to transport two to three pre-reform heavy army divisions at a time.[51]

Such operations are highly challenging in terms of the number of troops, equipment, and wounded troops to be transported. According to the PLA Logistics Academic Research Center, the entire operation would require about 3,000 train trips, 1 million vehicle trips, 2,100 aircraft sorties, 15 oil pipeline battalions [*dadui*, 大队], and more than 8,000 ship voyages.[52] There has been little mention of operational tempo in open-source research papers, though it appears the PLA wants group armies to complete the loading of outbound materiel within 24 hours, and brigades and regiments within 4 hours.[53]

To complete these tasks, the PLA has built both aviation- and sea-based delivery forces, but problems remain. By the end of 2017, the PLA could transport less than two brigades, or regiments, of armed paratroopers when 80 percent of its Y-20, Il-76, and Y-8C transport aircraft were ready for action.[54] There is still a considerable difference between that figure and the projected four to five combined arms brigades needed to accomplish an initial blitzkrieg-style invasion of Taiwan. Moreover, military helicopters, though capable of making up some of the shortfall created by insufficient transport aircraft, had the problem of being "of one same type, incapable of transporting heavy equipment and large amounts of materiel for emergency use," a condition that lasted at least until early 2020.[55]

Much attention has been given to the use of civilian aircraft in supplementing military airlift. Nevertheless, the civil aircraft fleet can perform only some wartime functions because features such as cabin door sizes, cabin sizes, and cabin floor bearing loads do not necessarily meet military requirements.[56] Other problems include loading and unloading facilities at airports and other technical limits. Therefore, in an island landing, the civil aircraft fleet can transport troops and materiel only to designated assembly areas or points of departure. Also, only after the PLA has paralyzed Taiwan's air defense system and taken control of a main airport could these civil aircraft begin to transport troops and materiel. During the critical early stages of a campaign, the PLA must therefore rely solely on its own organic air transport assets to execute sea-crossing troop and materiel transportation missions.

Several similar deficiencies are apparent in the military's sealift force. First, there is a shortage of standardized active delivery equipment. Problems with the PLA's marine transportation include "a severe shortage of large standardized ocean-going logistics vessels and an even smaller number of ships that can be used to carry troops across the strait to conduct amphibious landing operations, with existing ships small in tonnage and capable of carrying only a small number of troops."[57] In the first half of 2018, it was estimated that even if the PLA used all the transport ships and landing vessels at its disposal, it could project only two army brigades and four marine corps–reinforced battalions across the Taiwan Strait[58]—a far cry from the goal of sending two to three pre–military reform heavy divisions. PLA analysts have also noted as another issue the "failure to provide logistics support of various sorts for large-scale operations."[59]

Second, the PLA would attempt to bridge the gap in military sealift by enlisting civilian ships. Yet, while the PLA established the first civilian seaborne strategic delivery support fleet in Shanghai in July 2013,[60] roll-on/roll-off ships suitable for carrying heavy equipment for rapid delivery are assessed as insufficient.[61] As discussed in Conor Kennedy's chapter in this volume, the PLA also continues to rely on civilian merchant fleets. Such forces, however, seldom if ever participate in maritime training and important missions, which can directly diminish the effectiveness of mobilization of troops for seaborne strategic delivery.[62] As of early 2020, the problem of "landing ships being too diverse in type, scattered in deployment, and relatively weak in systematic delivery support" also remained.[63] In sum, the PLA's logistics support capabilities for large-scale joint operations, in terms of materiel supply, medical service, and transportation and delivery support, are presently unable to support the goal of a quick battle for a quick result.

Adapting the Logistics Mobilization System

In 2016, PLA Academy of Military Sciences National Defense Comprehensive Research Office Deputy Director Han Qinggu wrote that a large-scale joint operation is a strategic joint warfare campaign organized by the high command and executed jointly by one or several theater commands and units of different services and service branches under them.[64] "Partial mobilization" by a single theater command is insufficient given the immense logistics requirements of this joint warfare campaign.[65] Therefore, different levels of logistics mobilization must be launched in adjacent theaters depending on combat needs in specific areas or conditions.[66] This section first describes how the mobilization system is organized to meet these requirements and then describes the attendant challenges.

Post-Reform Mobilization System

PLA reforms have produced a top-down mobilization system that would organize support for forces during a Taiwan contingency. The system would be led by a logistics support department within the CMC JOCC. Below this level, joint logistics command and defense mobilization command mechanisms would be established under the Eastern Theater Command JOCC to collect and distribute resources in this and other theaters. The mobilization bureau under the Eastern Theater's Joint Staff Department would coordinate with provincial, municipal, and county national defense mobilization commissions to form different levels of joint mobilization command organizations.[67] This bureau would select options from among mobilization plans prepared in advance, adjusting according to the status and limitations of national defense mobilization. The bureau would then provide mobilization orders to various units and enact timely adjustments depending on the battle's progress.[68]

Provincial military districts are key to the success of the mobilization. In peacetime, the districts are led by the CMC National Defense Mobilization Department and carry out such functions as organizing militia units to participate in search and rescue, security, policing, anti-terror, and social order maintenance missions.[69] In wartime, districts would be placed under the theater joint operations command mechanism to handle "organizing and commanding national defense mobilization," "organizing reserve troops to provide support to combat action," and "supporting combat troops' trans-regional maneuvers."[70]

Given the anticipated scope of a cross-strait campaign, resources in several geographic locations would be mobilized. First, provinces and cities within the Eastern Theater Command would be regarded as basic mobilization areas [*jiben dongyuan qu*, 基本动员区], implying full mobilization in all areas.[71] By 2019, Shanghai City and Fujian Province, both located within this theater, had completed national defense mobilization systems covering the whole city or province. These wider mobilization systems appear to have solved or greatly reduced information problems and improved integration between previously fragmented mobilization systems.[72]

Second, provinces and cities adjacent to the Eastern Theater Command would be regarded as auxiliary mobilization areas [*fuzhu dongyuan qu*, 辅助动员区]. These zones would mobilize resources and personnel to a more limited extent to make up for resource deficiencies in the basic mobilization areas.[73] As troops and materials from other theaters are transported to the Eastern Theater, the provinces they transit will form "troop maneuver support command mechanisms" based on provincial military districts and national defense mobilization commissions to mobilize personnel, economic resources, transportation means, and civil air defense facilities to provide logistics support to troops and materials.[74]

Third, anticipating a possible expansion of the conflict through what Chinese strategists refer to as *chain reaction warfare*, other theaters may be regarded as stand-by mobilization areas [*yubei dongyuan qu*, 预备动员区], which implement target-specific mobilization in limited areas, such as territorial air defense, border defense, maintenance of social order, production of military items, and evacuation. Logistics mobilization in these areas can ensure the effective neutralization of armed conflicts and disruptive activities incited by domestic and hostile elements overseas.[75]

In early 2016, the Eastern Theater Command was notably tasked with the experimental mission of establishing a "theater command military-local coordination mechanism that supports the military and provides frontline support" [*zhanqu yong jun zhi qian jun di xietiao jizhi*, 战区拥军支前军地协调机制].[76] The command formulated relevant regulations with the local governments of the Shanghai, Jiangsu, Zhejiang, Anhui, Fujian, Jiangxi, and Guangdong provinces, specifying rules for civilian support for military operations. Supplemental measures—such as the establishment of joint meetings, situation reports, and inspection and assessment systems—have also been approved.[77] These regulations suggest that the moment the PLA uses forces against Taiwan, Guangdong Province, within the Southern Theater Command's area of responsibility, will execute full mobilization similar to the six provinces and cities within the Eastern Theater Command's area of responsibility.

In addition to area-specific "partial mobilization," large-scale joint operations against Taiwan would also involve "specific mobilization" [*zhuanxiang dongyuan*, 专项动员] covering multiple specialty areas, including the information, transportation, materiel, medical service, building, energy, and business sectors, all of which would be mobilized to differing extents. Based on available evidence, the information, communication, oil, and energy sectors would enforce full mobilization.[78]

Mobilization System Weaknesses

Although highly praised in Chinese media reports, the PLA's national defense mobilization system still faces various problems. First, there are command and control issues. Provincial military districts, which are responsible for preparing for mobilization in peacetime, remain outside the theater command structure and instead report to the CMC National Defense Mobilization Department. Whether this arrangement will affect the mobilization system's integration into the joint operations command mechanism during wartime remains under debate in the PLA. Moreover, there is virtually no peacetime communication link between theaters and civil government agencies capable of providing resources. Therefore, mobilization command departments established under theater commands during wartime will surely need time to get on track.

Second, there is evidence of poor planning in the provincial military districts. In the 2020 pandemic response, some districts acted in impromptu ways rather than according to plan. This experience could demonstrate that the PLA, in drafting its mobilization plans, focuses only on active troops without giving much attention to reserve troops or civilian resources. PLA scholars also report that plans for military operations other than war and government emergency response plans are not closely linked.[79] This assessment suggests that, in terms of advance planning, the PLA's national defense mobilization system has yet to make the improvements necessary to meet the requirements for an invasion of Taiwan.

Third, there are human capital and technical problems. For instance, provincial military districts generally do not have specialized units or personnel, nor are their examination criteria compatible with local norms. Insufficient informatization has also resulted in failure to achieve seamless alignment with real combat requirements.[80] In addition, the national defense mobilization command mechanism faces self-described problems such as outdated communications equipment, lack of unified data standards, poor integration of military and local government information systems, and an unsound assessment system.[81]

Follow-On Improvements

Due to the continuing weaknesses of the joint logistics and national defense mobilization systems, the PLA will likely make additional improvements. This section considers several changes that may be made in both systems in three areas: strengthened infrastructure; enhanced force capability, especially among reserve and militia logistics forces; and increased capacity to transport forces, equipment, and wounded personnel.

Strengthened Infrastructure

One set of changes will involve strengthening the basic infrastructure needed to provide logistics support. PLA sources describe the need to implement logistics support at three points:[82]

- "strategic rear area logistics support points," which are responsible for the collection of strategic materials, long-distance projection, and long-distance evacuation
- "campaign logistics support points," which engage in the collection, storage, and transportation of campaign-level materials
- "tactical field logistics support points," which conduct logistics support missions near the frontlines.[83]

Other sources argue that provincial military districts should work with local governments to establish "key area mobilization centers" [*zhongdian quyu dongyuan zhongxin*, 重点区域动员中心] along major traffic routes.[84] This could form the basis of a "prepositioning mobilization" model leveraging civilian and military resources.

Aside from supply points, the PLA will also likely strengthen transportation facilities such as large ports and airports near the coast, as well as comprehensive logistics support bases.[85] Also likely will be an expansion of specialized capabilities needed to load and unload military supplies, such as field mechanized railway platforms, multipurpose pontoons, floating jetties, heavy equipment, roll-on/roll-off regulating platforms, and tying and fastening devices for ships. Some coastal ports may be asked to install loading/unloading equipment to handle heavy containers.[86]

Complementing the increase in "hard" infrastructure, PLA logistics forces will also continue to build more robust information systems. Compared with traditional models, recent PLA discussions of "informatized joint logistics" place more emphasis on integrated logistics for whole area, precision, and active distribution support.[87] The PLA plans to further upgrade the ability of its joint logistics information-handling centers to automatically generate logistics support proposals according to operational missions, support missions, support resources, and other support-related information for theater units. Similarly, PLA researchers argue that the PLA should learn from the United States and utilize information technologies such as radio frequency identification technology, global positioning technology, satellite communications, big data, and cloud computing to build an advanced national defense mobilization command information system.[88] During wartime, more capable and reliable information systems will permit mobilization authorities to transmit orders, exchange real-time data, and share mobilization status.[89]

Enhanced Force Capability

In the coming years, the PLA will continue to build up active, reserve, and militia logistics forces. For instance, one PLA article describes the need for a reserve logistics force that can facilitate the integration of civilian and military resources during wartime. The authors recommend establishing logistics reserve troops at two levels: strategic and campaign.[90] Through infrastructure improvements and a more mature logistics force, the PLA hopes that by 2025 it will be able to execute the loading of outbound standard material for group armies within 24 hours and for brigades and regiments within 4 hours, thus supporting a quicker tempo for an island landing.[91]

Further improvements will also likely be made to militia units responsible for logistics. In a Taiwan scenario, their duties would include helping with production, mobilization, and other frontline support missions and providing materiel and personnel support to active units in such areas as information, electronic warfare, air defense, transportation, engineering, and maintenance.[92] To increase capacity, mainland China has sped the incorporation of "newly developed districts, economic development zones, state enterprises, and high and new technology industries" into the militia system.[93] Moreover, the CMC National Defense Mobilization Department has described "companies joining the militia system" as a positive factor in the evaluation of provincial military districts' party-building efforts.[94] Communication, cyberspace, and information technology industries have also been asked to organize employees categorized as "new types of militia" into "regular type, reservist type, and specialist type."[95] There will likely be additional efforts in the future to strengthen and integrate these supporting forces into the mobilization system.

Increased Transportation and Delivery Capacity

To overcome insufficient transportation and delivery capacity, the PLA has begun taking several measures and will continue to build on them in the coming years. First, the introduction of large military transport aircraft such as the Y-20 has strengthened the air force's airlift capability—and this fleet is poised to continue growing.[96] Second, efforts have been made to increase strategic- and campaign-level helicopter forces with the aim of increasing medium- and long-range strategic delivery capability. Third, ocean-going comprehensive supply ships, amphibious transport docks, and amphibious assault ships have been or are being built to satisfy troops' needs for seaborne strategic delivery, transport, and supply. Fourth, the maritime strategic delivery reserve force has been expanded. Chinese sources note that marine transportation groups will be established in each coastal province to form a maritime strategic delivery reserve force that can be readily deployed on demand.[97] Fifth, Chinese researchers have explored the development of specialized transportation vehicles and supporting equipment most suitable for beachhead loading/unloading operations to provide sea-crossing and logistics support in large-scale joint operations against Taiwan. Such vehicles are adaptable to all types of terrain in Taiwan, are highly maneuverable, have good armor protection, and can satisfy the needs of troops landing on the island.[98]

Given the PLA's need to quickly evacuate wounded personnel in a cross-strait campaign, further reforms will likely increase the PLA's medical support capacity. After reviewing its performance in the fight against the 2020 pandemic, for instance, PLA authors have proposed a shift from the model of evacuating personnel by symptom level to a "three-dimensional" model using various platforms, such as medical service trains, cars, planes, rescue helicopters, and hospital ships. The intent of these and other reforms would be to improve the efficiency of treatment and evacuation for seriously wounded personnel.[99]

Conclusion

To achieve the goal of fighting a quick battle for a quick result in an invasion of Taiwan, the PLA must prepare hundreds of thousands of soldiers and vast amounts of materiel in the shortest time possible. It must then project those forces by ship and plane to medium- to long-range destinations. In the meantime, the PLA must ensure that the delivery process is agile and resilient enough to handle interference by China's opponents. Throughout the process, the PLA's joint logistics and national defense mobilization systems will play key roles. The PLA has made significant efforts in recent reforms to enhance these systems' capabilities to support large-scale joint operations. Given perceptions of continuing weaknesses in these areas, the PLA likely will continue to improve these systems to lay the basis for a large-scale operation across the Taiwan Strait.

The PLA's acquisition of a stronger logistics mobilization capability means that it will not only greatly reduce the time it needs to send troops and materials mobilized from around China to sea and land areas around Taiwan but also lower the chance of having its combat rhythm interrupted by delays or mistakes happening in the process of transporting reinforcements and delivering materials. This places the Taiwan military at a disadvantage in two respects. First, reduced warning time will diminish Taiwan's ability to transition its armed forces from a peacetime to wartime footing and to mobilize reserve troops. Second, it will be increasingly difficult for the military to take the initiative and get the time it needs to turn the tide.

Considering these difficulties, the Taiwan military should promote several measures. First is improving its ability to transition from a peacetime footing to wartime operations. Second is strengthening intelligence-gathering and intelligence-analysis capabilities, thereby increasing early-warning time by grasping vital clues about the PLA's mobilization of materials and transportation forces. Third is integrating long-range precision attack weapons systems to enhance Taiwan's "joint suppression warfare" [*lianhe zhiya zuozhan*, 联合制压作战] capabilities based on the Overall Defense Concept. These strike systems should be combined with cyber and information warfare to launch attacks on the PLA's logistics mobilization nodes to disrupt its combat rhythm and strive for strategic space and time. These measures can exploit existing weaknesses in PLA logistics support and mobilization and help offset future improvements in PLA capabilities. After all, if the PLA wants to gain a quick victory in a Taiwan invasion, it must rely on smooth operations of its logistics support and mobilization plan. Therefore, it will be critical for the Taiwan military to sabotage PLA logistics and mobilization systems at the start of the war.

Notes

[1] Cao Zhengrong [曹正荣], Sun Longhai [孙龙海], and Yang Ying [杨颖], eds., *Army's Information Warfare* [信息化陆军作战] (Beijing: National Defense University Press, 2015), 113.

[2] Joel Wuthnow, "Responding to the Epidemic in Wuhan: Insights into Chinese Military Logistics," *China Brief* 20, no. 7 (April 13, 2020), available at <https://jamestown.org/program/responding-to-the-epidemic-in-wuhan-insights-into-chinese-military-logistics/>.

[3] PLA General Political Department [解放军总政治部], *A Selection of Xi Jinping's Remarks on National Defense and Military Building* [习近平关于国防和军队建设重要论述选编] (Beijing: PLA Press, 2014), 61.

[4] "Central Military Commission Opinions on Deepening National Defense and Military Reforms" [中央军委关于深化国防和军队改革的意见], Xinhua [新华网], January 1, 2016, available at <http://www.xinhuanet.com//mil/2016-01/01/c_1117646695.htm>.

[5] See LeighAnn Luce and Erin Richter, "Handling Logistics in a Reformed PLA: The Long March Toward Joint Logistics," in *Chairman Xi Remakes the PLA: Assessing Chinese Military Reforms*, ed. Phillip C. Saunders et al. (Washington, DC: NDU Press, 2019), 257–292.

[6] Nong Qinghua [农清华], "Reform of the PLA Logistic Support System in the Past 40 Years" [人民解放军后勤保障体制改革攻坚40年], *Military History* [军事历史], no. 1 (2019), 15.

[7] Ibid.

[8] PRC Ministry of National Defense, "MND Press Conference on Joint Logistics Support System Reform" [国防部举行联勤保障体制改革专题新闻发布会], September 13, 2016; Zan Wang [昝旺], Niu Yongjie [牛永界], and Xi Zhaoming [席兆明], "Evaluation of Support Capability of Joint Logistic Support Center Based on Fuzzy AHP" [基于模糊层次评价法的联勤保障中心保障能力评估], *Command, Control, and Simulations* [指挥控制与仿真] 21, no. 2 (2019), 73.

[9] Deng Zeqin [郑泽钦], Li Yuanyuan [李媛媛], and Guo Jianke [郭健科], "Reflection on the Construction of the Network Chain of Flexible Logistics Support in the Battlefield Under the New System" [新体制下战场柔性后勤保障网链建设], *National Defense Science and Technology* [国防科技] 40, no. 3 (2019), 85.

[10] Nong, "Reform of the PLA Logistic Support System," 15.

[11] Ibid., 16.

[12] Liu Xue [刘学] and Gao Fei [高飞], "Research on Military Material Supply Chain Model Under the New System" [新体制下军用物资供应链模型研究], *Military Operations Research and Systems Engineering* [军事运筹与系统工程] 31, no. 2 (2017), 36.

[13] Zan, Niu, and Xi, "Evaluation of Support Capability," 73.

[14] Nong, "Reform of the PLA Logistic Support System," 16.

[15] Zan Wang [昝旺] et al., "Essential Issues to Be Considered During Wartime Employment of the Joint Logistic Support Center" [联勤保障中心战时运用应把握的关键问题], *Journal of Military Transportation University* [军事交通学院学报] 20, no. 12 (2018), 55.

[16] Ibid.

[17] Nong, "Reform of the PLA Logistic Support System," 15–16.

[18] Ibid., 17.

[19] Ibid.

[20] Ibid., 16.

[21] Huang Tianxin [黄天信], "Reflections on How to Improve the Building of the Joint Logistic Support Force's Organization System Under the New Institutions" [对新体制下加强联勤保障部队组织体系建设的思考], *National Defense* [国防], no. 1 (2019), 44.

22   Yang Xueming [杨学铭], Xun Ye [荀烨], and Li Xidong [李锡栋], "Study on Theater Ground Force Supplies Distribution and Support Mode Under the New System" [新体制下战区陆军物资配送保障模式研究], *Logistics Technology* [物流技术] 21, no. 2 (2018), 126–127.

23   Ibid.

24   Ibid.

25   Liu and Gao, "Research on Military Material Supply Chain Model," 35–36.

26   PLA Logistics Academic Research Center [全军后勤学术研究中心], *Combat Logistics Support* [作战后勤保障] (Beijing: PLA Logistics Academic Research Center, 2015), 1.

27   Ibid., 28.

28   Ibid.

29   Cao, Sun, and Yang, *Army's Information Warfare*, 113.

30   Ibid., 2.

31   Tang Shengpeng [唐胜鹏] and Long Peng [龙鹏], "Some Thoughts on Advancing the Building of the Joint National Defense Mobilization System" [对推进联合动员体系建设的几点思考], *National Defense* [国防], no. 4 (2019), 37.

32   PLA Logistics Academic Research Center, *Combat Logistics Support*, 29.

33   Wan Haiou [万海鸥] et al., "Analysis of the Landing Operation POL Sea-Crossing Transport Consumption and Demand Based on MS" [基于MS的登岛作战油料跨海输送消耗与需求分析], *Journal of Ordnance Equipment Engineering* [兵器装备工程学报] 39, no. 7 (2018), 144.

34   PLA Logistics Academic Research Center, *Combat Logistics Support*, 58.

35   Ibid.

36   Ibid., 59.

37   Ibid.

38   Ibid., 30.

39   Ibid.

40   Yang Zhuotie [杨卓铁], "Looking at the Future Battlefield Graded Treatment from the Perspective of Epidemic Prevention and Control" [从疫情防控看未来战场分级救治], *PLA Daily* [解放军报], March 31, 2020, 7.

41   PLA Logistics Academic Research Center, *Combat Logistics Support*, 79.

42   Ibid.

43   Ibid., 80.

44   Ibid.

45   Huang Bingliang [黄炳亮] and Lu Liyang [吕立阳], "Discussion on Medical Support in Theater Joint Operations Under the Large Joint Logistics System" [大联勤体制下战区联合作战卫勤保障问题探讨], *Practical Journal of Medicine & Pharmacy* [实用医药] 25, no. 11 (2008), 1400.

46   Ibid.

47   Mao Zhenglu [毛正禄] et al., "Medical Service Based on Airborne Operation of Island Airborne Troops" [基于岛屿空降作战的卫勤保障], *Military Medical Journal of South China* [华南国防医学] 33, no. 5 (2019), 354.

48   Wang Jingtao [王景涛], Hai Jun [海军], and Ding Zhanfeng [丁展锋], "A SWOT-Analysis-Based Study of the Counter-Measures for the Construction and Development of Aviation Strategic Delivery Equipment" [基于SWOT分析的航空战略投送装备建设发展对策研究], *National Defense Transportation Engineering and Technology* [国防交通工程与技术], no. 4 (2018), 10.

49   PLA Logistics Academic Research Center, *Combat Logistics Support*, 48, 126.

50   Ibid.

51   Ibid., 48.

52 Ibid., 30.

53 Wei Yaocong [魏耀聪], Long Mianwei [龙绵伟], and Yin Linxuan [尹林喧], "Military Logistics Capability Construction Under New System" [新体制下军事物流能力建设研究], *Journal of Military Transportation University* [军事交通学院学报] 20, no. 5 (2018), 53.

54 Wang, Hai, and Ding, "A SWOT-Analysis-Based Study," 11.

55 Hu Haijun [胡海军] and Yao Yuan [姚远], "Transformation and Construction of Army Transportation Delivery Support Capability in Theater" [战区陆军运输投送保障能力转型建设], *Journal of Military Transportation University* [军事交通学院学报] 22, no. 4 (2020), 2.

56 Xu Duo [许多], Yao Qingkai [姚庆锴], and Song Hongchao [宋宏超], "Accelerate the Deep Development of Civil-Military Integration in Aviation Strategic Delivery System" [加快推进航空战略投送体系军民融合深度发展], *China Storage & Transport* [中国储运], no. 11 (2017), 118.

57 Zhang Jian [张健] and Wu Juan [吴娟], "Mobilization and Application of Offshore Civil Transport Ship in Large-Scale Combat" [大规模作战海上民用运输船舶动员与运用], *Journal of Military Transportation University* [军事交通学院学报] 19, no. 11 (2017), 3.

58 This is an estimate based on data made public by the Republic of China Ministry of National Defense with the exclusion of figures related to air-delivered personnel and materiel. See ROC Ministry of National Defense, *2018 China Military Power Report* (Taipei: Ministry of National Defense, 2018), 38.

59 Ibid.

60 Xu Jinzhang and Shen Peixin Ru Xiaolong, "Chinese Military's Logistics Development Moves Toward Realistic Training" [中国军队后勤向实战化聚力], *Red Flag* [红旗], March 6, 2014, available at <http://www.hongqi.tv/wwjz/2014-03-06/5471.html>.

61 Liu Jiasheng [刘嘉生], Sun Datong [孙大同], and Peng Fubing [彭富兵], "Development of Carriers for Strategic Projection in Response to National Security Needs" [基于国家安全需求的战略投送载运工具建设], *Journal of Military Transportation University* [军事交通学院学报] 21, no. 2 (February 2019), 12.

62 Cao Yang [曹杨], "Thoughts on Construction of Maritime Strategic Projection System in the New Era" [新时代海上战略投送体系建设的思考], *Journal of Military Transportation University* [军事交通学院学报] 21, no. 2 (2019), 3.

63 Hu and Yao, "Transformation and Construction of Army Transportation Delivery Support Capability," 2.

64 Han Qinggui [韩庆贵] and Liu Ning [刘宁], "A Preliminary Study on the Logistics Mobilization of Large-Scale Joint Operations" [大规模联合作战后勤动员初探], *National Defense* [国防], no. 12 (2016), 29.

65 Ibid.

66 Ibid.

67 Yue Shengjun [岳胜军] and Yu Chao [于超], "Analysis on the Operation Mechanism of National Defense Mobilization in Theaters" [战区国防动员运行机理探析], *National Defense* [国防], no. 3 (March 2017), 17.

68 Ibid.

69 Yu Zhonghai [于中海], "Focusing on the Main Duty and Main Business to Push Forward the National Defense Mobilization Preparation by the System of Provincial Military Commands" [聚焦主责主业，推进省军区系统国防动员准备], *National Defense* [国防], no. 10 (2019), 36.

[70] Ibid.; Zhoukoudian Prefectural Military Command [周口店军分区], "A Preliminary Inquiry into the Issue of the Provincial Military Commands System Supporting Cross-Theater Maneuvering by Operational Forces" [省军区系统保障作战部队跨区机动问题初探], *National Defense* [国防], no. 2 (2019), 31.

[71] Han and Liu, "A Preliminary Study on the Logistics Mobilization of Large-Scale Joint Operations," 29-31.

[72] Wang Fang [王芳], Guo Jing [郭静], and Wang Jizhen [王纪震], "Construction of a Smart Defense Mobilization Information System" [智能国防动员信息系统构建], *National Defense Technology* [国防科技], no. 321 (2020), 51.

[73] Han and Liu, "A Preliminary Study on the Logistics Mobilization of Large-Scale Joint Operations," 29-31.

[74] Zhoukoudian Prefectural Military Command, "A Preliminary Inquiry into the Issue of the Provincial Military Commands System," 32.

[75] Han and Liu, "A Preliminary Study on the Logistics Mobilization of Large-Scale Joint Operations," 29-31.

[76] "Eastern Theater Command Joins Hands with Seven Provinces and Cities to Promote Inclusion of 'Promoting the Military and Providing Frontline Support' Mechanism in Joint Operations System" [东部战区与七省市携手推动拥军支前融入联合作战体系], *China Military Online* [中国军网], December 19, 2017.

[77] Ibid.

[78] Han and Liu, "A Preliminary Study on the Logistics Mobilization of Large-Scale Joint Operations," 29-30.

[79] Linghu Yajun [令狐亚军], "Reflections on Building a Command System for 'Intelligent Mobilization'" [关于构建 "智慧动员" 指挥体系的思考], *National Defense* [国防], no. 10 (2019), 39.

[80] Xia Junyou [夏俊友], "Taking Multiple Measures Simultaneously and Making Innovations in Work to Concentrate Efforts on Improving the Development of National Defense Mobilization Potential in the New Era" [聚力提升新时代国防动员潜力建设水平], *National Defense* [国防], no. 12 (2019), 42.

[81] Ibid.

[82] For details, see Chung Chieh and Andrew N.D. Yang, "Crossing the Strait: Recent Trends in PLA 'Strategic Delivery' Capabilities," in *The PLA Beyond Borders: Chinese Military Operations in Regional and Global Context*, ed. Joel Wuthnow et al. (Washington, DC: NDU Press, 2021), 51-72.

[83] Ibid.

[84] Xia, "Taking Multiple Measures Simultaneously and Making Innovations in Work," 43.

[85] Wei, Long, and Yin, "Military Logistics Capability Construction," 54.

[86] Ibid., 53.

[87] Xiong Biao [熊彪] et al., "Evaluation Model and Simulation for Command and Decision of Joint Logistics Support" [联勤保障指挥决策评估模型构建与仿真分析], *Journal of Academy of Armored Forces Engineering* [装甲兵工程学院学报] 32, no. 3 (2018), 8.

[88] Tang and Long, "Some Thoughts on Advancing the Building of the Joint National Defense Mobilization System," 39.

[89] Sun Xinjian [孙新建] et al., "Design Research on Platform of Theater National Defense Mobilization Commanding and Coordination" [战区国防动员指挥协调平台设计研究], paper presented at the 6th China Command and Control Conference [第六届中国指挥控制大会], Beijing, July 2, 2018, 126.

90   Wei, Long, and Yin, "Military Logistics Capability Construction," 53.

91   Ibid.

92   Pan Jinkuan [潘金宽], "Mobilization of People's War Under Modern Conditions According to Law" [现代条件下人民战争依法动员], *China Defense Conversion* [中国军转民], no. 10 (2019), 81–82.

93   Yang Qinggan [杨清淦] and Liu Haixuan [浏海轩], "Some Thoughts on Strengthening the Work on People's Armed Forces in State-Owned Enterprises in the New Era" [加强新时代国有企业武装工作的几点思考], *National Defense* [国防], no. 9 (2019), 49.

94   Ibid., 50.

95   Zhong Fu [钟孚] and Zhang Renlong [章仁龙], "Issues to Be Considered in Developing Militia Cyber Elements" [民兵网络分队建设需关注的问题], *National Defense* [国防], no. 11 (2019), 64.

96   Chen Yu [陈瑜], Li Jiansi [李剑肆], and Zeng Yu [曾宇], "Research on Development of Overseas Strategic Airlift Capability" [境外空中战略投送能力建设研究], *Journal of Military Transportation University* [军事交通学院学报] 21, no. 2 (2019), 6.

97   Liu Ming [刘铭], "Maritime Strategic Projection Requirement and Force Construction of Our Armed Forces" [我军海上战略投送需求与力量建设], *Journal of Military Transportation University* [军事交通学院学报] 21, no. 4 (2019), 4.

98   Wei, Long, and Yin, "Military Logistics Capability Construction," 53.

99   Yang, "Looking at the Future Battlefield Graded Treatment from the Perspective of Epidemic Prevention and Control."

CHAPTER 10

Who Does What? Chinese Command and Control in a Taiwan Scenario

Joel Wuthnow

S timulated by the lack of progress on the "core interest" of unification, combat operations against Taiwan have been among primary planning scenarios of the People's Liberation Army (PLA) since the early 1990s.[1] Chinese planning has centered on joint campaigns either to persuade Taipei to capitulate, as would be the goal in a firepower strike or blockade, or to seize and occupy the island through a joint island landing campaign. The PLA has thus articulated doctrine for cross-strait campaigns, increased multidomain training, and sought to build forces that could execute the war plans. Significant attention was also given to constraining the U.S. ability to intervene on Taiwan's behalf. For two decades, however, the PLA lacked a modern joint command structure to take charge of those operations. China's Soviet-inspired military regions had limited ability to command naval and air forces, which weakened its ability to plan and train for joint operations, while a temporary realignment of authority in wartime would have created delays and provided a valuable warning for China's opponents.

Reforms led by Xi Jinping have reduced those weaknesses. Command arrangements for a Taiwan contingency are nested within the PLA's new joint command structure, consisting of key decisionmaking nodes at the national and theater levels. As a result, the PLA now has the system in place to prosecute the war, reducing delays and enabling stronger coordination among the services and support forces in peacetime. Yet several important constraints remain, including Leninist structures that reduce a commander's authority to execute decisions (these have been strengthened under Xi's desire to promote the role of the Chinese Communist Party in the army), an emphasis on centralization that increases the possibility of micromanagement and buck-passing, theater commanders' lack of direct authority over key support forces, and a risk-averse organizational culture aggravated by lack of experience.

The implications of a maturing PLA command structure for China's adversaries are mixed. On one hand, Taiwan and the United States must prepare for a PLA that could act more cohesively and expeditiously in a conflict and that is more confident in its own ability to command forces and thus more willing to ramp up coercion in peacetime. On the other hand, U.S. planners should consider how the apparent fragilities and tensions in the command structure can be exploited to strengthen Taiwan's defenses and buy time for U.S. intervention. Efforts should be made to complicate Chinese decisionmaking through rapid, intense, and hard-to-predict operations, including ones that aim to reduce the cohesion of China's fragmented joint operations system. Such operations would depend in part on conventional precision strikes in multiple domains, but the need to manage escalation risks would place greater emphasis on nonkinetic capabilities, such as cyber, electronic, and psychological warfare.

This chapter develops these arguments in three sections. The first describes current command arrangements for a Taiwan contingency and addresses the effects of recent reforms. The second section speculates about some of the potential weaknesses of these arrangements, focusing on issues of centralization and lack of experience. The third derives implications for the United States and Taiwan and develops principles for weakening China's ability to control its forces in a conflict. The chapter is based on a mix of Chinese doctrinal publications, authoritative Chinese media reports, and secondary works assessing the reforms. Nevertheless, much about the current system remains unknown or ambiguous, including the precise division of responsibilities between echelons, operational structures below the theater level, and how support forces are integrated into the theater commands (TCs). As a result, some of the judgments remain circumstantial or tentative.

An Improving Command System

China's previous command structure was poorly suited for joint campaigns across the Taiwan Strait. The military regions (MRs) lacked peacetime authority over naval and air forces, and Chinese doctrine suggested that hastily improvised joint commands would have been created to take charge of operations in a war zone. Under recent reforms, the PLA can now prepare for a conflict using the same command arrangement that would lead the war, consisting of the Joint Staff Department (JSD) and the Eastern Theater Command (ETC). This system not only facilitates better joint planning and training but also reduces delays associated with the transition from peacetime to wartime operations. There is also now stronger integration of the forces that would execute the war plans at the theater level, though the reforms stopped short of giving the ETC control over all relevant forces: Some are assigned to independent support forces or are "national assets" directly led by the services or the Central Military Commission (CMC).

A New Joint Command Structure

Prior to the recent reforms, PLA doctrinal writings suggested that an ad hoc joint headquarters would have been established to oversee joint campaigns. Chinese authors described various potential arrangements, with the final choice determined by the scope of the conflict. The most straightforward option involved converting the Nanjing MR into a joint "war zone" [*zhanqu*, 战区], with the MR commander appointed war zone commander. This plan would have followed existing MR boundaries but granted additional authority over air force, naval, and Second Artillery Corps forces, which reported to their respective service headquarters rather than the MR in peacetime. Another option, which would have been more likely in a large-scale contingency, envisioned establishing a new headquarters with boundaries beyond those of a single MR. PLA writings suggested that some of the commanders and staff, instead of relying on the Nanjing MR, would have been seconded from the General Staff Department in Beijing.[2]

A major flaw in this approach was that it was not optimized for a rapid transition to wartime operations.[3] First, MR responsibilities for administering land forces and lack of authority over naval and air forces meant less attention to joint training and operations, thus reducing combat readiness.

Second, the process of revising lines of authority could have created friction if those roles and responsibilities were unclear or disputed. Moreover, if officers from the General Staff Department took charge, they would have needed to quickly become familiar with subordinate commanders and forces not typically under their command. Third, the process of setting up ad hoc headquarters and accelerating joint training to promote combat readiness in the weeks and months prior to a conflict would have provided warning of a conflict to Taiwan and the United States. Recognizing these problems, the 2013 *Science of Strategy* called for building a command system "adapted to the needs and requirements of joint operations," including "a consistent peacetime-wartime joint command institution."[4] This vision reflected a desire to follow other foreign models more closely, such as the U.S. combatant command system, but was perhaps even more ambitious. For example, in the U.S. system, operational forces are typically retained by the Services and then transferred to a joint task force in wartime; Chinese planners advocated an organizational design that would eliminate such steps.[5]

Although these problems were discussed well before the recent reforms, bureaucratic resistance meant that previous CMC chairmen Jiang Zemin and Hu Jintao were unable to institute fundamental structural changes.[6] The 2015–2016 reform aimed to complete that unfinished business given Xi's better control over the bureaucracy. The pivotal contribution was establishing a permanent two-tiered joint command structure.[7] At the national level, the General Staff Department evolved into a JSD under direct CMC oversight and fully focused on joint command, with responsibilities for ground forces delegated to a new army headquarters. The JSD also manages a new joint operations command center (JOCC) whose nominal "commander in chief" is Xi himself (who appeared there in a camouflage uniform in April 2016).[8] At the theater level, five TCs were established to replace the MRs; the ETC now takes charge of cross-strait operations as well as those in the East China Sea. Similar to the national level, theater army components were established to free the theater headquarters to focus on joint operations, and theater JOCCs were created to facilitate operational planning and coordination.[9] In short, rather than standing up a command structure, the command system that would direct the war would already be in place.

In the context of a Taiwan campaign, the creation of a two-tiered structure conflicted with the emphasis of some PLA writings on collapsing command arrangements into a single overarching joint headquarters; however,
it reflected the complex responsibilities that would have to be managed in a
war.[10] First, a joint headquarters at the national level was needed to handle
contingencies not confined to a single TC. Preparing for such contingencies
appeared to be part of a national exercise in the summer of 2019 when the
JSD reportedly directed all five theaters and multiple services.[11] Given its position above the theaters and services, other JSD-level responsibilities also
likely include allocating resources that the CMC chooses to hold onto due to
scarcity or political sensitivity (such as space and cyber units) and managing
operations outside the geographic boundaries of the theater system (such as
counterintervention operations beyond the First Island Chain).[12]

Second, creating joint headquarters at the theater level reflected an operational imperative to devolve authority to those most familiar with specific
regional contingencies. One Academy of Military Science (AMS) author favor-
ably compared the U.S. system, based on geographic combatant commands,
with the Russian system, in which the concentration of power within the general staff creates a situation "which is not conducive to the deepening of jointness."[13] He stated more directly that systems with "a lower center of command
have greater joint depth than those with a higher center of command."[14] Authoritative sources thus describe the theaters as the "highest joint operations
command within their strategic direction," with responsibilities to organize
joint training, develop operational plans, and coordinate across services.[15] Giv-
en this peacetime focus, it is logical that the ETC would lead the primary campaigns in wartime, with the JSD focusing on national-level and cross-theater
issues. Nevertheless, the delineation of national and theater responsibilities remains somewhat ambiguous, and as discussed below, there are circumstances
in which the division of labor could break down in practice.[16]

Below the theater level, the peacetime chain of command runs through
the theater service components to operational units (see figure). However,
the wartime command structure at lower levels has not been clarified. Previous PLA writings suggested that task-oriented operations groups would be
established under the joint campaign command, organized either by function, such as intelligence, information, and firepower, or by domain.[17] Under

Figure. Notional C2 Construct for a Taiwan Campaign

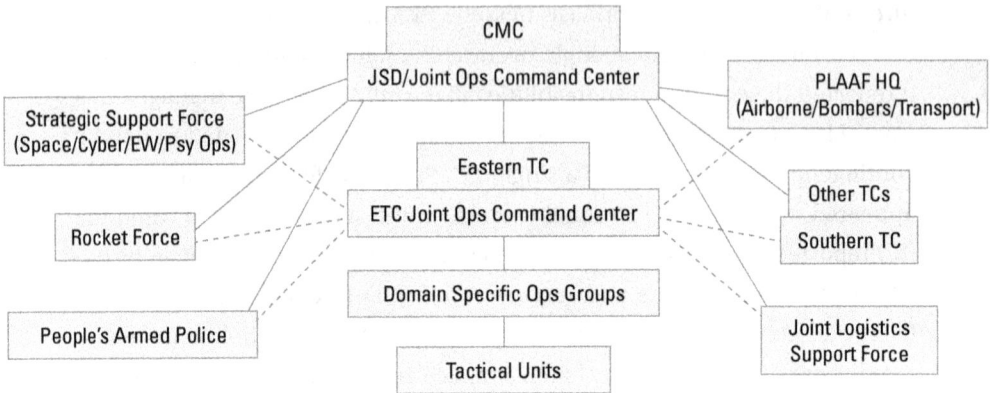

Key: CMC: Central Military Commission; EW: electronic warfare; ETC: Eastern Theater Command; HQ: headquarters; JSD: Joint Staff Department; PLAAF: PLA Air Force; TC: theater command.

Note: Straight lines = direct authority. Dashed lines = supporting/coordinating relationships.

the new structure, some of these functions may be carried out by the theater JOCC, and the theater service components might be placed in charge of certain domain-specific activities (for example, the ETC navy may be appointed as the lead for a maritime operations group). Yet the complexity of joint operations might also require the PLA to establish joint commands at lower levels. For instance, recent amphibious exercises have involved the use of frontline joint command posts to organize troops and process tactical intelligence, surveillance, and reconnaissance data.[18] China has also revealed new mobile truck-based joint command posts.[19] Nevertheless, it is presently unclear whether the ETC has standing joint command organs below the theater; however, more consistent joint training and planning would likely reduce delays if such arrangements needed to be set up on a temporary basis.

Stronger Horizontal Integration
One consequence of the lack of a permanent joint command structure was poor horizontal integration of forces that would participate in the primary cross-strait campaigns. The reforms corrected this problem, in part by transferring peacetime operational control over MR air and naval forces from their respective service headquarters to the theaters. This change was accompanied by greater "jointness" within the theaters. For example, there is now a

higher concentration of non–ground force senior officers in the ETC headquarters compared to the Nanjing MR, promoting more effective interservice
coordination and planning. As of 2019, four of five ETC deputy commanders
and two of five senior leaders in the ETC joint staff department were from the
navy and air force. By contrast, in 2014, the last full year before the reforms,
only two of five Nanjing MR deputy commanders and none of its headquarters department senior leaders were from outside the ground forces.[20]

A less obvious benefit of the reforms has been better integration of support
forces into the theater construct. Forces that might have to support the ETC
commander in wartime include conventional missile forces under the PLA
Rocket Force (PLARF), the airborne corps under PLA Air Force headquarters,
space and cyber troops under the Strategic Support Force (SSF), logistics resources managed by the Joint Logistic Support Force (JLSF), rear-area support
provided by the People's Armed Police (PAP), and forces assigned to other TCs.[21]
Chinese writings emphasize the need to ensure smooth coordination of these
forces into theater operations. AMS scholar Zhang Peigao notes that counterintervention operations would seek to merge theater forces with "elite units" [jin-
grui budui, 精锐部队] outside the theater structure, including those responsible
for the electromagnetic and "socio-psychological" domains.[22] Han Guangsong,
a professor at the PLA National Defense University (NDU) Joint Operations College, writes that joint commands must coordinate with "neighboring troops in
accordance with a clear coordination and support relationship."[23]

While the ETC commander does not possess de facto control over these
capabilities, the theater's mandate to supervise joint campaigns implies the
need for stronger coordination. Nevertheless, the degree to which forces
outside the theater commander's direct control have been integrated into
theater training, planning, and operations has varied. The discussion that follows categorizes forces into three tiers based on level of integration with the
ETC (see table 1). Key variables include whether the ETC JOCC has officers
seconded from those forces, participation in recent ETC exercises, inclusion
in the ETC's annual joint training plans, and whether units from those forces
are based within the ETC's geographic boundaries. These are, of course, tentative judgments given limited open-source reporting.

The first tier currently consists only of the conventional PLARF brigades. The
PLARF, unlike the other services, has neither a service component command

Table 1. Integration of Supporting Units with the Eastern Theater Command

	Officers in ETC JOCC	Participation in ETC Exercises	Coordinated in ETC Joint Training Plan	Units Based in ETC AOR
Tier 1				
PLARF (Conventional)	X	X	X	X
Tier 2				
SSF		X		X
JLSF		X	X	X
PAP		X		X
Tier 3				
Other TCs				
Airborne Corps				

Key: AOR: area of responsibility; ETC: Eastern Theater Command; JLSF: Joint Logistic Support Force; PAP: People's Armed Police; PLARF: PLA Rocket Force; SSF: Strategic Support Force; TCs: theater commands.

within the theater nor a commander who serves concurrently as theater deputy commander. There is, however, evidence of a strong coordinating relationship between the PLARF and the ETC. Short-range ballistic missiles under Base 61, which commands the PLARF brigades within the ETC region, would be central to a joint firepower campaign. As the lead organizer for theater joint campaigns, the ETC commander would likely be able to incorporate short-range missile systems into theater campaign plans and direct their use during a war.

By contrast, a differentiation of responsibilities within the command structure, and the desire by the center to retain control of "strategic" systems, make it likely that long-range missiles designed for counterintervention purposes would be handled at the JSD or CMC level.[24] In March 2016, ETC commander Liu Yuejun suggested as much by including rocket forces among those that "conduct joint operations and non-war military operations" in his theater.[25] More specific signs of close coordination include PLARF officers assigned to the ETC JOCC,[26] inclusion of a PLARF base in the 2018 ETC joint training plan [*zhanqu lianhe xunlian jihua*, 战区联合训练计划],[27] and participation of PLARF units in ETC exercises.[28] Moreover, Roderick Lee observes that joint duty offices within PLARF bases have been designated as "theater conventional missile sub-command centers," indicating closer collaboration with the theater compared with other supporting forces.[29]

The second tier includes three support forces that would participate in a cross-strait campaign but appear somewhat less well integrated with the TCs than the PLARF: the SSF, JLSF, and PAP.[30]

Strategic Support Force. The SSF was created in 2016 to consolidate control over space, cyber, electronic warfare, and psychological warfare capabilities. Within the ETC region, the SSF operates Base 311, which has long been responsible for carrying out psychological operations against Taiwan, and various cyber units (including Unit 61398, which has targeted Taiwan).[31] PLA theoretical discussions suggest that the technical reconnaissance bases, which are responsible for cyber operations, could be attached to theater JOCCs in wartime. However, there does not yet appear to be conclusive open-source evidence that those bases report to the theaters in peacetime.[32] Evidence that SSF units are coordinating with the theaters includes their reported role in an August 2020 ETC island-landing exercise intended to "further test and improve the joint combat capabilities of multiple services,"[33] as well as their inclusion in exercises in adjacent theaters.[34]

Joint Logistic Support Force. Established in September 2016, the JLSF is organized into five joint logistic support centers (JLSCs), which in turn supervise a network of supply bases and mobile logistics units.[35] During peacetime, the JLSCs fall under the JLSF headquarters but, according to one JLSF officer, could be placed under theater control in wartime.[36] Within the ETC region, the Wuxi JLSC is the prime element of the JLSF. Evidence of fairly strong coordination between joint logistics forces and the ETC includes the Wuxi JLSC's inclusion in the 2018 ETC joint training plan and direct support from JLSC units to ETC air force and army units during routine operations.[37] The Wuxi JLSC also oversees the assembly of civilian aviation and maritime support fleets, which have supported naval operations in the "near seas" and could be mobilized for strategic sealift and other purposes during a Taiwan contingency (see the chapter by Conor Kennedy in this volume for details).[38] This capability almost certainly requires the JLSC to coordinate with theater planners.

People's Armed Police. While primarily responsible for maintaining social control in restive regions within China, the PAP has certain wartime functions, such as guarding facilities and maintaining infrastructure, and has been involved in previous joint exercises.[39] Recent reforms firmly placed the PAP within the military command structure by eliminating the previous system that granted deployment powers to provincial leaders.[40] Within the ETC region, the PAP presence includes provincial contingents and a new mobile contingent [*jidong zongdui*, 机动总队] based in Fuzhou.[41] This unit, which possesses a mix of capabilities (including engineering, transportation, and special operations), is well placed to support rear-area operations in a Taiwan scenario. Whether the PAP has been formally integrated into ETC joint training plans is unclear; however, PAP units have taken part in some ETC exercises,[42] and the second mobile contingent was temporarily placed under ETC authority during 2020 flood relief operations.[43]

The third tier consists of forces with the lowest level of integration into ETC training and operations. One is the airborne corps, which continues to be a "national asset" under the direct authority of air force headquarters (for a discussion, see the chapter by Roderick Lee in this volume).[44] Airborne units are based in the Central Theater Command, and there is no open-source evidence of their participation in ETC-sponsored exercises.[45] The other TCs also fit into this category. In theory, forces in other TCs might be mobilized to augment the ETC: for instance, the Central TC functions as a strategic reserve for all the theaters while the Southern TC has a variety of naval and air force capabilities that could be integrated into a joint campaign. The PLA has conducted transregional exercises since 2006, suggesting a desire to improve the ability of troops to support contingencies in other theaters. However, it is unclear whether any of those troops were placed under the Nanjing MR or ETC commander.[46] In sum, command for a cross-strait campaign has benefited from a new command structure that would reduce the transition to a wartime footing and has, despite some variation, strengthened the integration of disparate units into theater joint training and planning.

Persistent Weaknesses

Despite these improvements, several continuing problems could reduce the PLA command system's effectiveness in wartime by complicating decisionmaking and slowing operations. These include a Leninist organizational culture that retains consensus decisionmaking through Party committees and values control at the highest possible level, which could limit the ETC commander's ability to quickly execute the war plan and make adjustments; lead to continued fragmentation between the ETC and the national, service, and external theater forces needed to support it; and create a lack of proficiency in joint operations among the commanders and staff officers charged with enabling the system to function smoothly at both the theater and the national levels.

Decisions by Consensus

Chinese strategists struggle to reconcile the military imperative of concentrating authority in the hands of a single commander given the Leninist prescription that decisions be reached collectively through Party committees and the dual leadership system (commanders and political commissars). Zhang Peigao writes that neither individual nor collective leadership should be "overemphasized at the expense of the other." Referencing PLA political work regulations, Zhang states that in "critical situations," joint campaigns can be handled ad hoc by "senior officers," who must then "promptly report to the party committee and receive an inspection."[47] A PLA treatise states that one must "correctly handle the relationship between the Party committee's decisions and the commander's resolutions." The distinction between the two is vague, with the former responsible for decisions on operational concepts, policies, and principles, and the latter assuming "concentrated power" over "joint campaign activities," albeit "under the Party committee's unified leadership."[48] Recent reforms did not resolve this tension; instead, reforms have emphasized the role of Party committees to retain unified control over operations.[49]

The political pressures of a Taiwan contingency could intensify the contradiction between individual and collective leadership. Any war against Taiwan would implicate the Party's "core interests," and political officers would be expected to monitor the commander to ensure that operational decisions do not damage those interests.[50] Those tendencies could be exacerbated by the character of modern conflicts, in which tactical actions (for example, a strike on a specific U.S. platform) could have profound strategic effects. Whether political scrutiny would lead to interference or even sanctions, though, would depend on idiosyncratic variables, including the ways in which individual services and units have interpreted the dual leadership system,[51] the nature of relationships between individual officers, and differences in judgment about the likely consequences of a course of action.[52] There is also a chance that theater or lower commanders, wary of reprimand either during or after the conflict, could seek a consensus prior to acting (which could range from a simple conversation to a decision punted to the Party committee, which also includes deputy commanders and political commissars). Those dynamics could slow decisionmaking, especially in circumstances in which the perceived risks of failure or escalation are high.

Micromanagement and Buck-Passing

A division of labor in which the ETC assumes primary responsibility for executing an island-landing or other cross-strait operation would require the CMC to delegate significant authority to the theater and provide national assets that typically reside outside theater control. This situation rests uneasily and may be difficult to reconcile given the countervailing tendency in Leninist systems to centralize authority among the smallest group of leaders at the highest possible level. Reflecting this tradition, Zhang writes that, in joint commands, centralization should be primary and supplemented by decentralized command (not the other way around); joint campaigns should therefore not "blindly follow" the dictum that "whoever is in charge of operations is in command" [*shei zhuzhan, shei zhihui,* 谁主战, 谁指挥].[53] The emphasis on centralizing—rather than distributing—control is also evident in recent decisions to break up the former general departments and place their remnants within the CMC, the increasing power of central supervisory organs within the PLA, and Xi's apparent interventions in personnel decisions down to the level of corps commander.[54]

Centralization could complicate efforts to achieve an effective balance of responsibilities between the JSD and theater levels in two ways. First is micromanagement: the CMC chairman and his associates may decide that theater operations require close personal oversight. Unlike contemporary gray zone operations, in which the risks of a strategic disaster are low, the direct connection between the outcome of a Taiwan campaign and the regime's (and Xi's or his successor's personal political) survival may heighten the temptation to keep a tight rein on activities at the theater level. (This tendency would be greatest in the "imploding China" scenario discussed in Andrew Scobell's chapter in this volume.) Xi, with little military experience of his own, would task his key lieutenants, including the CMC vice chairman responsible for operations and the JSD chief of staff, to scrutinize decisions made by the ETC commander or even override them in cases of differences in judgment. Those officials may in turn task officers in the national JOCC to liaise with the ETC.

Several factors, however, could push against the tendency to micromanage and support a delegation of power back to the theaters. The dominant countervailing factor would be widespread acceptance of the principle that power should be devolved; that acceptance could be higher among younger officers more attuned to the imperatives of modern operations. But other factors could also be instrumental. JSD officials with service in the Nanjing MR or ETC might be more confident in their ability to issue operational guidance, but those without such experience might be more comfortable yielding decisionmaking authority to the theaters (where, in any case, the theater commanders could be blamed for errors in judgment). As table 2 demonstrates, in recent years only a few JSD officials had operational experience in the ETC, potentially mitigating the impetus to micromanage. Another factor would be the nature of the relationship between officials at both levels. For example, good working relationships would facilitate more rapid and effective transfer of responsibility back to the theaters compared with situations in which officials did not know each other well or had conflicting personalities.[55]

Table 2. Backgrounds of Senior Joint Staff Department Officials, 2016–2019

Name	Position	Service	Years	Previous Positions				
				Group Army (Home)	GSD/ GD	ETC/ Nanjing	Other MR/TC	Service HQ
GEN Fang Fenghui	COS	GF	16–17	21st (Lanzhou)	X		X	
ADM Sun Jianguo	DCOS	Navy	16–17	N/A				X
GEN Wang Jianping	DCOS	GF	16	40th (Shenyang)				X (PAP)
GEN Xu Fenlin	DCOS	GF	16–	17th (Lanzhou)			X	
GEN Wang Guanzhong	DCOS	GF	16–17		X			

Name	Position	Service	Years	Previous Positions				
				Group Army (Home)	GSD/ GD	ETC/ Nanjing	Other MR/TC	Service HQ
GEN Qi Jianguo*	DCOS	GF	16–17	1st (Nanjing)	X			
LTG Yi Xiaoguang*	DCOS	AF	16–17	N/A	X	X	X	X
LTG Ma Yiming	DCOS	GF	16–	20th (Jinan)	X		X	
GEN Li Zuocheng	COS	GF	17–	41st (Guang-zhou)			X	X
LTG Shao Yuanming	DCOS	RF	17–	N/A				X
LTG Chang Dingqiu	DCOS	AF	17–	N/A			X	X
RADM Jiang Guoping	Asst. to COS	Navy	17–19	N/A				
MG Chen Guangjun	Asst. to COS	RF	17–	N/A				
MG Han Xiaodong	Asst. to COS	GF	18–	Unknown	X			
MG Jia Jiancheng	Dir., Ops. Bureau	GF	18–	Unknown	X			
MG Zhang Jian*	Dir., Ops. Bureau	GF	17–18	42nd (Guang-zhou)			X	

Key: AF: Air Force; COS: chief of staff; DCOS: deputy chief of staff; ETC: Eastern Theater Command; GD: General Department; GF: Ground Force; GSD: General Service Department; HQ: headquarters; MR: military region; PAP: People's Armed Police; RF: Rocket Force; TC: theater command.

Sources: 2016–2019 PRC Directories of Military Personalities and various People's Republic of China Web sites.

Notes:
* Signifies operational experience in the Nanjing MR or ETC.
† MG Zhang spent 1 year (February 2016–March 2017) as Eastern Theater Command army chief of staff. He was later promoted to ETC army commander.

The second way in which centralization could affect decisionmaking is buck-passing—hesitance by theater commanders to implement decisions without explicit approval. Risk aversion among commanders remains a persistent theme of PLA self-critiques, and regulations have attempted to clarify that officers' promotions and assignments will not be affected by mistakes due to a willingness to take initiative.[56] Yet the political stakes for a cross-strait campaign, including the possibility that Party leaders would fix the blame for any failures on the mistakes of those charged with carrying out the war plans, could lead ETC officials to err on the side of seeking higher authorization for even minor decisions. For instance, the ETC Party committee could collectively decide to transfer a decision to the next-highest Party committee, at the CMC level. In decisions with high risks of failure or embarrassment, it is also possible to imagine an amalgamation of two tendencies: the JSD putting off decisions to theater leaders, who could be more easily blamed, combined with bottom-up pressures to send decisions up to the center, leading to delays or paralysis with no one willing to take responsibility.

Stovepiping

While reforms have produced a higher level of jointness within the theaters, integration of support forces and other capabilities into the theater joint command system remains incomplete due to a combination of political, operational, and bureaucratic factors. One impediment is the conflict between the political imperative to centralize control over sensitive capabilities and the operational goal to devolve authority to the theater commanders who may need to employ those assets. Indeed, the merging of forces previously under MR control into the SSF and JLSF has in fact increased the Central Military Commission's ability to manage assets at the expense of the theaters.[57] The center also consolidated authority over the PAP as well as the provincial military districts, responsible for reserve and militia forces, which were transferred from the MRs to a new national defense mobilization department under the CMC. These changes reveal a preference for prioritizing central control over the empowerment of theater commanders.

China's complex security environment also creates an operational logic to distribute forces away from a single theater. Because the PLA must prepare for a variety of contingencies other than Taiwan, it makes sense for the center to directly manage scarce resources such as space, cyber, and logistics forces that may need to be employed elsewhere. The theaters themselves must address diverse threats, reducing their ability to act as a supporting actor for the ETC. Even in a cross-strait campaign, the other theaters would need to deter other rivals and thus prevent what Chinese strategists call "chain reaction warfare" [*liansuo fanying zhanzheng*, 连锁反应战争] while also dealing with U.S. intervention threats across China's littorals.[58] For instance, former Nanjing MR deputy commander Lieutenant General Wang Hongguang states that a key role of the Southern TC would be to serve as a "blocker," preventing U.S. intervention along China's southern flank.[59] These conflicting missions reduce the availability of forces from other theaters to assist the ETC either in joint training or wartime operations.

In other cases, a conflux of bureaucratic and operational reasons reduces the potential for theater-level integration of forces. A prime example is the consolidation of authority by air force headquarters over the airborne corps as well as select transport divisions and special mission aircraft.[60] Bureaucratically, control over these assets reflects a tacit concession to the air force headquarters, which otherwise has ceded operational authority to the theaters and is thus a source of leverage that the air force is likely to argue should remain in its purview. Operationally, these capabilities constitute scarce resources that may need to support not only cross-strait operations but also a range of other combat and nontraditional security missions domestically, regionally, and farther afield, thus strengthening the argument for centralization.[61] The combination of these factors creates a ceiling on the ETC's ability to integrate other forces into its training and operational planning processes.

Inadequate Joint Expertise

The effectiveness of both tiers of the joint command structure in a Taiwan contingency would also depend on the quality of the officers assigned to the ETC and JSD. Improving the ability of PLA officers to plan and execute joint operations has been a goal of PLA training and military education reforms for more than two decades.[62] However, recognizing the insufficiency of earlier reforms, Xi-era changes have focused on improving joint skills through a new CMC Training and Administration Department, which establishes standards and dispatches teams to evaluate theater joint training programs,[63] and by expanding education on joint operations to focus on younger officers, most notably through a new NDU Joint Operations College.[64] Moreover, the ETC, along with the other theaters, has instituted training programs for commanders and staff officers aimed at improving their ability to operate JOCCs and plan theater-specific campaigns.[65]

Nevertheless, several factors could weaken the PLA's ability to improve human capital. First is the lack of experience in conducting real-world joint operations.[66] The PLA has gained some recent combat experience at a very small scale in the 2020 border clash with Indian forces and has practiced higher end joint operations in wargames and simulations. However, no one serving in the PLA has experience executing any of the primary cross-strait campaigns. Second is the lack of a rotational assignment system. The PLA, unlike the post–Goldwater-Nichols system in the United States, does not require officers to rotate through joint assignments, nor does it require commanders to attain education in this area until reaching the corps commander level.[67] The limited flow of officers between joint organizations at the national and theater levels is also a problem to the extent that it reduces mutual understanding of roles and responsibilities at both levels. Third, as suggested above, the Leninist tendency toward centralization limits the PLA's ability to develop a culture of empowering lower level commanders.[68] Taken together, these weaknesses in the new joint command structure could reduce the system's effectiveness in a Taiwan campaign and provide opportunities for China's opponents.

Implications for the United States and Taiwan

From a U.S. and Taiwan perspective, China's evolving command and control system has mixed implications. On one hand, the new system has several advantages for China that are likely to promote more effective control of PLA operations:

- a stronger ability to manage and redistribute scarce resources through the JSD, SSF, and JLSF
- quicker transitions to war since most of the system that would take charge of operations (except for ad hoc structures below the theater level) is already in place
- consolidated theater authority over land, air, and naval forces in peacetime
- stronger integration of conventional missile and, to a lesser degree, other support forces into the ETC
- greater proficiency in joint operations as training and educational reforms begin to take hold.

Given those advantages, U.S. and Taiwan defense planners must update operational concepts to account for reduced warning times and a stronger

PLA ability to execute joint campaigns. Moreover, both Washington and Taipei should anticipate that greater cohesion in the command structure would give Beijing a higher degree of confidence in the PLA's ability to manage risks and thus pursue a wider range of coercive activities in peacetime.[69]

On the other hand, the foregoing analysis identified several potential weaknesses that may be exploited to gain operational advantages or at least buy additional time to allow U.S. forces to arrive. PLA decisionmaking would likely be slower and more convoluted than that of its opponents due to several factors:

- tensions between individual and collective decisionmaking and potential interference from political officers and Party committees
- temptations by the center to micromanage conflicts
- impulses at lower levels to pass decisions back up the chain of command, reducing the ETC commander's ability or willingness to execute timely decisions
- the PLA's lack of experience conducting joint operations and a risk-averse organizational culture that the PLA has been slow to correct.

The best way to leverage these weaknesses is, according to the 2018 National Defense Strategy, to "expand the competitive space" by conducting intense, rapid, and unpredictable operations, including those in multiple domains and from multiple directions.[70]

Conventional strikes launched from submarines, long-range bombers, mobile ground-based missiles, and other strike platforms constitute one way to achieve these effects.[71] Chinese strategy, of course, aims to deny those forces the ability to operate within the Western Pacific. However, doctrine being developed by the U.S. Services is focused on enabling those platforms to operate more effectively inside China's antiaccess/area-denial envelope.[72] The problem is that such kinetic actions incur significant risks of escalation, especially when used against targets inside China, and thus might be harder for U.S. political leaders to consent to in the first place. Moreover, Taiwan's defense planners should consider how long-range strike assets such as the Hsiung Feng IIE might also be used in such operations (for more information, see Drew Thompson's chapter in this volume).

As an alternative, U.S. planners might consider expanding operations in the information domain (for example, deception, misinformation, false signals), utilizing cyber, special operations/psychological warfare, and electronic warfare capabilities. Such operations, whether unilateral or in coordination with Taiwan's armed forces, should aim to reduce the confidence of Chinese civilian leaders and PLA senior officers in the likely effectiveness of operational units, inducing caution prior to a decision to use force or, barring that, disrupting the PLA's ability to execute its war plans. Attention to these solutions, however, may require greater investments and coordination between U.S. combatant commands.[73]

U.S. operations might also exploit the fragmentation of the PLA joint operations system. The system that has developed in practice is not the singular joint campaign command envisioned in conceptual PLA writings, but rather a complex system involving various actors segregated by geography and function. Key nodes include the national JOCC (Beijing), SSF headquarters (Beijing), ETC JOCC and ETC air force headquarters (Nanjing), Base 61 (Huangshan), naval headquarters (Ningbo), army headquarters (Fuzhou), and JLSC headquarters (Wuxi), along with potential tactical joint command posts in variable locations.[74] For the system to operate effectively, reliable communications need to be maintained throughout the chain of command and across the supporting-supported relationships. Whereas U.S. forces have strengths in operating in a communications-degraded environment, in part due to comfort with a "mission command" philosophy, it is doubtful the PLA would be able to operate with similar efficacy if, say, mobile command posts were cut off from the ETC headquarters or if theater commanders faced complications in communicating with the center.

Degrading the links between these organizations would create a specific dilemma that the PLA would have to resolve, thus complicating its decision-making and denying it the ability to coordinate effectively across echelons. Anticipating such threats, the PLA has instituted "robust, redundant communications networks to improve commanders' situational awareness."[75] Thus, U.S. and Taiwan defense planners need to think through the range of potential vulnerabilities and response options. Again, a basic choice is between kinetic strikes against key nodes in the communications infrastructure and nonkinetic means. To reduce the risks of escalation, offensive cyber tools might be used to reduce the reliability of key networks or inject false information, creating confusion at different points in the chain of command. Consideration should also be given to targeting weaknesses in logistics information systems, which may be more widely accessible and thus less well defended than command and control systems.

U.S. operations could also reduce the cohesiveness of China's joint operations systems by creating dilemmas beyond the Taiwan Strait. Horizontal escalation, in this context, would aim to stress the JSD's ability to manage a war on multiple fronts, divert resources from the main theater, and ultimately force the PLA to deviate from its timelines and improvise responses to unexpected U.S. actions. While attractive in concept, this approach may prove difficult to execute in practice due to a high level of Chinese resolve once a decision to use force against Taiwan has been made (the Party would not back down lightly), scarce U.S. resources, limited U.S. political will to get into a broader conflict with China, the unwillingness of third parties to allow U.S. forces to operate from their territory, and a theater command system that would be in a heightened state of readiness. As a matter of planning, though, consideration should be given to whether strikes against Chinese naval targets beyond the Taiwan Strait,[76] blockades of Chinese oil imports,[77] or information operations that point to an incipient crisis elsewhere would be sufficient to disorient Chinese decisionmaking and have enough effect in the main theater to justify the risk.

Conclusion

U.S. and Taiwan planners need to consider not only how to defeat specific PLA platforms and operate within an increasingly difficult antiaccess/area-denial environment but also how to leverage weaknesses in the broader PLA structure to complicate the ability of PLA commanders to utilize those systems effectively. Chinese strategists are aware of faults in their own system and have advocated for structural changes designed to increase the cohesiveness of joint operations. Recent reforms have put some of their suggestions into practice. Yet changes to the organizational culture of the PLA that would help produce more efficient decisionmaking and operations, such as eliminating Party committees or clearly delegating authority over sensitive capabilities to the theaters, have eluded reformers and may not even be possible in a Leninist system. Lack of combat experience would also continue to pose problems until the PLA actually finds itself in a war. This situation creates opportunities for exploitation by China's adversaries. Prudent planning and investments, especially in nontraditional domains, are necessary if those continuing weaknesses are to be converted to operational advantage.

For helpful comments on previous drafts, the author thanks David Chen, Fiona Cunningham, Scott W. Harold, Colonel Rafael Lopez, USA, and Phillip C. Saunders.

Notes

¹ M. Taylor Fravel, *Active Defense: Chinese Military Strategy Since 1949* (Princeton: Princeton University Press, 2019), 182–216. See also David M. Finkelstein, "China's National Military Strategy: An Overview of the 'Military Strategic Guidelines,'" in *Right Sizing the People's Liberation Army: Exploring the Contours of China's Military*, ed. Roy Kamphausen and Andrew Scobell (Carlisle, PA: Strategic Studies Institute, 2007), 69–140.

² For depictions of alternative models, see Xue Yanxu [薛彦绪] and Fan Jiabin [范嘉宾], *Joint Operations Command and Coordination Under High-Tech Conditions* [高技术条件下联合作战指挥与协同] (Beijing: National Defense University Press, 2003), 88–97. In the context of an island-landing campaign, see Zhang Peigao, *Lectures on Joint Campaign Command* [联合战役指挥教程] (Beijing: Academy of Military Science [AMS], 2012), 192–193. For analyses, see Dean Cheng, "The PLA's Wartime Structure," in *The PLA as Organization v2.0*, ed. Kevin Pollpeter and Kenneth Allen (Vienna, VA: Defense Group, Inc., 2015), 458–461; Mark A. Stokes, "Employment of National-Level PLA Assets in a Contingency: A Cross-Strait Conflict as Case Study," in *The People's Liberation Army and Contingency Planning in China*, ed. Andrew Scobell et al. (Washington, DC: NDU Press, 2015), 140–141.

³ For PLA self-assessments, see Dang Chongmin [党崇民] and Zhang Yu [张羽], *Science of Joint Operations* [联合作战学] (Beijing: PLA Press, 2009), 249; Wang Xiaohui [王晓辉], "What Strategic Preparations Should China's Military Make in a Transition Era?" [转型期中国军队要做哪些战略准备], *National Defense Reference* [国防参考], October 27, 2015; Fang Yongzhi [房永智], "When Will the Chinese Military Set Up Its Joint Operations Command?" [中国军队何时设立联合作战司令部?], *China Youth Daily* [中国青年报], March 28, 2014, available at <http://zqb.cyol.com/html/2014-03/28/nw.D110000zgqnb_20140328_1-10.htm>.

⁴ AMS Military Strategy Studies Department, *Science of Strategy* [战略学] (Beijing: Military Science Press, 2013), 201.

⁵ Thanks to Rafael Lopez for this observation.

⁶ Concerns about parochialism hobbling reforms have been longstanding for the PLA. See Kenneth W. Allen et al., *Institutional Reforms of the Chinese People's Liberation Army: Overview and Challenges* (Arlington, VA: CNA, 2002), 67–69.

⁷ For a general overview, see Joel Wuthnow, "A Brave New World for Chinese Joint Operations," *Journal of Strategic Studies* 40, no. 1–2 (2017), 169–195; Edmund J. Burke and Arthur Chan, "Coming to a (New) Theater Near You: Command, Control, and Forces," in *Chairman Xi Remakes the PLA*, ed. Phillip C. Saunders et al. (Washington, DC: NDU Press, 2019), 227–255.

⁸ "President Xi Visits CMC Joint Operations Command Center," *China Military Online*, April 21, 2016.

⁹ For a description of the Eastern Theater Command Joint Operations Command Center (JOCC), see "'Gunpowder Smoke' Is Strong in the Eastern TC Joint Operations Command Center" [东部战区联合作战指挥中心 "硝烟味" 浓烈], *Jiefangjun Bao* [解放军报], February 16, 2016, available at <http://military.people.com.cn/n1/2016/0216/c1011-28126703.html>.

¹⁰ On reducing command layers, see Dong and Zhang, *Science of Joint Operations*, 248.

¹¹ "Hong Kong Media: The Five Theater Commands Are Moving Together, the Central Military Commission Takes the Lead, Taiwan-Focused Drill Is Just One Part of the Large Exercise" [港媒: 大陆五大战区齐动中央军委牵头对台军演仅为大军演一部分], *Zao Bao* (Singapore), August 2, 2019, available at <https://www.zaobao.com.sg/realtime/china/story20190802-977728>; "The Five Major Branches of the People's Liberation Army May Participate in Military Exercises in the Southeast Coast" [解放军五大军种或将悉数参加在东南沿海军演], *Huanqiu Shibao* [环球时报], July 15, 2019, available at <https://mil.news.sina.com.cn/china/2019-07-15/doc-ihytcerm3686362.shtml>.

¹² Joel Wuthnow, *System Overload: Can China's Military Be Distracted in a War over Taiwan?* China Strategic Perspectives No. 15 (Washington, DC: NDU Press, 2020), 19–22; Phillip C. Saunders, *Beyond Borders: PLA Command and Control of Overseas Operations*, INSS Strategic Forum No. 306 (Washington, DC: NDU Press, 2020).

¹³ Xu Xuesong [许雪松], "Historic Development and Fundamental Rules of Joint Operation Command System of Foreign Military Forces" [外军联合作战指挥体制的历史发展及其基本规律], *Military History* [军事历史], no. 3 (2019), 104–105.

¹⁴ Ibid.

¹⁵ Liang Liqiang [梁力强] and Sun Bingxiang [孙炳祥], "How to Develop Joint Operations Command Talent? The Southern TC Has Developed a Blueprint" [联战指挥人才如何培养? 南部战区绘制人才成长蓝图], *Jiefangjun Bao* [解放军报], November 12, 2018, available at <http://www.mod.gov.cn/power/2018-11/12/content_4829238.htm>; "Military Media: Each Theater Can Fight Independently and Support Each Other at Any Time" [军媒: 每一个战区都可以独立作战, 相互间又能随时支援], *The Paper* [澎湃新闻], February 4, 2018, available at <https://www.thepaper.cn/newsDetail_forward_1982789>.

¹⁶ Sorting out respective roles and responsibilities was an initial focus of the reforms, even if few authoritative details have been released on the results of these efforts. During an inspection of the Center Military Committee (CMC) JOCC in February 2017, Xi enjoined the PLA to "quickly straighten out relevant major relationships and to improve the joint operations command mechanism" and to standardize "command powers and responsibilities." A Joint Staff Department commentary similarly observed the need to "improve the organization, optimize procedures, clarify responsibilities, and improve the joint operation command and operational modes." See Lin Qiang [林强], "Strive to Build a Strong Joint Operations Command Structure" [努力建设过硬联合作战指挥机构], *People's Daily* [人民日报], February 28, 2017, available at <http://theory.gmw.cn/2017-02/28/content_23857525.htm>; "This Article Signed 'CMC Joint Staff Department' Is Worth a Read" [这篇署名 "中央军委联合参谋部" 的文章值得一读], Ministry of National Defense, August 20, 2016.

¹⁷ Jeffrey Engstrom, *Systems Confrontation and System Destruction Warfare* (Santa Monica, CA: RAND, 2018), 28–36.

[18] For instance, an October 2020 Eastern Theater Command landing exercise included a forward command post synthesizing tactical intelligence, surveillance, and reconnaissance and directing firepower strikes. See "The Eastern TC Discloses a Complete Landing Exercise, Taiwan Media Calls It a 'Warning'" [东部战区披露的这次完整登陆演练, 台媒直呼有 "警告" 意味], *Beijing Youth Daily* [北京青年报], October 11, 2020, available at <https://m.us.sina.com/gb/china/sinacn/2020-10-11/detail-ihaauwts5940528.shtml>.

[19] "Official Media Reveals State-Produced New-Type Joint Operations Mobile Command Truck 'Foresight'" [官媒揭秘国产新型联合作战机动指挥车 "远谋"], available at <https://mil.news.sina.com.cn/china/2021-09-30/doc-iktzscyx7136684.shtml>.

[20] Information provided in the *Directory of PRC Military Personalities* (Washington, DC: Department of Defense, 2014 and 2019).

[21] Stokes, "Employment of National-Level PLA Assets in a Contingency," 143–145.

[22] Zhang, *Lectures on Joint Campaign Command*, 212–213.

[23] Han Guangsong [韩光松], "Joint Operation Command and Control Based on Modern Control Theory" [基于现代控制理论的联合作战指挥控制], *Fire Control & Command Control* [火力与指挥控制], no. 5 (2020), 18.

[24] Longer range systems used for operations beyond the Taiwan Strait might be centralized within the Joint Staff Department or CMC; this would preserve political control and accord with a notional division of labor between the two echelons.

[25] "Eastern TC Commander Liu Yuejun Speaks About Construction of Joint Operations Command Capabilities" [东部战区司令员刘粤军谈联合作战指挥能力建设], *Caixin* [财新], March 3, 2016, available at <http://china.caixin.com/2016-03-03/100915681.html>.

[26] Zhang Hui, "PLA Rocket Force Names 100 Officers to Commands," *Global Times*, April 12, 2016, available at <https://www.globaltimes.cn/content/978291.shtml>; "How to Build a Joint Operations Command Platform? Look Here" [联合作战指挥平台咋搭建? 到这里看看], *China Military Online* [中国军网], September 21, 2017, available at <http://www.81.cn/2017jj90/2017-09/21/content_7765599.htm>.

[27] "The Eastern Theater Command: Joint Training Proceeds Under Legal Routes" [东部战区: 联合训练, 在法治轨道运行], *Jiefangjun Bao* [解放军报], January 2, 2018, available at <http://www.mod.gov.cn/power/2018-01/02/content_4801252.htm>.

[28] "The 'Rim of Taiwan' Military Exercise in the Eastern Theater Command's New Weapon Will Deter 'Taiwan 'Independence'" [东部战区 "环台湾" 军演 这款新列装武器将震慑 "台独"], *Ordnance Technology* [兵工科技], August 18, 2020, available at <https://mil.news.sina.com.cn/zhengming/2020-08-18/doc-iivhvpwy1653868.shtml>. See also David C. Logan, "Making Sense of China's Missile Forces," in Saunders et al., *Chairman Xi Remakes the PLA*, 393–435.

[29] Roderick Lee, "Integrating the PLA Rocket Force into Conventional Theater Operations," *China Brief* 20, no. 14 (August 14, 2020), available at <https://jamestown.org/program/integrating-the-pla-rocket-force-into-conventional-theater-operations/>.

[30] This category may also include provincial military districts, which report to the CMC National Defense Mobilization Department.

[31] Nevertheless, cyber units are less tied to geography; presumably, the Eastern Theater Command could assume control over Strategic Support Force cyber units physically based in other regions.

[32] John Chen, Joe McReynolds, and Kieran Green, "The PLA Strategic Support Force: A 'Joint' Force for Information Operations," in *The PLA Beyond Borders*, ed. Joel Wuthnow et al. (Washington, DC: NDU Press, 2021), 151–179.

33 "The 'Rim of Taiwan' Military Exercise in the Eastern Theater Command's New Weapon Will Deter 'Taiwan Independence'"; "News of an Eastern TC Exercise Contains Three 'Rares'" [东部战区演训消息包含三个 "罕见"], *Global Times* [环球时报], August 13, 2020, available at <https://news.sina.com.cn/c/2020-08-14/doc-iivhuipn8528837.shtml>.

34 See, for example, "A Certain Brigade of the Central TC Army and a Certain Base of the Strategic Support Force Conduct Confrontation Exercises to Explore the Cross-Service Joint Training Mechanism" [中部战区陆军某旅与战略支援部队某基地开展对抗演练 探索跨军种联合训练机制], *Jiefangjun Bao* [解放军报], October 14, 2018, 2; and "Treading the Waves and Fortifying the Soldiers" [踏浪砺精兵 大洋战歌飞], *Jiefangjun Bao* [解放军报], February 19, 2019, 9.

35 For background, see Statement of Kevin McCauley, *Modernization of PLA Logistics: Joint Logistic Support Force*, Testimony Before the U.S.-China Economic and Security Review Commission, February 15, 2018; LeighAnn Luce and Erin Richter, "Handling Logistics in a Reformed PLA: The Long March Toward Joint Logistics," in Saunders et al., *Chairman Xi Remakes the PLA*, 257–292.

36 "Expert Explains the Relationship Between the CMC Logistic Support Department and the CMC Joint Logistic Support Force" [专家详解军委联勤保障部队与军委后勤保障部是何种关系], *The Paper* [澎湃], November 27, 2016, available at <https://www.thepaper.cn/newsDetail_forward_1569162>.

37 "When 'Old Joint Logistics' Meets 'New Joint Logistics'" [当 "老联勤" 遇到 "新联勤"], *Jiefangjun Bao* [解放军报], April 18, 2017, 5; "Demystifying the Newly Established Central Military Commission Joint Logistic Support Force" [揭秘新成立的中央军委联勤保障部队], *China Youth Daily* [中国青年报], January 19, 2017, available at <http://military.people.com.cn/n1/2017/0119/c1011-29035648.html>.

38 On the civil transport fleets, see Conor M. Kennedy, *Civil Transport in PLA Power Projection*, China Maritime Report No. 4 (Newport, RI: U.S. Naval War College, 2019), 4–17.

39 See Joel Wuthnow, *China's Other Army: The People's Armed Police in an Era of Reform*, China Strategic Perspectives No. 14 (Washington, DC: NDU Press, 2019), 22.

40 Ibid., 9–16.

41 This is the second mobile contingent. The first is based in Shijiazhuang. See ibid., 13.

42 "The Eastern TC Commanded More than 10,000 PLA and PAP Troops Around Chaohu Lake" [东部战区指挥万余名解放军，武警部队官兵沿环巢湖大堤奋战排险], Anhui News Network [安徽新闻网], July 31, 2020, available at <http://www.hf365.com/2020/0731/1305206.shtml>.

43 "The PLA and PAP Scientifically Deploy Rescue Forces to Fight Floods and Conduct Disaster Relief" [解放军和武警部队科学调配救援力量，全力抗洪救灾], China National Radio Military Channel [央广军事], July 23, 2020, available at <http://www.taihainet.com/news/military/zgjq/2020-07-23/2408594.html>.

44 Strategic transport aircraft also remain under PLA Air Force headquarters. See *PLA Aerospace Power: A Primer on Trends in China's Military Air, Space, and Missile Forces* (Washington, DC: China Aerospace Studies Institute, 2019), 11.

45 However, airborne troops were involved in a seminar on joint operations held in Beijing. See *Military and Security Developments Involving the People's Republic of China 2020* (Washington, DC: Office of the Secretary of Defense, 2020), 53.

46 On transregional exercises, see Dennis J. Blasko, "The Biggest Loser in Chinese Military Reforms: The PLA Army," in Saunders et al., *Chairman Xi Remakes the PLA*, 366–370.

⁴⁷ Zhang Peigao [张培高], *Science of Joint Campaign Command* [联合战役指挥学] (Beijing: Military Science Press, 2009), 104. Zhang quotes nearly verbatim from the 2003 *PLA Political Work Regulations* [中国人民解放军政治工作条例].

⁴⁸ Xu Guxian [徐国咸] et al., *Study of Joint Campaigns* [联合战役研究] (Beijing: Yellow River Press, 2004), 5.

⁴⁹ Instead, a consistent theme has been strengthening Party-building in the PLA. For instance, a *Xuexi Shibao* article describing new regulations on Party-building within the PLA enjoined Party committees to "strengthen political leadership and effectively control the troops, organize and command major tasks and operations, and hold onto major issues related to combat readiness." See Donghe Weidong [东何卫东] and He Ping [何平], "Scientific Guidelines for Comprehensively Strengthening Party Building of the Army in the New Era" [全面加强新时代军队党的建设的科学指引], *Xuexi Shibao* [学习时报], October 16, 2020, available at <http://www.qstheory.cn/llwx/2020-10/16/c_1126618351.htm>.

⁵⁰ The exact role of the political commissar is not clear, but Zhang writes that that officer would be expected to conduct political work and "coordinate with the commander." See Zhang, *Lessons on Joint Campaign Command*, 39.

⁵¹ On the PLA Navy, see Jeff Benson and Zi Yang, *Party on the Bridge: Political Commissars in the Chinese Navy* (Washington, DC: Center for Strategic and International Studies, 2020). The authors report that on certain ships there is evidence of Party committees, rather than ship captains, making tactical decisions.

⁵² It is worth noting that political commissars receive similar education in military arts as commanders. For instance, both commanders and political officers attend the senior-level joint operations course at the PLA National Defense University.

⁵³ Zhang, *Lectures on Joint Campaign Command*, 2-3.

⁵⁴ Phillip C. Saunders and Joel Wuthnow, "Large and In Charge: Civil-Military Relations Under Xi Jinping," in Saunders et al., *Chairman Xi Remakes the PLA*, 519–555.

⁵⁵ Notably, the reforms appeared to promote a system in which commanders and political commissars, both within the same level and up and down the chain of command, do not know each other well, ostensibly to reduce the prevalence of patronage networks and corruption. This system was achieved by rotating officers out of one of those positions, but not both. For a discussion, see Saunders and Wuthnow, "Large and In Charge," 536–537.

⁵⁶ Statement of Dennis J. Blasko, *PLA Weaknesses and Xi's Concerns About PLA Capabilities*, Testimony Before the U.S.-China Economic and Security Review Commission, February 7, 2019, 9.

⁵⁷ As John Costello and Joe McReynolds write in the context of the SSF, "This new centralization of information power may be more a function of persistent paranoia and the need for control than a desire to explore innovative means of warfighting." See John Costello and Joe McReynolds, *China's Strategic Support Force: A Force for a New Era*, China Strategic Perspectives No. 13 (Washington, DC: NDU Press, 2018), 55.

⁵⁸ Ibid. On chain reaction warfare, see Wuthnow, *System Overload*, 10–11; M. Taylor Fravel, "Securing Borders: China's Doctrine and Force Structure for Frontier Defense," *Journal of Strategic Studies* 30, no. 4–5 (2007), 716.

⁵⁹ "Lieutenant General Wang Hongguang: After the Eastern TC Exercise, the Southern TC Conducted a Big Maneuver!" [王洪光中将: 东部战区军演之后, 南部战区又一大动作!], *Daily Headline* [今日头条], February 21, 2020.

⁶⁰ *PLA Aerospace Power*, 11.

⁶¹ In the context of expeditionary operations, see Cristina L. Garafola and Timothy R. Heath, *The Chinese Air Force's First Steps Toward Becoming an Expeditionary Air Force* (Santa Monica, CA: RAND, 2017). On the broad range of missions for the PLA Air Force, see Michael S. Chase and Cristina L. Garafola, "China's Search for a 'Strategic Air Force,'" *Journal of Strategic Studies* 39, no. 1 (2016), 4–28.

⁶² See, for example, Kevin Pollpeter, "Towards an Integrative C4ISR System: Informationization and Joint Operations in the People's Liberation Army," in *The PLA at Home and Abroad: Assessing the Operational Capabilities of China's Military*, ed. Roy Kamphausen, David Lai, and Andrew Scobell (Carlisle, PA: Strategic Studies Institute, 2010), 212–220.

⁶³ "CMC Training and Management Department Organizes Joint Theater Training and Service and Branch Training Supervision" [军委训练管理部组织开展战区联合训练和军兵种战役训练监察], *Jiefangjun Bao* [解放军报], November 16, 2017, available at <http://www.xinhuanet.com/mil/2017-11/16/c_129742096.htm>.

⁶⁴ "NDU's 'Elimination System' Cultivates Military Joint Operations Staff Talents" [国防大学全程 "淘汰制" 培养军队联合作战参谋人才], Xinhua, April 3, 2019, available at <http://www.xinhuanet.com/2019-04/03/c_1124322788.htm>. For a discussion of joint education at the PLA National Defense University and other military universities, see Joel Wuthnow and Phillip C. Saunders, "A Modern Major General: Building Joint Commanders in the PLA," in Saunders et al., *Chairman Xi Remakes the PLA*, 304–306.

⁶⁵ "Reshaping the System, Forging a Winning Division" [体系重塑, 锻造胜战之师], *Jiefangjun Bao* [解放军报], September 21, 2017.

⁶⁶ For a broader discussion of PLA human capital problems, see Michael S. Chase et al., eds., *China's Incomplete Military Transformation* (Santa Monica, CA: RAND, 2015), 43–68.

⁶⁷ Wuthnow and Saunders, "A Modern Major General," 293–323.

⁶⁸ Notably, the U.S. military itself continues to struggle with implementing decentralized decisionmaking. See, for example, Andrew Hill and Heath Niemi, "The Trouble with Mission Command: *Flexive Command* and the Future of Command and Control," *Joint Force Quarterly* 86 (3ʳᵈ Quarter 2017), 94–100.

⁶⁹ The increase in Chinese provocations toward Taiwan in 2020 could reflect, among other things, greater confidence in the PLA's command and control system. For a description of events, see Joel Wuthnow, *Projecting Strength in a Time of Uncertainty: China's Military in 2020*, Testimony Before the U.S.-China Economic and Security Review Commission, September 9, 2020.

⁷⁰ Such themes are already present in a variety of recent U.S. doctrinal expositions. See, for example, David G. Perkins, "Multi-Domain Battle: Joint Combined Arms Concept for the 21ˢᵗ Century," Association of the United States Army, November 14, 2016, available at <https://www.ausa.org/articles/multi-domain-battle-joint-combined-arms>; Robert B. Brown, "The Indo-Pacific and the Multi-Domain Battle Concept," U.S. Indo-Pacific Command, March 21, 2017, available at <https://www.pacom.mil/Media/News/News-Article-View/Article/1125682/the-indo-asia-pacific-and-the-multi-domain-battle-concept/>; Terrence J. O'Shaughnessy, Matthew D. Strohmeyer, and Christopher D. Forrest, "Strategic Shaping: Expanding the Competitive Space," *Joint Force Quarterly* 90 (3ʳᵈ Quarter 2018), 10–15.

⁷¹ Thomas G. Mahnken et al., *Tightening the Chain: Implementing a Strategy of Maritime Pressure in the Western Pacific* (Washington, DC: Center for Strategic and Budgetary Assessments, 2019).

[72] Examples include the navy's concept of distributed lethality, air force concepts of distributed operations, army multidomain operations, and marine corps expeditionary advanced base operations.

[73] One sign that these approaches are gaining traction is comments from former Pacific Air Forces Commander General Charles Q. Brown, Jr., who noted that deception is "something we've done in the past. . . . What I really believe [is] it's something we, as a department, probably need to start paying more attention to." See Marcus Weisgerber, "U.S. Military Should Deepen Its Use of Deception, Pacific Air Forces General Says," *Defense One*, December 18, 2019, available at <https://www.defenseone.com/threats/2019/12/us-military-should-add-deception-its-playbook-pacific-air-forces-general-says/161982/>. See also Kyle Rempfer, "SOCOM Needs to Step Up Its Propaganda Game, Pentagon Deputy Says," *Military Times*, February 6, 2019, available at <https://www.militarytimes.com/news/your-military/2019/02/06/socom-needs-to-step-up-its-propaganda-game-pentagon-deputy-says/>.

[74] For a description, see Peter Wood, "Snapshot: China's Eastern Theater Command," The Jamestown Foundation, March 14, 2017, available at <https://jamestown.org/program/snapshot-chinas-eastern-theater-command/>.

[75] *China Military Power: Modernizing a Force to Fight and Win* (Washington, DC: Defense Intelligence Agency, 2019), 27.

[76] For instance, former Department of Defense official Michèle Flournoy has argued that, at least for deterrence purposes, the U.S. Navy should have the ability to sink all of China's surface combatants as a counter to PLA aggression toward Taiwan. See Joe Gould, "Congress Wrestles with Deterring China—Beyond Nukes," *Defense News*, January 16, 2020, available at <https://www.defensenews.com/congress/2020/01/16/congress-wrestles-with-deterring-chinabeyond-nukes/>.

[77] See T.X. Hammes, *Offshore Control: A Proposed Strategy for an Unlikely Conflict*, INSS Strategic Forum No. 278 (Washington, DC: NDU Press, June 2012); Gabriel Collins, "A Maritime Oil Blockade Against China—Tactically Tempting but Strategically Flawed," *Naval War College Review* 71, no. 2 (2018), 1–30.

IV

Strengthening Taiwan's Defenses

CHAPTER 11

A Net Assessment of Taiwan's Overall Defense Concept

Alexander Chieh-cheng Huang

P eace has been generally maintained across the Taiwan Strait since the Second Taiwan Strait Crisis in 1958. However, relative peace has become more fragile than ever as the military balance between Taiwan and the mainland has incrementally shifted in favor of the People's Liberation Army (PLA). This has resulted from China's rapid economic development and defense modernization over the past 40 years, including the ambitious program of "deepening defense and military reform" introduced by General Secretary Xi Jinping at the end of 2015.

To cope with the possibility that China may attempt to achieve unification by force, Taiwan's military has spent the past decade debating the tradeoffs between retaining a conventional legacy force and building a more asymmetrical military capability. The combination of an expanded Chinese military threat and Taiwan's limited military and budgetary resources has contributed to the gradual realization that an effective and affordable defense should prioritize balanced investments and force-building plans. In this context, the Overall Defense Concept (ODC) [*zhengti fangwei gouxiang*, 整體防衛構想] has emerged as the leading thought in developing Taiwan's force-building and operational guidelines.

This chapter examines the key contents, challenges, and future possibilities of the ODC (which continues to be elaborated and enriched) through an assessment of Taiwan's national security environment, the timeline of a possible armed conflict, available financial and human resources that may be committed to implementing the concept, and, most important, the ODC's operational utility and implications. This chapter is divided into three parts: the first section briefly reviews the evolution of Taiwan's military strategy since 1949. The second section discusses the ODC's emergence as a new concept in Taiwan defense policy and military strategy. The third section analyzes challenges that could complicate the ODC's implementation and provides suggestions for further developing the concept.

The Evolution of Taiwan's Military Strategies

Securing Taiwan's democratic institutions and way of life in the face of a Chinese invasion threat has been a constant challenge since the Nationalist government retreated to Taiwan after losing the Chinese Civil War in 1949. Recognizing changes in the international power structure, military balance across the Taiwan Strait, military technology, and operational concepts, one should not write off the devotion, sacrifice, defense strategy, and acquisitions policy of previous governments when discussing a new defense strategy for Taiwan today.

Over the past 70 years, Taiwan's defense has closely depended on the United States for weapons systems procurement, doctrinal development, training and exercises, and organizational innovation. More broadly, both Taiwan's defense policy and military strategy have generally adhered to larger U.S. regional strategy and interests.[1] At the outset, China's intervention in the Korean War in 1950 changed the seemingly neutral U.S. position on the Chinese Civil War and led Washington to provide Taiwan with critically needed military assistance. The U.S.–Republic of China (ROC) Mutual Defense Treaty, signed in 1954, frustrated President Chiang Kai-shek's intention of retaking the mainland by force and altered his "offensive" military strategy. However, it also played a significant role in the relative success of Taiwan's offshore islands operations, for example by enabling the successful withdrawal of Taiwan's forces from the Tachen archipelago off the Zhejiang coast in 1955 and by providing military support during the Jinmen campaign in 1958.

The normalization of U.S.-China relations in 1971 and the switch of U.S. diplomatic recognition from Taipei to Beijing in 1979 led Taiwan to gradually abandon the offensive element of its military strategy. The termination of the Mutual Defense Treaty and the U.S. Military Assistance and Advisory Group, along with the subsequent withdrawal of U.S. military personnel from the island, left Taiwan in a long period of self-reliant defense planning. After several years of study, Taiwan started the annual series of Han Kuang joint military exercises in 1984, based initially on war scenarios that did not assume U.S. intervention in a Taiwan contingency.

Another pivot in Taiwan's military strategy occurred during and after the 1995–1996 Taiwan Strait Crisis. Between July 1995 and March 1996, China lobbed missiles into the waters near Taiwan and conducted joint exercises along the Fujian coast to protest Washington granting a visa to Taiwan President Lee Teng-hui and his high-profile visit to Cornell University, his alma mater. The missile crisis sounded an alarm to both Taipei and Washington that the defensive military strategy of an isolated Taiwan was inappropriate and risked endangering the interests of both Taiwan and the United States. The United States, acknowledging the lack of understanding of Taiwan's defense planning and capability and the commitment codified in the Taiwan Relations Act, began a series of proactive efforts to promote closer military ties and reengage Taipei with gradually increased exchanges and assistance in defense reorganization and modernization. (*Resolute defense* and *effective deterrence* were two key terms used for Taiwan's military strategy to address a possible armed conflict in the Taiwan Strait.)

A final shift has taken place over the past decade. When Xi assumed the chairmanship of the Central Military Commission (CMC) in 2012, the PLA had already undergone several military doctrinal changes, from fighting and winning a "war under modern conditions" to "local wars under high-tech conditions" and "informatized conditions." Xi further transformed China's military strategy to a new doctrine of "winning informatized local wars."[2] In association with his articulation of the "great rejuvenation of the Chinese nation" by 2049, Xi initiated an ambitious military reform plan at the end of 2015 that included reforming the CMC, reorganizing seven military regions into five theater commands emphasizing integrated joint operations, and modernizing key naval and air systems with greatly improved force projection capability.[3] Since then, the PLA has conducted more provocative military activities beyond China's coastline (for a discussion of Chinese coercive activities across the Taiwan Strait, see the chapter by Mathieu Duchâtel in this volume). As the military balance has tilted decisively in China's favor, many hawkish elements on the mainland, from retired military officers to netizens, have in recent years advocated "unification by force."

In response to growing and urgent military pressure and intimidations, Taiwan has again modified its military strategy to focus on resolute defense and multidomain deterrence. The shift is a tacit recognition that Taiwan can no longer compete against the PLA and effectively defend Taiwan based on the previous symmetrical approach of force-building and operational planning. Defense planners, including those on the joint staff, finally must look seriously into asymmetric operational concepts that have been proposed and debated for years.

Development of Asymmetrical Concepts for Taiwan's Defense

The ODC is a campaign- and theater-level operational concept based on input from defense professionals in Taiwan's Ministry of National Defense (MND) and the Pentagon over the past decade. Even before the Xi era, the concept of a more asymmetrical defense approach was mentioned by then–Assistant Secretary of Defense for Asia-Pacific Affairs Wallace Gregson in a keynote speech delivered in October 2009 at the U.S.-Taiwan Defense Industry Conference in Charlottesville, Virginia:

> As a result of the PRC [People's Republic of China]'s rapid economic growth and military modernization, Taiwan will never again have the luxury of relying on quantitative advantages over the PRC. Instead Taiwan must look to its qualitative advantages through focusing on innovation and asymmetry. I realize that words like "innovation" and "asymmetry" are often thrown around, but these concepts are much more than just popular military buzz words. They are essential components of a modern security strategy.[4]

The words *innovation* and *asymmetry* were then adopted widely and appeared in the MND's public statements, strategic documents, and white papers, but without clearly defined conceptualization and authoritative consensus by Taiwan's senior political and military leaders.[5] Between 2010 and 2012, the MND set up an ad hoc task force to study and flesh out the two concepts; however, no information about these efforts was made available to the public.

Cross-strait relations took a sharp downturn after the pro-independence Democratic Progressive Party regained power in May 2016. As the threat of the Chinese military taking Taiwan by force becomes more likely, the asymmetric and innovative approaches to Taiwan's defense modernization and operational plans proposed by the U.S. Department of Defense have emerged as Taiwan's official operational concept, as detailed in the *2019 ROC National Defense Report*:

> *In accordance with the military strategy of "resolute defense and multidomain deterrence," the MND has developed an ODC of "force protection, decisive battle in the littoral zone, and destruction of enemy at the landing beach" to make use of natural trenches and geographic advantages, apply "innovative/asymmetric" operational thinking, integrate capabilities of the three services, take battlefield initiatives, deal a deadly blow to the enemies, and ultimately "frustrate enemies' invasion mission."*[6]

In an interview with *United Daily News* on November 15, 2020, Taiwan's former Chief of the General Staff Lee Hsi-ming stated that the ODC is a "joint operations outline" [*lianhe zuozhan gangyao*, 聯合作戰綱要] developed through numerous meetings with the joint staff in the MND.[7] This statement demonstrates that the ODC resulted from nearly a decade-long exploration of asymmetrical and innovative operational concepts based on collaborative work by stakeholders in both Taiwan and the United States.

For Taiwan's defense leaders, the ODC is an operational concept that supports the military strategy of resolute defense and multidomain deterrence. Like the U.S. military's joint doctrine, the ODC promotes asymmetrical principles that guide the employment of Taiwan's armed forces in integrated actions against an invasion. It also provides a common perspective from which the MND can plan, train for, and conduct joint operations. The operational concept is not designed to cover full-spectrum military scenarios. Its original concept, as illustrated in the *2019 ROC National Defense Report*, does not deal with such areas as military responsibilities and requirements before or after an all-out invasion.

According to the *2019 ROC National Defense Report*, the ODC centers on three major elements: force protection, decisive battle in the littoral zone, and destruction of the enemy on the landing beaches. It is primarily designed for active-duty fighting forces to counter an all-out Chinese invasion through the application of asymmetric operational concepts. Key principles informing the concept include mobility [*jidong*, 機動], camouflage [*weizhuang*, 偽裝], concealment [*yinbi*, 隱蔽], deception [*qidi*, 欺敵], lethality [*zhiming*, 致命], precision [*jingzhun*, 精準], inexpensive systems [*pianyi*, 便宜], operational redundancy [*daliang*, 大量], and dispersion [*fensan*, 分散].[8] These principles will help ensure that Taiwan's armed forces are not severely damaged in the initial stages of a war, thus preserving their strength and maintaining the flexibility required to conduct a counterattack against the invading enemy.

Strengthening the ODC

In examining the functions and utilities of the new asymmetric-minded ODC, several key problems must be identified and incorporated into the future development of the concept. These include estimating the Chinese Communist Party (CCP)'s timeline for unification, addressing the problem of a Taiwanese public perhaps not ready for war, clarifying the deterrent and other peacetime roles the ODC can play, supporting capability development through budgetary increases, and strengthening U.S.-Taiwan defense cooperation to avoid the prospect of an isolated Taiwan. Fortunately, the ODC is framed as an "overall" concept, especially when articulated in the original Chinese connotation—*zheng ti* [整體]—that gives it the flexibility and potential for enrichment. This section analyzes both the problems inherent in the ODC and potential ways to mitigate those concerns.

Estimating China's Timeline

In a meeting with President Bill Clinton in Beijing in late 1998, after the 1995–1996 Taiwan Strait Crisis and the resumption of cross-strait dialogue in 1998, Chinese leader Jiang Zemin stated that "the cross-strait problem should not be postponed indefinitely and there is a need of a timetable."[9] Jiang's remarks generated anxiety and wide discussion in Taiwan, but his successors have never repeated such calls for a formal timeline. However, when Xi suggested that "national unification is an integral part of achieving the great rejuvenation of the Chinese nation," observers naturally pointed to the timetable he set for the fulfillment of the Chinese dream: to achieve "basic prosperity in all sectors" in 2020; to realize "a modernized socialist country" in 2035; and to reach the status of a "prosperous, powerful, democratic, harmonious, and beautiful socialist modern country" by 2049.[10] This proposal implied that Xi intended for unification to be completed, by force if necessary, by midcentury.

More alarmingly, in his address to the fifth plenary session of the 19th Party Congress in October 2020, Xi set a new goal for the centennial of the PLA in 2027, albeit without further elaboration.[11] The year 2027 is also when Xi is expected to complete his third term as general secretary of the CCP and chairman of the CMC. Because the ODC emerged as an official joint operations outline only in 2019, it is crucial to assess whether there is a CCP timetable for national unification. The answer has important implications for how much time Taiwan has for the ODC's implementation of changes in force planning and buildup, doctrinal formulation, and validation through joint military exercises.

Enhancing Social Endurance

Taiwan has not needed to mobilize for war since the 1958 Jinmen campaign. Expert views on growing Chinese military threats are not widely shared by the public. The MND's public relations efforts, such as the opening of army barracks, naval stations, and air bases, while extremely popular, did not translate into a strong recruitment record for volunteer military service. Civil and air defense drills have been too short and small in scale to raise awareness of tensions across the Taiwan Strait.

Increased PLA air and naval intimidation around Taiwan's Air Defense Identification Zone and waters, and the occasional incursion of PLA fighter jets past the median line of the Taiwan Strait, have prompted hatred toward the Chinese Communist regime but have rarely created real anxiety among Taiwan's civilian population. War scenarios in general fall outside the bounds of citizens' daily lives. The possible disruption of electricity, water, gas, food, health care, Internet, and other daily public services during wartime is generally dismissed by politicians and the public, and the definite impact on military maneuvering and the psychological effect on fighting forces on the frontlines are largely ignored.

Under the assumption of failure in both littoral and beachhead battles, in an article coauthored with Democratic Progressive Party think tank executive

Enoch Wu, Admiral Lee advocated the establishment of a "territorial defense force" through the mobilization and reorganization of the existing reserve force.[12] The idea is to "capitalize on all available military and civilian assets to muster a whole-of-society effort" to conduct guerrilla-type urban warfare.[13] In other words, initial discussions have already been held in Taiwan about expanding the ODC, both outward and inward, in a way that is much larger than the original operational concept and that extends beyond the responsibility of the active-duty fighting force.

Expanding the Aims Supported by the ODC

Maintaining peace and stability in the Taiwan Strait is the objective of Taiwan's defense. To meet this goal, the defense policy is to build military capability and capacity to prevent war and deter Chinese aggression. Should deterrence fail, the Taiwan military will aim to fight and win at the operational level and achieve a lasting peace. In this prevent-deter-fight-win equation, the ODC, as a joint operations outline, is designed to address the "warfighting" stage. However, in building a Taiwan military with asymmetric capabilities and capacity for sustainment, a successful force buildup adhering to the ODC can also help complicate Chinese invasion plans and lower the probability of a Beijing decision to wage a war. For instance, the ODC's deterrence function could be presented in Taiwan's investment priorities on improved command, control, communications, computers, intelligence, surveillance, and reconnaissance capabilities; better protection of critical infrastructure; and highly mobile and long-range strike systems. The extended functions of the ODC in deterrence and prevention should be elaborated and supported within the military ranks and by the people.

The ODC also needs to clarify the role of Taiwan's armed forces beyond wartime missions. While building the capability and capacity to fight against a Chinese invasion is the main mission of Taiwan's military, peacetime responsibilities and responding to "gray zone" coercion have also been frequent and costly military missions. Indeed, these activities help maintain peace and stability in the Taiwan Strait. For example, regular Taiwan naval and air force patrols have made significant contributions to the freedom and safety of navigation in the Taiwan Strait and between the Miyako Strait and Bashi Channel.

Asymmetric operational concepts and related investment requirements have little connection to these peacetime responsibilities. Responding to scenarios such as China's encirclement of offshore islands without attacks, intimidation against the Taiwan-held Dongsha Island (Pratas) and Taiping Island (Itu Aba) in the South China Sea, interdiction or quarantine of maritime shipping en route to Taiwan, announcement of a partial naval blockade, notification to foreigners living in Taiwan to leave or recommendation of a noncombatant evacuation operation, and many other gray zone tactics are all beyond the ODC's original emphasis on force protection, decisive battle in the littoral zone, and destruction of the enemy on the landing beaches.

In an article published in *The Diplomat*, Admiral Lee Hsi-ming writes, "The ODC's three tenets for force buildup are force preservation, conventional capabilities, and asymmetric capabilities."[14] The conceptualization and interpretation of the ODC have already begun to expand to address military responsibilities and scenarios short of all-out invasion, as evidenced by sources ranging from the *2019 ROC National Defense Report*, which explained that the ODC focuses on operations in the littoral area and beachhead, to Admiral Lee's 2020 article that addresses additional requirements for gray zone and peacetime missions.

Resourcing the ODC

The search for innovative ways of dealing with China's looming military threat is necessary due to the PLA's rapid modernization and the changing cross-strait military balance. Taiwan's limited financial resources cannot cover all requirements in building both conventional and asymmetric capabilities. The ODC faces the same dilemma, which is why a rebalance of defense investments, involving fewer high-end conventional legacy weapons systems and more asymmetric capabilities, is required.

However, given the scheduled payments for committed arms procurement items from the United States and the estimated cost of developing indigenous systems such as submarines, it is extremely difficult to locate new funding to procure asymmetric systems. One should also keep in mind that smaller, survivable, mobile systems have command, control, communications, and logistics requirements that also cost a great amount. Therefore, continued and reasonable defense budget increases will be essential to the success of the ODC. Since Tsai Ing-wen assumed the presidency in 2016, Taiwan has averaged a 2 percent annual defense budget increase, with expenditures rising to USD $15 billion in fiscal year 2021, partly to meet the requirement for increased U.S. arms sales to Taiwan in the latter half of the Donald Trump administration. Among the arms sales items, a few are already in line with asymmetrical operational concepts (for details, see the chapter by Drew Thompson in this volume).

Even a limited budget increase, however, cannot solve the problem of funding requirements to fully implement the ODC. Possible solutions include exploiting operational concepts that enable asymmetrical applications of traditional weapons and equipment and focusing future defense acquisition on weapons systems that could better execute the ODC.

Strengthening U.S.-Taiwan Defense Cooperation

In the 20th century, the offshore islands of Jinmen and Matzu served as the frontline for Taiwan's defense. However, these islands were too close to the Chinese coast and thus had an extremely low probability for resupply, reinforcement, or maritime and air cover from the main island of Taiwan during wartime. Therefore, the guidance for offshore islands defense operations was always "independent resolute defense" [*duli gushou*, 獨立固守], meaning that Taiwan forces on these outposts would fight as an isolated fortress with no external support. It was expected that those forces could deplete the enemy and delay its actions, possibly altering their operational tempo to protect Taiwan.

Similarly, from a U.S. perspective, Taiwan itself could be viewed as an isolated offshore island too close to the Chinese mainland that needs to be built as a hardened fortress and that must conduct military operations independently without the expectation of immediate external reinforcement. Taiwan is surrounded by water and heavily depends on open sea lines of communication for critical energy and food supply. The ODC is an ideal and necessary operational concept to defend against a PLA invasion, but a fortress can hardly be sustained if its external logistics support is cut off.

To mitigate the probability of Taiwan becoming an isolated fortress because of a Chinese air and naval blockade, U.S. forces must play a proactive role in preventing China from disrupting Taiwan's shipping lanes and providing maritime escort beyond Taiwan's territorial sea and contiguous zones or areas of operation. The asymmetric capability built on the basis of the ODC could be better employed with advanced situational awareness derived not only from Taiwan military units but also from data shared through the U.S. intelligence, surveillance, and reconnaissance network in the U.S. Indo-Pacific Command area of responsibility.

More broadly, support from the United States will be crucial in further developing the ODC. As one potential step, Admiral Lee suggests that Washington and Taipei establish a joint working group to augment the existing bilateral security dialogues and promote better understanding, implementation, and institution of the ODC.[15] In my keynote speech delivered at the 2018 U.S.-Taiwan Defense Industry Conference, I also suggested the idea of extending the ODC into a "unified defense concept" shared by both militaries at the theater level—creating better synchronized communication and courses of action.[16] The shared interests of Taiwan and the United States are peace and stability in the Taiwan Strait. With limited national power, Taiwan cannot "shape" an environment conducive to peace in the region without external assistance, especially from Washington.

Conclusion

Although most senior military officers recognize that joint operations involving asymmetric capabilities are key to Taiwan's defense, the term *ODC* disappeared in the 2021 Quadrennial Defense Review. This reflects an inherited Chinese bureaucratic culture in Taiwan that discourages leaders from adopting the signature policies of their predecessors but does not symbolize a drop in support for the principles embraced by the ODC. It is my view that we should not be too cynical about the future development of the ODC, nor should we associate the concept with specific individuals.

The ODC meets the two most important components of the defense of Taiwan: prevention and sustainability. Its focus on asymmetric systems and capabilities, and innovative concepts of force buildup and force employment, could complicate China's calculations and operational plans, preventing and detering a war in the Taiwan Strait. An expanded ODC could also address the requirements of peacetime missions and the challenges of dealing with gray zone threats prior to a possible PLA invasion. Additionally, it could guide joint civil-military territorial defense should the war not be won in the littoral and beach areas. Over the course of 10 years of debate and deliberation, with the gradual evolution of asymmetrical operational concepts, the ODC was officially presented to the public in the *2019 ROC National Defense Report*. As this chapter discusses, the ODC is like a joint venture between the United States and Taiwan in the creation of an innovative theater-level operational concept for the island's defense along with the potential to advance bilateral military cooperation.

Even with the welcome support of interlocutors in the Pentagon and the broader U.S. defense community, the ODC must expand the numbers of domestic stakeholders who have the resolve and mindset to embrace new thinking about Taiwan's defense policy, military strategy, and operational concepts. Taiwan's leaders' ability to communicate and persuade audiences about the ODC's necessity will be critical for public support. After all, the ODC is a product with many stakeholders within Taiwan's joint staff and among defense policymakers who contributed to its formulation.

The form and characteristics of the ODC will continue to be shaped by an evolving security threat; the state of the relationships among the United States, China, and Taiwan; the legacy of traditional force structure; the availability of financial resources; the acquisition of desired weapons systems; successive governments; and the ever-shifting makeup of Taiwan's defense leadership in the coming years. Ultimately, the ODC is not a total or permanent solution for Taiwan's defense and security, but it is a useful operational concept or joint doctrine that can help guide, build, and employ asymmetrical capabilities more effectively to deter, defend against, and defeat a Chinese invasion. Given the ODC's utility and flexibility, defense leaders should continue to enrich and refine its elements without falling into the trap of making changes in name only.

Notes

[1] Another timeline categorization of the evolution can be seen in Alexander Chieh-cheng Huang, "Homeland Defense with Taiwanese Characteristics: President Chen Shui-bian's New Defense Concept," in *The Costs of Conflict: The Impact on China of a Future War*, ed. Andrew Scobell (Carlisle, PA: Strategic Studies Institute, 2001), 129–161.

[2] Sergio Miracola, "The Evolution of China's Army and Military Strategy," Italian Institute for International Political Studies, September 27, 2019, available at <https://www.ispionline.it/en/pubblicazione/evolution-chinas-army-and-military-strategy-24040>.

[3] For an overview, see Phillip C. Saunders et al., eds., *Chairman Xi Remakes the PLA: Assessing Chinese Military Reforms* (Washington, DC: NDU Press, 2019).

⁴ Wallace C. Gregson, "Remarks to the U.S.-Taiwan Business Council Defense Industry Conference," U.S.-Taiwan Business Council, September 28, 2009.

⁵ Ministry of National Defense, National Defense Report Compilation Committee [國防部 "國防報告書" 編纂委員會], *2011 ROC National Defense Report* [中華民國壹百年國防報告書] (Taipei: Northern Print Shop, Armaments Bureau, Ministry of National Defense, 2011), 71.

⁶ 2019 National Defense Report Compilation Committee [中華民國108年國防報告書編纂委員會], *2019 ROC National Defense Report* [中華民國108年國防報告書] (Taipei: Northern Print Shop, Armaments Bureau, Ministry of National Defense, 2019), 58.

⁷ Cheng Chia-wen, "Former Chief of Staff Li Hsi-ming Pushed for the 'Overall Defense Concept,'" *United Daily News*, November 15, 2020, available at <https://vip.udn.com/vip/story/121160/5016849>.

⁸ Lee Hsi-ming, "Exclusive: First Interview with Former Chief of Staff Lee Hsi-ming," Formosa TV, video, 53:13, November 1, 2020, available at <https://www.youtube.com/watch?v=9xOBVpCbT6w&ab_channel=民視讚夯FormosaTVThumbsUp>.

⁹ Jiang Zemin [江澤民], *Volume II Selected Works of Jiang Zemin* [江澤民文选 第二卷] (Beijing: People's Press, 2006), 152.

¹⁰ State Council of the People's Republic of China, "CPC Central Committee's Proposals for China's 14ᵗʰ Five-Year Plan for National Economic and Social Development and the Long-Term Goals Through 2035" [中共中央关于制定国民经济和社会发展第十四个五年规划和二〇三五年远景目标的建议], November 3, 2020, available at <http://www.gov.cn/zhengce/2020-11/03/content_5556991.htm>.

¹¹ Ibid.

¹² Lee Hsi-ming [李喜明] and Enoch Y. Wu [吳怡農], "The Transformation of Backup: Establishment of the Territorial Defense Force" [後備的轉型：建立國土防衛部隊], *Apple Daily* [蘋果日報], October 8, 2020, available at <https://tw.appledaily.com/forum/20201008/COZCM6LDPJF3DGPN2W3JDHGEQE/>.

¹³ Lee Hsi-ming and Eric Lee, "Taiwan's Overall Defense Concept, Explained," *The Diplomat*, November 3, 2020, available at <https://thediplomat.com/2020/11/taiwans-overall-defense-concept-explained/>.

¹⁴ Ibid.

¹⁵ Ibid.

¹⁶ U.S.-Taiwan Business Council Defense Industry Conference archive.

CHAPTER 12

Winning the Fight Taiwan Cannot Afford to Lose

Drew Thompson

Taiwan's defense approach has long relied on purchases of U.S. equipment and attempts to emulate U.S. doctrine. The U.S. military, however, has focused on projecting power to fight smaller adversaries around the world, while Taiwan faces the prospect of defending its homeland from China's increasingly capable People's Liberation Army (PLA). The United States is deeply committed to defending Taiwan, particularly as it becomes increasingly clear that Taiwan's military needs to adapt to the rising threat posed by the PLA and the risk that Xi Jinping might seek to use force to compel unification. China has long had the ability to blockade or to launch missiles or air strikes against Taiwan, but a defiant Taipei could resist such coercion and refuse to surrender. Beijing can only be certain that it can compel unification if it can mount an invasion. Deterring invasion is, therefore, the ultimate objective for the United States and Taiwan. Maintaining cross-strait stability in the face of an increasingly well-resourced and modernizing PLA requires continual innovation and adaptation, including the updating of defense concepts.

While casual observers of the U.S.-Taiwan defense relationship focus on highly visible arms sales announcements, the extent of deep, substantive engagement between the two militaries is arguably even more valuable to en-suring cross-strait deterrence. Military-to-military exchanges take place from the highest political-security levels to operational exchanges, to the level of units and individual soldiers, and all the way down to the midshipmen and cadets from Taiwan studying at each of the U.S. Service academies. In each of these engagements, ideas are exchanged, trust is developed, and friendships are forged by the common bond of two democracies seeking to deter aggres-sion and preserve peace and stability in the Western Pacific.

Beginning in 2007, U.S. experts from the Department of Defense began collaborating with senior Taiwan military officials to jointly analyze the prog-ress and implications of Chinese military modernization. Senior and mid-lev-el civilian officials and military officers, experienced veterans, and defense planners all worked together to assess how Taiwan could transform its mili-tary to adapt to growing PLA power-projection capabilities.[1] A generation of Taiwan defense policymakers and planners spent years, both independently and collaboratively with U.S. colleagues, studying cases, challenging assump-tions, and developing, simulating, modeling, and testing concepts. Everyone involved recognized the significance of this intellectual endeavor in deterring Beijing from using force to unify Taiwan and, if that failed, preventing a PLA invasion from succeeding. They called a PLA invasion "the fight Taiwan can-not afford to lose." Failure to deter China or stop an invasion would imperil Taiwan's survival and raise the specter of nuclear war between the U.S. and China. Taiwan's defense planners ultimately determined that avoiding this outcome depended on Taiwan transforming its military to address the grow-ing PLA threat by adopting an asymmetric strategy.

Origins of the Overall Defense Concept

In 2017, Taiwan's then Chief of the General Staff, Admiral Lee Hsi-ming, qui-etly proposed a revolutionary new approach to Taiwan's defense called the Overall Defense Concept (ODC).[2] The ODC is at its core an asymmetric strat-egy that, if effectively implemented, could increase the chance of preventing China from being able to take Taiwan by force.

Mainland China considers Taiwan a rogue province—an unresolved remnant of the Chinese Civil War that otherwise ended in 1949 when Chiang Kai-shek's defeated forces retreated to Taiwan under the protection of the U.S.

Navy. Afterward, the U.S. military maintained a presence in Taiwan until the normalization of U.S. diplomatic relations with China in 1979. China has stated its intent to reunify Taiwan by force, if necessary, with Xi Jinping threatening in 2013 that the Taiwan issue "should not be passed down generation after generation."[3] To that end, China has built its military to be able to invade Taiwan and prevent the U.S. military from coming to the island's defense in time, a strategy the U.S. Defense Department labeled *antiaccess/area denial* (A2/AD).

Taiwan has historically depended on the United States to help deter China through both the threat of U.S. intervention and the provision of arms. The Taiwan Relations Act requires the United States to maintain the ability to defend Taiwan and to provide it with "arms of a defensive character."[4] Taiwan's military has closely mirrored its U.S. counterpart in miniature for years, sending its officers to U.S. military schools, training together, acquiring new and used military platforms sold by the U.S. Government, and basing Taiwan's own doctrine on concepts that originated in the United States. Taiwan's military capabilities are a hodgepodge of U.S. and indigenously built systems. Its U.S.-sourced systems range from antique to cutting edge. Taiwan's arsenal includes Vietnam-era U.S. systems, such as M-60 tanks, *Knox*-class frigates, and F-5 fighters, though many are slated for replacement under a much-needed recapitalization program. At the higher end, Taiwan's AH-64E Apache attack helicopter is newer than the model fielded by the U.S. Army in the U.S. Indo-Pacific Command's area of responsibility. Taiwan's F-16s are being retrofitted to include new capabilities that make U.S. Air Force pilots jealous.

The problem with copying the American approach to warfare is that the U.S. military's doctrine is to project power over great distances and to maximize mobility and networks to take the fight to the enemy with overwhelming superiority. Taiwan, on the other hand, needs the opposite: short-range and defensive systems that can survive an initial bombardment from a larger adversary and that are suitable for deployment close to home in defense of the island should it come under blockade or attack. Despite emulating the U.S. military in its doctrine, training, and capabilities for decades, Taiwan has begun to chart its own course.

Taiwan's defense planners have long expressed a willingness to employ innovative and asymmetric strategies, but implementation has been slow and challenging. Taiwan's Quadrennial Defense Reviews, published in 2009, 2013,

2017, and 2021, endorsed the concept of asymmetric and innovative methods. The 2017 review, for example, reiterated Taiwan's intent to adopt asymmetric and innovative approaches "to present multiple dilemmas to the enemy and deter aggression" before describing its strategy of a war of attrition, where Taiwan would "resist the enemy on the other shore, attack the enemy on the sea, destroy the enemy in the littoral area, and annihilate the enemy on the beachhead."[5] While the rhetoric used by Taiwan's defense planners supported a new approach to defense, Taiwan's services and some politicians continued to favor the acquisition of large, expensive, conventional systems from the United States, along with U.S. doctrine and training to support Taiwan's long-established "defense-in-depth" strategy by fighting the PLA from the mainland, across the Taiwan Strait, to the beaches of Taiwan itself.

Contours of a New Defense Approach

The ODC describes an asymmetric defense approach where Taiwan maximizes its defense advantages and targets an invading force when it is at its weakest: in Taiwan's littoral. While Taiwan's previous strategy focused on fighting across the entire Taiwan Strait and defeating the enemy through attrition, the new concept divides Taiwan's defense operations into three phases: force preservation, decisive battle in the littoral zone, and destruction of the enemy at the landing beach. Each phase takes place closer to Taiwan's shores where the lines of communication are short and Taiwan's forces can benefit from land-based air denial and more effective surveillance and reconnaissance. As Admiral Lee explains, "The ODC *redefines winning the war* as foiling the PLA's mission of successfully invading and exerting political control over Taiwan. Taiwan must abandon notions of a traditional war of attrition with the PLA."[6] The following sections describe each of the ODC's phases and then highlight the specific role played by sea mines and antiship missiles.

Force Preservation. Force preservation is the first phase of the ODC. Defense planners presume that a PLA campaign would begin with a blockade, followed by missile strikes intended to destroy Taiwan's military and demoralize its public. The ODC calls for large numbers of affordable, small, mobile systems that can sortie out from bases; employ deception, camouflage, and decoys to make targeting difficult; and ensure that sufficient capabilities survive initial strikes. The survival and continued effectiveness of

Taiwan's military following initial PLA strikes has taken on greater urgency considering China's larger and more accurate ballistic and cruise missile forces, while PLA A2/AD capabilities are anticipated to slow a U.S. military response. Taiwan is already experienced in hardening its military infrastructure to withstand attacks, but the ODC calls for additional investments in key capabilities, including mobility, deception, camouflage, concealment, jamming, redundancy, rapid repair, and reconstitution. While these attributes are often neglected by militaries because they are not visible or prestigious, the new defense concept recognizes that they are critical to Taiwan's credible deterrence and prioritizes them in the competition for scarce defense dollars.

Decisive Battle in the Littoral. The second phase is the decisive battle in the littoral, which extends up to 100 kilometers from the island. Key capabilities at this phase include sea mines and large surface vessels equipped with Taiwan's capable, domestically manufactured antiship cruise missiles, the Hsiung Feng 2 and 3. Taiwan's surface fleet includes larger vessels from the legacy force, such as French-built *Lafayette*-class frigates, *Kidd*-class destroyers, and U.S.-designed *Perry*-class frigates armed with both Hsiung Feng and Harpoon missiles, and a new class of domestically built, fast attack *Tuojiang*-class catamarans that carry 16 Hsiung Feng missiles. These large surface combatants and the aluminum-hulled *Tuojiang* catamarans will likely suffer severe losses in the opening phases of a cross-strait conflict as they seek to counter Chinese surface vessels in a symmetrical contest that favors the PLA Navy (PLAN)'s larger number of ships armed with longer range antiship missiles, which can also be launched by the PLA's land-based fighters.

The heart of Taiwan's asymmetric strategy is the use of mobility, low observability, camouflage, swarm tactics, and innovative approaches to complicate the PLA's ability to find and destroy Taiwan's platforms, particularly in the opening phases of a conflict. Taiwan currently fields truck-mounted Hsiung Feng antiship missiles, which can disperse to survive initial strikes, then set up later when PLAN ships, particularly the high-value amphibious vessels carrying an invasion force, are crossing the strait. These land-based mobile antiship systems are expected to survive after Taiwan's capital ships have been destroyed and may be able to further extend their survivability by moving after firing to avoid counter-fire strikes. On October 26, 2020, the U.S. Government notified Congress of its intent to sell Taiwan 100 Harpoon Coastal

Defense Systems and 400 RGM-84L-4 Harpoon Block II Surface Launched Missiles in a deal valued at $2.37 billion, giving Taiwan greater depth and capacity to hold a Chinese invasion fleet at risk from the sanctuary of Taiwan's urban and mountainous terrain.[7] Most recently, in August 2021, the Joseph R. Biden administration notified Congress of its intent to sell Taiwan $750 million worth of new and upgraded M109A6 Paladin self-propelled howitzers, giving the Taiwan army the improved capability to attack enemy forces in the littoral and on the beach.[8] This capability to survive an initial bombardment, then "shoot-and-scoot" from concealment, is the hallmark of an asymmetric strategy and a key component of the ODC.

Destruction of the Enemy at the Landing Beach. The third phase of the ODC seeks to annihilate the enemy at the "beach area," which extends approximately 40 kilometers out from the anticipated invasion beaches.[9] This phase calls for Taiwan's navy to lay mines in both the deep and shallow waters off suspected landing beaches. A new fleet of automated, fast minelaying ships are being built for that mission, with the first vessel of the class launched in August 2020.[10] Mine-launching rails can be installed on several classes of surface vessels and will be incorporated into the design of future corvettes. While invading ships are slowed by mine fields, swarms of small fast attack boats and truck-launched antiship cruise missiles will target key PLA ships, particularly amphibious landing ships carrying the initial assault wave and roll-on/roll-off vessels carrying follow-on vehicles and armor.[11]

The Taiwan army comes into play during this phase, laying beach mines and targeting PLAN ships, including minesweepers, with precision fires. Joint precision fires artillery will target any vessels and troops reaching shore, using area-effects weapons that have large blast and fragmentation radii to destroy all personnel and lightly armored vehicles or vessels in a target zone. Examples of area-effects weapons include indigenously built multiple launch rocket systems with cluster munitions and the U.S.-built High Mobility Artillery Rocket System (HIMARS), the sale of which was also notified to Congress in October 2020.[12] Attack helicopters, including AH-1W Super Cobras and AH-6E Apaches, are also key army systems that may be used during these operations.

According to the ODC, the Taiwan air force will seek to deny Chinese fighters, bombers, and drones the ability to operate effectively within Taiwan's battlespace by deploying integrated air defenses, including Patriot

PAC-3 batteries and domestically manufactured Tian Kung-2 surface-to-air missiles designed to defend air bases and critical infrastructure. Smaller mobile air defense systems operated by the army and navy, such as U.S.-provided Stinger man-portable air defense systems (MANPADS) and Avenger systems, aim to prevent the PLA Air Force from providing close-in air support to their invading forces.

Mines and Missiles. Sea mines and antiship cruise missiles are critical capabilities at the heart of the ODC and thus warrant a more detailed discussion. Because the ODC prioritizes countering an amphibious invasion force in Taiwan's littoral and beach zones, these two inherently asymmetric systems favor the smaller defender against the larger aggressor, taking advantage of short lines of communication and Taiwan's complex terrain.

Coastal defense mines are a key component of Taiwan's defense strategy and a bellwether of institutional support for the ODC. Historically, sea mines have proved difficult to counter by an invasion force. In the Korean War, for instance, the U.S. invasion force at Incheon landed before North Koreans could deploy sea mines. U.S. forces landed quickly, met heavy resistance ashore, and found warehouses full of mines after they cleared the beach. At the attack on Wonson a month later, sea mines were deployed offshore before the planned invasion. Two minesweepers were destroyed by mines while under fire from shore-based artillery and clearing operations took two weeks. U.S. Marine and Army units embarked on transports had to wait offshore for 5 days for lanes to be cleared, which only happened after North Korean forces abandoned their positions.[13]

Taiwan has asked the United States to provide Quickstrike MK-64 air-delivered sea mines to supplement its inventory and give it a rapid-deployment capability at the outset of a conflict, but that system has not been notified to the U.S. Congress to date.[14] Taiwan possesses World War II–era MK-6 mines acquired from the United States, which have been periodically refurbished. Modern mines were produced by the government-led National Chung Shan Institute for Science and Technology (NCSIST), Taiwan's main designer and manufacturer of defense articles, around 2002, and the navy actively practices deploying them, but little is known about their quantity.

President Tsai Ing-wen brought considerable attention to mine warfare, however, when she visited the shipyard building Taiwan's new fast mine-laying vessel and the new missile corvette, which will be fitted with mine-rails on the stern, demonstrating a political intersection between the asymmetric strategy and Taiwan's policy objective of building its defense industrial base.[15] Following President Tsai's visit in 2019, the first fast mine-laying vessel was launched in August 2020.[16]

NCSIST is currently developing two new types of shallow- and deep-water influence mines that they plan to deploy by 2021, but little progress has been reported and the program is believed to be well behind schedule.[17] They are also developing a self-propelled mine with a planned deployment date around 2025.[18] Until then, Taiwan has been refurbishing its current mine inventory, which includes domestically manufactured Wan Xiang mines and U.S.-made MK-6 mines.

The Hsiung Feng 2 and 3 antiship missiles are the other weapons at the heart of the ODC. These missiles are fielded by surface ships or fired ashore from a handful of vulnerable fixed batteries and batteries of vehicle-mounted launchers. Mobile vehicle-mounted antiship missiles are inherently survivable, making them effective at the critical moments when a PLA amphibious force is approaching Taiwan and preparing to offload troops and armor.

History has proved how difficult it is for an adversary to find and destroy mobile transporter-erector-launchers (TELs) in a conflict. During the 1991 Gulf War, U.S. and British special forces, along with coalition aircraft, hunted in vain for Scud TELs in the flat and featureless western Iraqi desert. Despite coalition air superiority and multiple special operations units on the ground assigned to hunt TELs, Iraq fired a total of 88 extended-range Scuds against targets in Israel, Saudi Arabia, and Bahrain. Furthermore, Iraqi forces used decoys and deception, as well as shoot-and-scoot tactics, to enhance those missile systems' survivability and add to the uncertainty of coalition forces, leading a postwar Pentagon assessment to conclude, "[T]here is no indisputable proof that Scud mobile launchers—as opposed to high-fidelity decoys, trucks, or other objects with Scud-like signatures—were destroyed by fixed-wing aircraft."[19]

Taiwan's shoreline, which is infinitely more complex than the Iraqi desert, is particularly well suited for concealing mobile missile launchers. Comprised of agricultural areas interspersed with suburban areas, coastal zones in Taiwan feature a complex infrastructure that supports the defender, including sea walls, paddy fields, bridges, tunnels, and overpasses, as well as mountainous zones not far from the coast where TELs and their supporting vehicles can hide. Taiwan has reportedly camouflaged cruise missile battery support vehicles to look like commercial trucks.[20] Taiwan's NCSIST, the maker of Hsiung Feng missiles and launchers, is aware of the possibilities of mounting missiles in structures configured like shipping containers, as Russia does.[21] Using advanced camouflage techniques, the existence of both camouflaged and conventional launchers, and the use of high-tech decoys complicates targeting Taiwan's TELs. It also greatly increases PLA uncertainty about whether they have destroyed Taiwan's antiship capabilities before launching an amphibious attack.

Expecting that Taiwan's large surface ships will be primary initial targets for the PLA, the ODC also relies on small fast attack vessels, such as the 170-ton displacement, 112-foot long Kuang Hwa fast attack craft. That vessel mounts four Hsiung Feng missiles and can be quickly reloaded in austere locations, such as the small fishing ports that dot Taiwan's coastline. The Taiwan navy is reportedly acquiring another small, 50-ton vessel based on a catamaran hull, with the first test-bed platform called *Glorious Star* [光榮之星], carrying four missiles.[22] NCSIST is upgrading missiles and increasing production of antiship cruise missiles, land attack cruise missiles, and surface-to-air missiles to arm new ships and launchers, deepen magazines, and ensure that Taiwan's armed forces have sufficient munitions to hold out for an extended period. While the ODC does not prescribe that the Taiwan military retire its large conventional weapon systems or neglect peacetime missions, it highlights the importance of investments in asymmetric, survivable capabilities and doctrine that directly target an invasion.

Orphans of the Overall Defense Concept. The ODC is animated by the most critical mission of the Taiwan military: denying China the ability to land and resupply an invasion force. Beijing can use blockades, coercion, hybrid warfare, or gray zone pressure, but the only thing that guarantees that Beijing can achieve its political objective of Taiwan's surrender is putting PLA boots on the ground and physically seizing control of the island. Preventing that outcome is, therefore, the most fundamental mission of Taiwan's military, but it is not the only one.

Taiwan's military also has a multitude of peacetime missions and other potential contingencies for which it must prepare. Taiwan will therefore continue to invest in platforms that do not directly support the asymmetric warfighting concept, or which are unlikely to survive the initial waves of fire strikes prior to an invasion. Unpublished Taiwan Ministry of National Defense (MND) depictions of the ODC include icons of Taiwan's fixed-wing aircraft, capital ships, large unmanned aerial vehicles, large submarines, and fixed sites such as the powerful Pave Paws surveillance radar atop Leshan Mountain that are unlikely to survive initial air and missile strikes, denoting that they are an integral part of the ODC in the military's eyes, despite their lack of an asymmetric pedigree. The published depiction of the ODC in Taiwan MND's 2019 National Defense Report emphasizes the ODC's focus on the littoral zone and landing beach, as well as the role of coastal defense missiles, area-effects weapons, mines, and small attack craft (see figure).[23]

Taiwan's vulnerable runways and the inability to disperse outside the range of Chinese air and missile strikes make it unlikely that the Taiwan air force's fixed-wing assets will survive initial bombardments. Patriot and Tian Kong surface-to-air missile batteries, runway repair capabilities, and the underground facility at Jiashan Air Base that is intended to shelter a portion of the air force are insufficient to protect or reconstitute fixed-wing capabilities in the face of the PLA Rocket Force's numerical advantage in ballistic missiles or air-to-surface munitions delivered by the PLA Air Force. As a conflict progresses, the Taiwan air force will eventually be forced to make its warfighting contributions without functioning runways destroyed by repeated strikes, resorting to mobile air defenses, small drones, and maintaining critical command, control, communications, computers, intelligence, surveillance, and reconnaissance infrastructure to enable a joint defense.

The Taiwan navy is building large amphibious transport vessels and a future large air defense destroyer, which are also likely to be targeted and sunk in the early phases of a conflict. It is unclear what role Taiwan's future Indigenous Defense Submarine will play in targeting the surface ships of an invasion force since it is expected to be a large, conventional diesel electric design similar to Taiwan's existing two *Hai Lung*-class submarines, which are optimized for deep, open water, rather than the shallows found in the Taiwan Strait. Taiwan's submarines could present a threat to PLA surface combatants outside the strait, particularly if they seek to operate on the east side of Taiwan, but U.S. Navy submarines are expected to be operating in those areas in defense of U.S. surface action groups and carriers,

Figure. Diagram of the Overall Defense Concept

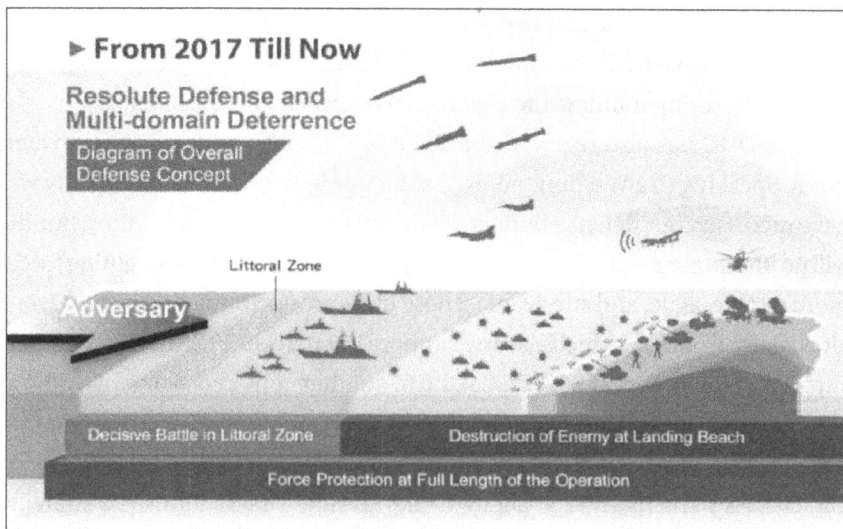

Source: *2019 National Defense Report* (Taipei: Ministry of National Defense, 2019), 69, available at <https://www.ustaiwandefense.com/tdnswp/wp-content/uploads/2020/02/Taiwan-National-Defense-Report-2019.pdf>.

necessitating a robust water space management regime to ensure Taiwan submarines are not eliminated by friendly forces.

Investments in submarines, large surface vessels, and fighter aircraft are necessary for Taiwan to recapitalize its aging legacy force so the air force and navy can continue to provide peacetime deterrence and resist PLA gray-zone pressure. The challenge for Taiwan is ensuring that there is adequate defense funding for these large, prestige-enhancing platforms that are the darlings of their service chiefs, while also funding the small, maneuverable, and surviv-able asymmetric systems that are critical to Taiwan's survival.

Obstacles to Implementation

While Taiwan's Ministry of National Defense has embraced the ODC, sup-port for it is not unconditional and implementation has been uneven. The ODC was mentioned for the first time in Taiwan MND's biennial defense re-port in 2019. Its presence in the widely coordinated document indicates that a consensus has been reached about its centrality to the "resolute defense and multi-domain deterrence" strategy that MND has employed since 2017.

The annual 2019 Han Kuang exercises, which focused on littoral combat and beach defense, were described by the MND's spokesperson as an exercise to implement the ODC, indicating that it is evolving past the concept stage and already informing training and potentially doctrinal development.[24]

The ODC has also received President Tsai's public endorsement several times. Speaking to a Washington, DC, audience in 2019, she said, "Already we have increased our defense budget over the past 2 years in a row. These funds will go into strategies, techniques, and capabilities that make our fighting force more nimble, agile, and survivable. These ideas are encompassed by the Overall Defense Concept, which has my support 100 percent."[25] She reiterated her support again in August 2020, speaking to another conference organized by a Washington, DC, think tank, by stating, "I am committed to accelerating the development of asymmetric capabilities under the overall defense concept."[26] The ODC is particularly well aligned with President Tsai's industrial strategy to develop Taiwan's indigenous defense industry. The numerous small, maneuverable, affordable platforms called for in the ODC can generally be made by domestic firms or NCSIST. In addition to supporting the ODC, increasing spending on domestic defense contractors benefits Taiwan's economy and increases domestic support for more defense spending, while also reducing reliance on the United States as Taiwan's sole supplier of weapons.

However, support for the ODC within the Ministry of National Defense is mixed. Service chiefs generally feel that the ODC constrains their acquisition prerogatives, forcing them to work harder to justify acquiring expensive, large platforms as part of the recapitalization of Taiwan's legacy force. According to serving and recently retired officers, the most-senior officers in MND rarely, if ever, mention the ODC. One- and two-star general and flag officers likewise keep their personal preferences to themselves as they navigate service politics. The Chief of the General Staff from January 2020 until June 2021, Admiral Huang Shu-kuang, was personally opposed to the ODC and succeeded in preventing it from being mentioned in Taiwan's 2021 Quadrennial Defense Review (QDR). Though the QDR recognizes the importance of asymmetric forces for Taiwan's defense, it also embraces the conventional defense-in-depth principle, calling for larger, conventional systems which would be able to strike the mainland during the early stages of an invasion, even though those conventional systems are assessed to be less survivable and vulnerable to PLA initial fire strikes. The current Chief of the General Staff, General Chen Pao-yu, is believed to be supportive of the asymmetric and innovative principles embedded in the ODC concept, but internal debate within the ministry about the role of mainland strikes and offensive cyber is ongoing. Some are referring to this debate somewhat glibly as "ODC 2.0," while others assert that thinking in MND has evolved "beyond ODC" in response to developments in PLA capabilities. At the time of writing, the ODC term is not expected to appear in the MND's 2021 annual defense report, and it is doubtful that the concept will resurface in the future as the ministry continues to explore conventional defense-in-depth concepts.[27]

The majority of mid-level staff officers are openly enthusiastic about the ODC because they recognize the intrinsic value of adopting an asymmetric strategy against the PLA, but they too have little incentive to challenge senior officers.[28] The unwillingness of the senior-most officers in Taiwan's MND and services to openly support an asymmetric strategy reveals Admiral Lee's sponsorship of the ODC during his tenure as Chief of the General Staff as a courageous decision, which was noted by President Tsai at his retirement ceremony.[29]

Acquisitions are at the heart of contentions over the ODC's asymmetric focus, with services championing their preference for large, expensive systems, including the Taiwan air force's F-16Vs and Indigenous Defense Fighter and the navy's Indigenous Defense Submarine, future destroyer, and landing platform dock ship. Proponents of the ODC argue that these expensive systems are unlikely to survive initial PLA fire strikes or to be effective at attritting invasion forces as they approach Taiwan's littoral zone, while their big price tags squeeze a small defense budget that is growing ever-so-slowly under President Tsai. To their credit, the services have invested in some asymmetric systems, such as small unmanned aerial vehicles, MANPAD missiles, coastal defense cruise missiles, a fast mine-laying vessel, and fast missile corvettes. Budget pressures, however, have caused the delay of some small, mobile, asymmetric systems, such as the "micro-class missile assault boat."[30]

The ODC does not specifically designate some weapon systems as asymmetric and others as conventional, giving military leaders and lobbyists considerable latitude to associate their preferred platform with the ODC strategy or to argue that a particular system is necessary for the defense of Taiwan. It is therefore very difficult to judge whether a particular system being acquired is "good" or "bad" for Taiwan's total defense, since one could argue the need for expensive platforms for peacetime deterrence, and for smaller, numerous, asymmetric capabilities that can survive to counter an invasion force. With limited acquisition resources, however, Taiwan's defense planners face a challenging situation. There is strong political support to prioritize expensive, imported U.S.-made systems, which have considerable value as a political deterrent to PLA aggression. However, the ODC favors cheaper, smaller, locally made systems whose larger numbers and mobility are more likely to survive initial fire strikes and be waiting on the beaches for the PLA to arrive.

What Is Missing from the ODC?

Most discussion about the ODC in Taiwan revolves around procurement of weapon systems. Proponents of large, conventional legacy systems argue that the Taiwan military faces other critical missions besides littoral and beach defense (such as disaster relief), while forward-looking thinkers argue that the ODC's asymmetric capabilities must be fulfilled first to protect the homeland and win "the fight Taiwan cannot afford to lose" before spending on conventional capabilities for peacetime missions. What has been noticeably absent from ODC discussions, however, are two critical issues: personnel and logistics.

Personnel. Taiwan's decision to transition to an all-volunteer force affects all aspects of the armed forces and necessitates a thorough review to understand how it will affect Taiwan's defense planning processes. The ODC must take those personnel issues into account. The transition to a volunteer force has already increased personnel costs and resulted in a downsized force.[31] Taiwan's low birth rate—the second lowest in the world—puts additional pressure on the volunteer force structure, as the military will need to compete even harder with the private sector for recruits from a shrinking pool of candidates every year.

Taiwan's military recruitment targets range between 18,000 and 28,000 per year, but the total annual number of births is between 180,000–200,000 per year (and declining steadily). Taking low figures of each, Taiwan's military must attempt to recruit roughly 10 percent of the 18-year-olds entering the workforce each year to maintain its current force size.[32] By comparison, the U.S. military sought to recruit 171,000 enlisted soldiers for the Active-duty force in 2019 from a population of four million live births in 2002, or approximately 4 percent of the total.[33] The personnel challenges that Taiwan's military faces, ranging from recruiting, training, sustaining, and retaining soldiers, have not been addressed by senior political or military leaders despite their centrality to ODC and to Taiwan's future defense capability.

One area where personnel issues have been raised in the context of the ODC is Taiwan's reserves. The decision to transition to an all-volunteer force during the Ma Ying-jeou administration from 2009 to 2011 was not accompanied by a robust discussion within the military about how it would affect the force, including Taiwan's reserves. Historically, Taiwan maintained a strategic reserve made up of able-bodied adult males who had all completed 2 years of military service under the conscription system. The end of meaningful conscription undermines the all-out mobilization system and necessitates the need for a professional reserve force to support and complement the professional Active-duty force.[34]

How that reserve force supports the ODC strategy is undetermined at this point, but several analysts, including the now-retired Admiral Lee, have proposed that Taiwan form a territorial force of reservists who are "trained for localized operations with decentralized command, as the nature of warfare will be urban and guerrilla. . . . During peacetime, the territorial defense force would be responsible for localized disaster relief, and during war, protection of critical infrastructure and defense of secondary enemy landing sites."[35] The concept of a territorial force was proposed directly to President Tsai by a visiting high-level delegation of U.S. Government officials in 2020, potentially stimulating discussion of the future role of Taiwan's reserves at the highest levels of government and MND.[36]

Logistics. Dwight Eisenhower once said, "You will not find it difficult to prove that battles, campaigns, and even wars have been won or lost primarily because of logistics."[37] Unfortunately, like personnel, logistics has not been raised in the context of the ODC. The ODC's premise of taking advantage of short lines of communication and fighting close to Taiwan's shores can be seen as an advantage, but its emphasis on force preservation at the outset of a conflict means that forces will be dispersing, relying on mobility to survive. This requires the ODC to consider a dynamic approach to supporting those forces on the move. Because the Taiwan army and navy will need to sortie out from their bases at the outset of a conflict to survive the expected initial PLA missile strikes, Taiwan's military logistics system also will need to disperse to survive. How Taiwan supports forces, including the delivery of war reserve munitions to functioning units in the field in the later stages of a conflict, will strongly influence the effectiveness of the ODC.

Managing war reserve munitions is also a critical challenge for Taiwan's military. Determining what levels of stocks are adequate, acquiring them from a perceived fickle United States that has often deliberated over arms sales for long periods, and then maintaining those stocks as they age is a massive, expensive undertaking. Taiwan's defense planners and decisionmakers have historically taken a conservative view of munitions requirements and refrained from "over-ordering" munitions. This conservatism is due to tight budgets and resource competition in each service, a military training culture that limits live-fire training activities, the high cost of sustaining stored munitions, and a belief that stored munitions do not play a meaningful role in deterrence compared to highly visible platforms, such as tanks, planes, and ships. Congressional notifications for both the Patriot and Harpoon Coastal Defense Systems indicate that Taiwan ordered only enough missiles to support purchased batteries without ordering "reloads."[38]

Taiwan cannot rely on the United States to resupply munitions at the outset of a conflict for two key reasons. First, the area around Taiwan would be contested by PLA air and surface units, which undoubtedly will consider the vulnerable planes or ships supplying Taiwan priority targets. Second, U.S. war reserve stocks in the Pacific would be earmarked for U.S. forces that would be coming to Taiwan's defense. Producing new munitions in the United States or finding and supplying them from Department of Defense global stockpiles would probably not arrive in Taiwan until the air and sea space around Taiwan were secure. Taiwan's logistics experts will need to develop strategies to preserve war reserve munitions stocks so they are not destroyed in their bunkers and storage depots. Ensuring that the right stocks are available at the right place and time would require dispersing them quickly to highly mobile units employing asymmetric, shoot-and-scoot tactics, in addition to anticipating firing and reloading locations in advance of units arriving.

U.S. Interests in the ODC

U.S. national interests in sustaining Taiwan as a free and open society in the Asia-Pacific, as well as the commitment in the Taiwan Relations Act to provide Taiwan with defensive arms and maintain the U.S. capacity to resist the use of force or coercion, make Taiwan a crucial credibility test for U.S. security assurances to other states in the region. The United States is, therefore, a critical stakeholder in Taiwan's defense planning process and a key partner incentivized to help Taiwan effectively implement the ODC.

DOD broadly supports the ODC because it is Taiwan's own defense concept and aims to maximize Taiwan's comparative advantages. Various U.S. officials have publicly voiced their support for the ODC, while also reflecting a recognition that the concept promises to be an effective plan against a much larger adversary.[39] That said, U.S. officials have also consistently approved the sale of high-profile, expensive U.S.-made arms. These systems have key benefits that are consistent with the ODC's strategic objective of deterring aggression, even if they are less survivable than asymmetric ones. Conventional U.S.-made systems are a tangible measure of U.S. commitment to Taiwan's defense, which boosts morale in Taiwan and increases uncertainty in Beijing. Possession of these U.S.-made systems also helps MND in recruiting efforts, capturing the imagination of Taiwan youth who want to join a cutting-edge military, operating advanced weapon systems.

Taiwan's acquisition of U.S. and indigenous long-range strike weapons with ranges beyond 300 kilometers provides an added dimension to the ODC. Taipei's top China-watchers will need to determine for themselves whether the prospect of missile strikes on major Chinese cities will achieve the most important strategic objective of deterring an attack on Taiwan, while defense planners are focused on the operational impact of mainland strikes on the PLA. Systems such as the indigenous Hsiung Feng 2E land-attack cruise missiles and the air-launched Wan Chien air-to-ground cruise missile have been in Taiwan's inventory for over 10 years, while the supersonic, long-range Yun Feng cruise missile is reportedly being modified to launch small satellites.[40] These capabilities are joined by recent acquisitions from the United States—a marked departure from Washington's previous practice of avoiding selling long-range weapons to Taiwan. U.S. sales include the AGM-84H Standoff Land Attack Missile Expanded Response, notified in October 2020, and the AGM-154C Joint Stand-Off Weapon, notified in June 2017, to give the Taiwan air force additional options to strike mainland targets.[41] The U.S. decision in October 2020 to sell HIMARS gives the Taiwan army a defensive long-range strike capability that can reach portions of China's coastline, potentially placing embarkation points for a PLA invasion force at risk.

After China has initiated attacks on Taiwan, long-range counter-strike options give Taiwan considerable flexibility in determining how to respond. The most strategic objective for initiating mainland strikes is boosting the morale of the Taiwan people, giving them the will to resist, even in the face of strikes on Taiwan. The military effects of those initial counterstrikes need not be large to be powerful, much as the Doolittle Raiders boosted U.S. morale in the early days of World War II. Taiwan defense strategists can consider the relative benefits of striking military or economic centers to achieve specific effects to disrupt society, the economy, or military capabilities and then determine the optimal capability to deploy at the optimal time. For example, the 300 kilometer–range HIMARS artillery might be well suited to attack mainland command and control targets or coastal embarkation points to disrupt an invasion force or degrade coastal integrated air defense systems, while Taiwan's ground and air-launched land attack cruise missiles might target urban areas to demoralize China's population, cause economic effects, or complicate war-mobilization efforts.

In addition to mainland strikes, Taiwan may also carry out cyber attacks to deter China or degrade its ability to carry out an invasion as part of an expanded ODC. It is unclear whether the threat of cyber attacks would deter Beijing due to the difficulty of signaling in this domain, or whether cyber attacks on critical infrastructure and defense networks in China would support Taiwan's defense effort by hampering Chinese mobilization efforts. The threat of U.S. intervention remains the most critical factor, but as the PLA continues to modernize and expand, including with A2/AD capabilities designed to challenge a U.S. intervention, Taiwan's own defense capabilities to counter a PLA invasion become an increasingly important deterrent.

One challenge for the United States supporting Taiwan is that Taiwan's defense needs are diverging from the expertise and systems the U.S. military can readily provide. For example, the U.S. Marine Corps does not have a dedicated opposing force that Taiwan could train with to hone their skills in defending beaches. Nowhere in the U.S. Marine Corps is there a center of excellence or red team that specializes in beach defenses; opposed beach landings are long gone from U.S. Marine Corps doctrine. Commanders of Taiwan's squadrons of small fast attack boats can find no counterpart in the U.S. Navy with whom to train. The U.S. Navy mine warfare community is underresourced, unappreciated, and mines are generally considered a problem, not a solution, by the Navy's legions of surface warfare officers.

Nevertheless, with every challenge comes opportunity. As the U.S. Army develops its multidomain battle concept and applies it to the Indo-Pacific, it will increasingly realize that China is the challenge, the battlespace is Taiwan, and cooperation with Taiwan is a laboratory for developing innovative future warfare concepts. When Admiral Harry Harris, then commanding U.S. Pacific Command, spoke at the Association of the United States Army conference in 2016, he reduced the U.S. Army's key task to a quip, "Army's got to be able to sink ships."[42] The U.S. Army should find solutions and opportunities for expanding their reach into the maritime domain by studying and innovating alongside their counterparts in Taiwan.

Reliance on U.S. systems may also increase Taiwan's interoperability with the U.S. military and possibly other countries in the region. Taiwan's proximity to China is an advantage which could benefit networked U.S. forces operating at greater stand-off distances if those forces are networked with their Taiwan counterparts. For example, a sensor operated by Taiwan could feed data to networked U.S. planes and ships operating at safe distances to increase their awareness of threats and improve targeting. While not explicit in the ODC, the notion of a Taiwan sensor linked to a U.S. "shooter" is exactly the sort of innovation the concept advocates. Furthermore, the recent notification of new U.S. weapon systems, such as unmanned aerial vehicles and the Harpoon Coastal Defense System, with its integrated radars and sensors, increases the feasibility of linking U.S. and Taiwan forces. Interoperability makes Taiwan a potentially significant offset capability for U.S. platforms, which could leverage Taiwan's proximity to an invading adversary. Taiwan's sensors feeding targeting data to U.S. weapon systems operating at greater stand-off distances would make those U.S. forces more accurate and effective against the invader.

Underscoring the significance of the cooperative aspects of the U.S.-Taiwan defense relationship, Admiral Lee has suggested establishing a joint U.S.-Taiwan working group to support implementation of the ODC, along similar lines to the joint working group established in 2007 to assess the threat and consider Taiwan's options. Admiral Lee proposed, "Through conducting contingency simulations and exercises, U.S. officials could offer their operational experience and expertise to guide Taiwan's force restructuring and doctrinal reforms, with an emphasis on military doctrine, force planning, and logistical support, as well as operational tactics."[43] As the ODC becomes central to Taiwan's defense planning, coordination and cooperation between the two sides is critical to help ensure that Taiwan is able to maximize the benefits of their own strategy and find innovative ideas and synergies from joint planning with the United States.

Conclusion

The beauty of Admiral Lee's Overall Defense Concept is that it embraces an asymmetric strategy, does not seek to compete with China's larger military head on, and focuses Taiwan's resources on targeting the greatest threat while ensuring Taiwan's military survives long enough as an effective fighting force to enable third-party intervention. It eschews traditional symmetrical warfighting of surface action groups, fighter planes, or tanks slugging it out head-to-head with corresponding PLA forces. Instead, it takes a page from guerrilla warfare and envisions large numbers of small, affordable, highly mobile units taking advantage of Taiwan's complex terrain to defeat a larger enemy. Like all good strategies, this concept has both strategic and operational objectives that are clearly set out.

The coalition effort to destroy TELs in the Iraqi desert in 1990 failed in its operational objective to destroy Iraq's missile launchers, but it did achieve its strategic objective of reassuring Israel that all possible measures were being taken to hunt Scuds, which kept Israel from attacking Iraq and undermining the U.S.-led coalition. Likewise, the ODC is not only intended to achieve an operational objective of ensuring the survival of the Taiwan armed forces in a high-intensity conflict with China; its strategic objective is to deter China from using force in the first place by creating uncertainty about the PLA's prospects of launching a successful invasion.

The ODC will undoubtedly continue to be debated internally within Taiwan's defense planning community and at the highest levels of the MND. Deliberation will likely evolve beyond the binary choices of symmetrical and asymmetrical capabilities, expanding to a broader focus on capabilities that will affect China's political and military calculations. Advocates for greater investments in conventional long-range strike capabilities observe that they buy time for Taiwan to mobilize its forces, including its reserves, who are expected to play a role defending beaches and invasion routes. Once the strategy for littoral and beachhead operations is well-developed and capabilities for fighting in those zones have been acquired, planners can expand the ODC to incorporate new concepts, or expend remaining resources for capabilities that support other missions, such as disaster relief, and the conventional capabilities that offer defense-in-depth options, such as long-range strike. The major unresolved challenge, however, is Taiwan's stagnant defense budget, which is unable to support sufficient investment in both asymmetric littoral defense and conventional long-range strike capabilities.

While approaches to implementing the ODC may differ among competing stakeholders, there is no debate that in 2017, Admiral Lee made a courageous proposal to set Taiwan on this crucial course that contributes to cross-strait stability and ensures Taiwan's survival despite an existential threat from a larger, increasingly capable adversary.

Notes

[1] *NIDS China Security Report 2017: Change in Continuity: The Dynamics of the China-Taiwan Relationship* (Tokyo: National Institute for Defense Studies, 2017), 55.

[2] This section of the paper draws on Drew Thompson, "Hope on the Horizon: Taiwan's Radical New Defense Concept," *War on the Rocks*, October 2, 2018, available at <https://warontherocks.com/2018/10/hope-on-the-horizon-taiwans-radical-new-defense-concept/>.

[3] Richard C. Bush, "8 Key Things to Notice from Xi Jinping's New Year Speech on Taiwan," *Brookings Order from Chaos* blog, January 7, 2019, available at <https://www.brookings.edu/blog/order-from-chaos/2019/01/07/8-key-things-to-notice-from-xi-jinpings-new-year-speech-on-taiwan/>. See also Article 8 of China's 2005 Anti-Secession Law, available at <http://www.china-embassy.org/eng/zt/999999999/t187406.htm>.

[4] U.S. Congress, *Taiwan Relations Act*, Public Law 96-8, 22 U.S.C. 3301 et seq., 96th Cong., 1st sess., January 1, 1979, available at <https://www.ait.org.tw/our-relationship/policy-history/key-u-s-foreign-policy-documents-region/taiwan-relations-act/>.

[5] *2017 Quadrennial Defense Review* (Taipei: Ministry of National Defense, 2017), 38–39.

⁶ Lee Hsi-ming and Eric Lee, "Taiwan's Overall Defense Concept, Explained," *The Diplomat*, November 3, 2020, available at <https://thediplomat.com/2020/11/taiwans-overall-defense-concept-explained/>.

⁷ Taipei Economic and Cultural Representative Office in the United States (TECRO), "RGM-84l-4 Harpoon Surface Launched Block II Missiles," news release, U.S. Defense Security Cooperation Agency, October 26, 2020, available at <https://www.dsca.mil/press-media/major-arms-sales/taipei-economic-and-cultural-representative-office-united-states-17>.

⁸ Mike Yeo, "U.S. Government Clears $750 Million Artillery Sale to Taiwan," *Defense News*, August 6, 2021, available at <https://www.defensenews.com/global/asia-pacific/2021/08/06/us-government-clears-750-million-artillery-sale-to-taiwan/>.

⁹ For more information about potential invasion beaches on Taiwan, see Ian Easton, *The Chinese Invasion Threat: Taiwan's Defense and American Strategy in Asia* (North Charleston, SC: CreateSpace Independent Publishing Platform, 2017).

¹⁰ Xavier Vavasseur, "Taiwan Starts Construction on Improved Catamaran Corvette and Minelayers," *Naval News*, May 26, 2019, available at <https://www.navalnews.com/naval-news/2019/05/taiwan-starts-construction-on-improved-catamaran-corvette-minelayers/>.

¹¹ Robert Beckhusen, "China Now Using a Cruise Ship to Haul Troops and Tanks," *Wired*, August 31, 2012, available at <https://www.wired.com/2012/08/chinacruise/>.

¹² TECRO, "HIMARS, Support, and Equipment," U.S. Defense Security Cooperation Agency, October 21, 2020, available at <https://www.dsca.mil/press-media/major-arms-sales/taipei-economic-and-cultural-representative-office-united-states-15>.

¹³ Theodore L. Gatchel, *At the Water's Edge: Defending Against the Modern Amphibious Assault* (Annapolis, MD: Naval Institute Press, 2013), 173–185.

¹⁴ Scott Morgan, "Taiwan Military Mulls Purchase of U.S. Autonomous Helicopters, Mines," *Taiwan News*, November 5, 2018, available at <https://www.taiwannews.com.tw/en/news/3568309>.

¹⁵ Matthew Strong, "Taiwan Starts Building Missile Corvettes and Minelayers," *Taiwan News*, May 24, 2019, available at <https://www.taiwannews.com.tw/en/news/3709758>. See also Joseph Trevithick, "Taiwan's Next Batch of Stealthy Catamarans Will Have Serious Mine-Laying Capabilities," *The Drive*, May 24, 2019, available at <https://www.thedrive.com/the-war-zone/28201/taiwans-next-batch-of-stealthy-catarmans-will-have-serious-mine-laying-capabilities>.

¹⁶ "1ˢᵗ Locally Built Fast Minelayer Launched in Taiwan," *Taiwan Today*, August 5, 2020, available at <https://taiwantoday.tw/news.php?unit=2&post=182648>.

¹⁷ Author interviews with a Taiwan defense analyst, October 2020. See also "Navy Counters the CCP's Military Disturbance to Taiwan, Deploys State-Made Wan Xiang Sea Mines in 192 Naval Exercise" [海軍反制共軍擾台 192艦隊操演施放國造萬象水雷], Central News Agency, June 23, 2020, available at <https://www.cna.com.tw/news/firstnews/202006230195.aspx>; and "1 Piece, 100 Million [Yuan] but of No Use: Navy Refuses Chinese Academy of Sciences Sea Mine" (1顆1億卻不管用 海軍婉拒中科院水雷), *Liberty Times Net* (自由時報), October 20, 2015, available at <https://news.ltn.com.tw/news/politics/breakingnews/1481053>.

¹⁸ "1 Piece, 100 Million [Yuan] but of No Use; see also "Mine," National Chung-Shan Institute of Science and Technology, available at <http://www.ncsist.org.tw/ENG/csistdup/products/product.aspx?product_id=255&catalog=38>.

¹⁹ William Rosenau, *Special Operations Forces and Elusive Enemy Ground Targets: Lessons from Vietnam and the Persian Gulf War* (Santa Monica, CA: RAND, 2001), 29–44.

[20] John Reed, "Taiwanese Cruise Missile Batteries Are Disguised as Delivery Trucks," *Foreign Policy*, February 27, 2013, available at <https://foreignpolicy.com/2013/02/27/taiwanese-cruise-missile-batteries-are-disguised-as-delivery-trucks/>.

[21] Robert Beckhusen, "Missiles in a Box and More at Russia's Bizarro Arms Show," *War Is Boring*, September 11, 2013, available at <https://medium.com/war-is-boring/missiles-in-a-box-and-more-at-russias-bizarro-arms-show-ef345d4cf39c>.

[22] Wang Jionghua [王烱華], "Counter-CCP Warship, We've Built a Missile Assault Boat" [抗中共戰艦 我造飛彈突擊艇], *Taipei Times* [台北報導], January 8, 2018, available at <https://tw.appledaily.com/headline/20180108/PW6YEEU7UQ4JIZDN6NVN2IZQNY/>.

[23] *2019 National Defense Report* (Taipei: Ministry of National Defense, 2019), 68–69, available at <https://www.ustaiwandefense.com/tdnswp/wp-content/uploads/2020/02/Taiwan-National-Defense-Report-2019.pdf>.

[24] "National Army's 108 'Hanguang 35 Exercise Plan,'" Taiwan Ministry of National Defense, press conference, February 27, 2019, available at <https://www.mnd.gov.tw/Publish.aspx?p=76033>.

[25] "The Taiwan Relations Act at Forty and U.S.-Taiwan Relations," remarks by Taiwan President Tsai Ing-wen, Center for Strategic and International Studies, Washington, DC (via video), April 9, 2019, available at <https://www.csis.org/analysis/taiwan-relations-act-forty-and-us-taiwan-relations>.

[26] See "President Tsai Ing-wen Discusses the Diplomatic, Security, and Economic Challenges Facing Taiwan," remarks by Taiwan President Tsai Ing-wen, Hudson Institute, Washington, DC (via video), August 12, 2020, available at <https://www.hudson.org/research/16300-transcript-president-tsai-ing-wen-discusses-the-diplomatic-security-and-economic-challenges-facing-taiwan>.

[27] Author interviews with a senior Taiwan Ministry of National Defense official and a senior military officer in a service branch, September 2021.

[28] This is true both in my personal experience engaging with mid-level officers and in my interviews with senior military leaders conducted in fall 2020.

[29] Teng Pei-ju, "Taiwan Chief of the General Staff Conferred Highest Military Award Ahead of Retirement," *Taiwan News*, June 26, 2019, available at <https://www.taiwannews.com.tw/en/news/3732486>.

[30] "Explaining and Clarifying the Matter Regarding the Media Coverage of '60 Micro-Class Missile Assault Boats Reduced from the Initially Recorded $1.67 Billion to Merely $1.04 Million,'" Ministry of National Defense, press release, September 2, 2019, available at <https://www.mnd.gov.tw/English/Publish.aspx?title=News%20Channel&SelectStyle=Defense%20News&p=76674>.

[31] Steven Lee Myers and Javier C. Hernández, "With a Wary Eye on China, Taiwan Moves to Revamp Its Military," *New York Times*, August 30, 2020, available at <https://www.nytimes.com/2020/08/30/world/asia/taiwan-china-military.html>. See also Yimou Lee, "For Taiwan Youth, Military Service Is a Hard Sell Despite China Tension," Reuters, October 29, 2018, available at <https://www.reuters.com/article/us-taiwan-military-idUSKCN1N20U3>.

[32] "Population Policy Data Collection," Department of Household Registration, Taiwan Ministry of the Interior, available at <https://www.ris.gov.tw/documents/data/en/4/Population-Policy-Data-Collection.pdf>.

[33] Lawrence Kapp, *Defense Primer: Active Duty Enlisted Recruiting*, IF11147 (Washington, DC: Congressional Research Service, January 28, 2021), available at <https://fas.org/sgp/crs/natsec/IF11147.pdf>. See also Joyce A. Martin et al., "Births: Final Data for 2002," *National Vital Statistics Reports* 52, no. 10 (December 17, 2003), 1–113.

[34] Ian Easton, Mark Stokes, Cortez A. Cooper III, and Arthur Chan, *Transformation of Taiwan's Reserve Force* (Santa Monica, CA: RAND, 2017), available at <https://www.rand.org/pubs/research_reports/RR1757.html>.

[35] Lee and Lee, "Taiwan's Overall Defense Concept, Explained."

[36] Interviews with a senior U.S. Government official, in Washington, DC, and a Taiwan government official, October 2020.

[37] Major General Charles R. Hamilton and Lieutenant Colonel Edward K. Woo, "The Road to Predictive Logistics: Perspectives from the 8th Theater Sustainment Command," Indo-Pacific Command, October 2, 2019, available at <https://www.pacom.mil/Media/News/News-Article-View/Article/1977957/the-road-to-predictive-logistics-perspectives-from-the-8th-theater-sustainment/>.

[38] *Taiwan: Major U.S. Arms Sales Since 1990*, RL30957 (Washington, DC: Congressional Research Service, January 5, 2015, available at <https://www.everycrsreport.com/files/20150105_RL30957_222a5c3ccea779f9e46979c29e185f3858cf8bd3.pdf>.

[39] Rebeccah L. Heinrichs, "Interview with Assistant Secretary of Defense Randall Schriver on Security in the Indo-Pacific," transcript, Hudson Institute, December 19, 2019, available at <https://www.hudson.org/research/15578-interview-with-assistant-secretary-of-defense-randall-schriver-on-security-in-the-indo-pacific>. See also David Helvey, Keynote Remarks, U.S. Taiwan Business Council Defense Industry Conference, October 28, 2018, available at <https://www.us-taiwan.org/wp-content/uploads/2020/04/2018_october29_david_helvey_dod_keynote.pdf>; and "Taiwan Must Focus on Cost-Effective Defense: U.S. Official," *Taipei Times*, October 10, 2019, available at <https://www.taipeitimes.com/News/taiwan/archives/2019/10/10/2003723717>.

[40] Keoni Everington, "Taiwan's Upgraded 'Cloud Peak' Missiles Could Reach Beijing," *Taiwan News*, January 25, 2018, available at <https://www.taiwannews.com.tw/en/news/3349525>.

[41] TECRO, "AGM-84H Standoff Land Attack Missile-Expanded Response (SLAM-ER) Missiles," news release, U.S. Defense Security Cooperation Agency, October 21, 2020, available at <https://www.dsca.mil/press-media/major-arms-sales/taipei-economic-and-cultural-representative-office-united-states-16>. See also TECRO, "AGM-154C Joint Standoff Weapon (JSOW) Missiles," news release, U.S. Defense Security Cooperation Agency, June 29, 2017, available at <https://www.dsca.mil/press-media/major-arms-sales/taipei-economic-and-cultural-representative-office-tecro-united-1>.

[42] Admiral Harry Harris, Commander, U.S. Pacific Command, speech, Association of the United States Army conference, October 4, 2016, available at <https://www.pacom.mil/Media/Speeches-Testimony/Article/963703/association-of-the-united-states-army-ausa-conference/>.

[43] Lee and Lee, "Taiwan's Overall Defense Concept, Explained."

CONTRIBUTORS

Joel Wuthnow is a senior research fellow in the Center for the Study of Chinese Military Affairs (CSCMA), Institute for National Strategic Studies (INSS), at the National Defense University. He also serves as an adjunct professor in the Edmund A. Walsh School of Foreign Service at Georgetown University. Dr. Wuthnow has worked as a China analyst at CNA, a postdoctoral fellow in the China and the World Program at Princeton University, and a predoctoral fellow at the Brookings Institution. Dr. Wuthnow holds degrees from Princeton University (AB, summa cum laude, in public and international affairs), Oxford University (M.Phil. in modern Chinese studies), and Columbia University (Ph.D. in political science).

Arthur S. Ding is a professor emeritus at the National Chengchi University (NCCU), Taipei. He is now an adjunct professor at both the NCCU and Taiwan's National Defense University. His research focuses on China security, including China's security policy and defense, party-military relations, and China's defense industry. He holds degrees from National Taiwan University (AB in anthropology) and the University of Notre Dame (MA and Ph.D. in political science).

Phillip C. Saunders is director of the Center for the Study of Chinese Military Affairs and a distinguished research fellow in the Institute for National Strategic Studies at the National Defense University. Dr. Saunders previously worked at the Monterey Institute of International Studies from 1999 to 2003, where he directed the East Asia Nonproliferation Program at the James Martin Center for Nonproliferation Studies. He served as an officer in the Air Force from 1989 to 1994. Dr. Saunders is coauthor, with David Gompert, of *The Paradox of Power: Sino-American Strategic Restraint in an Era of Vulnerability* (NDU Press, 2011) and editor of eight books on Chinese military and security issues. Dr. Saunders attended Harvard College and received his MPA and Ph.D. in international relations from the School of Public and International Affairs at Princeton University.

Andrew Scobell is a distinguished fellow for China at the United States Institute of Peace. Previously, he was a senior political scientist at RAND. His recent publications include *China's Grand Strategy: Trends, Trajectories, Long-Term Competition* (RAND, 2020), *Command and Control in U.S. Naval Competition with China* (RAND, 2020), and *Chairman Xi Remakes the PLA: Assessing Chinese Military Reforms* (NDU Press, 2019). He was born in Hong Kong and earned a Ph.D. in political science from Columbia University.

Andrew N.D. Yang is the secretary general of the Chinese Council of Advanced Policy Studies (CAPS). He is a leading international authority on the dynamic relations among Taiwan, the United States, and China. CAPS primarily focuses on studying and analyzing the strategic and security aspects of the People's Republic of China (PRC)'s domestic and international situation, particularly its cross-strait relations. Since 1987, Mr. Yang has been in charge of organizing a series of international conferences on the People's Liberation Army that have earned international acclaim and recognition in the academic field of security and defense studies.

Joshua Arostegui is a Department of the Army senior intelligence analyst who has specialized in Chinese military capabilities for the past 10 years. He has also served for more than 25 years in the Navy as a Chinese interpreter and a cryptologic warfare officer in both Active and Reserve capacities. He is a graduate of the Marine Corps Command and Staff College and holds an MA in international relations from Salve Regina University and a MA in history from the University of Nebraska at Kearney. He is also a graduate of the Defense Language Institute's Basic and Intermediate Chinese courses and completed an executive Chinese language program at the Beijing Institute of Economic Management.

Michael Casey is a military analyst with the Department of Defense, where he looks at security developments in the Indo-Pacific region—particularly the growth and evolution of the Chinese People's Liberation Army (PLA) and China's growing threat to Taiwan. His work focuses on how the PLA's new-found capabilities shape its military planning and how it may apply those capabilities in real-world combat. He previously received a master's degree from the George Washington University with a focus on security studies, and a Bachelor of Arts from the University of Michigan, where he focused on East Asian security issues.

Chung Chieh is an assistant research fellow at the National Policy Foundation in the Republic of China (ROC). Earlier, he served as the chief of staff in a congressional office from 1997 to 2015, with a specific focus on the Foreign Affairs and National Defense Committee, formerly known as the National Defense Committee, from 2001 to 2015. His expertise includes People's Liberation Army military reform, the ROC's national defense policy, the ROC's South China Sea policy, and coercive diplomacy.

Mathieu Duchâtel is director of the Asia Program at Institut Montaigne, Paris. He was previously senior policy fellow and deputy director of the Asia and China Programme at the European Council of Foreign Relations (2015–2018), senior researcher and the representative in Beijing of the Stockholm International Peace Research Institute (2011–2015), research fellow with the Asia Centre in Paris (2007–2011), and associate researcher based in Taipei with the Asia Centre (2004–2007). He holds a Ph.D. in political science from the Institute of Political Studies (Sciences Po, Paris). He has spent 9 years in Shanghai (Fudan University), Taipei (National Chengchi University), and Beijing, and has been visiting scholar at the School of International Studies of Peking University (2011–2012), the Japan Institute of International Affairs (2015), and the Institute for National Defense and Security Research, Taiwan (2020).

Alexander Chieh-cheng Huang is a professor in the Institute of Strategic Studies at Tamkang University and founder and chairman of the Council on Strategic and Wargaming Studies in Taiwan. Dr. Huang previously served in the Republic of China (Taiwan) government as Deputy Minister of the Mainland Affairs Council and has worked closely with consecutive governments on foreign and security policy matters. Dr. Huang did his graduate work in the School of Foreign Service (MS in foreign service) at Georgetown University, and in the Department of Political Science at George Washington University, where he received his doctoral degree. Dr. Huang specializes in Asian and Chinese foreign and security affairs and has been frequently interviewed by international news agencies and local media. He has also been a syndicated columnist for the *United Daily*, the *China Times*, and many newspapers and online media in Taiwan since 2011.

Conor Kennedy is a research associate at the China Maritime Studies Institute of the Naval War College in Newport, Rhode Island. He received his MA from the Johns Hopkins University–Nanjing University Center for Chinese and American Studies. His research focuses on Chinese maritime and military affairs, including work on maritime militia and amphibious warfare development.

Roderick Lee is director of research at the Air University's China Aerospace Studies Institute (CASI), where he oversees research on Chinese military aerospace forces and the Chinese civilian aerospace sector as it relates to the military. Prior to joining CASI, he served as an analyst with the Navy, covering Chinese naval forces. He earned his MA from the George Washington University's Elliott School of International Affairs.

Sale Lilly is a senior policy analyst at RAND, focusing on Chinese military and economic analysis and wargame design. Sale previously served as an officer in the Navy and as a management consultant in the financial service industry. He holds degrees from the Naval Academy (BA in economics) and dual degrees from Oxford University (M.Sc. in modern Chinese studies and a M.Phil. in economic and social history).

Drew Thompson is a visiting senior research fellow in the Lee Kuan Yew School of Public Policy at the National University of Singapore and a senior research scientist at CNA. From 2011 to 2018, he was director for China, Taiwan, and Mongolia in the Office of the Secretary of Defense. He previously worked at the Center for Strategic and International Studies and the Center for the National Interest and held management roles in U.S. companies based in China, where he lived for 10 years. He has a master's degree in government from the Johns Hopkins University, a certificate from the Johns Hopkins–Nanjing University Center for Chinese and American Studies, and a BA in Asian studies from Hobart College.

INDEX

www.ingramcontent.com/pod-product-compliance
Lightning Source LLC
Chambersburg PA
CBHW071344280326
41927CB00039B/1678